W9-AXY-518

14w

Pg. 41-46

The Skilled mastery

Reader 4,5,6

Second Edition

D. J. Henry

Daytona State College

Homework

58, 19, 20, in selection from the

Black

1-10 each

comprehension

New York   Boston   San Francisco
London Toronto Sydney Tokyo Singapore Madrid
Mexico City Munich Paris Cape Town Hong Kong Montreal

Acquisitions Editor: Kate Edwards
Development Editor: Janice Wiggins-Clarke
Marketing Manager: Thomas DeMarco
Senior Supplements Editor: Donna Campion
Production Manager: Ellen MacElree
Project Coordination, Text Design, and Electronic Page Makeup: Nesbitt Graphics, Inc.
Cover Design Manager: Wendy Ann Fredericks
Cover Designer: Nancy Sacks
Cover Photos: Wallenrock/Shutterstock.com
Photo Researcher: Jody Potter
Senior Manufacturing Buyer: Dennis J. Para
Printer and Binder: Quebecor World–Taunton
Cover Printer: Phoenix Color Corps

For permission to use copyrighted material, grateful acknowledgment is made to the copyright holders on pp. 617–619, which are hereby made part of this copyright page.

Library of Congress Cataloging-in-Publication Data on file with the Library of Congress.

Please visit us at http://www.ablongman.com/henry

ISBN 13: 978-0-205-57318-9 (Student Edition)
ISBN 10:   0-205-57318-5 (Student Edition)

ISBN 13: 978-0-205-57049-2 (Instructor's Edition)
ISBN 10:   0-205-57049-6 (Instructor's Edition)

4 5 6 7 8 9 10—WCT—10 09 SE Edition
3 4 5 6 7 8 9 10—WCT—10 09 AIE Edition

Brief Contents

Detailed Contents

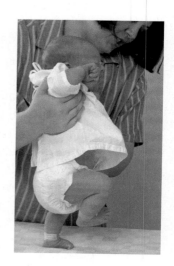

Preface

Dear Colleagues:

In our college's library hangs a poster that bears the face of Fredrick Douglass and the following words: "Once you learn to read, you will be forever free." The poster serves as a daily reminder of two ideals: Reading empowers an individual life, and our work as reading instructors is of great and urgent importance. Many of our students come to us lacking the basic skills that make skilled reading and clear thinking possible. Too often their struggles have left them unable to find much joy or success in working with the printed word. For them, text is a barrier. *The Skilled Reader,* Second Edition, has been designed to address these challenges.

New to This Edition

- Twenty-five percent of the short and long reading selections and accompanying pedagogy in the book have been revised, giving students even more lively, thought-provoking reading material. The new topics honor cultural diversity by offering high-interest readings about the people, traditions, and values of Hispanic, Asian, Native American, and African American cultures. In addition, a significant number of new readings deal with communication, relationships, science, health, and pop culture.

- Coverage of SQ3R in Chapter 1, "A Reading System for Skilled Readers," has been enhanced with graphics that illustrate the reading process. Throughout the book, SQ3R prompts have been revised to better activate reading strategies.

- A new appendix, "ESL Reading Tips," offers reading strategies and activities to aid students who are in the process of acquiring English.

- Visual Vocabulary exercises in each chapter have been revised, providing students with new opportunities to interact with photographs and graphics by completing captions and answering skill-based questions.

Guiding Principles

The Skilled Reader, Second Edition, was written to develop in students the essential abilities that will enable them to become skilled readers and critical thinkers.

Practice and Feedback

An old Chinese proverb says, "I hear and I forget. I see and I remember. I do and I understand." We all know that the best way *to learn* is *to do.* Thus, one of the primary aims of this text is to give students plentiful opportunities to practice, practice, practice!

For every concept introduced in the book, there is an **explanation** of the concept; an **example** with an explanation of the example; and a **practice or sets of practices**. Each chapter also has a **chapter review quiz, brief skill applications, four review tests**, and **six mastery tests**. Two more review tests and two more mastery tests are available on the book's website. For students in Florida and Texas, the website includes practice diagnostic and achievement tests for the state-mandated tests:

The Florida College Basic Skills Exit Test for Florida students

The Texas Higher Education Assessment Test for Texas students

High-Interest Reading Selections

For many, enthusiasm for reading is stimulated by reading material that offers high-interest topics written in a direct, energetic style. Every effort has been made to create reading passages in examples, exercises, reviews, and tests that students will find lively and engaging. Topics are taken from popular culture and textbooks; some examples are music, sports figures, interpersonal relationships, gangs, movies, weight loss, drug use, nutrition, inspiration and success stories, role models, stress management, football, and aerobics.

Integration of the Reading Process and Reading Skills

Skilled readers blend individual reading skills into a reading process such as SQ3R. Before reading, skilled readers skim for new or key vocabulary or main ideas. They create study questions and make connections to their prior knowledge. During reading, skilled readers check their comprehension. For example, they annotate the text. They notice thought patterns and the relationship between ideas. They read for the answers to the questions they created before reading. After reading, skilled readers use outlines, concept maps, and summaries to review what they have read and deepen their understanding. Students are taught to integrate each skill into a reading process in Part One.

In Chapter 1, "A Reading System for Skilled Readers," students are introduced to SQ3R. In every other Part One chapter, students actively apply SQ3R strategies in "Before Reading" and "After Reading" activities. "Before Reading" activities are pre-reading exercises that appear at the beginning of each chapter. These activities guide the student to review important concepts studied in earlier chapters, build on prior knowledge, and preview upcoming material. "After Reading" activities are review activities that appear after the review tests in each chapter. These activities guide students to reflect upon their achievements and assume responsibility for learning.

Since many students are visual learners, a new graphic representation of the SQ3R reading process has been added to Chapter 1. In addition, "Before Reading" and "After Reading" activities are signaled with reading process icons.

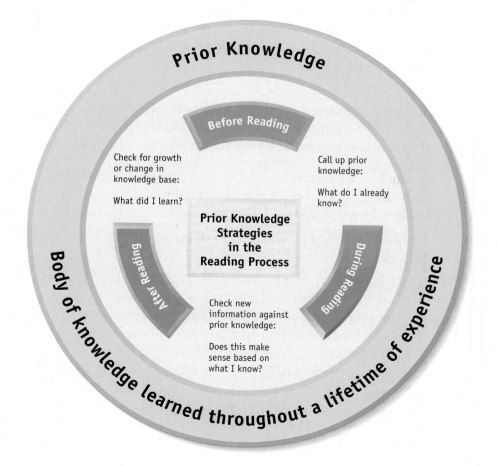

Prior Knowledge

Before Reading

Check for growth or change in knowledge base:

What did I learn?

Call up prior knowledge:

What do I already know?

Prior Knowledge Strategies in the Reading Process

After Reading

During Reading

Check new information against prior knowledge:

Does this make sense based on what I know?

Body of knowledge learned throughout a lifetime of experience

Multiple practice exercises throughout each chapter teach comprehension strategies during the reading process.

Comprehensive Approach

The Skilled Reader, Second Edition, offers several levels of learning. First, students are given an abundance of practice. Students are able to focus on individual reading skills through a chapter-by-chapter workbook approach. In each of the skills chapters of Part One, Review Test 4 offers a multiparagraph passage with items on all the skills taught up to that point. In addition, Chapter 1 ("A Reading System for Skilled Readers") teaches students how to apply their reading skills to the reading process before, during, and after reading by using SQ3R. Students also learn to apply all the skills in combination in Part Two, "Additional Readings," and Part Three, "Combined-Skills Tests." The aim is to provide our students with varied and rich opportunities to learn and practice reading skills and to apply reading processes.

Textbook Structure

To help students become skilled readers and critical thinkers, *The Skilled Reader,* Second Edition, introduces the most important basic reading skills in Part One and then provides sections of additional readings (in Part Two), combined-skills tests (in Part Three), and reading enrichment (in Part Four).

Part One, Becoming a Skilled Reader

Essential reading skills are introduced individually in Part One to help students become skilled readers.

- Chapter 1, "A Reading System for Skilled Readers," guides students through the stages of the SQ3R reading process. Each step of this process is explained thoroughly with ample opportunities for practice and mastery. The aim is to show students how to apply the skills they acquire in each of the skills chapters before, during, and after reading.
- Chapter 2, "Vocabulary in Context," fosters vocabulary acquisition during reading by using a mnemonic technique: SAGE stands for **S**ynonyms, **A**ntonyms, **G**eneral context, and **E**xamples.

- Chapter 3, "Vocabulary-Building Skills," develops language skills by demonstrating how to determine word meanings from prefixes, roots, and suffixes. The chapter also provides extensive instruction in dictionary skills.

- Chapter 4, "Topics and Main Ideas," offers both verbal and visual strategies to help students see the building-block relationship between topics and main ideas.

- Chapter 5, "Locating Stated Main Ideas," builds on the foundation laid in the previous chapter by explaining strategies to locate main ideas along with extensive practice in doing so.

- Chapter 6, "Supporting Details," identifies the differences between major and minor details. This chapter uses a visual method to demonstrate the increasing level of specificity in a paragraph from topic sentence to major details to minor details.

- Chapter 7, "Outlines and Concept Maps," reinforces the skills of locating main ideas and identifying major and minor supporting details. This chapter teaches the students the structure of a text by offering instruction and practice with outlines and concept maps.

- Chapter 8, "Transitions and Thought Patterns," introduces the fundamental thought patterns and the words that signal those patterns. Students are given numerous opportunities to practice identifying the signal words and their relationship to the thought patterns they establish. The chapter includes the time order, space order, listing, and classification patterns.

- Chapter 9, "More Thought Patterns," introduces the more complex thought patterns and the words that signal those patterns. Just as in Chapter 8, students are given extensive practice opportunities. Chapter 9 introduces the comparison-and-contrast pattern, the cause-and-effect pattern, the generalization-and-example pattern, and the definition pattern.

- Chapter 10, "Implied Main Ideas," furthers students' understanding of the main idea by explaining the unstated main idea and offering extensive practice in identifying implied main ideas.

- Chapter 11, "Inferences," addresses this advanced skill carefully by dividing the necessary mental processes into understandable units of activity. Students are taught the basic skills necessary to evaluate an author's purpose and choice of words.

Part Two, Additional Readings

Part Two is a collection of ten reading selections followed by skills questions designed to give students real reading opportunities and the opportunity to gauge their growth as readers. This section begins with a key discussion about the relationship between reading and writing and offers a few pointers on basic writing skills. The readings, which include magazine articles, textbook excerpts, and a short story, were chosen to engage, encourage, and motivate the reader. Each selection is followed by skills questions so that students can practice all the skills taught in Part One. The skills questions are followed by discussion and writing topics so that students can practice making connections among listening, speaking, reading, and writing.

Part Three, Combined-Skills Tests

Part Three is a set of 15 reading passages and combined-skills tests. This section offers students ample opportunity to apply reading skills and strategies and to become more familiar with a standardized testing format to help prepare them for exit exams, standardized reading tests, and future content course quizzes, tests, and exams.

Part Four, Reading Enrichment

Supplementary material is provided here for three important skills.

- Appendix A, "ESL Reading Tips," addresses some of the particular challenges of students who are learning English as an additional language. Students first learn about the difference between literal and figurative language. They then learn how to understand idioms, similes, and metaphors to become skilled readers. Since every chapter of *The Skilled Reader,* Second Edition, teaches specific skills and strategies that are helpful to students learning to read English, students are first guided through a survey of the entire textbook.

- Appendix B, "Reading Graphics," offers basic guidelines for reading and analyzing graphics, followed by specific examples and explanations of tables, line graphs, bar graphs, pie charts, diagrams, and pictograms.

- Appendix C, "Word Parts," is an in-depth list of prefixes, roots, suffixes, their meanings, and sample words. This section supplements Chapter 3, "Vocabulary-Building Skills."

Chapter Features

Each chapter in Part One features elements that work together to help students become skilled readers.

Before Reading About . . . : "Before Reading About . . ." activities appear at the beginning of Chapters 2–11 in Part One. These activities are pre-reading exercises based on SQ3R: they review important concepts studied in earlier chapters, build on prior knowledge, and preview the chapter. For example, students may be asked to create study questions based on the chapter preview and then record the answers to those questions as they read the chapter. Or, students may review relevant information from previous chapters. Sometimes these pre-reading activities direct students to skim the chapter and create a skeleton outline that they complete as they study the chapter. The purpose of "Before Reading About . . ." is to actively teach students to develop a reading process that applies individual reading skills as they study.

After Reading About . . . : "After Reading About . . ." activities appear after Review Test 4 in Chapters 2–11 of Part One. Based on SQ3R, "After Reading About . . ." activities teach students to reflect on their achievements and assume responsibility for their own learning. These activities check their comprehension of the skill taught in the chapter. Students learn to integrate individual reading skills into a reading process; they learn the value of reviewing material; and finally, students create a learning journal that enables them to see patterns in their behaviors and record their growth as readers.

Instruction, example, explanation, and practice: The chapter skill is broken down into components, and each component is introduced and explained. Instruction is followed by an example, an explanation of the example, and a practice. For example, Chapter 2, "Vocabulary in Context," is divided into four components: synonyms, antonyms, general context, and examples. Each of these components has its own instruction, example and explanation, and practice exercises.

Textbook
Skills

Textbook Skills: As the last section of each chapter's instruction, students are shown the ways in which the skills they are learning apply to reading college textbooks. These activities, signaled by the icon to the left, present material from a college textbook and direct the student to apply the chapter's skill to the reading passage or visual. In a concerted effort to prepare students to be skilled readers in their content courses, activities that foster college textbook skills across the curriculum are also carefully woven throughout *The Skilled Reader,* Second Edition. The Textbook Skills icon signals these activities.

Visual Vocabulary: The influence of technology and media on reading is evident in the widespread use of graphics in newspapers, magazines, and college textbooks. The "Textbook Skill" on page 59 zeroes in on the much-needed skill of blending information in visuals—such as photographs, charts, and graphs—with text for full comprehension. Throughout *The Skilled Reader,* Second Edition, visual vocabulary is presented as part of the reading process, and students interact with these visuals by completing captions or answering skill-based questions. The aim is to teach students to value photos, graphs, illustrations, and maps as important sources of information.

Chapter Review: Every chapter includes a fill-in review of the information about a particular reading skill. Students complete statements with words from a word box. The chapter review serves as a comprehension check for the reading concepts taught in that chapter.

Applications: Immediately following the chapter review, brief application exercises give students the opportunity to apply each component of the reading skill they've just acquired.

Review Tests: Each chapter has a total of six review tests, four in the book and two on the book's website. Review Tests 1 through 3 are designed to give opportunity for practice on the specific skill taught in the chapter; Review Test 4 offers a multiparagraph passage with questions based on all the skills taught up to and including that particular chapter. Review Test 4 also gives discussion and writing topics so that teachers have the opportunity to guide students as they develop critical thinking skills.

Mastery Tests: Each chapter also includes eight Mastery Tests, six in the book and two on the website. Most of the Mastery Tests are based on excerpts from science, history, psychology, social science, and literature textbooks.

Review Tests 5 and 6 and Mastery Tests 7 and 8 are available on the book's website. To access these tests, go to **http://www.ablongman. com/henry**. Click on *The Skilled Reader,* then select "More Review and Mastery Tests." These tests can be electronically scored and the scores entered into the instructor's gradebook, if desired.

The Longman Teaching and Learning Package

The Skilled Reader, Second Edition, is supported by a series of innovative teaching and learning supplements.

The **Annotated Instructor's Edition (AIE)** is a replica of the student text, with all answers included. Ask your Longman sales representative for ISBN 0-205-57049-6.

The **Instructor's Manual,** prepared by Mary Dubbé of Thomas Nelson Community College, features teaching strategies for each textbook chapter, plus additional readings that engage students with a variety of learning styles and encourage active learning through class, group, and independent practices. Each chapter includes an introduction designed to hook the students, reproducible handouts, and study-strategy cards. Also included are a 10-item quiz for each chapter and a summary of corresponding activities in the Companion Website. A supplemental section provides a sample syllabus, readability calculations for each reading in *The Skilled Reader,* Second Edition, five book quizzes to encourage independent reading and the creation of book groups, sample THEA and Florida State Exit Exams, and a scaffolded book review form. ISBN 0-205-56696-0.

The **Test Bank,** prepared by Mary Dubbé of Thomas Nelson Community College, features four preformatted quizzes/tests per chapter, plus a midterm exam and a final exam. It is available both in electronic format and printed format. Ask your Longman sales representative for a copy, or download the content at **http://www.ablongman.com/henry** (Instructor Resources section). Your sales representative will provide you with the username and password to access these materials. ISBN 0-205-57384-3.

PowerPoint Presentations for each chapter can be downloaded from the Instructor's Resource Center.

The **Companion Website** offers additional review tests and mastery tests for students as well as sample THEA and Florida State Exit Exams.

The **Lab Manual,** prepared by Mary Dubbé of Thomas Nelson Community College, is designed as a student workbook and provides a collection of 65 activities that provide additional practice, enrichment, and assessment for the skills presented in *The Skilled Reader*, Second Edition. The activities for each chapter include practice exercises, one review test, and two mastery tests that mirror the design of *The Skilled Reader*, Second Edition and emphasize the reading skills and applications students need in order to succeed in college. The lab activities give students realistic practice, encourage them to use the strategies they have learned, and offer an opportunity for students to continue to build a base of general, background knowledge. This lab manual can be used to strengthen students' reading skills, to allow them to assess their own progress, and to measure their success and readiness for college level reading. The lab manual is available packaged with *The Skilled Reader*, Second Edition for an additional cost. ISBN 0-205-57659-1.

Developmental Reading Student Supplements

Longman Annotated Literature Series Now, timeless texts are complemented by engaging pedagogy and illuminating content. Essay and review questions, activities, and discussion journals allow students to directly engage the story and gain a fuller sense of the material. In addition to utilizing reading skills, students will sharpen their vocabulary, critical thinking, and writing skills. Please visit **www.ablongman.com/devenglish** for more information.

Longman Literature for College Readers Series Literature anthologies, edited by Yvonne Sisko, help students maximize their reading and writing abilities with supportive pedagogy and experience literature like never before. Please visit **www. ablongman.com/devenglish** for a list of the anthologies and additional information.

Vocabulary Skills Study Card (Student / 0-321-31802-1) Colorful, affordable, and packed with useful information, Longman's Vocabulary Study Card is a concise, 8-page reference guide to developing key vocabulary skills, such as learning to recognize context clues, reading a dictionary entry, and recognizing key root words, suffixes, and prefixes. Laminated for durability, students can keep this Study Card for years to come and pull it out whenever they need a quick review.

Reading Skills Study Card (Student / 0-321-33833-2) Colorful, affordable, and packed with useful information, Longman's Reading Skills Study Card is a concise, 8-page reference guide to help students develop basic reading skills, such as concept skills, structural skills, language skills, and reasoning skills. Laminated for durability, students can keep this Study Card for years to come and pull it out whenever they need a quick review.

The Longman Textbook Reader, 2nd Edition (with answers: Student / 0-321-48629-3 or without answers: Student / 0-205-51924-5) Offers six complete chapters from our textbooks: psychology, mathematics, biology, history, literature, and business. Each chapter includes additional comprehension quizzes, critical thinking questions, and group activities.

The Longman Reader's Portfolio and Student Planner (Student / 0-321-29610-9) This unique supplement provides students with a space to plan, think about, and present their work. The portfolio includes a diagnostic area (including a learning style questionnaire), a working area (including calendars, vocabulary logs, reading response sheets, book club tips, and other valuable materials), and a display area (including a progress chart, a final table of contents, and a final assessment), as well as a daily planner for students including daily, weekly, and monthly calendars.

The Longman Reader's Journal, by Kathleen McWhorter (Student / 0-321-08843-3) The first journal for readers, The Longman Reader's Journal offers a place for students to record their reactions to and questions about any reading.

The Longman Planner (Student / 0-321-04573-4) Ideal for organizing a busy college life! Included are hour-by-hour schedules, monthly and weekly calendars, an address book, and an almanac of tips and useful information.

What Every Student Should Know About Study Skills (Student / 0-321-44736-0) This supplement teaches students the study skills they need to master for college success. The strategy-development activities throughout the book allow students to assess their learning styles, improve time management and stress management, and become active learners.

***Newsweek* Discount Subscription Coupon (12 weeks) (Student / 0-321-08895-6)** *Newsweek* gets students reading, writing, and thinking about what's going on in the world around them. The price of the subscription is added to the cost of the book. Instructors receive weekly lesson plans, quizzes, and curriculum guides as well as a complimentary *Newsweek* subscription. *Package item only.*

Interactive Guide to *Newsweek* (Student / 0-321-05528-4) Available with the 12-week subscription to *Newsweek*, this guide serves as a workbook for students who are using the magazine.

Research Navigator Guide for English, H. Eric Branscomb and Michelle D. Trim (Student / 0-321-49601-9) Designed to teach students how to conduct high-quality online research and to document it properly, Research Navigator guides provide discipline-specific academic resources; in addition to helpful tips on the writing process, online research, and finding and citing valid sources. Research Navigator guides include an access code to Research Navigator™, providing access to thousands of academic journals and periodicals, the *New York Times* Search by Subject Archive, Link Library, Library Guides, and more.

The Oxford American Desk Dictionary and Thesaurus, Second Edition (ISBN 0-425-18068-9) From the Oxford University Press and Berkley Publishing Group comes this one-of-a-kind reference book that combines both of the essential language tools—dictionary and thesaurus—in a single, integrated A-to-Z volume. The 1,024-page book offers more than 150,000 entries, definitions, and synonyms so you can find the right word every time, as well as appendices of valuable quick-reference information including signs and symbols, weights and measures, presidents of the United States, U.S. states and capitals, and more.

The Oxford Essential Thesaurus (ISBN 0-425-16421-7) From Oxford University Press, renowned for quality educational and reference works, comes this concise, easy-to-use thesaurus—the essential tool for finding just the right word for every occasion. The 528-page book includes 175,000 synonyms in a simple A-to-Z format, more than 10,000 entries, extensive word choices, example sentences and phrases, and guidance on usage, punctuation, and more in the exclusive "Writers Toolkit."

Penguin Discount Novel Program In cooperation with Penguin Putnam, Inc., Longman is proud to offer a variety of Penguin paperbacks at a significant discount when packaged with any Longman title. Excellent additions to any developmental reading course, Penguin titles give students the opportunity to explore contemporary and classical fiction and drama. The available titles include works by authors as diverse as Toni Morrison, Julia Alvarez, Mary Shelley, and Shakespeare. To review the complete list of titles available, visit the Longman-Penguin-Putnam website at **http://www.ablongman.com/penguin.**

Multimedia Offerings

Interested in incorporating online materials into your course? Longman is happy to help. Our regional technology specialists provide training on all of our multimedia offerings.

MyReadingLab (www.myreadinglab.com) MyReadingLab is the first and only online learning system to diagnose both students' reading skills and reading levels. This remarkable program utilizes diagnostic testing, personalized practice, and gradebook reports to allow instructors to measure student performance and help students gain control over their reading. Specifically created for developmental students, MyReadingLab is a website that provides diagnostics, practice, tests, and reporting on student reading skills and student reading levels. Student reading skills are improved through a mastery-based format of exercises and tests. Exercises include objective-based questions, open-ended questions, short answer questions, combined skills exercises and more. Student reading level is assessed through a Lexile framework (developed by Metametrics™, an educational measurement expert). Once diagnosed, students are assigned a Lexile number, which indicates their reading comprehension skills, and throughout the program, the Lexile number rises as the students' reading level improves. The result of this skills and level combination is a personalized student study plan to address individual needs and quantifiable data that measures individual student reading level advancement.

The Longman Vocabulary Website (http://www.ablongman.com/vocabulary) This unique website features hundreds of exercises in ten topic areas to strengthen vocabulary skills. Students will also benefit from "100 Words That All High School Graduates Should Know," a useful resource that provides definitions for each of the words on this list, vocabulary flashcards, and audio clips to help facilitate pronunciation skills.

Longman Study Skills Website (http://www.ablongman.com/studyskills) This site offers hundreds of review strategies for college success, time and stress management skills, study strategies, and more. Students can take a variety of assessment tests to learn about their organizational skills and learning styles, with follow-up quizzes to reinforce the strategies they have learned.

Developmental Reading Instructor Resources

Printed Test Bank for Developmental Reading (Instructor / 0-321-08596-5) Offers more than 3,000 questions in all areas of reading, including vocabulary, main idea, supporting details, patterns of organization, critical thinking, analytical reasoning, inference, point of view, visual aides, and textbook reading. (Electronic also available; see CDs.)

Electronic Test Bank for Developmental Reading (Instructor / CD 0-321-08179-X) Offers more than 3,000 questions in all areas of reading, including vocabulary, main idea, supporting details, patterns of organization, critical thinking, analytical reasoning, inference, point of view, visual aides, and textbook reading. Instructors simply choose questions, then print out the completed test for distribution OR offer the test online.

The Longman Guide to Classroom Management (Instructor / 0-321-09246-5) This guide is designed as a helpful resource for instructors who have classroom management problems. It includes helpful strategies for dealing with disruptive students in the classroom and the "do's and don'ts" of discipline.

The Longman Guide to Community Service-Learning in the English Classroom and Beyond (Instructor / 0-321-12749-8) Written by Elizabeth Rodriguez Kessler of California State University–Northridge, this monograph provides a definition and history of service-learning, as well as an overview of how service-learning can be integrated effectively into the college classroom.

The Longman Instructor's Planner (Instructor / 0-321-09247-3) This planner includes weekly and monthly calendars, student attendance and grading rosters, space for contact information, Web references, an almanac, and blank pages for notes.

State-Specific Supplements

For Florida Adopters

Thinking Through the Test: A Study Guide for the Florida College Basic Skills Exit Test, by D. J. Henry. This workbook helps students strengthen their reading skills in preparation for the Florida College Basic Skills Exit Test. It features both diagnostic tests to help assess areas that may need improvement and exit tests to help test skill mastery. Detailed explanatory answers have been provided for almost all of the questions.

Reading Skills Summary for the Florida State Exit Exam, by D. J. Henry (Student / 0-321-08478-0) An excellent study tool for students preparing to take the Florida College Basic Skills Exit Test for Reading, this laminated reading grid summarizes all the skills tested on the Exit Exam.

For Texas Adopters

The Longman THEA Study Guide, by Jeannette Harris (Student / 0-321-27240-0) Created specifically for students in Texas, this study guide includes straightforward explanations and numerous practice exercises to help students prepare for the reading and writing sections of THEA Test.

TASP Test Package, Third Edition (Instructor / Print ISBN 0-321-01959-8) These 12 practice pre-tests and post-tests assess the same reading and writing skills covered in the Texas TASP examination.

For New York/CUNY Adopters

Preparing for the CUNY-ACT Reading and Writing Test, edited by Patricia Licklider (Student / 0-321-19608-2) This booklet, prepared by reading and writing faculty from across the CUNY system, is designed to help students prepare for the CUNY-ACT exit test. It includes test-taking tips, reading passages, typical exam questions, and sample writing prompts to help students become familiar with each portion of the test.

CLAST Test Package, Fourth Edition (Instructor / Print ISBN 0-321-01950-4) These two, 40-item objective tests evaluate students' readiness for the Florida CLAST exams. Strategies for teaching CLAST preparedness are included.

Acknowledgments

As I worked on the second edition of this reading series, I felt an overwhelming sense of gratitude and humility for the opportunity to serve the learning community as a textbook author. I would like to thank the entire Longman team for their dedication to providing the best possible materials to foster literacy. To every person, from the editorial team to the representatives in the field, all demonstrate a passion for students, teachers, and learning. It is a joy to be part of such a team. Special thanks are due to the following: Kate Edwards, Acquisitions Editor, and Janice Wiggins-Clarke, Developmental Editor, for their guidance and support; Kathy Smith with Nesbitt Graphics, Inc. for her tireless devotion to excellence; Ellen MacElree and the entire production team for their work ethic and gracious attitudes, including Katherine Grimaldi and Genevieve Coyne. I would also like to thank Mary Dubbé for authoring the Lab Manual and the Instructor's Manual that supplement this reading series.

For nearly twenty-five years, I worked with the most amazing group of faculty from across the State of Florida as an item-writer, reviewer, or scorer of state-wide assessment exams for student learning and professional certification. The work that we accomplished together continues to inform me as a teacher, writer, and consultant. I owe a debt of gratitude to this group who sacrificed much for the good of our students. In particular, I owe thanks to the following for their mentorship: Dr. Dan Kelly, University of Florida; Don Tighe, Valencia Community College; Dr. Willa Wolcott, University of Florida; and Pat Hare, Brevard Community College.

I would also like to acknowledge several of my colleagues at Daytona Beach Community College: Dustin Weeks, Librarian; Dr. Rhodella Brown, Dean of the Virtual College; and Sandra Offiah-Hawkins, reading professor. As Tennyson extols in "Ulysses," these are the "souls that have toiled, and wrought, and thought with me." Their influence and support has made me a better person, teacher, and writer.

Finally, I would like to gratefully recognize the invaluable insights provided by the following colleagues and reviewers. I deeply appreciate their investment of time and energy: Patricia Davis, *Houston Community College;* Ivan Dole, *Northlake College;* Maria Elizabeth Garcia, *Laredo Community College;* Rebecca Ingraham, *St. Charles Community College;* Jocelyn Jacobs, *Lee College;* Sandra Thomson, *Northwest Vista College;* Kristine Volpi, *Broward Community College;* and Quakish Williams, *Miami Dade College.*

D. J. Henry
Datytona Beach, FL

Introduction

Congratulations! If you are reading this textbook, you have come face to face with a life-changing fact: Reading is a vital tool for success.

Reading is one of the most important skills we can gain. Good reading skills give us access to better-paying jobs. Reading well makes everyday life easier and more interesting. As skilled readers, we can stay well informed about events that affect our lives by reading newspapers and magazines. We can understand contracts and help our children with their homework. As skilled readers, we also find joy in a well-told story or a well-crafted argument.

A few semesters ago, Jamie, a former reading student of mine who had struggled with math for years, burst into my office beaming with pride. "I am doing great in math," she boasted with a wide grin. "Did you know there are words—not just numbers but words, too—in a math textbook? Once I learn the vocabulary for each chapter, the formulas begin to make sense. And everything I learned in reading class works in my math class." Jamie passed her math course with one of the highest grade point averages in her class. She had become a skilled reader.

What Is a Skilled Reader?

Just what is a skilled reader? A skilled reader is one who has a positive attitude, who wants to learn, who finds good reasons to read, who gets rid of distractions, and who stays focused. This textbook has been written and designed to teach you how to become such a reader, but here are some quick pointers to get you started.

How to Stay Focused

- Create a place for studying. Study in that one place as often as you can, and don't play, sleep, or watch TV there.
- Manage your time. Make a plan for how you will spend your time, and stick to it. Create a weekly plan. Once you see how much you can accomplish in a week, change your next weekly plan so it is even more realistic.

- Let go of distractions. If you find your mind wandering when you are trying to study, start a list. Jot down reminders of your distracting thoughts on a separate piece of paper. Once you have stored them on paper, you can put them out of your mind.

- Set goals, and work toward them. To reach goals, you have to set them first. For example, you probably want to graduate from college. What are your other goals? Write them down. Keep track of each time you reach a goal you have set, and give yourself a pat on the back for your success.

How to Succeed in College

- Attend class. To get the most out of college and to learn from your courses, you need to go to class. And your instructors will expect you to know what has been covered in class.

- Read assignments before class. Complete all reading assignments so that you will have a basic understanding of the subject before the lecture and class discussion. Think about questions you'd like to ask about the reading.

- Review your lecture notes after class. Within a day after a class, review your notes and fill in the blanks while the lecture is still fresh in your mind. If you didn't understand part of the discussion, ask your instructor or your classmates for help.

- Learn about the campus. Find out where the library is and what hours it is open. Become familiar with the college offices so you will know how to get things done.

Previewing This Text

This textbook is designed to help you become a skilled reader. Knowing how the book is set up and what features it has will help you make the most of your studies.

Reading Skills and Practice Materials

Each chapter addresses a specific reading skill. For example, Chapters 2 and 3 deal with vocabulary. Take a moment to look over the table of contents, which is on pages v–x. Answer the following questions:

1. How many reading skills (chapters) are in Part One? 11

2. What skill is taught in Chapter 4? Topic and main idea

In each chapter, the skill is explained and examples are given. Practice exercises follow to help you practice each skill. In addition, each chapter includes review tests and mastery tests (with scorecards) so that you and your instructor can track your progress.

The tests have been designed to give you lots of opportunities to practice test-taking skills in preparation for the standardized tests you will face in your academic career. Look in Chapters 4 and 5 at the review tests and mastery tests, and answer the following questions:

3. How many review tests does each chapter have? ___/___

_____

4. How many mastery tests does each chapter have? _/_

_____

Textbook Skills

One of the main goals of a reading course is to prepare you for college-level textbook reading; therefore, "Textbook Skills" have been included in every chapter for your benefit. Featured passages are taken from college textbooks that are used in business courses, the humanities, the social sciences, and the physical sciences. Textbook skills are marked with an icon as seen at left:

Textbook
Skills

5. Look through Chapter 8. What are three pages that include the Textbook Skills icon? 306, 312

_____

6. In Chapter 8, does Review Test 3 deal with Textbook Skills? Yes

Additional Readings

Part Two of the book contains ten additional readings. Each reading is introduced, and a list of vocabulary words and definitions is given. After each reading are questions to help you test your vocabulary and your understanding of the reading. Discussion questions are also given to help get a conversation about the reading started.

7. Look at a reading in Part Two. What is the list of vocabulary words before the reading called? _____

8. What is the title of Reading Selection 1? _____

Combined-Skills Tests

Part Three contains 15 tests that combine all the skills you are learning. Most of the tests have a short reading selection and questions that follow it.

9. Look at Test 7. What is the title of the reading selection? _____

_____

10. How many questions does Test 7 have? _____

Visual Vocabulary

More and more academic and everyday readings include photographs, charts, graphs, or some other kind of visual or graphic aid to help make a point clear. Therefore, each chapter of this textbook also teaches visual literacy skills, asking you to study photographs or graphics and answer questions about them.

11. Look at the graphic on page 387. What does the graphic show? _____

_____

12. Sometimes the visuals are part of the reading selections. How many of the numbered reading selections in Part Two include photos? _____

Reading as Power

Reading is a great source of power and joy. It is my sincere hope that your semester is both productive and rewarding as you discover the joyful power of reading. Here is to your success as a skilled reader both now and in your future coursework.

                                                                D. J. Henry

Becoming a
Skilled Reader

Daryl Lawrence   09/29/09

A Reading System for Skilled Readers

CHAPTER PREVIEW

Many people think that reading involves simply passing our eyes over the words in the order that they appear on the page. But reading is much more than that. Once we understand the **reading process**, we can follow specific steps and apply strategies that will make us skilled readers.

Reading is an active process during which you draw information from the text to create meaning. When you understand what you've read, you've achieved **comprehension** of the material.

> **Comprehension** is an understanding of information.

Before we examine the reading process in detail, it is important to talk about the role of prior knowledge.

Prior Knowledge

We all have learned a large body of information that we have acquired throughout a lifetime of experience. This body of information is called **prior knowledge**.

Knowledge is gained from experience and stored in memory. Everyday, prior knowledge is expanded by what is experienced. For example, a small child hears the word *hot* as her father blows on a spoonful of steaming soup. The hungry child grabs for the bowl and cries as some of the hot liquid spills on her hand. The child has learned and will remember the meaning of *hot*.

> **Prior knowledge** is the large body of information that is learned throughout a lifetime of experience.

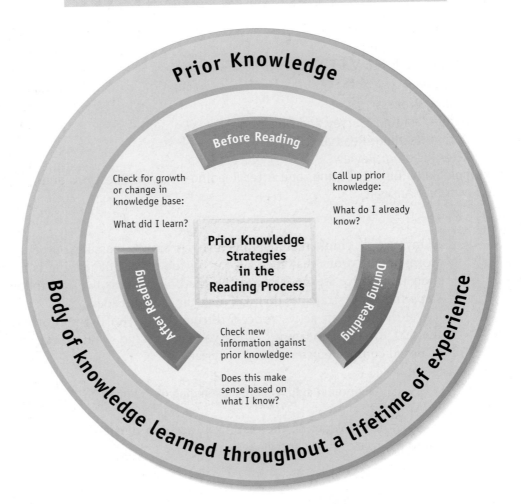

EXAMPLE   Read the following paragraph. In the space provided, list any topics from the paragraph about which you already have prior knowledge.

A computer virus is programmed to raid and attack existing computer programs. The virus is sent by an e-mail or activated through a download. The virus program then infects the whole computer system. The virus attaches itself to other programs in the computer and copies itself. Some computer viruses are terrible; they erase files or lock up systems. Viruses must not go untreated.

EXPLANATION If you know about computer programs, this passage makes more sense to you than it does to someone who does not understand how computer programs work. However, even if you do not know much about computers, you may have helpful prior knowledge about some of the ideas in the passage. For example, most of us have been sick with a virus. We understand that a virus can affect our entire body, and we understand the need for treatment to help the body repair itself. Our prior knowledge about human viruses helps us understand how serious a computer virus can be.

The more prior knowledge we have about a topic, the more likely we are to understand that topic. The more you know, the easier it is to learn. This is why skilled readers build their knowledge base by reading often!

PRACTICE 1

Read the passage, and answer the questions that follow it.

Give Water a Chance!

[1]Water is the most common substance on earth. [2]In fact, all living things are made mostly of water. [3]For example, the human body is about two-thirds water.

[4]Your body uses the water in your blood to supply nutrients and carry away wastes. [5]A lack of water can cause fats and toxins to remain in your body. [6]Instead of drinking water, you may reach for coffee, soft drinks, or alcohol. [7]Wine, coffee, tea, and soft drinks are all liquids, but they don't have the life-giving effects of plain water. [8]Caffeine strains the heart and causes high blood pressure. [9]Alcohol and soft drinks contain too much sugar. [10]Even diet soft drinks contain too much salt. [11]Your kidneys can't use contaminated water, so your liver must filter it. [12]If your liver is busy filtering water, it isn't free to process blood and break down fat. [13]Thus the more water you drink, the more likely you are to flush fat out of your system rather than store it. [14]Health experts recommend that we drink eight large glasses of water every day.

1. What did you already know about water? That is, what was your prior knowledge about water? _____

2. When you think of water, what do you think of? Describe ideas and experiences that come to mind when you think of water and being thirsty.

   _____

3. Was this an easy passage to understand? How does your prior knowledge about water affect your understanding of this passage? _____

   _____

4. List the statements in the passage that you had no prior knowledge about.

   _____

VISUAL VOCABULARY

This photo illustrates _____ water.

   a. purified
   b. contaminated

The Reading Process

Prior knowledge helps the skilled reader get a head start on the reading process. Skilled readers break reading into a three-step process. Each step uses its own thinking activities.

1. Before reading, look over or preview the material. (Previewing brings up prior knowledge.) Ask questions about the material you are about to read.

2. During reading, test your understanding of the material.

3. After reading, review and react to what you have learned.

One well-known way to apply this reading process is called **SQ3R.**

> **SQ3R** stands for
> Survey
> Question
> Read
> Recite
> Review

SQ3R activates prior knowledge and offers strategies for each phase of the reading process. The following graphic illustrates the phases of the reading process through SQ3R. Skilled readers repeat or move among phases as needed to repair comprehension.

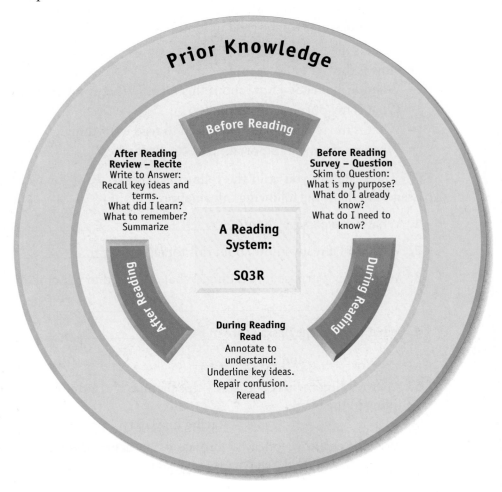

Before Reading: Survey and Question

Survey

Quickly look over, or **skim**, the reading passage for clues about how it is organized and what it means.

To skim effectively, look at *italic* and **boldface** type and take note of titles, introductions, and headings. Also look at pictures and graphs. Finally, read the first paragraph, summaries, and questions. Each of these clues provides important information.

Glossary

skim read quickly

Question

To aid in comprehension, ask questions before you read. The following list of prereading questions can be used in most reading situations:

- What is the passage about?
- How is the material organized?
- What do I already know about this idea? (What is my prior knowledge?)
- What is my purpose for reading?
- What is my reading plan? Do I need to read everything?
- What are the most important parts to remember?

EXAMPLE   Before you read the following passage word for word, skim the passage and fill in the following information.

1. What is the passage about? _____

2. What do I already know about this topic? _____

3. What is my purpose for reading? What do I need to remember? _____

   _____

4. What ideas in the passage are in **bold** type? _____, _____,

   _____, and _____

5. After reading the passage, study this picture, and complete the caption by filling in the blank.

Racing for Safety

The challenge for each Indianapolis 500 car team is the same every year. Designers need to develop a race car that is safe, durable, and competitive in

VISUAL VOCABULARY

This track in Daytona Beach, Florida, is an oval track with banked turns and long straightaways; thus it is a

_____.

a. short oval
b. speedway

different racing conditions. Durability is required to complete the 16-race schedule. In addition, cars must meet the demands of four different types of racing circuits, with each course requiring a different aerodynamic and mechanical setup.

Street: A narrow, temporary course ranging from 1.6 to 2.1 miles in length, with tight turns and a long straightaway. The Long Beach circuit (lap record, 108 mph) tests the durability of the gearbox, braking system, and low-speed acceleration.

Road: Laguna Seca Raceway (lap record, 112 mph) is an example of a road course with hills. A road course is a wide-open track that ranges in length from 1.9 to 4 miles. It has both slow and high-speed corners and is wide enough for passing. The suspension system, downhill braking, and power are stressed on this type of course.

Short Oval: Phoenix International Raceway (lap record, 172 mph) is a 1-mile-long oval track. Short straightaways and banked turns are typical of this type of track. The short oval tests the suspension and aerodynamic setup of the car.

Speedway: The speedway is an oval track with banked turns and long straightaways. The one-lap record at the Michigan International Speedway (2-mile oval) is 234 mph. At Indianapolis (2.5-mile oval), the record is 232 mph. High sustained speed requires aerodynamic efficiency.

The job of the team engineer is to prepare a competitive, safe car that can be adjusted quickly. Currently, the Indy cars are considered the safest race cars in the world.

—Adapted from "Car Development," *NAS Systems Development at NASA Ames Research Center,* Homepage, 9 Sept. 2001.

EXPLANATION

1. *What is the passage about?* The title of the passage gives us a clue: "Racing for Safety." So does the first paragraph. This passage is about the need to make race cars safe for four different types of tracks.

2. *What do I already know about this idea?* This answer will vary for each of you. Racing fans already know a great deal that will help them understand the details in this passage. Others may not follow the sport. Yet most of you probably drive or ride in cars and can relate to the need for safety on different types of roads, so you can connect your driving experience to the information in the passage.

3. *What is my purpose for reading?* You read to learn new information. *What do I need to remember?* You might need to remember the four types of racetracks.

4. *What ideas in the passage are in* **bold** *type?* The four types of racetracks are in bold: street, road, short oval, and speedway.

5. Based on information in the passage, the track in Daytona Beach is a speedway.

Applying the Before Reading Step: "Before Reading" Activities

The "Before Reading" activities in this book will help you turn reading skills into reading strategies. The rest of the chapters in Part One start with a "Before Reading" activity. These activities use SQ3R strategies. Sometimes, the activity directs you to review skills taught in earlier chapters. At other times, you are asked to skim the chapter and create study questions. Then you answer these questions as you read about the skill. For example, in Chapter 4's **Before Reading About Stated Main Ideas,** you will create several questions based on the chapter preview. Notice that every chapter has a set of preview topics listed under the chapter's title.

During Reading: Read and Recite

After you have surveyed and asked questions about the text, it's time to read the entire passage.

A. Read

As you read, think about the importance of the information by continuing to ask questions:

- Does this new information agree with what I already knew?
- Do I need to change my mind about what I thought I knew?
- What is the significance of this information? Do I need to remember this?

In addition to asking questions while you read, acknowledge and resolve any confusion as it occurs.

- Create questions based on the headings, subheadings, and words in **bold** print and *italics*.
- Reread the parts you don't understand.
- Reread when your mind drifts during reading.
- Read ahead to see if the idea becomes clearer.
- Determine the meanings of words from the context.
- Look up new or difficult words.
- Think about ideas even when they differ from your own.

B. Recite

Make the material your own. Make sure you understand it by repeating the information.

- Create a picture in your mind or on paper.
- Restate the ideas in your own words.
- Write out answers to the questions you created based on the headings and subheadings.

EXAMPLE   Before you read the following passage, take the time to use your surveying skills by answering the following questions.

1. What is the passage about? _____

2. What do I already know about this topic? What is my prior knowledge?

_____

_____

_____

3. What is important about this passage? What do I need to remember?

_____

_____

_____

4. What are the words in **bold** type? _____ , _____ ,

and _____

As you read, monitor your understanding or comprehension. Once you have surveyed the information, read the passage. Record the answers to the questions based on the ideas in **bold** print.

Drug Abuse: *A, B, C*

5. What new or difficult words do I need to look up?

_____

_____

6. How does alcohol act as a depressant?

_____

_____

7. How do barbiturates act as a depressant?

_____

_____

8. How does cocaine act as a stimulant?

_____

_____

Drug abuse is a serious problem in modern society. Drugs are available at school, on the street, and even in our homes. Depression, stress, and peer pressure can make the use of drugs as an escape very appealing. Three drugs in particular—alcohol, barbiturates, and cocaine—cause millions of people great loss of income, health, and peace of mind. One way to combat drug abuse is to learn some facts about these drugs.

Alcohol is a depressant that affects the central nervous system. It slows the action of nerve cells called *neurons*. Alcohol numbs the part of the brain that controls behavior. It makes the user feel happy and relaxed. However, as little as $1\frac{1}{2}$ ounces of alcohol affect the body and judgment. Muscle control is lost, and speech becomes slurred. Some people become loud and violent; others insist on driving. Too much alcohol taken in during a short period of time can cause breathing to stop, which can lead to coma or even death. Alcohol is the oldest and most commonly used social drug.

Barbiturates are also depressants that affect the central nervous system. In small doses, they relieve tension. In large doses, they cause a deep sleep. A large dose that does not result in sleep causes a feeling of being high. This feeling is similar to the effect of alcohol. Barbiturates can be grouped by how long their effect lasts. The longest-lasting barbiturates stay in the body for 6 to 24 hours. The short-term barbiturates last 3 to 6 hours and are the most widely used. These are the ones doctors give to people who complain about sleep problems. Barbiturates are often used in suicide attempts.

Cocaine is a stimulant that causes short, intense bursts of energy. When cocaine is taken into the body by chewing coca leaves, stomach acids reduce the effect. However, when the drug is sniffed through the nose or injected directly into a vein, the drug becomes more dangerous. Mild use causes confusion and anxiety. A large dose leads to dizziness, tremors, and convulsions. Overdoses cause the heart to stop and breathing to cease.

`EXPLANATION`   Compare your answers to the ones given here. Your wording and examples may be different.

Before Reading: Survey and Question

1. The passage is about drug abuse.

2. Details of your prior knowledge will vary.

3. What is important to remember are the characteristics of the three types of drugs and the dangers of each drug.

4. The words in **bold** type are *alcohol*, *barbiturates*, and *cocaine*.

During Reading: Read and Recite

5. Words you need to look up may include *depressant, neurons, stimulant,* and *convulsions.*

6. Alcohol slows down the brain and causes loss of muscle control. Loss of muscle control causes unclear speech and poor driving. Alcohol can cause a person to become violent or to make poor decisions and can lead to a coma or death.

7. Depending on the dose and type, barbiturates can help a person relax, cause a deep sleep, or lead to coma or death.

8. Cocaine causes confusion, anxiety, dizziness, tremors, and convulsions. Cocaine in large doses brings the heart and lungs to a stop.

9. Identify here any ideas you needed to reread to understand. _____

_____

After Reading: Review

Once you have read the entire selection, go back over the material to review it.

- Summarize the most important parts.
- Revisit and answer the questions raised by headings and subheadings.
- Review new words and their meanings based on the way they were used in the passage.

As part of your review, take time to think and write about what you have read.

- Connect new information to your prior knowledge about the topic.
- Form opinions about the material and the author.
- Notice changes in your opinions based on the new information.
- Write about what you have read.

PRACTICE 2

Now that you have learned about each of the three phases of the reading process, practice putting all three together. Think before, during, and after reading. Apply SQ3R to the following passage. Remember the steps:

- **Survey:** Look over the whole passage.
- **Question:** Ask questions about the content. Predict how the new information fits in with what you already know about the topic.
- **Read:** Continue to question, look up new words, reread, and create pictures in your mind.
- **Recite:** Restate the ideas in your own words. Write out questions and answers, definitions of words, and new information.
- **Review:** Think about what you have read and written. Use writing to capture your opinions and feelings about what you have read.

Before Reading: Survey and Question

The following passage is adapted from a speech delivered by Connecticut Senator Joseph Lieberman. Skim the passage and answer the following questions.

1. What is this passage about? _____

2. What do I already know about this topic? _____

   _____

3. What do I need to remember? _____

   _____

4. What ideas are in **bold** print? _____ ,

   _____ , _____ ,

   _____ , and _____

5. What new or difficult words do I need to look up?

_____

_____

_____

6. What indicates a breakdown of the old rules and limits?

_____

_____

_____

7. How are the media the new teacher of values?

_____

_____

_____

8. What is the immoral television show mentioned by Lieberman?

_____

_____

_____

_____

During Reading: Read and Record

As you read this statement by Senator Joseph Lieberman, answer the questions raised by the ideas in **bold** type.

The Social Impact of Music Violence

Our children are often better armed than our police. We applaud celebrities like the NBA's Dennis Rodman with each brazen elbow he throws at an opponent and/or a cameraman. And we don't seem to blink when big businesses sell music to our children that celebrates violence, including the murder of police, gang rape, and sexual perversity, including pedophilia.

These events speak of a **breakdown in the old rules and limits** that once governed our public lives and the way we raised our children. We are left with a vacuum, a values vacuum, in which our children learn that anything goes, and which I believe is at the heart of our society's worst problems.

This vacuum is troubling in its own right. It is all the more profoundly upsetting when we consider how the **media are the new teacher of values**. More and more, in our society, the television and movie producers, the fashion advertisers, the gangsta rappers and shock rockers, and a host of other players within the electronic media are teaching our children new values. They have an extremely powerful hold on our culture and our children in particular, and they often show little sense of responsibility for the harmful values they are selling.

As a result, the marketplace is flooded with **immoral television shows** like Fox's _When Animals Attack,_ which treats real-life terror as a form of entertainment; with video games like Postal, in which the player acts as a deranged gunman trying to wipe out an entire town and whose marketing brochure promises "chilling realism as victims actually beg for mercy, scream for their lives, and pile up on the streets." And the inexcusable ads of Calvin Klein told a generation threatened by heroin use that it is cool to look and be strung out.

Music lyrics are sometimes a piece of this problem with their messages. Consider a song like "Slap-a-Hoe" by the group Dove Shack, which praises a machine that automatically smacks a wife or girlfriend into line; or the vile work of the death metal band Cannibal Corpse, which recorded one song describing the rape of a woman with a knife. These songs are helping to create a

9. How are music lyrics a piece of the problem?

_____

_____

_____

_____

10. According to Lieberman, what is *gangsta rap*?

_____

_____

_____

_____

culture of violence that is increasingly enveloping our children, hardening them to consequences and ultimately cheapening the value of human life.

Social science can tell us about the impact that violent and antisocial music has on its listeners. But we should also take a close look at the real-life experiences in the world of **gangsta rap**, a part of the music industry that has glorified murder and mayhem on CDs and then lived it on the streets. The story of Tupac Shakur is well known. He and many other rappers recorded rhymes that help make killing cool. It was the same kind of gangsterism they celebrated that claimed Shakur's life and has landed several other rappers in jail. Before he was killed, Tupac Shakur himself said he went beyond "representing" violence—"I represented it too much. I was thug life."

This music, reinforced by television through MTV that presents the gangster life as the high life, has spawned its own subculture, setting standards for how to dress, how to treat women, and how to resolve conflict cleanly with a bullet.

I hope the music industry will consider improving its one-size-fits-all labeling system to give parents the basic information they need to make informed judgments for their kids.

—Adapted from Lieberman, "The Social Impact of Music Violence." The Governmental Affairs Committee Subcommittee on Oversight.

After Reading: Review

11. What do you think that Senator Lieberman wants to happen based on the views he offers in this passage? _____

_____

_____

12. Which of Senator Lieberman's opinions do you agree with? _____

_____

_____

13. Which of Senator Lieberman's opinions do you disagree with? _____

_____

_____

14. Have your opinions changed after reading Senator Lieberman's view? Why or why not? _____

_____

_____

15. Why is Senator Lieberman's opinion important on this issue? _____

_____

_____

Applying the After Reading Step: "After Reading" Activities

"After Reading" activities will help you turn reading skills into reading strategies. "After Reading" activities appear in Chapters 2–11 as a final review and comprehension check before the mastery tests. After you have completed the review tests, you will be asked questions that focus on your studies. These questions ask you to reflect on what you have learned about the skill taught in the chapter. As you write your answers, you are creating a learning log or journal that tracks your growth as a reader.

Textbook
Skills

Before, During, and After Reading— Asking Questions and Recording Answers

A vast number of textbooks use titles, headings, **bold** print, and *italics* to organize ideas. A skilled reader applies the questioning and recording steps to these pieces of information. For example, before reading, turn titles and headings into questions. Write these questions out. During or after reading, write out the answers to these questions.

EXAMPLE   Before you read the following passage from a health textbook, skim the information and write out four questions based on the title and the words in **bold** print. After you read, answer the questions you have created.

Three Types of Eating Disorders

Throughout our lives, most of us wage a running battle with food. We eat too much, we gain weight, and a few days go by when we are not concerned about what we are putting into our mouths and what all that food is doing to our hips, our buttocks, or other body parts. On occasion, over one-third of all Americans are obese and obsessed with diet.

For a growing number of people, chiefly young women, this obsessive bond with food develops into a persistent, chronic eating disorder known as **anorexia nervosa**. Anorexia is a condition marked by deliberate food restriction and severe, life-threatening weight loss. **Bulimia nervosa** is an eating disorder marked by binge eating, which is followed by improper steps to avoid weight gain. These steps include purging (self-induced vomiting), laxative abuse, or excessive exercise. **Binge eating disorder** (BED) is an eating disorder of regular binge eating, without steps to avoid weight gain. Binge eaters are clinically obese.

—Donatelle, *Access to Health*, 7th ed., p. 280.

1. _____

_____

2. _____

_____

3. _____

_____

4. _____

_____

EXPLANATION   Compare your questions and answers to the ones given here.

1. *What are the three types of eating disorders?*

The three types of eating disorders are anorexia nervosa, bulimia nervosa, and binge eating disorder (BED).

2. *What is anorexia nervosa, and what is it marked by?*

Anorexia nervosa is the severe restriction of food intake, marked by an avoidance of food and dangerous weight loss.

3. *What is bulimia nervosa, and what is it marked by?*

Bulimia is binge eating and then taking drastic steps to avoid gaining weight.

4. *What is binge eating disorder, and what is it marked by?*

Binge eating disorder is binge eating without any steps to avoid weight gain, resulting in obesity.

PRACTICE 3

Before you read the following passage from an interpersonal communication textbook, skim the information and write out *five* questions based on the title and the words in **bold** print. After you read, answer the questions you have created.

Self-Awareness and the Four Selves

Since you control your thoughts and behaviors to the level that you understand who you are, it's crucial to develop a high sense of self-awareness. We can begin this discussion by looking at the four selves.

Your Open Self. Your **open self** represents all the information, behaviors, attitudes, feelings, desires, motives, and ideas that are you. The type of information might vary from your name and sex to your age, religion, and batting average. The size of your open self changes based on the situation you are in and the people you are with. Some people may make you feel comfortable. To them, you would open yourself wide. To others, you might want to leave most of yourself closed and unknown.

Your Blind Self. Your **blind self** represents all the things about yourself that others know but of which you are not aware. These may include your habit of rubbing your nose when you get angry, your defense mechanisms, and your repressed experiences. You can shrink your blind area, but you can never totally get rid of it.

Your Hidden Self. Your **hidden self** contains all that you know of yourself but that you keep to yourself. This area includes all your secrets. This includes everything you have not revealed and seek actively to hide.

Your Unknown Self. Your **unknown self** represents truths that exist but that neither you nor others know. We infer this unknown self from dreams, psychological tests, or therapy. For example, through therapy you might become aware of your need for acceptance.

—DeVito, *Messages: Building Interpersonal Communication Skills*, 4th ed., pp. 42–3.

1. _____

_____

_____

2. _____

_____

_____

3. _____

_____

_____

4. _____

_____

_____

5. _____

_____

_____

_____

Chapter Review

Test your understanding of what you have read in this chapter by filling in each blank with a word from the box. Use each word only once.

after reading	comprehension	prior knowledge	review	survey

1. _____ is an understanding of information.

2. _____ is the large body of information that is learned throughout a lifetime of experience.

3. Skilled readers divide the reading process into the following three phases:

a. Before reading   c. _____
b. During reading

4. SQ3R stands for _____, question, read, recite, and

_____.

Applications

Application 1: **Prior Knowledge**

Read the paragraph, and answer the questions that follow it.

Cellular Phones

For most people, cell phones are a welcome addition to a busy, on-the-go lifestyle. Cell phones offer many benefits. Because of wireless phones, parents are more likely to keep up with their teenage children. Drivers faced with roadside emergencies can reach help. Some cell phones even allow access to e-mail and the Internet. This access helps workers stay in touch with their offices. However, cell phones also present some real problems. Dialing while driving takes attention from the road, and in an instant, a car can drift off the road or into oncoming traffic. Talking while driving presents the same risk. Surprising or bad news can cause the driver to think about the conversation instead of the traffic. Finally, some experts fear cell phones because cell phones use radio frequency waves. Experts question the safety of constantly putting radio frequency waves close to the head. Overall, cell phones do create immediate contact, but they may also present some risks.

1. What is your prior knowledge about the benefits of cell phones? _____

   _____

   _____

   _____

2. What is your prior knowledge about the dangers of cell phones? _____

   _____

   _____

   _____

3. What is your reaction to the information about the safety of using cell

   phones? _____

   _____

   _____

Application 2: Before Reading

Survey the passage by answering the following questions.

1. What is the passage about? _____

_____

2. What do I already know about these ideas? _____

_____

3. What do I need to remember? What is my purpose for reading? _____

_____

_____

4. What words are in **bold** type? _____, _____, and

_____

Three Steps to Success

Successful people tend to follow three steps to achieve their goals.

Setting goals is the first step. Success comes from a clear goal, and a clear goal comes from a strong desire. For example, to successfully lose 10 pounds and keep those pounds off, a person must first want to do so. This goal is based on the strong desire to look and feel better.

Staying focused is the second step. For example, a student sets a clear goal to earn a high grade in a class, understanding that the grade represents a level of knowledge. Cheating on a test or assignment for a higher grade would distract from the goal of becoming educated. Staying focused leads to hard work and follow-through.

Solving problems is the final step to success. The path to every goal has a set of barriers or problems that need to be overcome. Sometimes the barrier is a lack of a skill. At other times, the problem may be an attitude or habit that needs to be changed. Often unplanned events must be dealt with. No matter what the barrier, successful people find ways to solve the problem and reach the goal. Successful people set goals, stay focused, and solve problems.

Application 3: During Reading

As you read the following passage, record your answers to the following questions.

1. What new words do I need to look up? _____

_____

2. What is another name for therapeutic cloning ? _____

_____

3. What is a **blastocyst**? _____

_____

4. Why are stem cells harvested? _____

_____

5. How may therapeutic cloning be used in the future? _____

_____

_____

_____

Therapeutic Cloning

When the media report on cloning, they usually talk about only reproductive cloning. Reproductive cloning creates a genetic twin of another animal. However, there are different types of cloning. One other type is therapeutic cloning.

Therapeutic cloning is also called "embryo cloning." This type of cloning produces human embryos for use in research. The goal of this process is not to clone human beings. Instead, the goal is to harvest stem cells. These stem cells can be used to study human development and to treat disease. **Stem cells** can be used to generate virtually any type of specific cell in the human body. Stem cells are extracted from the egg after it has divided for 5 days. The egg at this stage of development is called a **blastocyst**. The extraction process destroys the embryo. Destroying the embryo does raise a variety of ethical concerns.

Therapeutic cloning may some day be used in humans to produce whole organs from single cells. Or it may produce healthy cells to replace damaged cells in diseases such as Alzheimer's or Parkinson's. Many researchers hope that one day stem cells can serve as replacement cells to treat heart disease, cancer, and other diseases.

—Adapted from U.S. Department of Energy Office of Science.
"Cloning Fact Sheet" 29 August 2006. http://www.ornl.gov/
sci/techresources/Human_Genome/elsi/cloning.
shtml#animals

VISUAL VOCABULARY

Cloned human _____, created at Centre for Life in Newcastle upon Tyne, is seen three days after nuclear transfer took place.

Which word best completes the caption?

a. blastocyst
b. stem cell

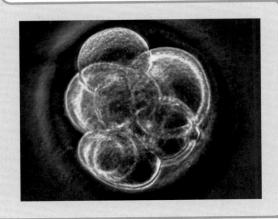

Application 4: After Reading

Read the passage, practicing your before reading and during reading skills. Once you have finished reading the selection, answer the questions that follow it.

Gangs

Although gangs can be found anywhere these days, two of the best known are the Crips and the Bloods from California. To cope with the problems gangs bring to a community, it is important to understand what a gang is and why people join gangs.

Why join a gang? There are at least five reasons that gangs are attractive to young people. First, some young men thrill at the idea of parties, girls, and drugs, which they assume gang membership will provide. Second, gangs often satisfy the desire to escape poverty by providing money for food and clothes through drug dealing and theft. Third, some young people crave power and respect and see gang membership as a way to gain both. Fourth, some feel the need to belong to and be accepted by a peer group or regard the gang as the family they never had. Fifth, some people join gangs for protection against the violence in their neighborhood.

What is a gang? Most gangs share at least five traits. First, like the Crips and the Bloods, gangs have names. Even large gangs like these two have smaller groups with local names. Second, most gangs mark out a territory with graffiti. The graffiti are a way of warning enemies or advertising a drug sale. Third, gangs are known for their violence. Often the violence starts over a trivial issue like an insult. Violence can also be a part of initiation into the gang, or it can occur as the gang commits another crime such as robbery. Fourth, the bond between members is deep. Gang members become almost inseparable. The strength of the gang comes from the amount of time the members spend together. Finally, gangs usually wear clothing or other items to identify their gang membership.

1. What five things make gangs attractive?

a. _____

b. _____

c. _____

d. _____

e. _____

2. What five traits do most gangs share?

a. _____

b. _____

c. _____

d. _____

e. _____

VISUAL VOCABULARY

Based on the passage, the best meaning of graffiti is _____

a. artistic expression.
b. vandalism.

REVIEW **Test 1**

During Reading

Read the paragraph. As you read, answer the accompanying questions.

1. What happened in 1952?

_____

_____

2. What happened in 1975?

_____

_____

3. What happened in 1978?

_____

_____

_____

4. What happened in 1979?

_____

_____

On April 29, 1952, Ralph Dale Earnhardt was born in Kannapolis, North Carolina. Although he was the son of a NASCAR winner, Ralph Earnhardt, no one could have known just how great a race car driver young Dale Earnhardt would become. In 1975, Dale started for the first time in a Winston Cup event, the World 600. In 1978, he finished in second place in the World Service Life 300 at Charlotte. That race made him a star as he battled Bobby Allison for the win. In 1979, Dale was named Winston Cup Rookie of the Year. A brilliant career was on its way.

REVIEW **Test 2**

Before and During Reading

A. Before you read, survey the passage by skimming for the following information.

1. What is the passage about? _____

2. What are the ideas in *italics*? _____, _____,

_____, and _____

3. What do I already know about this topic? _____

_____

4. What do I need to remember? _____

_____

_____

_____

B. Read the passage. As you read, answer the accompanying questions.

5. How much of the earth's surface do tropical rain forests cover?

_____

6. What percentage of the earth's species live in tropical rain forests?

_____

7. What is the effect of rich soil and a hot, wet climate?

_____

_____

8. What are hot spots?

_____

_____

9. What fraction of forest plant species live in hot spots?

_____

10. What do insects and birds do to help other species survive?

_____

_____

_____

Tropical Rain Forests

The *beauty and value* of tropical rain forests are their great diversity of life. Tropical rain forests cover about 6 percent of the earth's surface and are home to half of the world's species.

Of all the known insects in the world, 80 percent are found in tropical forests. Several factors explain why so many different types of life thrive in tropical forests. *Rich soil* and a *hot, wet climate* create ideal growing conditions. Heavy rainfall and abundant energy from the sun produce dense plant growth. Some tropical rain forests have more variety of life than others. Forests that have a great variety of life are known as *hot spots*. Hot spots contain more than one-fourth of all forest plant species. The different species that live in a tropical rain forest need one another to survive. Insects and birds pollinate flowers, allowing fruit to develop. And the fruits of the forest feed the animals and people who live there.

VISUAL VOCABULARY

The beauty and value of tropical rain forests are their great

_____ of life.

a. species
b. diversity

REVIEW Test 3

Before and During Reading

A. Before reading, survey the following excerpt from the website, and answer these questions.

   1. What is my purpose for reading? _____

   _____

   2. What kinds of information should I be looking for to understand and remember? _____

   _____

   _____

B. Read the information. As you read, answer the following questions.

   3. What is the main ingredient in this dish? _____

   4. How does Calorie-Count rate this dish? _____

   _____

   5. Which of the following words best describes the ratings for the levels of cholesterol and sodium? _____ healthful _____ unhealthful

calorie-count
from About.com Health

Calories in SOUTH BEACH DIET
FROZEN ENTREES ENTREE- CAPRESE
STYLE CHICKEN WITH BROCCOLI &
CAULIFLOWER
Frozen Entrees

Add item to food log

Create a free account

Manufactured by South Beach Diet

Nutrition Facts

Serving Size 1 serving (297.0 g)

Amount Per Serving

Calories 250   Calories from Fat 72

	% Daily Value*
Total Fat 8.0g	**12%**
Saturated Fat 2.0g	**10%**
Cholesterol 95mg	**32%**
Sodium 1350mg	**56%**
Total Carbohydrates 12.0g	**4%**
Dietary Fiber 3.0g	**12%**
Sugars 6.0g	
Protein 35.0g	

Vitamin A 15%   •   Vitamin C 25%
Calcium 20%   •   Iron 10%

* Based on a 2000 calorie diet

Legend
☐ Fat
☐ Protein
☐ Carbs
■ Alcohol
☐ Other

Calorie Breakdown (2)

Daily Values (2)

Tags - south beach, lunch, dinner

Nutritional Analysis

Nutrition Grade

42%
confidence

B-

Bad Grade?

Bad points
High in cholesterol
Very high in sodium

Source: © 2007, calorie-count.com. Reprinted by permission.

REVIEW Test 4

Before, During, and After Reading

A. Before reading, survey the poem, and answer the following questions.

1. What is this poem about? _____

_____

_____

2. What do I already know about this topic? _____

_____

_____

B. Read the poem. As you read, answer the accompanying questions.

3. How many people are identified as "Nobody"?

_____

4. How is a "Somebody" described?

_____

I'm Nobody! Who are you?
Are you—Nobody—too?
Then there's a pair of us!
Don't tell! They'd banish us—you know!

How dreary—to be—Somebody!
How public—like a Frog—
To tell your name—the livelong June—
To an admiring Bog!

—Emily Dickinson, 1861

C. After you have read it, put the poem into your own words. Use two or three sentences.

5. _____

_____

_____

_____

SKILLED READER Scorecard

A Reading System for Skilled Readers

Test	Number Correct		Points		Score
Review Test 1	_____	×	25	=	_____
Review Test 2	_____	×	10	=	_____
Review Test 3	_____	×	20	=	_____
Review Test 4	_____	×	20	=	_____
Review Test 5 (website)	_____	×	20	=	_____
Review Test 6 (website)	_____	×	25	=	_____

Enter your score on the Skilled Reader Scorecard: Chapter 1 Review Tests inside the back cover.

Before you read the following passage from a textbook on physical fitness, skim the information and write out *five* questions based on the words in **bold** print. Then read the passage and answer the questions you have created.

Textbook
Skills

Weight Training

Weight training is an excellent way to control weight, tone muscles, and build bones. However, many people begin lifting weights with very little understanding about the proper way to get the most out of a workout. Understanding a few workout terms will help you execute your workout routine.

Repetitions or reps. Repetitions are the number of times that you perform an exercise. For example, one rep for a bench press occurs when you pick up the bar, lower it, pause, and lift it up. If you perform that same movement a second time, you have completed a second repetition.

Sets. A set is a series of repetitions that ends when the muscle reaches muscular failure. Muscular failure occurs when the buildup of lactic acid in the muscle makes it impossible to complete another rep with proper form.

Rest interval. A rest interval is the amount of time you rest between sets. For example, a rest interval of 60 seconds means you sit inactive for 60 seconds before beginning another set.

Modified compound supersets. A modified compound superset occurs when you pair exercises, usually for opposing muscle movements or opposing muscle groups (such as push and pull). First, you perform one exercise, rest, and then perform the second exercise. For example, first you do the biceps, then do the triceps. Then you rest and return to the first exercise.

Supersets. A superset is a combination of exercises performed right after each other with no rest in between. There are two ways to do this. The first way is to do two exercises for the same muscle group at once. The second and best way to superset is by pairing exercises of opposing muscle groups.

—Adapted from Villepigue & Rivera, *The Body Sculpting Bible for Women: The Way to Physical Perfection*, p. 46.

1. _____

_____

_____

2. _____

_____

_____

3. _____

_____

_____

4. _____

_____

_____

_____

5. _____

_____

_____

Read the paragraph; then answer the questions that follow it.

Attendance Policy

Regular attendance and **class participation** are crucial. Therefore, students who miss more than **three class hours** put their grades at risk. Students who regularly miss class can expect to fail. The instructor records attendance and participation. The **student must officially drop** the class to avoid receiving the grade of F for too many absences.

1. What is this passage about? _____

What are the ideas in **bold** print?

2. _____

3. _____

4. _____

5. _____

What are the two most crucial items in the attendance policy?

6. _____

7. _____

8. What will happen to a student who misses class regularly? _____

_____

9. How can a student who has missed class a lot avoid getting an F? _____

_____

10. What do I need to remember about this paragraph? _____

_____

_____

Name _____ Section _____

Date _____ Score (number correct) _____ × 10 = _____ %

A. Survey the passage below before reading it, and answer the following questions.

1. What is this passage about? _____

2. What are the nine ideas in **bold** print and *italics* ?

_____

_____

_____

_____

_____

_____

_____

_____

_____

_____

B. Now read the passage. As you read, answer the accompanying questions.

3. How did Banneker show his love of learning?

_____

_____

_____

4. How did Banneker show his love of work?

_____

_____

_____

_____

Benjamin Banneker: A True Genius

Benjamin Banneker, born a free black man, lived in Elliot Mills, Maryland, from 1731 until 1806. His life was marked by a love of learning, a love of work, and a love of justice.

A love of learning. Banneker had to teach himself. Throughout his childhood, he spent most of his days working beside his mother and father in their tobacco fields. His farm duties meant that he could attend school only during the winter months. Banneker's love of learning was evident even in his early years. In a one-room school, he learned reading, writing, and mathematics. He excelled in *mathematics*. He was curious about everything, and he spent much of his time observing the sky, earth, clouds, rain, and seasons. He read as much and as

39

5. What is an almanac?

_____

_____

_____

_____

6. How many years did Banneker write and publish his almanac?

_____

_____

7. What did President Washington appoint Banneker to?

_____

_____

_____

8. How did Banneker show his love of justice?

_____

_____

_____

9. What was the attitude of slave owners?

_____

_____

10. What about Banneker impressed Thomas Jefferson?

_____

_____

often as he could. However, books were scarce. So most of what he learned, he had to learn firsthand.

A love of work. As much as Banneker loved to learn, he also loved to use his knowledge. He became a hardworking and successful _farmer_. He was also an inventor, writer, and publisher. For example, by the time he was 22, he had built a handmade clock. This clock was probably the _first clock made on American soil_. He shaped the clock and each gear out of hardwood with a knife, and the clock kept time for more than 20 years.

From 1792 until 1802, Banneker _wrote and published his own almanac_. An almanac is a book that shows the times the sun sets and rises, phases of the moon, and times of high and low tides. Farmers used almanacs to help them in many ways. For example, a farmer could reset a stopped clock or plan the best time to plant a crop.

Banneker's success brought him to the attention of the president, George Washington. The United States was about to build the nation's capital. _President Washington appointed Banneker_ to the team of civil engineers and surveyors who would _plan the nation's capital_. Banneker helped select the sites for the U.S. Capitol building, the U.S. Treasury, and the White House. At one point in the process, the plans for the capital disappeared. President Washington feared the work would not be finished. However, Banneker had memorized the plans, and the work continued.

A love of justice. Although Benjamin Banneker was a free black man, racial limits were placed on free blacks as well as slaves. Slave owners tried to convince the nation that blacks were not as smart or hardworking as whites. Many whites began to fear well-educated free blacks. Banneker was the _first black person to take a stand against the unfair treatment of blacks_. In fact, he wrote a letter to Thomas Jefferson. Jefferson, the author of the Declaration of Independence, owned slaves. In his letter, Banneker talked about Jefferson's owning slaves. Along with the letter, Banneker sent a copy of his almanac. Banneker's education and success impressed Jefferson.

Textbook Skills

A. Survey the following passage before reading it. Answer these questions.

1. What is this passage about? _It is about President Roosevelt passing a bill._

2. What are the ideas in **bold** print? _the new deal_, _the first lady_, _women_, _African americans mexican americans_, and _native americans_

3. What do I need to remember about this passage? _That everything that happened in life still effects us today._

B. Now read the passage. As you read, answer the accompanying questions.

4. What was the New Deal?

refers to the programs President Franklin D. Roosevelt created to deal with the problems of the great Depression of the 1930's.

5. For what reforms does Eleanor Roosevelt deserve credit?

aimed at helping minorities she was the first president's wife to take a strong public stand on these issues

6. In what roles did women predominate prior to the Great Depression?

Social work and the voluntary associations she provided charities for the poor and unemployed.

The New Deal, Women, and Minority Groups

The New Deal: The term *New Deal* refers to the programs President Franklin D. Roosevelt created to deal with the problems of the Great Depression of the 1930s. These programs were designed to provide relief, recovery, and reform.

The First Lady: Eleanor Roosevelt deserves much of the credit for the reforms aimed at helping minorities. Mrs. Roosevelt was the first president's wife to take a strong public stand on these issues. She supplied moral strength to the New Deal. The First Lady worked tirelessly to convince her husband and the government to hire skilled women and African Americans. In 1933 alone, she traveled 40,000 miles, visiting families and checking on welfare programs. Some thought she was more courageous than her husband. She did not hesitate to take a public stand on civil rights. When the Daughters of the American Revolution refused in 1939 to allow the black contralto Marian Anderson to sing in Washington's Constitution Hall, Mrs. Roosevelt arranged for her to perform a concert on the steps of the Lincoln Memorial on Easter Sunday.

Women: Women made some progress under the New Deal. Prior to the depression, women had dominated both social work and the voluntary associations that provided charity for the poor and unemployed. Since the same skills were needed to combat

41

7. How did Harold Ickes support civil rights?

He place seven African americans on his Staff. He also poured federal funds into black and hospitals in the south.

8. How did the Farm Security Administration try to help Mexican Americans?

Created camps for migrants farm workers in California. The wpa hired jobless mexican americans on relief Job.

9. How did federal grant money help Native Americans?

Yes it ded. It allowed them to buy new land, have there own government and custom there speak and languges.

the depression, women joined the throngs of professionals who rushed to Washington to work in New Deal programs.

African Americans: Roosevelt named Mary McLeod Bethune, an African American educator, to the advisory committee of the National Youth Administration (NYA). Thanks to her efforts, African Americans received a fair share of NYA money. The Works Progress Administration (WPA) was colorblind. The WPA was a federal program that put millions of jobless people to work. These workers built or repaired bridges, highways, and parks. Blacks in northern cities benefited from its work relief programs. Harold Ickes, a member of Roosevelt's cabinet, was a strong supporter of civil rights. He placed several African Americans on his staff. He also poured federal funds into black schools and hospitals in the South.

Mexican Americans: The New Deal offered Mexican Americans some help. The Farm Security Administration created camps for migrant farm workers in California. The WPA hired jobless Mexican Americans on relief jobs. Many, however, did not qualify for relief because they had no home address. Additionally, migrant farm workers were not able to collect benefits under workers' compensation or Social Security.

Native Americans: The Indian New Deal was the only bright spot in President Roosevelt's treatment of minorities. President Roosevelt created the Indian Emergency Conservation Program (IECP), which hired more than 85,000 Native Americans. In 1934, Congress passed laws to help Native Americans. They were allowed to buy new land. They were allowed to have their own government. And they were able to follow their customs and speak their own language. That same year, federal grants gave money to schools, hospitals, and social services to help Native Americans.

—Adapted from Martin et al., *America and Its Peoples: A Mosaic in the Making,* 3rd ed., pp. 848–49.

C. Now that you have read the passage, answer the following question.

10. What were the three purposes of the New Deal? *to help people get Jobs, help provide for women, and assist americans*

Name *Daryl Lawrence*　　　　　　　Section ＿＿＿＿＿

Date *10-31-10*　Score (number correct) ＿＿＿ × 20 = ＿＿＿ %

Textbook Skills

A. Survey the passage before reading it. Answer the following questions.

1. What is this passage about? *a group of people resuing some stranded people in a rain forest.*

2. What is the purpose for reading this passage? *to read and understand what happened in and why people need to be resued.*

B. Now read the passage. As you read, complete the study notes with details from the passage.

3. The *life cycle* is the sequence of life stages that lead from the adult of one generation to the adults of the next.

4. *sexual reproduction* is the making of offspring from the union of a sperm and egg.

5. *asexual reproduction* is the making of offspring without a sperm or egg.

Rain Forest Rescue

In 2002, the small shrub *Cyanea kuhihewa* was among the rarest of the rare; only a single known plant remained alive in nature. So when this lone *C. kuhihewa* bloomed, scientists from the National Tropical Botanical Garden on Kauai saw an opportunity. Their goal was to promote sexual reproduction. **Sexual reproduction** involves fertilization, the union of a sperm and an egg. Using a fine brush, the botanical rescuers transferred pollen from a garden-grown plant onto the wild bloom. The pollen contained the sperm, and the wild bloom contained the egg. If sperm and egg join, the fertilized egg may soon divide into two cells. If development proceeds, the resulting cells will continue to divide and eventually form an embryo and then a seed. Upon germination of the seed, the embryo may develop into a juvenile and later into an adult plant.

Development is one phase of a multicellular organism's life cycle. The **life cycle** is the sequence of life stages that lead from the adults of one generation to the adults of the next. The other phase of the life cycle is reproduction. Reproduction is the formation of new individuals from existing ones.

Unfortunately, the *C. kuhihewa* rescue attempt failed. Even worse, the last remaining wild plant died in 2003. But hope remains. The garden's botanists are trying asexual reproduction. **Asexual reproduction** is the production of an offspring without the involvement of a sperm or egg.

—Adapted from Campbell, Reece, Taylor, and Simon. *Biology: Concepts and Connections*, 5th ed., Benjamin Cummings, 2005, pp. 124–125.

VISUAL VOCABULARY

Without a sperm or egg, an amoeba makes an offspring through _____

a. sexual reproduction.
b. asexual reproduction.

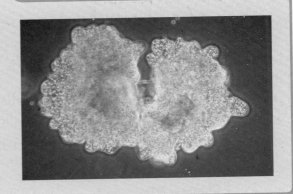

Name *Daryl Lawance* _____ Section _____

Date *10-31-10* Score (number correct) _____ × 10 = _____ %

Textbook
Skills

A. Before reading the passage, survey the information. Answer the following questions.

1. What is this passage about? *What happens before you getting into a situation and the consequences*

B. Now read the passage. As you read, answer the accompanying questions.

2. What can you do to make conflict more productive?

One useful idea's to prepare for the conflict ahead of time and use it as a method of growth.

3. Why should you fight in private?

Because when you are airing your conflicts in front of others you grow a wide variety of other problems

4. Why should you fight only about problems that can be solved?

You should because if you done it situation can get intense

5. What can you learn from the conflict?

You can learn and think about how you can handle the conflict more differently.

Before and After a Conflict

Make conflict with your partner truly useful. Use these ideas both for preparing for the conflict ahead of time and for using the conflict as a method of growth after the conflict.

Before the Conflict

Fight in private. When you air your conflicts in front of others, you create a wide variety of other problems. You might not be willing to be totally honest when others are present. You may feel you have to save face and win at all costs. This might lead you to use strategies to win the argument rather than to solve the problem. Also, you run the risk of embarrassing your partner in front of others. Embarrassment may lead to bitterness and anger.

Focus on the problem. Make sure you are both free of other problems and ready to deal with the conflict at hand. Confronting your partner when she or he comes home after a hard day of work may not be the right time for resolving a conflict. Choose a good time to deal with your conflict.

Know what you are fighting about. Sometimes people become so hurt and angry that they lash out just to vent their frustration. The problem at the center of the conflict is merely an excuse to express anger. For example, getting upset over the uncapped toothpaste tube is not the real problem. The underlying problem may be a need to feel respected.

Fight about problems that can be solved. Fighting about past behaviors or about family members over

6. What does it mean to keep the conflict in perspective?

To not take things so extreme and blow so out of proportion

7. Why reward each other?

Rewarding each others shows you have respect for one another.

which you have no control doesn't help. Instead, it creates additional problems. Any attempt at resolution is doomed since the problems can't be solved.

After the Conflict

Learn from the conflict. Think about the process you went through in trying to resolve the problem. For example, can you identify the fight strategies that aggravated the situation?

Keep conflict in perspective. Be careful not to blow it out of proportion. In most relationships, conflicts actually occupy a very small part of the couple's time, and yet in their recollection, they often loom extremely large. Don't view yourself, your partner, or your relationship as a failure just because conflicts sometimes arise.

Attack your negative feelings. Often such feelings arise because unfair fight strategies were used to challenge the other person—for example, blame or verbal attacks. Resolve to avoid such unfair tactics in the future, but at the same time, let go of guilt or blame for yourself or your partner.

Reward each other. Increase the exchange of rewards and cherishing behaviors. These will show your positive feelings and that you're over the conflict and want the relationship to survive.

—DeVito, *Messages: Building Interpersonal Communication Skills*, 4th ed., pp. 297–98.

C. Now that you have read the passage, answer the following question by filling in the blanks.

What are the steps to making conflict useful?

Before the conflict:

8. *fight in private*

Focus on the problem.
Know what you are fighting about.
Fight about problems that can be solved.

After the conflict:

9. *learn from the conflict*

Keep conflict in perspective.
Attack your negative feelings.

10. *reward each other*

Vocabulary in Context

Daryl Lawrence

10/06/09

CHAPTER PREVIEW

Before Reading About Vocabulary in Context
The Importance of Words
Context Clues: A SAGE Approach
    Synonyms
    Antonyms
    General Context
    Examples
Textbook Skills: Visual Vocabulary

Before Reading About Vocabulary in Context

Chapter 1 taught you the importance of surveying material before you begin reading by skimming the information for **bold** or *italic* type and noting graphs, charts, and boxes. Throughout this textbook, key ideas are emphasized in bold or italic print where they appear in the passage. Often they are also set apart visually in a box that gives the definition or examples of the term. Skim this chapter for key ideas in bold or italic print and ideas highlighted in boxes. Refer to these key ideas and create at least six questions that you can answer as you read the chapter. Write your questions in the following spaces (record the page number for the key term in each question):

_____ (page_____)?

_____ (page_____)?

_____ (page_____)?

_____ (page_____)?

_____ (page_____)?

_____ (page_____)?

Compare the questions you created with the following questions. Then write the ones that seem most helpful in your notebook, leaving enough space between each question to record the answers as you read and study the chapter.

What is vocabulary (page 48)? What is a context clue (page 49)? What is a SAGE approach (page 49)? What are synonyms (page 49)? What are the signal words for synonyms (page 49)? What are antonyms (page 51)? What are the signal words for antonyms (page 52)? What does the term *general context* mean (page 54)? What are the signal words for examples (page 57)? What is visual vocabulary (page 59)?

The Importance of Words

Words are the building blocks of meaning. Have you ever watched a child with a set of building blocks, such as Legos? Hundreds of separate pieces can be joined together to create buildings, planes, cars, or even spaceships. Words are like that, too. Individual words have meaning. Words properly joined create greater meaning. A large set of building blocks increases the size and number of items a child can build. Likewise, a large set of words expands your ability to create meaning.

> **Vocabulary** is all the words used or understood by a person.

How many words do you have in your **vocabulary**? By the age of 18, most people know about 60,000 words. During your college studies, you will most likely learn an additional 20,000 words. Each subject you study will have its own set of words.

Learning so many new words may seem overwhelming. However, as you add words to your vocabulary, you increase your skill and pleasure in reading. You first learned words by interacting and practicing. You heard the word; you connected the word to its meaning; you heard the word again and again; you used the word. A skilled reader follows that same pattern.

Context Clues: A SAGE Approach

Skilled readers learn new words in a number of ways. One way is to use **context clues**. The meaning of a word is influenced by the words surrounding it—by its context. Skilled readers use context clues to learn new words.

A **context clue** is the information that surrounds a new word, used to understand its meaning.

Four most common types of context clues are:

- Synonyms
- Antonyms
- General context
- Examples

Notice that the first letter of each type of context clue, reading down, spells the word *SAGE*. *Sage* means "wise." Using context clues is a wise—a SAGE—reading strategy.

Synonyms

A **synonym** is a word that has the same or nearly the same meaning as another word. For example, the words *funny* and *humorous* are synonyms. Many times, an author will place a synonym near a new or difficult word as a context clue to the word's meaning. Often the words *or* and *that is* introduce the synonym. Sometimes a synonym is used later in the sentence. A synonym may also be set off with a pair of dashes, a pair of parentheses, or a pair of commas before and after it.

Synonym Signal Words	
or	*that is*

EXAMPLES Each of the following sentences has a key word in **bold** type. In each sentence, circle the synonym for the word in **bold**.

1. Ashamed of his **flaccid**—flabby—muscles, Glenn joined the local gym.

2. A **cross-section** (slice) of the leaf is studied under the microscope.

3. The Vietnam Memorial in Washington, D.C., is a **memorial**, or tribute, to honor the men and women who gave their lives in service to their country.

VISUAL VOCABULARY

The Vietnam _____

is in our nation's capital.

   a. Cross-section
   b. Memorial

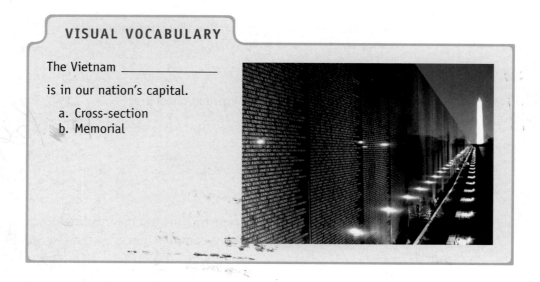

EXPLANATIONS

1. The synonym for **flaccid** is *flabby.* The synonym *flabby* immediately follows the word *flaccid.* It is set off with a pair of dashes.

2. The synonym for **cross-section** is *slice.* The synonym *slice* immediately follows the term *cross-section,* enclosed in a set of parentheses.

3. The synonym for **memorial** is *tribute.* Notice that the synonym *tribute* immediately follows the word *memorial* and has the signal word *or* before it. The phrase *or tribute* is enclosed by a pair of commas.

PRACTICE **1**

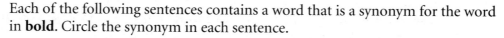

Each of the following sentences contains a word that is a synonym for the word in **bold**. Circle the synonym in each sentence.

1. **Toxic** (poisonous) steroids can affect the heart, liver, and kidneys.

2. Hot and tired, Chantel became **huffy**—irritable—after striking out during her turn at bat.

3. Mother delivered another one of her **homilies**, that is, sermons, on the value of hard work.

4. In **marshes** or swamplands, the croaking of frogs and chirping of cicadas become unbelievably loud in the evening.

VISUAL VOCABULARY

The Florida Everglades is a

massive _____

  a. marsh.
  b. cicada.

---

5. Samuel was **erroneous** or mistaken in his assessment of the facts.

6. Samantha's parents **indulged**, that is, spoiled, her with expensive clothes and cars.

7. Christina's use of curses and personal attacks against the waitress **mortified**—embarrassed—everyone.

8. Mr. and Mrs. Rutherford Danbury built a house of a **palatial** or regal scale that sits on four acres and overlooks the river.

9. Most students look forward to spring break as a much needed **respite** or rest from the demands of a long academic semester.

10. The **smudge**, that is, spot, of lipstick on Jonathan's shirt collar did not match the color lipstick his girlfriend was wearing.

Antonyms

An **antonym** is a word that has the opposite meaning of another word. For example, *heavy* and *light* are antonyms. So are *early* and *late*. Antonyms help you determine a word's meaning by showing you what the word does *not* mean. Antonyms are usually introduced with words and phrases of contrast or difference. Contrast words such as *not* or *unlike* often act as signals that an antonym is being used. These signal words alert you to expect a change.

Antonym Signal Words				
as opposed to	however	not	rather than	yet
but	in contrast	on the other hand	unlike	

Sometimes antonyms can be found next to the new word. In those cases, commas, dashes, or parentheses may set them off from the new word. At other times, antonyms are placed in other parts of the sentence to emphasize the contrast between the ideas.

EXAMPLES In each sentence, circle the antonym for the word in **bold**. In the blank, write the letter of the word that best defines the word in **bold**.

___c___ **1.** Trying to save money by putting off going to the doctor may have a **detrimental**, not helpful, result.
  a. useful   c. positive
  b. harmful   d. pleasant

___d___ **2.** A person possessed of **fortitude** rather than indecision has great purpose and strength.
  a. kindness   c. success
  b. determination d. honor

___d___ **3.** Sandra was a **sociable** child; in contrast, her sister was very shy.
  a. annoying   c. loving
  b. cute   d. outgoing

___b___ **4.** One physical sign of starvation is a **distended**, not flat, stomach.
  a. swollen   c. hard
  b. shrunken   d. soft

EXPLANATIONS

1. The antonym for **detrimental** is *helpful. Detrimental* means (b) "harmful." Notice the signal word *not* and the pair of commas before and after the antonym phrase.

2. The antonym for **fortitude** is *indecision. Fortitude* means (b) "determination." Notice the signal words *rather than.*

3. The antonym for **sociable** is *shy. Sociable* means (d) "outgoing." Notice the signal words *in contrast.* Also note that the antonym *shy* appears at the end of the sentence.

4. The antonym for **distended** is *flat. Distended* means (a) "swollen." Notice the signal word *not* and the set of commas that signal the antonym *flat.*

PRACTICE 2

In each sentence, circle the antonym for the word in **bold**. In the blank, write the letter of the word that best defines the word or phrase in **bold**.

___b___ **1.** Instead of being so **severe** in your attitude, please try to be more open-minded.
    a. rigid   c. gentle
    b. unhappy   d. depressed

___c___ **2.** In short stories, some characters remain **static** (not dynamic) in their beliefs and actions.
    a. shocking   c. fixed
    b. changing   d. confused

___d___ **3.** Mothers Against Drunk Driving urges young people to **abstain from**—rather than indulge in the use of drugs and alcohol.
    a. enjoy   c. apply
    b. avoid   d. learn

___d___ **4.** Beyond rational thought, a person suffering from anorexia nervosa has a **fixation** with being thin.
    a. interest   c. obsession
    b. diet   d. failure

___C___ **5.** In contrast to the leanness of anorexia, obesity is marked by **adiposity.**
    a. fattiness   c. thinness
    b. size   d. weight

VISUAL VOCABULARY

_____ This person suffers from

    a. adiposity.
    b. anorexia nervosa.

___b___   **6.** Julie Ann refused to remain **illiterate**; instead she worked to become well educated.
    a. poor
    b. uneducated
    c. helpless
    d. depressed

___b___   **7.** Paul's reactions to problems seem to be expressed by a **dearth**, not an excess, of emotions.
    a. lack
    b. surplus
    c. dread
    d. acceptance

___c___   **8.** The **obscurity** of Professor Bailey's lecture was in direct contrast to the clarity of Professor Brown's presentation.
    a. certainty
    b. success
    c. vagueness
    d. stupidity

___d___   **9.** The employee received not a **commendation** but a rebuke for working overtime.
    a. punishment
    b. warning
    c. reward
    d. demand

___c___   **10.** The identical twins Roger and Ted have very different attitudes; Roger remains **complaisant**, unlike Ted, who is often disobedient.
    a. unruly
    b. wild
    c. obedient
    d. weak

General Context

Often you will find that the author has not provided a synonym clue or an antonym clue. In that case, you will have to rely on the **general context** to figure out the meaning of the unfamiliar word. This requires that you read the entire sentence, or read ahead for a few sentences, for information that will help you understand the new word.

Information about the word can be included in the passage in several ways. Sometimes a definition of the word may be provided. Often vivid word pictures or descriptions of a situation can give a sense of the word's meaning. At times, you may need to figure out the meaning of an unknown word by using prior knowledge, logic, and reasoning skills.

EXAMPLES In the blank, write the letter of the word that best defines the word in **bold**.

 1. The children lived in **squalor**: soiled and stained clothes covered every piece of furniture, dirty dishes filled the sink and cluttered the stove and counters, the floor was sticky with food, and the house smelled of rotted food, sweat, and urine.
　　a. confusion　　　　c. freedom
　　b. filth　　　　　　d. hope

 2. Kashada decorated her room with a **hodgepodge** of posters of everything from country music stars to hard rock groups.
　　a. unity　　　　　　c. mixture
　　b. theme　　　　　 d. group

3. A climber must think about the harmful impact high mountain **elevations** can have on her body.
　　a. heights　　　　　c. widths
　　b. depths　　　　　 d. scenes

EXPLANATIONS

1. Squalor means (b) "filth." The details of this passage vividly describe a very dirty place: *soiled, stained, dirty, cluttered, sticky, smelled,* and *rotted.*

2. Hodgepodge means (c) "mixture." Kashada doesn't seem to have a favorite kind of group or music. Instead she seems to collect posters based on a wide range of taste.

3. Elevations means (a) "heights." The words *climber, high,* and *mountain* all suggest height.

PRACTICE **3**

Each of the following sentences has a word in **bold** type. In the blank, write the letter of the word that best defines the word in **bold**.

 1. Too often, the **indigenous** people of the rain forests are considered backward; however, they have lived successfully in their homelands for thousands of years.
　　a. native　　　　　c. uneducated
　　b. poor　　　　　　d. displaced

_____ **2.** California power companies had **blackouts** because there was not enough energy to supply the residents' electrical needs.
   a. fainting spells
   b. power failures
   c. rate hikes
   d. lower prices

_____ **3.** Rebecca was accused of **slander** when she spread lies about Ross after they broke up.
   a. stalking
   b. damage to a person's reputation
   c. burglary
   d. hatefulness

_____ **4.** Jordan demonstrated his **agility** when he caught the football, turned in midair, outran the defense, and scored a touchdown.
   a. clumsiness and fear
   b. determination
   c. quickness and grace
   d. courage

_____ **5.** The **perimeter** of a figure is the total distance around the edge of the figure.
   a. border
   b. inside
   c. center
   d. value

_____ **6.** Marie smiled and whistled as she **obligingly** helped her father wash the car.
   a. resentfully
   b. agreeably
   c. reluctantly
   d. skillfully

_____ **7.** Mark and Sandi made no advance plans for their trip; they simply **meandered** across the country for two weeks.
   a. ran
   b. drifted
   c. rushed
   d. drove

_____ **8.** The **emergence** of the butterfly from its cocoon surprised and delighted the young child.
   a. beauty
   b. appearance
   c. change
   d. shape

_____ **9.** Kaye **coerces** the other children to give their allowance to her by threatening to beat them up.
   a. forces
   b. limits
   c. helps
   d. discourages

_____ **10.** The Lincoln Memorial in Washington, D.C., is an **enduring** reminder of the strength, wisdom, and sacrifice of Abraham Lincoln.
   a. temporary
   b. lasting
   c. humble
   d. final

Examples

Many times, an author will show the meaning of a new or difficult word with an example. Often the signal words *such as, including,* or *consisting of* introduce the example as a context clue. Colons and dashes can also indicate examples. Sometimes the example is incorporated into the sense of the sentence.

Example Signal Words		
consisting of	for instance	like
for example	including	such as

EXAMPLES   Using example clues, choose the correct meaning of the word in **bold**.

 1. Many wealthy people take up **altruistic** causes; for instance, film star Angelina Jolie volunteers as a spokesperson with the United Nations on the behalf of refugees.
   a. unselfish   c. political
   b. horrible   d. harmful

 2. Sports figures, including Michael Jordan, Tiger Woods, Dale Earnhardt, and Maria Sharapova, become **paragons** of excellence in our society.
   a. people   c. heroes
   b. role models   d. rulers

 3. The player seemed **suspended** in midair as she jumped as high as the basket to score the winning point in the game.
   a. pushed   c. slapped
   b. shocked   d. hanging

EXPLANATIONS

1. **Altruistic** means (a) "unselfish." Angelina Jolie could use her time and energies to enjoy her own life of privilege; instead she gives up countless hours to help others in need.

2. **Paragons** are (b) "role models." Each of these people has risen to the height of success in sports and set a new standard for excellence.

3. **Suspended** means (d) "hanging." "Jumped as high as the basket" suggests that the player's feet were off the ground.

PRACTICE 4

Using example clues, choose the correct meaning of the word in **bold**.

_____c__ 1. Many television ads use **fallacious** thinking—such as half-truths and exaggerations—to sell products.
   a. factual   c. honest
   b. deceitful   d. creative

_____c__ 2. People from different parts of the United States speak using different **dialects**, including the fast, clipped northern accent and the slow southern drawl.
   a. language patterns   c. interests
   b. value systems   d. jobs

_____b__ 3. **Illicit** drugs, like marijuana, cocaine, and heroin, bring great wealth to those who buy and sell them in large amounts for a living.
   a. dangerous   c. illegal
   b. legal   d. expensive

_____a__ 4. **Lagomorphs** (which include rabbits and hares) used to be thought of as rats.
   a. animals with scales   c. animals with large front teeth
   b. animals with wings   d. animals without fur

_____a__ 5. Mrs. Powell served a plate of tasty **hors d'oeuvres** that included cheese, crackers, and bite-size meatballs before dinner.
   a. main courses   c. desserts
   b. appetizers   d. drinks

_____b__ 6. **Salutations**, such as "Hello," "How do you do?" and "How are you?," are common courtesies.
   a. insults   c. greetings
   b. snubs   d. questions

_____c__ 7. Carbon monoxide, chlorine vapor, and ammonia are **noxious** chemicals that can cause severe health problems or lead to death if not handled properly.
   a. harmless   c. natural
   b. expensive   d. poisonous

_____d__ 8. Some authors use **pseudonyms**; for example, American author Mark Twain's real name was Samuel L. Clemens.
   a. disguises   c. false names
   b. body guards   d. autographs

_____ *C* **9.** A **chronic** illness, such as asthma or arthritis, usually gets increasingly worse.
  a. short-term   c. painful
  b. long-term   d. curable

_____ *d* **10. Predators**, such as owls, catch and eat other animals.
  a. birds   c. hunters
  b. animals   d. victims

Textbook
Skills **Visual Vocabulary**

Textbooks often make information clearer by providing a visual image such as a graph, chart, or photograph. Take time to study these visual images and their captions to figure out how each one ties in to the information.

  EXAMPLE Study the following image and its caption. Answer the question that follows.

◀ Land **parched** from lack of rain

_____ *a* What does **parched** mean?
  a. rich   c. dry
  b. moist   d. overgrown

  EXPLANATION *Parched* means (c) "dry."

PRACTICE 5

Study the following image and its caption. Then answer the question accompanying it.

◄ A good **compost** for use as fertilizer is made up of "greens" such as vegetables and "browns" such as fall leaves.

_____ What does **compost** mean?
   a. mixture of organic matter   c. dessert
   b. menu item   d. vegetable

Chapter Review

Test your understanding of what you have read in this chapter by filling in each blank with a word or phrase from the box. Three words are each used twice.

antonym	example	image	vocabulary
context	general	SAGE	
context clues	general context	synonym	

1. ___*Sage*___ is all the words used or understood by a person.

2. *general context* is the information that surrounds a new word, used to understand its meaning.

3. Skilled readers use ___*vocabulary*___ to learn new words.

4. List the four most common types of context clues:

   a. ___*example*___   c. ___*image*___

   b. ~~*vocabulary*~~ *context*   d. *context clues*

5. The first letter of each of the four common context clues spells the word ___*general*___.

6. A ___*antonym*___ is a word that has the same or nearly the same meaning as another word.

7. An _synonym_ is a word that has the opposite meaning of another word.

8. The _____ context requires you to read the entire sentence or to read ahead for a few sentences.

9. Often the signal words *such as* or *including* introduce a(n) _antonym_ as a context clue.

10. Many times, textbooks make information clearer by providing a visual _____ such as a graph, chart, or photograph.

Applications

Application 1: Synonyms as Context Clues

Circle the synonym for each word in **bold**.

1. Juan faced the **daunting**, or challenging, task of moving to a new country with hope and courage.

2. Jan always has an **optimistic**—hopeful—attitude about life.

3. The nurse **sterilized** the needle by cleansing it with alcohol.

4. To reduce crime, various **factions** (groups) in the community had to unite.

5. A **rogue** since childhood, Mark lived the life of a rebel.

Application 2: Antonyms as Context Clues

In each sentence, circle the antonym for the word in **bold**. In the blank, write the letter of the word that best defines the word in **bold**.

 1. **Comprehension**, unlike confusion, results in knowledge.
   a. understanding   c. studying
   b. ignorance   d. work

 2. If a part of a chromosome is lost, the remaining chromosome has a **deletion**, not an addition.
   a. added part   c. finished part
   b. missing part   d. important part

 3. Charlie Anne has a **phobia** for dogs, yet she tries to act as if she has some liking for them.
   a. courage   c. fear
   b. concern   d. joy

_a_   4. **Obese** people (unlike thin people) may suffer social problems because of their weight.
    a. tall
    b. overweight
    c. skinny
    d. rejected

_a_   5. **Geriatric** citizens are concerned about the cost of health care; in contrast, youthful citizens are concerned about finding a job.
    a. elderly
    b. young
    c. helpless
    d. independent

Application 3: General Context as a Clue

Write the letter of the word that best defines the word in **bold**.

_c_   1. Suddenly, there was a **lull** in the hard-driving rain and wind; after hours of hearing the howling wind, the silence was strange.
    a. increase
    b. outbreak
    c. pause
    d. strength

_b_   2. Katie's **belligerence** surprised everyone. She threw her book across the room, glared at Chris, and then pushed him to the floor.
    a. carefulness
    b. hostility
    c. courage
    d. honesty

_b_   3. The pupil of the eye **dilates** to adjust to darkness, sometimes becoming as large as the eye's iris.
    a. closes
    b. opens
    c. agrees
    d. contracts

_a_   4. John's **sentimental** card expressed his deep and undying love for Amy.
    a. cheap
    b. unemotional
    c. emotional
    d. expensive

_d_   5. After eating three helpings of turkey and dressing, four helpings of sweet potatoes, and three pieces of pumpkin pie, Andy's hunger was **satiated**.
    a. increased
    b. permanent
    c. satisfied
    d. worsened

Application 4: Examples as Context Clues

Write the letter of the word that best defines the word in **bold**.

_b_   **1.** The use of **mnemonics** is a good way to remember something by putting a name on it; for example, SAGE stands for *synonyms, antonyms, general context,* and *examples.*
    a. memory tools   c. discussion tools
    b. note-taking tools   d. reviewing tools

_c_   **2.** The **axial** skeleton of a human being includes the bones of the trunk, head, and neck.
    a. bottom   c. central
    b. inner   d. limb

_c_   **3.** A **spherical** object is a solid object on which all points on its surface are the same distance from the center of the figure; for example, the sun and the earth are spherical objects.
    a. large   c. round
    b. heavy   d. oval

_d_   **4.** The **characteristics** of cocaine withdrawal include depression, irritability, and strong cravings.
    a. denials   c. barriers
    b. symptoms   d. goals

_a_   **5.** Many type of **reflexes** are present at birth, including the moro or startle reflex, walking or stepping reflex, and the grasping reflex.
    a. automatic responses   c. planned responses
    b. thoughtful responses   d. unhappy responses

VISUAL VOCABULARY

This infant is showing the

_____ reflex.

    a. moro
    b. walking or stepping
    c. grasping

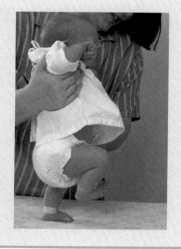

REVIEW **Test 1**

Using Context Clues

A. Read the sentences, and answer the questions that follow them.

Putting your work off until the last minute will have **adverse**—negative—effects on your learning.

_____ c   **1.** What does **adverse** mean?
    a. helpful   c. long-term
    b. harmful   d. short-term

_____ d   **2.** Identify the context clue you used.
    a. synonym   c. general context
    b. antonym   d. example

John took a **menial** job in the company, hoping to train and work his way into a more skilled and higher-paying position.

_____ b   **3.** What does **menial** mean?
    a. important   c. unskilled
    b. better   d. high-paying

_____ a   **4.** Identify the context clue you used.
    a. synonym   c. general context
    b. antonym   d. example

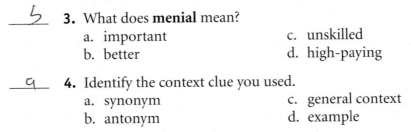

Inebriated from the effects of drinking too many beers, Marsha staggered through the house, unable to find any of the light switches or walk in a straight line.

_____ a   **5.** What does **inebriated** mean?
    a. sober   c. happy
    b. drunk   d. confused

_____ d   **6.** Identify the context clue you used.
    a. synonym   c. general context
    b. antonym   d. example

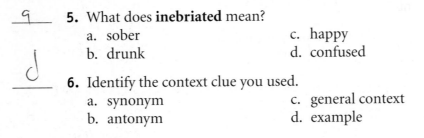

B. Using context clues, write the definition for each word in **bold**. Choose definitions from the box. Use each definition only once.

concluded	ground-breaking	mutual	worry

7. In a healthy marriage, giving should be **reciprocal**, not one-sided.

Definition of **reciprocal**: _ground - breaking_

8. The **angst**, or anxiety, of giving her speech weighed heavily on LaToya.

Definition of **angst**: _worry_

9. Although Justin and Robert were best friends, Justin refused to speak with or even look at Robert. After a few days of being ignored or treated rudely by Justin, Robert finally **inferred** that he had somehow angered his friend.

Definition of **inferred**: _concludee_

10. At a time when men were the ones to hold most of the high-powered jobs, a few women enjoyed **innovative** careers; for example, Ruth Handler created the Barbie doll, and Margaret Knight invented a machine that made the first flat-bottomed paper bag.

Definition of **innovative**: _mutual_

REVIEW Test 2   _Dorcy Lawrence   11-02-10_

Using Context Clues

Choose the best definition for each word in **bold**. Then identify the context clue used in each passage. A clue may be used more than once.

Context Clues

> **S**ynonym
> **A**ntonym
> **G**eneral context
> **E**xample

The folly of youth stands in stark contrast to the wisdom of age.

_C_ **1.** The word **folly** means
    a. strength.   c. foolishness.
    b. happiness.   d. decisions.

    2. Context clue: _wisdom_

Some recovering alcoholics still think they can control their habit. They believe they can start and stop drinking at any time. But after they have stopped, taking even one drink is a **perilous** decision.

  _c_   **3.** The word **perilous** means
      a. dangerous.   c. good.
      b. hopeful.   d. funny.

      4. Context clue: _____

A fat, orange moon hung low against a velvet black sky. A mist of fog swirled around the lamppost, and a black cat ran across the street. A werewolf howled. The **eerie** scene made me walk a little faster.

  _d_   **5.** The word **eerie** means
      a. beautiful.   c. relaxing.
      b. spooky.   d. inspiring.

      6. Context clue: _____

Some old **superstitions** are told in childhood sayings, for example, "Step on a crack, break your mother's back"; "Break a mirror, have seven years of bad luck"; and "If your nose itches, you're going to have company soon."

  _b_   **7.** The word **superstitions** means
      a. facts.   c. false ideas.
      b. details.   d. wise sayings.

      8. Context clue: _____

Simone carefully dressed for the prom; she **donned** her best shoes, a new gown, and her mother's pearls.

  _c_   **9.** The word **donned** means
      a. borrowed.   c. put on.
      b. bought.   d. laid out.

      10. Context clue: _____

Jeremy Bletz wandered in the desert for three weeks. **Dehydrated**, he looked for water by cutting open a cactus.

  _a_   **11.** The word **dehydrated** means
      a. thirsty.   c. hungry.
      b. tired.   d. lost.

      12. Context clue: _____

The drug addict who does not seek help may **regress** into more serious drug use; however, recovery is possible with counseling, hard work, and support from loved ones.

_____ C 13. The word **regress** means
    a. succeed.   c. depress.
    b. turn back.   d. overcome.

    14. Context clue: _____

Jane's fingerprints at the scene **refuted**, not proved, her innocence.

_____ C 15. The word **refuted** means
    a. confused.   c. denied.
    b. doubted.   d. approved.

    16. Context clue: _____

Some creatures can **regenerate** parts of themselves, such as a starfish growing a new arm or a lizard growing a new tail.

_____ c 17. The word **regenerate** means
    a. break off.   c. grow back.
    b. reattach.   d. relax.

    18. Context clue: _____

A short temper, constant fatigue, and a sense of hopelessness may be **symptomatic** of depression.

_____ b 19. The word **symptomatic** means
    a. characteristic.   c. hurtful.
    b. supportive.   d. stylish.

    20. Context clue: _____

REVIEW Test 3

Using Context Clues

A. Using context clues, write the definition for each word in **bold**. Choose definitions from the box. Use each definition only once.

corruption	refused	view
match	use of words that imitate sounds	worth imitating

1. The *Riverdance* dancers **synchronize** their movements so that they seem to move as one person.

   Definition of **synchronize**: _____

2. The **vice**, or evil, of violence threatens our schools across the nation.

   Definition of **vice**: _____

3. Dr. Martin Luther King Jr. was an **exemplary** human being; he was a man of strength, wisdom, and compassion.

   Definition of **exemplary**: _____

4. The **vista** from Diamond Head in Honolulu, Hawaii, is a breathtaking sight as the sun rises.

   Definition of **vista**: _____

5. Sybil **rebuffed** her brother's offer to lend her money with a brusque "no thanks."

   Definition of **rebuffed**: _____

6. **Onomatopoeia**, evident in words such as *sizzle, crackle, buzz,* and *whirr,* helps a reader's mind hear an idea while a text is being read.

   Definition of **onomatopoeia**: _____

B. Read the sentences, and answer the questions that follow them.

The hurricane **pummeled** the island with heavy rain and high winds for three days.

_____ **7.** What does **pummeled** mean?
   a. dumped   c. pounded
   b. embraced   d. frightened

_____ **8.** Identify the context clue you used.
   a. synonym   c. general context
   b. antonym   d. example

As Miguel grew older and tried to find a good job, he developed a **robust** desire for learning, a far cry from his weak commitment to school during his younger years.

_____ **9.** What does **robust** mean?
   a. halfhearted   c. happy
   b. strong   d. successful

_____ **10.** Identify the context clue you used.
   a. synonym   c. general context
   b. antonym   d. example

REVIEW Test 4

Using Context Clues

Textbook
Skills

Read the following passage adapted from the health textbook *The Dynamics of Drug Abuse*. Apply context clues to each of the words in **bold** print, and answer the questions that follow the passage.

The Tracks of My Tears

[1]Comedian Richard Pryor has entertained the world for almost three decades and intensely **engages** his audience when he tells the story of how his cocaine habit nearly killed him when he was thirty-nine years old. [2]Now over fifty, Pryor acts as a constant reminder that cocaine can kill in more than one way.

[3]According to police, Pryor was sitting in his luxurious home in suburban Los Angeles preparing to free-base cocaine when a **volatile** chemical exploded. [4]Flames from the explosion engulfed him. [5]An elderly aunt who was in the house quickly **smothered** the flames with a blanket. [6]But Pryor, who was in agonizing pain, threw off the blanket and bolted out of the house. [7]The police found Pryor **wandering** half a mile away. [8]His body was so burnt that they first thought he was wearing makeup.

[9]When the officers tried to stop him, Pryor murmured, "I can't stop. [10]If I stop, I'll die." [11]One officer walked with him until an ambulance arrived. [12]Before getting into the ambulance, Pryor said, "I done wrong. [13]They told me not to smoke that stuff." [14]Doctors **initially** put his survival odds at one in three. [15]When he responded well to treatment, however, his doctor said, "He's lucky to be alive. [16]He's been through a hell of a lot."

—Fishbein & Pease, *The Dynamics of Drug Abuse*, p. 163.

_____ **1.** What does **engages** mean in sentence 1?
   a. bores   c. involves
   b. frightens   d. hurts

_____ **2.** What does **volatile** mean in sentence 3?
   a. mixed   c. safe
   b. unstable   d. heavy

_____C_____ **3.** What does **smothered** mean in sentence 5?
    a. hurt   c. started
    b. ran from   d. put out

_____a_____ **4.** What does **wandering** mean in sentence 7?
    a. moving aimlessly   c. standing still
    b. stopping often   d. holding on

_____c_____ **5.** What does **initially** mean in sentence 14?
    a. sometime later   c. at first
    b. never   d. now

SKILLED READER Scorecard

Vocabulary in Context				
Test	**Number Correct**		**Points**	**Score**
Review Test 1	_____	×	10	=	_____
Review Test 2	_____	×	5	=	_____
Review Test 3	_____	×	10	=	_____
Review Test 4	_____	×	20	=	_____
Review Test 5 (website)	_____	×	5	=	_____
Review Test 6 (website)	_____	×	10	=	_____

Enter your score on the Skilled Reader Scorecard: Chapter 2 Review Tests inside the back cover.

After Reading About Vocabulary in Context

The reading system you learned in Chapter 1 will help you comprehend and retain large sections of information, such as this textbook chapter about vocabulary skills. Now that you have read and studied the chapter, take time to reflect on what you have learned before you begin the mastery tests. Check your comprehension of what you have studied. Answer the following questions. Write your answers in your notebook.

What did I learn about vocabulary in context?

What do I need to remember about vocabulary in context?

How has my knowledge base or prior knowledge about vocabulary in context changed?

More Review and Mastery Tests

For more practice, go to the book's website at **http://www.ablongman.com/henry** and click on *The Skilled Reader.* Then select "More Review and Mastery Tests." You will find the tests listed by chapter.

MASTERY **Test 1**

Textbook
Skills

Name _Daryl Lawrence_ Section _____

Date _12/03/16_ Score (number correct) _____ × 10 = _____ %

A. The following sentences are from a chapter in the textbook *With Respect to the Japanese: A Guide for Americans*. Read each sentence, and answer the questions that follow them.

> **Modesty** is a virtue, a social grace, in Japanese and American societies. For example, Japanese and Americans alike appreciate a hero who brushes off words of praise for his actions.

 1. What does **modesty** mean?
- a. humility
- b. goodness
- c. pride
- d. politeness

 2. Identify the context clue you used.
- a. synonym
- b. antonym
- c. general context
- d. example

> A boastful and **egotistical**, or self-centered, person is as tedious in Seattle as in Saporo.

 3. What does **egotistical** mean?
- a. selfless
- b. loud
- c. selfish
- d. self-confident

 4. Identify the context clue you used.
- a. synonym
- b. antonym
- c. general context
- d. example

> As a rule, Americans can risk sounding "overly modest" by American standards and still be within the **realm** of "appropriately modest" by Japanese standards.

 5. What does **realm** mean?
- a. kingdom
- b. range
- c. behavior
- d. kind

 6. Identify the context clue you used.
- a. synonym
- b. antonym
- c. general context
- d. example

73

B. Using context clues, write the definition for each word in **bold**. Choose definitions from the box. Use each definition only once.

| humility | saying | selling | value |

7. While there is something in American culture that allows or even encourages a person to "sell yourself," the notion of **merchandizing** oneself does not sit well with the Japanese.

   Definition of **merchandizing**: _____

8. A Chinese journalist describes the difference between Eastern and Western values, "You'll notice that Bruce Lee never shows how good he is until he has to act. Only the bad guys and the unskilled show off. That's not a part of the Bruce Lee character; that's an Asian **virtue**."

   Definition of **virtue**: _____

9. One **proverb** quoted by Japanese about Japanese values is: "The clever hawk hides his claws."

   Definition of **proverb**: _____.

10. The expression of **depreciation** is apparent in a variety of situations. For example, a Japanese personal advertisement might read, "Though I am not very good looking . . ."

    Definition of **depreciation**: _____

—Adapted from Condon, John C. (1984) *With Respect to the Japanese:
A Guide for Americans.* Intercultural Press, a Nicholas Brealey
Publishing Co. Yarmouth, Maine, pp. 51–52.

Textbook
Skills

A. The following sentences are from a chapter in the textbook *Communication @ Work*. Read each sentence, and answer the questions that follow.

> When working, how late is "late" for a meeting? How early is "early" for dinner? North Americans become **intolerant** after waiting for about ten minutes. But in some South American countries it is excusable if you show up four hours late.

 1. What does **intolerant** mean?
- a. unforgiving
- b. patient
- c. angry
- d. curious

 2. Identify the context clue you used.
- a. synonym
- b. antonym
- c. general context
- d. example

> **Kinesics** reflects the values of a culture. For example, in a Japanese company, if a person sits quietly, others assume that the person is thinking and will not interrupt. If the person stands and moves about, others will interact more freely.

 3. What does **kinesics** mean?
- a. attitude
- b. conversation
- c. body movement
- d. thoughts

_____ **4.** Identify the context clue you used.
- a. synonym
- b. antonym
- c. general context
- d. example

> "Cultural **chauvinism**" is the belief that one's culture is the only way to live. Cultural chauvinism is an intolerance of values, customs, and traditions different from one's own.

 5. What does the word **chauvinism** mean?
- a. value
- b. indifference
- c. prejudice
- d. tolerance

 6. Identify the context clue you used.
- a. synonym
- b. antonym
- c. general context
- d. example

B. Using context clues, write the definition for each word in **bold**. Choose definitions from the box. Use each definition only once.

fail	manners	space	timely

7. When working in another country, visitors risk making a negative impression unless they adapt their use of **spatial** distances. In one program, some Englishmen were trained to stand closer to Arabs, make more eye contact, touch more, and smile more.

   Definition of **spatial**: _____

8. Numerous websites and travel guides discuss customs and communication. These guidelines help prepare people to follow business **etiquette** across cultures.

   Definition of **etiquette**: _____

9. **Err** on the side of being too formal, rather than too informal. Develop relationships slowly.

   Definition of **err**: _____

10. Learn the culture's use of time and the practice of **punctuality**. Northern Europeans, Americans, and Japanese are the most punctual. In contrast, southern Europeans, Hispanics, Middle Easterners, and Filipinos are more relaxed about time.

    Definition of **punctuality**: _____

—Adapted from Kelly, Marylin S. (2006) *Communication @ Work.*
Boston: Allyn & Bacon, pp. 128–129.

Study the following words in their context. Then answer the questions that follow them.

constructed	Jeremiah **constructed** his house with natural materials.
	The beavers **constructed** a dam in the river within hours.
gelatinous	The blueberries simmered until they became **gelatinous** and coated the spoon.
	The **gelatinous** thickness of a blood clot blocks an artery.
impart	Parents **impart** values to their children through family traditions.
	The mushrooms **impart** a nutty taste to the rice.
properties	The **properties** of water are hydrogen and oxygen.
	The **properties** of salt make it essential for life.
scaffolding	A **scaffolding** was built for the window washers to reach the top floor windows of the high rise.
	To achieve success, many students rely on a **scaffolding** of learning skills such as attending class regularly, questioning, note taking, and forming study groups.

A. Match the word to its definition.

1. constructed   _____ jellied

2. gelatinous   _____ pass on

3. impart   _____ traits

4. properties   _____ framework

5. scaffolding   _____ built

B. Fill in the blank with a word from the list in the box. Use each word only once.

constructed	gelatinous	impart	properties	scaffolding

A Prized Delicacy

A popular dish in Chinese and Chinese-American culture is authentic bird's nest soup. This soup is made using the nest of the swiftlet, a small, sparrowlike bird found throughout Southeast Asia. (**6**) _____ in pitch-black caves where the swiftlet lives, the nests are made of seaweed. The tiny swallow secretes strands of (**7**) _____ saliva to hold the nest together. To harvest the nests, people climb bamboo (**8**) _____ to pry the nests from the walls. This is a dangerous job, and many harvesters die each year. Research proves that the birds' nests contain valuable (**9**) _____ such as protein, iron, and calcium. Although "raw" birds' nest have little flavor, they (**10**) _____ a delightful taste when cooked in stocks. The danger of harvesting the nests and their high demand make them a costly delicacy. The birds' nests industry generates billions of dollars.

Read the following passage adapted from the college communications textbook *The Media in Your Life: An Introduction to Mass Communication.* Then answer the questions that follow it.

Textbook
Skills

TALK RADIO

[1]Between 1990 and 1995, many more stations began **devoting**, or giving, the greater part of their on-air time to talk. [2]In fact, talk shows almost tripled, from 450 to 1,130. [3]With talk, radio stations discovered a new way to **boost** their ratings and bring in advertisers. [4]By the end of the 1990s, ratings made talk one of the top radio formats in the United States.

[5]Experts believe that talk radio **capitalizes on**, rather than avoids, emotion. [6]Issues like homosexuality may arouse anger and fear. [7]The talk show hosts know this. [8]They talk more about such subjects than may seem needed. [9]They start heated debates and push people to become excited. [10]That boosts ratings.

[11]The popularity of talk radio has created a wide range of hosts. [12]They range from **conservative** Rush Limbaugh to outrageous Howard Stern. [13]Even some politicians had their own shows. [14]For example, Pat Buchanan, who ran for President, was the first to understand the power of a talk show to get his ideas to the American people.

[15]A 1993 survey showed that almost one-third of adults had listened to political talk shows. [16]Many listeners said they strongly disagreed with the talk show host most of the time.

[17]Some critics of talk radio **speculate** about why it is so successful. [18]One reason given is that talk radio is the new town meeting. [19]In a society that is so **fragmented** (not unified or in touch with each other), radio offers a place to connect to each other. [20]In this new town meeting, the **populace** speaks rather than relying on official voices. [21]In fact, critics credit the public interest in talk radio to a rising **distrust** of public officials.

[22]Critics often attack talk radio as a harmful force. [23]Critics suggest that talk radio **exploits,** instead of educates. [24]Talk radio, they say, spreads fear and **paranoia**.

—Folkerts & Lacy, *The Media in Your Life: An Introduction to Mass Communication,* 2nd ed., pp. 194–95.

_____ C **1.** What does **devoting** mean in sentence 1?

      a. giving   c. talking

      b. taking away   d. growing

_____ C **2.** What does **boost** mean in sentence 3?

      a. hurt   c. stop

      b. raise   d. see

_____ d **3.** What does **capitalizes on** mean in sentence 5?

      a. ignores   c. tears down

      b. takes advantage of   d. furthers

_____ b **4.** What does **conservative** mean in sentence 12?

      a. extreme   c. simple

      b. crude   d. traditional

_____ g **5.** What does **speculate** mean in sentence 17?

      a. guess   c. gamble

      b. know   d. bet

_____ b **6.** What does **fragmented** mean in sentence 19?

      a. joined together   c. broken apart

      b. strong   d. afraid

_____ b **7.** What does **populace** mean in sentence 20?

      a. public   c. government

      b. private   d. popular

_____ d **8.** What does **distrust** mean in sentence 21?

      a. trust deeply   c. respect

      b. doubt   d. hate

_____ g **9.** What does **exploits** mean in sentence 23?

      a. takes advantage of   c. teaches

      b. helps   d. kills

_____ b **10.** What does **paranoia** mean in sentence 24?

      a. trust   c. mistrust

      b. hope   d. caution

Read the following passage adapted from the college sociology textbook *Women, Men, and Society*. Then answer the questions that follow it.

Textbook
Skills

GENDER AND HOUSEWORK:
WHO DOES WHAT?

[1]When it comes to housework, research consistently shows that wives spend more time on these chores than husbands do—as much as five times more hours per week, in fact. [2]Of course, this may not seem unfair if spouses are exchanging services according to the traditional marriage contract: She does the housework and he works in the paid labor force for their financial support. [3]However, this arrangement applies to only a small percentage of couples today.

[4]Most married women, like their husbands, are **employed** outside the home. [5]Although husbands in two-earner families spend more time on housework than men who are the only breadwinners, they still do less than their wives. [6]Husbands typically express a willingness to "help" their wives with the housework, but even among two-earner couples, the commonly held belief of both men and women is that housework is "women's work." [7]This is true no matter what other demands wives have on their time.

[8]Interestingly, men are less tolerant of gender **inequality** in the workplace than in their own homes. [9]Consequently, employed wives end up working what is called the "second shift." [10]They are wage earners for part of the day and then come home to still more, **albeit** unpaid, work.

[11]In fact, if you ask full-time homemakers what kind of work they do, they usually reply, "I don't work; I'm a housewife." [12]This is a **striking** answer, for housework, which is important and necessary work, is not considered real work. [13]Even the woman who is doing housework doesn't think of it as real work. [14]One reason housework is not considered real work is that it is **unspecialized**, covering by some guesses more than eighty different tasks. [15]It is also never ending; in a sense, it is never fully finished. [16]No sooner is a chore completed than it must be done again. [17]This is because housework produces items and services for immediate **consumption**.

[18]Another reason housework is not thought of as "real" work is that unlike work in the paid labor force, there is no fixed work schedule for housework. [19]Homemakers rarely get time off, not even holidays—who, for instance, cooks those large holiday meals? [20]Housework also differs from what we usually think of as real work in that it is **intertwined** with love and feelings of care. [21]It is also **privatized**. [22]We see people leaving their houses to go to work; we see them in public on the job. [23]But housework is done **in isolation** in the home, and much of it is done when other family members are elsewhere.

Deryl Lawrence 10/15/09

²⁴And of course, one of the main reasons housework is not considered real work is that it is unpaid. ²⁵In a society such as ours, individuals' **status**—how much people are valued by others as well as by themselves—often is measured by how much money they make.

—Renzetti & Curran, *Women, Men, and Society,* 4th ed., pp. 164–65.

a 1. What does **employed** mean in sentence 4?
   a. working   c. roaming
   b. staying   d. looking

b 2. What does **inequality** mean in sentence 8?
   a. fairness   c. strength
   b. unfairness   d. weakness

c 3. What does **albeit** mean in sentence 10?
   a. although   c. so
   b. and   d. for example

c 4. What does **striking** mean in sentence 12?
   a. hitting   c. weak
   b. powerful   d. sick

b 5. What does **unspecialized** mean in sentence 14?
   a. special   c. broad, general
   b. hard   d. focused

c 6. What does **consumption** mean in sentence 17?
   a. waste   c. work
   b. use   d. play

b 7. What does **intertwined** mean in sentence 20?
   a. broken apart   c. woven in
   b. free   d. replaced

b 8. What does **privatized** mean in sentence 21?
   a. made public
   b. controlled by a person or private group
   c. controlled by the government
   d. made secret

c 9. What does **in isolation** mean in sentence 23?
   a. alone   c. in large groups
   b. in small groups d. out of fear

a 10. What does **status** mean in sentence 25?
   a. worth   c. work
   b. height   d. friends

Read the following passage adapted from the college communications textbook *Listening: Attitudes, Principles, and Skills.* Then answer the questions that follow it.

Textbook
Skills

CONCEPT VERSUS FACT METHOD
OF LISTENING

[1]This method of listening focuses your attention on the main points of the message. [2]To use the **concept** versus fact technique, draw a vertical line down the center of your paper. [3]On the left side, jot down the speaker's main points as they occur. [4]In the right column, indicate any supporting evidence, examples, and other information used to **clarify** those concepts. [5]If the rate of presentation becomes too fast to get everything recorded, you will be able to make informed decisions about what information to include in your notes.

[6]Not only is the concept versus fact method easy to use, it also provides a quick **reference** when you need to recall information later on. [7]Study the example below. [8]This chart was created by listening to a speech about the effects of the sun.

Effects of Sun

Concept	Fact
[9]The sun is harmful (main **topic**)	
[10]Greeks' view of sun exposure—recognized only the benefits	Hippocrates—sun for health
[11]Today's scientific facts are different—sun viewed as harmful	Herodotus—necessary for recovery
	Tan is response to solar damage
	Sun has a negative **cumulative**—not single—effect
[12]Sun has many harmful effects	Heat stress—cramps, dizziness
	Heat exhaustion—nausea, faintness
	Heatstroke is life-threatening
	Skin and hair damage
	Stay away 10 A.M.–3 P.M.
	Sun is stronger at high altitudes
[13]Damage can be prevented	Tan slowly
	Wear a sunscreen

—Brownell, *Listening: Attitudes, Principles, and Skills,* 2nd ed., pp. 123–24.

83

_c_   **1.** What does **concept** mean in sentence 2?
   a. idea   c. fact
   b. dream   d. myth

_d_   **2.** What does **clarify** mean in sentence 4?
   a. argue   c. explain
   b. deny   d. create

_b_   **3.** What does **reference** mean in sentence 6?
   a. source   c. opinion
   b. recommendation   d. memory

_a_   **4.** What does **topic** mean in sentence 9?
   a. subject   c. fact
   b. support   d. paper

_d_   **5.** What does **cumulative** mean in sentence 11?
   a. small   c. dangerous
   b. total   d. healthy

CHAPTER
3

Vocabulary-Building Skills

CHAPTER PREVIEW

 ## Before Reading About Vocabulary-Building Skills

Two kinds of vocabulary-building skills are learning about word parts and using the dictionary and other similar resources. To aid your study, set up a note-taking system like the one that follows. Refer to the chapter preview and headings throughout the chapter, and create headings such as the following on notebook paper:

Key Term	Definition (or type of information)	Example
Word parts	Definition	Example
Roots (page 86)		
Prefixes (page 86)		
Suffixes (page 86)		

Dictionary	Type of Information	Example
Guide Words (page 95)		
Spelling (page 97)		
Syllabication (page 97)		

Leave enough space between each key term to record the definition and example as you read the chapter. Skim the chapter and record the page number where each key term is defined. Be sure to use all the key terms listed in the chapter preview to complete your note-taking system.

Word Parts

Just as ideas are made up of words, words are also made up of smaller parts. Learning about *word parts* can help you learn vocabulary more easily and quickly. Furthermore, knowing the meaning of the parts of words helps you understand a new word when you see it in context. In fact, word parts can help you unlock the meaning of thousands of words. A single word part may appear in hundreds or even thousands of different words. If you know the meanings of several parts of a word, you can often figure out the meaning of the word as a whole.

Root	The basic or main part of a word. Prefixes and suffixes are added to roots to make a new word.
	Example: *spect* means "look"
Prefix	A group of letters with a specific meaning added to the beginning of a word or root to make a new word.
	Example: *in-* means "into," so *inspect* means "look into"
Suffix	A group of letters with a specific meaning added to the end of a word or root to make a new word.
	Example: *-ator* means "one who," so *spectator* means "one who looks"

For example, the word *restatement* has three parts, and each part has its own meaning. The first part, the prefix *re-*, means "again"; the second part, the root *state*, means "say"; and the third part, the suffix *-ment*, means a condition of being. Thus a *restatement* is "something that is said again."

The overall meaning of the word changes if one part of the word changes. For example, in the word *overstatement,* the prefix is now *over-.* The prefix *over-* means "excessive" or "exaggerated." The new word means "something that is said in an exaggerated way."

A word can have two or more parts. For example, *prehistoric* has three parts. The first part of *prehistoric,* the prefix *pre-,* means "before"; the second part, the root *historia,* means "inquiry, learned"; the third part, the suffix, *-ic,* means "related to." *Prehistoric* means being related to times before formal learning was recorded or written.

This chapter defines and explains each of the three word parts in depth and offers you ample opportunity to practice combining word parts to explore meanings. Furthermore, Appendix C in the back of this book provides an additional list of word parts and their meanings for further study.

Many of the words in the English language are based on two other languages: Greek and Latin. Greek and Latin divided words into the following three parts: **roots**, **prefixes**, and **suffixes**. Skilled readers understand how the three word parts join together to make additional words.

EXAMPLES The following group of word parts has a root, prefix, and suffix. Make two new words by combining the word parts. The meaning of each part is in parentheses. You don't have to use all the parts to make a word.

Prefix: *im-*   (in)
Root: *port*   (carry)
Suffix: *-ation*   (action)

1. _____

2. _____

EXPLANATIONS

1. **Import**: The root *port* ("carry") joins with the prefix *im-* ("in"). The new word means "carry in."

   Companies in the United States now **import** many of their supplies from other countries.

2. **Importation**: The prefix *im-* ("in"), the root *port* ("carry"), and the suffix *-ation* ("action") join to form a word meaning "the action of carrying in."

Another kind of **importation** results when people move here and bring their own customs with them.

PRACTICE 1

Study the word parts. Using the meanings of the prefixes, the root, the suffixes, and context clues, put each word into the sentence that best fits its meaning. Use each word once.

Prefix	Meaning	Root	Meaning	Suffix	Meaning
in-	in, into	*spect*	look	*-acle*	quality
retro-	backward			*-or*	person

spect = "look"

inspector	retrospect	spectacle

1. In _____, after pulling a muscle running, Manny said, "I should have warmed up before exercising."

2. The fireworks created an awesome _____ in the night sky.

3. The _____ placed a sticker on each piece of fruit she checked for quality.

VISUAL VOCABULARY

These fruit _____ are checking for quality.

   a. spectators
   b. inspectors

Roots

The **root** is the basic or main part of a word. Many times a root combined with other word parts will create a whole family of closely related words. Even when the root is joined with other word parts to form new words, the meaning of the root does not change. Learning frequently used roots will help you develop a strategy for decoding the meaning of many new words. A list of common roots starts on page 609.

EXAMPLES The root *tract* means "drag" or "pull." Study the following words. Using the meaning of the root *tract* and the context of each sentence, put each word into the sentence that best fits its meaning. Use each word once.

tract = "drag, pull"

contract	extracted	traction	tractor

1. The _____ pulled the oak tree, roots and all, out of the ground.

2. The shoe factory and its workers agreed on a _____.

3. Cocaine is a drug _____ from the coca plant.

4. After he injured his back, Alex was placed in _____.

EXPLANATIONS Each word contains the root *tract* ("drag" or "pull"), and each word uses the meaning of "drag" or "pull" differently. The additional word parts—prefixes and suffixes—create the different meanings. However, the meaning of the root word and the context of the sentence should have helped you choose the correct word for each sentence.

1. **Tractor:** A tractor is a machine that pulls or drags objects.

2. **Contract:** A contract is a legal record that pulls people together into agreement.

3. **Extracted:** Extracted means "pulled out."

4. **Traction:** Traction pulls broken bones together by means of a special device.

PRACTICE 2

Study the following words. The root *port* means "carry." Using the meaning of the root *port* and context clues, put each word into the sentence that best fits its meaning. Use each word once.

port = "carry"

imported	portable	porter	report	support

1. Cantaloupes _____ from Mexico are larger and cheaper than local produce.

2. Many people buy laptop computers because laptops are _____ and allow work to be done in many different locations.

3. Al-Anon is a _____ group for people who live with alcoholics.

4. Could you give a _____ at tonight's meeting?

5. The hotel _____ brought our luggage to our rooms.

VISUAL VOCABULARY

_____ expect to receive tips from the people they help.

  a. Reporters
  b. Porters

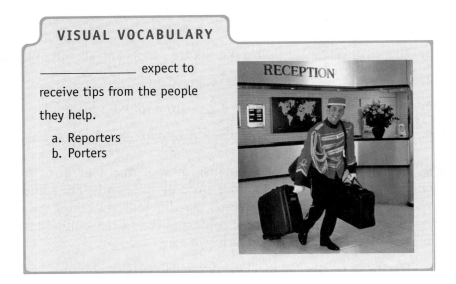

Prefixes

A **prefix** is a group of letters with a specific meaning added to the beginning of a word or root to make a new word. Although the basic meaning of a root does not change, a prefix changes the meaning of the word as a whole. A list of common prefixes starts on page 612.

For example, the prefix *ex-* means "out" or "from." When placed in front of the root *tract* (which means "pull" or "drag"), the word *extract* is formed. *Extract* means "pull or drag out." The same root *tract* joined with the prefix *con-* (which means "with" or "together") creates the word *contract*. A *contract* is a legal way to pull people together.

The importance of prefixes can be seen in the family of words that comes from the root *port,* which means "carry." Look over each of the following prefixes and their meanings. Then, in the examples given, note the change in the meaning of the whole word.

Prefix	Meaning	Root	Meaning	Example
ex-	out, from	*port*	(carry)	Oil is one **export** from the Middle East.
im-	in, into			Many countries **import** French wines.
re-	back, again			Bill's credit **report** was good.

EXAMPLES   Using the meanings of the prefixes, root, and context clues, put each word into the sentence that best fits its meaning. Use each word once.

Prefix	Meaning		Root	Meaning
e-	out, from		*mit*	send, let go
per-	through			
sub-	under, from below			

mit = "send, let go"

emit	permit	submitted

1. Jane _____ her request for a vacation to her boss.

2. Malcolm hoped his father would _____ him to use the car Saturday night.

3. Some factories _____ dangerous fumes.

EXPLANATIONS

1. **Submitted**: The prefix *sub-* means "under" or "from below." The root *mit* means "send." Jane is recognizing the authority of her boss by asking for the vacation time, so her request was "sent from below."

2. **Permit**: The prefix *per-* means "through." The root *mit* means "let go." Therefore, *permit* means "let go through." Malcolm hoped that his father would let his request for the car go through.

3. **Emit**: The prefix *e-* means "out of" or "from." The root *mit* means "send." Therefore, *emit* means "send out": Some factories send out fumes into the air.

PRACTICE **3**

Study the meaning of each of the following prefixes and roots.

Prefix	Meaning	Root	Meaning
auto-	self	*graph*	write
micro-	small	*scope*	see
tele-	far, from a distance		

Create five words by joining these prefixes and roots.

1. _____

2. _____

3. _____

4. _____

5. _____

VISUAL VOCABULARY

Use a _____ to study organisms up close.

a. telescope
b. microscope

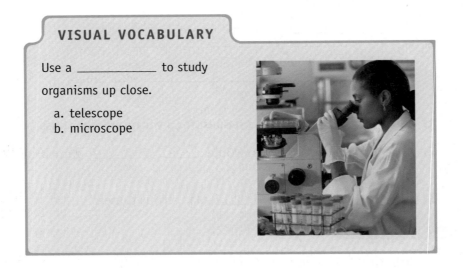

Suffixes

A **suffix** is a group of letters with a specific meaning added to the end of a word or root to make a new word. Although the basic meaning of the root does not change, a suffix can change the type of word and the way a word is used. (A list of common suffixes starts on page 614.) A word may contain more than one suffix. Look at the following examples.

Root	Meaning	Suffix	Meaning	Word	Meaning
bio	life	*-logy*	study of	*biology*	study of life
		-ist	person	*biologist*	person who studies life
		-ical	related to	*biological*	related to biology

EXAMPLES Using the meanings of the root, suffixes, and context clues, put each of the words in the box into the sentence that best fits its meaning. Use each word once.

Root	Meaning		Suffix	Meaning
grad	to go, take steps		*-al*	related to
			-ate	action of
			-ation	action, process
			-ly	in that manner

grad = to go, take steps

gradually	graduate	graduation

1. My sister's high school _____ is tonight.

2. Sondra is _____ becoming more self-confident.

3. Michael is going to _____ from West Point.

EXPLANATIONS

1. The answer is *graduation*. A graduation is an event that marks the completion of a step in the educational process.

2. The answer is *gradually*. Sondra is taking steps toward or is in the process of becoming self-confident. In this sentence, *gradually* describes how Sondra is becoming self-confident.

3. The answer is *graduate*. In this sentence, taking the step is stated in the form of an action.

PRACTICE 4

Using the meanings of the roots, suffixes, and context clues, put each word in the box into the sentence that best fits its meaning. Use each word once.

Root	Meaning		Suffix	Meaning
loc	place		*-ation*	action, process
eco	environment		*-logy*	study of
tact	touch		*-ile*	related to
equal	equal		*-ize*	cause to become
mot	movement		*-ive*	related to

ecology	equalize	location	locomotives	tactile

1. The three branches of American government were designed to _____, or balance, power.

2. To learn about animals and their habitats, one should study _____.

3. Knowing the _____ of the enemy is crucial to victory.

4. The skin receives _____ sensations.

5. Steam _____ used to be the main engines that pulled trains.

VISUAL VOCABULARY

In the past, steam _____ pulled trains.

a. locations
b. locomotives

Additional Word Parts

A skilled reader wisely invests time and effort in studying word parts and their meanings. Appendix C in the back of this book provides an additional list of word parts and their meanings for further study.

The Dictionary

Remember, some experts believe that most people by age 18 know around 60,000 words. Experts also believe that most adults actually use between 25,000 and 50,000 words. That seems like a large number, yet the English language has over one million words. Skilled readers use a dictionary to understand new or difficult words.

Most dictionaries provide the following information:

- Guide words (the words at the top of each page)
- Spelling (how the word and its different forms are spelled)
- Syllabication (the word divided into syllables)
- Pronunciation (how to say the word)
- Part of speech (the type of word)
- Definition (the meaning of the word, with the most common meaning listed first)
- Synonyms (words that have similar meanings)
- Etymology (the history of the word)

All dictionaries have guide words at the top of each page. However, dictionaries differ in the way they give other information about words. Some dictionaries give more information about the origin of the word; other dictionaries give long lists of synonyms. In addition to print dictionaries, computer technology has caused the development of electronic dictionaries. Dictionaries now come on CD-ROMs and as Web-based formats that are available through the Internet. Each dictionary will explain how to use its resources in the first few pages or in an introduction.

How to Find Words in the Dictionary

Guide words help you find a given word. **Guide words** are a pair of words printed in bold at the top of every page of a dictionary. Guide words show the first and last word printed on that page. Below is a copy of the top and bottom of a page from *Merriam-Webster's Collegiate Dictionary, Eleventh Edition*.

24 aged • aggressive

aged \'ā-jəd, 'ājd; 'ājd *for 1b*\ *adj* (15c) **1** : grown old: as **a** : of an advanced age <an ~ man> **b**: having attained a specified age <a man ~ 40 years> **2** : typical of old age — **ag·ed·ness**\'ā-jəd-nəs\ *n*

age–group \'ā-j-,grüp\ *n* (1904) : a segment of a population that is of approximately the same age or is within a specified range of ages

age·ism *also* **age·ism** \'ā-(,)ji-zəm\ *n* (1969) : prejudice or discrimination against a particular age-group and esp. the elderly — **age·ist** *also* **age·ist** \-jist\ *adj*

age·less \'āj-ləs\ *adj* (1651) **1** : not growing old or showing the effects of age **2** : TIMELESS, ETERNAL <~ truths> — **age·less·ly** *adv* — **age·less·ness** *n*

> **ag·gres·sion** \ə-'gre-shən\ *n* [L *aggression-, aggressio* attack, fr. *aggredi* to attack, fr. *ad-* + *gradi* to step, go — more at GRADE] (1611) **1** : a forceful action or procedure (as an unprovoked attack) esp. when intended to dominate or master **2** : the practice of making attacks or encroachments; *esp* : unprovoked violation by one country of the territorial integrity of another **3** : hostile, injurious, or destructive behavior or outlook esp. when caused by frustration
> **ag·gres·sive** \ə-'gre-siv\ *adj* (1824) **1 a** : tending toward or exhibiting aggression <~ behavior> **b** : marked by combative readiness <an ~ fighter> **2 a** : marked by obtrusive energy **b** : marked by driving forceful energy or initiative : ENTERPRISING <an ~ salesman> **3** : strong or emphatic in effect or intent <~ colors> <~ flavors> **4** : growing, developing, or spreading rapidly <~ bone tumors> **5** : more severe, intensive, or comprehensive than usual esp. in dosage or

Source: Used by permission. From *Merriam-Webster's Collegiate® Dictionary, Eleventh Edition* © 2005 by Merriam-Webster, Incorporated (www.Merriam-Webster.com)

The guide words are *aged* and *aggressive*. These guide words tell you that the words on this page fall alphabetically between them. When you are looking up a word, use the guide words to determine if the word you need is located on that page.

EXAMPLE   Place a check beside the three words that would appear on the page with the guide words **aged • aggressive.**

___affirm   ___agency   ___aggravate   ___age-old   ___airplane

EXPLANATION   The guide words **aged • aggressive** tell you that all the words on this page will begin with the letters *ag*. Thus *affirm* and *airplane* will not be found on this page of the dictionary.

PRACTICE **5**

In each of the following items, a pair of guide words is followed by five other words. Place a check next to the three words in each set that would be found on the page with the guide words that are given.

1. chairman • champ

___cesspit   ___chamber   ___challenge   ___chalet   ___cicada

2. pant • paper money

___papaw   ___pupil   ___pantry   ___popular   ___pantsuit

3. gender • genet

——gene ——genesis ——gladly ——general ——gimmick

How to Read a Dictionary Entry

The following entry from *Merriam-Webster's Collegiate Dictionary, Eleventh Edition,* will be used as an example for the discussions about the kinds of information a dictionary provides.

stol·id \'stä-ləd\ *adj* [L *stolidus* dull, stupid] (ca. 1600) **:** having or expressing little or no sensibility **:** UNEMOTIONAL   *syn* see IMPASSIVE — **sto·lid·i·ty** \stä-'li-d ə-tē, st ə-\ *n* — **stol·id·ly** \'stä-ləd-lē\ *adv*

Source: Used by permission. From *Merriam-Webster's Collegiate® Dictionary, Eleventh Edition* © 2005 by Merriam-Webster, Incorporated (www.Merriam-Webster.com)

Spelling and Syllables

The spelling of the word is given first in bold type. The word is also divided into syllables. A **syllable** is a unit of sound that includes a vowel. In our sample entry, *stolid* is divided into two syllables: *stol-id.*

Variants are given at the end of the entry. These are very helpful when letters are dropped from or added to the entry word to create another word. Variants of the word *stolid* are *stolidity,* which has four syllables (*sto-lid-i-ty*), and *stolidly,* which has three syllables (*stol-id-ly*).

EXAMPLES Use a dictionary to break the following words into syllables. In the space provided, rewrite each word, using a dot (•) to separate the syllables.

1. mural _____

2. extradite _____

3. immediately _____

EXPLANATIONS

1. Mural has two syllables: *mu · ral.*

2. Extradite has three syllables: *ex · tra · dite.*

3. Immediately has five syllables: *im · me · di · ate · ly.*

PRACTICE 6

Use a dictionary to break the following words into syllables. In the space provided, rewrite each word, using a dot (·) to separate the syllables.

1. inset _____

2. mutable _____

3. myology _____

4. psychoneurosis _____

Pronunciation Symbols and Accent Marks

Right after the word itself, the word's pronunciation is given in parentheses. The entry for *stolid* shows this information: \\'stä · ləd\\. Notice that accent marks and pronunciation symbols are used.

An **accent mark** is a dark mark above a word that looks like a slanted apostrophe or a tiny vertical bar ('). The accent mark indicates the syllable that gets the most emphasis when the word is spoken. For the word *stolid*, the dictionary places the accent mark before the first syllable, which means that the first syllable gets the emphasis. Often an additional stress mark, positioned below the syllable rather than above it, will indicate that a word has a lighter stress placed on that syllable.

EXAMPLES Study these words, and answer the questions that follow them.

1. tri · bal \\'trī-bəl\\

   a. How many syllables are in *tribal*? _____

   b. Which syllable is stressed? _____

2. mo · men · tous \\mō-'men-təs\\

   a. How many syllables are in *momentous*? _____

   b. Which syllable is stressed? _____

3. man · do · lin \\ˌman-də-'lin\\

   a. How many syllables are in *mandolin*? _____

   b. Which syllable is most strongly stressed? _____

EXPLANATIONS

1. **Tribal** has two syllables, and the first syllable is stressed.

2. **Momentous** has three syllables, and the second syllable is most strongly stressed.

3. **Mandolin** has three syllables, and the third syllable is most strongly stressed.

Note: Dictionaries vary in their use of accent marks; some dictionaries use bold and regular type to show the difference between the stressed syllables. Some dictionaries place the accent mark before the stressed syllable, and others place it after the syllable. Be sure to get to know your dictionary's approach.

Pronunciation symbols indicate the sounds of consonants and vowels. Dictionaries provide a pronunciation key so that you will understand the symbols used. Here is a sample pronunciation key:

Pronunciation Key

\ə\ **abut** \ᵊ\ **kitten, F table** \ər\ **further** \a\ **ash** \ā\ **ace** \ä\ **mop, mar**
\au̇\ **out** \ch\ **chin** \e\ **bet** \ē\ **easy** \g\ **go** \i\ **hit** \ī\ **ice** \j\ **job**
\ŋ\ **sing** \ō\ **go** \ȯ\ **law** \ȯi\ **boy** \th\ **thin** \t̲h̲\ **the** \ü\ **loot** \u̇\ **foot**
\y\ **yet** \zh\ **vision beige** \k̲, ⁿ, œ,ᴜe, ʸ\ *see* **Guide to Pronunciation**

Source: Used by permission. From *Merriam-Webster's Collegiate® Dictionary, Eleventh Edition* © 2005 by Merriam-Webster, Incorporated (www.Merriam-Webster.com)

Note that each letter and symbol is followed by a sample word. The sample word tells you how the letter represented by that symbol sounds. For example, \ā\ (long *a*) sounds like *a* in *ace*. And \ĭ\ (short *i*) has the sound of the *i* in *hit*. The symbol that looks like an upside-down *e* (ə) is called a *schwa*. The schwa has a sound like *a* and *u* in **ab**u**t**.

Different dictionaries use different symbols in their pronunciation keys, so be sure to check the key of the dictionary you are using.

EXAMPLES   Using our sample pronunciation key, answer questions about the following words. Write the letters of your answers in the given spaces.

_____ 1. **pit · fall** \ˈpĭt-ˌfȯl\
The *i* in *pitfall* sounds like the *i* in

a. *hit.*   b. *ice.*

_____ **2. ra·di·um** \'rā-dē-əm\
The *a* in *radium* sounds like the *a* in

    a. *ash.*   b. *ace.*

_____ **3. in·sole** \'ĭn-ˌsōl\
The *o* in *insole* sounds like the *o* in

    a. *boy.*   b. *go.*

EXPLANATIONS

1. The *i* in *pitfall* is a short *i* sound as in (a) *hit.*

2. The *a* in *radium* is a long *a* sound as in (b) *ace.*

3. The *o* in *insole* is a long *o* sound as in (b) *go.*

PRACTICE 7

Using your dictionary, find and write in the pronunciation symbols and accent marks for each of the following words.

1. bovine _____

2. comply _____

3. nocturnal _____

4. physicist _____

5. sextant _____

VISUAL VOCABULARY

This sailor is using _____ to fix a course.

    a. sextant
    b. nocturnal

Parts of Speech

Dictionary entries tell you what part of speech a word is—noun, verb, adjective, and so on. The part of speech is abbreviated and printed in italics. Your dictionary provides a full list of abbreviations. The following box lists the most common abbreviations for the parts of speech:

Parts of Speech			
adj	adjective	*prep*	preposition
adv	adverb	*pron*	pronoun
art	article	*vi, vt*	verb (intransitive,
conj	conjunction		transitive)
interj	interjection	*v aux*	verbal auxiliary
n	noun		

Review the dictionary entry for *stolid.*

stol·id \'stä-lied\ *adj* [L *stolidus* dull, stupid] (ca. 1600) **:** having or expressing little or no sensibility **:** UNEMOTIONAL   *syn* see IMPASSIVE — **sto·lid·i·ty** \stä-'li-də-tē, stə-\ *n* — **stol·id·ly** \'stä-ləd-lē\ *adv*

Source: Used by permission. From *Merriam-Webster's Collegiate® Dictionary, Eleventh Edition* © 2005 by Merriam-Webster, Incorporated (www.Merriam-Webster.com)

As the entry indicates, the word *stolid* is an adjective. The two variants of the word are identified as a noun (*stolidity*) and an adverb (*stolidly*).

EXAMPLES   Use your dictionary to identify the parts of speech for each of the following words. A word may be used as more than one part of speech.

1. pardon _____

2. without _____

3. rust _____

EXPLANATIONS

1. **Pardon** can be used as a noun or as a transitive verb.

2. **Without** can be used as a preposition, an adverb, a conjunction, or a noun.

3. **Rust** can be used as a noun, an intransitive verb, or a transitive verb.

PRACTICE 8

Use your dictionary to identify the parts of speech for each of the following words. A word may be used as more than one part of speech.

1. exclusive _____

2. like _____

_____

3. stream _____

Definitions

Most words have more than one meaning. When more than one definition is given in the dictionary, each meaning is numbered. The most common meaning is listed first. The dictionary may also provide examples of sentences in which the word is used.

EXAMPLES   Three definitions are given for the verb form of the word *run*. In the space provided, write the letter of the definition that best fits the meaning of the sentence.

> a. keep company
> b. go rapidly or hurriedly
> c. sing or play a musical passage rapidly

_____ **1.** Joanne ran with a gang when she was younger.

_____ **2.** John ran up the scale as practice on the piano.

_____ **3.** Thousands of people ran in the Boston Marathon.

EXPLANATIONS

1. The correct answer is (a) "keep company."

2. The correct answer is (c) "sing or play a musical passage rapidly."

3. The correct answer is (b) "go rapidly or hurriedly."

PRACTICE 9

Examine the following words, their definitions, and a sentence using each word. In the space provided, write the number of the meaning that best fits each sentence.

cross   **1** pass from one side to the other   **2** make or put a line across
3 combine the qualities of two things

_____   **1.** Jane is going to *cross* the river on her homemade raft.

sage   **1** a person known for being wise   **2** an herb in the mint family used in flavoring foods

_____   **2.** Rubbing a turkey with **sage** before cooking adds a savory flavor.

Synonyms

Often at the end of an entry, synonyms are given. A **synonym** is a word whose meaning is similar to that of another word. For example, a synonym for *angry* is *irate*. The abbreviation for *synonym* is *syn*. You may find it helpful to look up the synonym, too.

The entry for *stolid* includes this note: "***syn*** see IMPASSIVE." If you look up *impassive*, you will find a list of synonyms for the words *impassive* and *stolid*.

Etymology

Etymology is the study of a word's history. This information follows the part of speech and is found in brackets. In the entry for *stolid*, some facts about the word's history are given. Inside the brackets is the following information: "L *stolidus* dull, stupid." The letter *L* stands for *Latin*. The word *stolidus* is the Latin word from which the word *stolid* came; in Latin, its meaning was "dull" or "stupid." The entry also gives the date when a word was first recorded in a dictionary: "(ca. 1600)." The abbreviation *ca.* means "approximately," so the word *stolid* was first recorded in English around the year 1600. If even an approximate date cannot be given, the dictionary may indicate the century instead of the year, using the abbreviation *c*: thus "(16c)" would indicate that the word entered the English language in the 16th century.

Textbook
Skills
Textbook Aids for Learning Content Words

Content Words

Many students think they should be able to pick up a textbook and simply read it. However, a textbook is written for a content or subject area, such as math, history, or English. Each content area has its own vocabulary. For example, a history textbook takes a different approach than a literature textbook. Different courses may use the same words, but the words often take on new or different meanings in the context of the content area.

EXAMPLES   The following sentences all use the word *portfolio*. For each sentence, write the letter of the course that would use the word in its context.

_____ **1.** The **portfolio** included works of oils, watercolors, and chalk and line drawings.
  a. introduction to art
  b. business
  c. English

_____ **2.** A wise investor creates a **portfolio** of a wide range of investment stocks and bonds.
  a. introduction to art
  b. business
  c. English

_____ **3.** You will be required to turn in a **portfolio** that includes prewrites, drafts, and final copies of all your essays.
  a. introduction to art
  b. business
  c. English

EXPLANATIONS   Use context clues to determine your answers.

1. The word *portfolio* in this sentence is used in the area of art. So this term could be used in an introduction to art course (a).

2. The word *portfolio* in this sentence is used in the area of business or economics (b).

3. The word *portfolio* in this sentence is used in a writing class (c).

Textbook Definitions

You do not always need to use context clues or the dictionary to find the meaning of a word. In fact, many textbooks contain words or word groups that you cannot find in a dictionary. The content word is usually typed in bold or italic print. The definition follows, and many times an example is given. Sometimes the word and its definition are also repeated in the margin or at the top or bottom of the page.

EXAMPLES   Read the following passage from a biology textbook. Then answer the questions that follow it.

There are two alternating types of deep sleep. One type, **slow wave (SW) sleep**, is characterized by delta waves, which are fairly regular with strong bursts of brain activity. The other type of deep sleep is **REM sleep**, in which the brain waves are rapid and less regular, more like those of an awake state. During REM (rapid eye movement) sleep, the eyes move rapidly under the closed lids. The brain itself is highly active and may consume more oxygen than it does when awake.

—Campbell, Mitchell, & Reece, *Biology Concepts and Connections,* 5th ed., p. 582.

1. What are the two types of deep sleep? _____ and _____

2. What does REM mean? _____

EXPLANATIONS The two types of deep sleep are **slow wave sleep** and **REM sleep**. The words *slow wave sleep* and *REM sleep* are part of biology's content vocabulary. The authors know that these are new words for many students, so the words are typed in bold print and definitions are given. In fact, the definition for the term *REM* is put in parentheses next to it. *REM* means "rapid eye movement." Notice that the term *REM* is formed by taking the first letters of each word of its definition.

PRACTICE 10

Read each of the following textbook passages. Then write the definition for the words in bold print.

1. The way you talk to yourself affects the way you talk with others. Become aware of your **inner speech**—how you think about your thinking. Then you can become more effective when talking with others.

—Adapted from Brownell, *Listening: Attitudes, Principles, and Skills,* 2nd ed., p. 128.

inner speech _____

2. In the early 1830s, a new class of newspapers targeted to lower- and middle-class audiences earned the name **penny press** because they were sold for a penny a copy.

—Adapted from Folkerts & Lacy, *The Media in Your Life: An Introduction to Mass Communication,* 2nd ed., p. 84.

penny press _____

3.   Recreational cocaine users, including those known as **chippers** (occasional users), will often inhale cocaine in its powder form.

—Adapted from Fishbein & Pease, *The Dynamics of Drug Abuse*, p. 162.

chippers _____

Glossaries

Each subject or content area, such as science, mathematics, or English, has its own specialized vocabulary. Therefore, many textbooks provide an extra section in the back of the book called a *glossary*. A **glossary** is a list of selected language used in a specific area of study. Like a dictionary, a glossary is an alphabetized list of words, their spellings, and their meanings. However, unlike a dictionary entry, a glossary does not give parts of speech, word origins, or different forms or definitions of the word. In fact, the meanings given in a glossary are limited to the way in which the word or term is used in that content area.

   EXAMPLE   Read the following two word lists. Identify each one as follows:
      G = Glossary entry   D = Dictionary entry

_____ List 1:

Balanced budget A budget in which the legislature balances expenditures with expected revenues, with no deficit.

Barbary Wars Conflicts the United States fought in the early eighteenth century with North African states against their piracy.

Bicameral legislature A legislature divided into two houses: the U.S. Congress and the state legislatures are bicameral except Nebraska, which is unicameral.

—O'Connor et al., *American Government: Continuity and Change, 2004 Texas Ed.*, p. 1050.

_____ List 2:

¹**as·ter·oid** \ˈas-tə-ˌròid\ *n* [Gk *asteroeidēs* starlike, fr. *aster-, astēr*] (1802) **1** : any of the small rocky celestial bodies found esp. between the orbits of Mars and Jupiter **2** : STARFISH — **as·ter·oi·dal** \ˌas-tə-ˈròi-dᵊl\ *adj*
²**asteroid** *adj* (1854) **1** : resembling a star < ∼ bodies in sporotrichosis > **2** : of or resembling a starfish
asteroid belt *n* (1952) : the region of interplanetary space between the orbits of Mars and Jupiter in which most asteroids are found

Source: Used by permission. From *Merriam-Webster's Collegiate® Dictionary, Eleventh Edition* © 2005 by Merriam-Webster, Incorporated (www.Merriam-Webster.com)

EXPLANATION The first list is a glossary from a history textbook. The terms and meanings are specifically related to U.S. history. The second list is from *Merriam-Webster's Collegiate Dictionary, Eleventh Edition*. The second list includes much more information about the words, such as the pronunciation marks and several definitions of each term.

PRACTICE 11

Read the following sample from a glossary. In the spaces provided, write **T** if the statement is true and **F** if the statement is false.

Glossary

Absorption: Occurs when a drug reaches the bloodstream from surrounding tissue or organs
Abuse potential: Ability of a drug to give pleasure or pain; this ability increases the likelihood that the user will continue to use the drug and become dependent
Addictive personality: Character traits that may put an individual at risk for addictive behaviors, such as drug addiction, eating disorders, compulsive gambling, or other compulsive behaviors
Bazuko: Cocaine paste that is mixed with tobacco and smoked
Cold turkey: Abrupt withdrawal from an addictive drug without the help of other drugs to lessen withdrawal symptoms; most commonly linked with heroin withdrawal

—Adapted from Fishbein & Pease, *The Dynamics of Drug Abuse,* pp. 395–97.

_____ **1.** Surrounding tissues and organs do not absorb drugs from the bloodstream.

_____ **2.** Abuse potential comes from a drug's ability to give pleasure or relieve pain.

_____ **3.** An addictive personality does not put an individual at risk.

_____ **4.** "Bazuko" is taken into a person's system by smoking.

_____ **5.** Cold turkey is most commonly linked with heroin.

Chapter Review

Test your understanding of what you have read in this chapter by filling in each blank with a word from the box. Use each word once.

accent mark	etymology	guide words	pronunciation	syllable
content	glossary	prefix	suffix	word parts

1. _____ can help you learn vocabulary more easily and quickly.

2. A _____ is a group of letters with a specific meaning added before a word or root to make a new word.

3. A _____ is a group of letters with a specific meaning added to the end of a word or root to make a new word.

4. _____ are a pair of words printed in bold at the top of every page of the dictionary.

5. A _____ is a unit of sound that includes a single vowel sound.

6. An _____ is a dark mark above a word that indicates which syllable gets the most emphasis when the word is spoken.

7. _____ symbols indicate the sounds of consonants and vowels.

8. _____ is the study of a word's history.

9. Each _____ area has its own vocabulary.

10. Many textbooks provide a special section of definitions called a _____. This section provides a list of the words used in a content area and their meanings.

Applications

Application 1: Roots and Prefixes

A. Fill in each blank by using the **root word** that best fits the meaning of the sentence.

Root	Meaning
aqua	water
cap	head
ego	self
phobia	fear

1. Maxine has a _____ about flying and won't travel by airplane.

2. Be sure to put the _____ on the tube of toothpaste.

3. José has a big _____—he is always talking about himself.

4. The actress wore a beautiful _____ blue dress.

B. Study the following set of **prefixes** and **roots**:

Prefix	Meaning	Root	Meaning
dis-	apart	sect	cut
in-	in, into	spect	look
re-	back, again		

Using these prefixes and roots, create three words.

5. _____

6. _____

7. _____

Fill in each blank with a word from the box. Use each word once.

dissect	inspect	respect

8. We had to _____ a frog in science class today.

9. Children should _____ house rules.

10. The police officer needs to _____ the scene for evidence.

Application 2: Roots and Suffixes

A. Using the chart, fill in each blank with the word that best fits the meaning of the sentence.

Root	Meaning	Suffix	Meaning
dent	tooth	-al	of, like, related to, being
dynam	power	-ic	related to
log	speech, science, reason		

dental	dynamic	logic

1. My gums are sore from the _____ work Dr. White did on my teeth.

2. The energetic Robin Williams is an entertainer with a _____ personality.

3. The union president gave a speech explaining his _____ for threatening a strike.

B. Using the chart and the context of the sentences, fill in each blank with a word from the box. Use each word once.

Root	Meaning	Suffix	Meaning
psych	mind	*-ic*	related to
		-ist	person
		-logy	study of

psychiatric	psychiatrist	psychology

4. George is studying _____. He is learning about the mind and behavior.

5. George hopes to be a _____ who can help people understand the way they think and behave.

6. One day, George hopes to open a _____ clinic for homeless individuals who are suffering from mental illness.

Application 3: Using a Glossary and a Dictionary

A. Study the list of words from an ecology textbook glossary. Then answer the questions that follow it.

Textbook
Skills

> **Glossary**
>
> **age structure** The number of each age group within a population.
> **arroyo** A water-carved canyon in the desert.
> **bog** Wetland which has peat, acid conditions, and sphagnum moss.
> **calorie** Amount of heat needed to raise 1 gram of water 1 degree Celsius, usually from 15 to 16 degrees Celsius.
> **carnivore** Organism that feeds on animal tissue.
> **energy** Capacity to do work.
> **hybrid** Plant or animal resulting from a cross between genetically different parents.

—Adapted from Smith & Smith, *Elements of Ecology,* 4th ed., pp. 535–41.

Based on the definition of each word and the context of each sentence, label the statements below either true (**T**) or false (**F**).

___F___ **1.** A mule is an *arroyo* of a donkey and a horse.

___T___ **2.** The slopes of a desert level off into low basins, which receive waters that rush down from the hills and water-cut canyons or *hybrids*.

___F___ **3.** *Bogs* are wetlands that have sphagnum moss.

___+___ **4.** Many human beings are *carnivores*.

___T___ **5.** Plants get the *energy* they need from the sun and from the nutrients in the soil.

B. Study the excerpt based on *Merriam-Webster's Collegiate Dictionary, Eleventh Edition*, and then answer the questions that follow it.

---

half cock • hallucinosis

hal·lu·ci·nate \hə-'lü-sə-ˌnāt\ *vb* **-nat·ed; -nat·ing** [L *hallucinatus*, pp. of *hallucinari*, *allucinari* to prate, dream, modif. of Gk *alyein* to be distressed, to wander] *vt* (ca. 1834) **1 :** to affect with visions or imaginary perceptions **2 :** to perceive or experience as a hallucination ~ *vi* : to have hallucinations — **hal·lu·ci·na·tor** \-ˌnā-tər\ *n*
hal·lu·ci·na·tion \hə-ˌlü-sə-'nā-shən\ *n* (1629) **1 a :** perception of objects with no reality usu. arising from disorder of the nervous system or in response to drugs (as LSD) **b :** the object so perceived **2 :** an unfounded or mistaken impression or notion **:** DELUSION *syn* see DELUSION
hal·lu·ci·na·to·ry \hə-'lü-sə-nə-ˌtòr-ē, -'lüs -nə-\ *adj* (1830) **1 :** tending to produce hallucination <~ drugs> **2 :** resembling, involving, or being an hallucination <~ dreams> <a ~ figure>
hal·lu·ci·no·gen \hə-'lü-sə-nə-jən\ *n* [*hallucination* + *-o-* + *-gen*] (1954) **:** a substance that induces hallucinations — **hal·lu·ci·no·gen·ic** \-ˌlü-sə-nə-'jə-nik\ *adj or n*

Source: Used by permission. From *Merriam-Webster's Collegiate® Dictionary, Eleventh Edition* © 2005 by Merriam-Webster, Incorporated (www.Merriam-Webster.com)

___a___ **1.** Which of the words was first recorded in print?
   a. hallucinate
   b. hallucination
   c. hallucinatory
   d. hallucinogen

_a_ **2.** Which of the following is a synonym for *hallucination*?
   a. delusion
   b. hope
   c. drug
   d. disease

Based on the definition of each word given in the dictionary and the context of each sentence, fill in the blank with the word that best fits the sentence.

3. Many drug users _hallucinate_ or see visions while taking drugs.

4. The drug LSD often causes a _hallucination_ .

5. LSD is an illegal _hallucinatory_ drug.

REVIEW Test 1

Vocabulary-Building Skills

A. Using the chart and the context of each sentence, select the word from the box that best fits the meaning of the sentence. Use each word once.

Prefix	Meaning	Root	Meaning	Suffix	Meaning
hypo-	under	derm	skin	-ic	of, like, related to, being
hyper-	excessive	errat	wander	-logy	study of
				-ally	in that manner

dermatology	erratic	hyperactive	hypodermic

1. Eric is afraid of _erratic_ needles.

2. By the time we noticed the dog's _hyperactive_ behavior, it was too late to cure his case of rabies.

3. Some brands of cough medicine make Lana _hypodermic_ .

4. _dermatology_ is the study of the skin.

B. Look over the following entry from *Merriam-Webster's Collegiate Dictionary, Eleventh Edition*. Then mark each statement **T** (true) or **F** (false), based on the entry.

innards • in-process

in·no·vate \'i-nə-,vāt\ *vb* **-vat·ed; -vat·ing** [L *innovatus,* pp. of *innovare,* fr. *in-* + *novus* new — more at NEW] *vt* (1548) **1 :** to introduce as or as if new **2 :** *archaic* **:** to effect a change in <the dictates of my father were . . . not to be altered, *innovated,* or even discussed —Sir Walter Scott> ~ *vi* **:** to make changes **:** do something in a new way — **in·no·va·tor** \-,vā-tər\ *n* — **in·no·va·to·ry** \'i-nə-və-,tȯr-ē, -,tȯr- ; 'i-nə-,vā-tə-rē\ *adj*

Source: Used by permission. From *Merriam-Webster's Collegiate® Dictionary, Eleventh Edition* © 2005 by Merriam-Webster, Incorporated (www.Merriam-Webster.com)

___T___ **5.** The word *innovate* comes from a Latin word that means "new."

___F___ **6.** The date the word *innovate* was first recorded in English is not known.

___F___ **7.** The word *innovate* has four syllables.

___F___ **8.** The word *inside* would be found on this page of the dictionary.

C. Look over the terms from the glossary of the textbook *Government in America.* Based on the definition of each term and the context of the sentence, write the term that best fits the meaning of each of the sentences that follow the list.

Textbook
Skills

Glossary

affirmative action A policy designed to give attention to members of a group that had been deprived up to that time.
arms race A tense relationship beginning in the 1950s between the Soviet Union and the United States. One side's advance in weapons caused the other side to develop more weapons, and so on.

—Adapted from Edwards, Wattenberg, & Lineberry, *Government in America: People, Politics, and Policy,* 5th ed., Brief Version, p. 490.

9. The Soviet Union and the United States began an *arms race* in the 1950s.

10. Several minority groups have benefited from *affirmative action*

REVIEW Test 2

Vocabulary-Building Skills

A. Using the chart and the context of each sentence, select the word from the box that best fits the meaning of the sentence. Use each word once.

Prefix	Meaning	Root	Meaning	Suffix	Meaning
re-	back, again	fluct	flow	-ation	action, state of, like, related to, being
		pater	father	-al	
				-ity	quality

fluctuation	paternal	paternity	reflux

1. Heartburn is caused by a _reflux_ of stomach acid.

2. Graham demanded a _paternity_ test to determine if he was the child's father.

3. Arthur has strong _paternal_ feelings for his nieces and nephews.

4. Seasons of flood and drought cause a _fluctuation_ in the water supply.

B. Look over the following entry for *chop suey* from *Merriam-Webster's Collegiate Dictionary, Eleventh Edition*. Then mark each statement **T** (true) or **F** (false), based on the entry.

---

chopper • chowder

chop su·ey \,chäp-'sü-ē\ *n, pl* **chop sueys** [Chin (Guangdong) *jaahp-seui* odds and ends, fr. *jaahp* miscellaneous + *seui* bits] (1888) : a dish prepared chiefly from bean sprouts, bamboo shoots, water chestnuts, onions, mushrooms, and meat or fish and served with rice and soy sauce

---

Source: Used by permission. From *Merriam-Webster's Collegiate® Dictionary, Eleventh Edition* © 2005 by Merriam-Webster, Incorporated (www.Merriam-Webster.com)

___F___ **5.** *Chop suey* is a term that had its origin in China.

___T___ **6.** The word *suey* means "pig."

___F___ **7.** The word *chorus* would be found on this page of the dictionary.

C. Look over the list of words from the glossary of the textbook *The Family*. Based on the definition of each word and the context of the sentence, write the word that best fits the meaning of each sentence that follows the list.

Textbook
Skills

> **Glossary**
>
> **Gender** A term that refers to being male or female.
> **Gender role** The expected behaviors of a gender that are assigned by a given culture.
> **Househusband** A husband who stays at home and performs the domestic tasks and takes care of the children while his wife is employed full time.

—Adapted from Eshleman, *The Family*, 9th ed., p. 558.

8. Being a *househusband* is a new role for many men.

9. Giving toy cars to boys and dolls to girls is seen by some people as a way to teach children their proper *gender role*.

10. New medical breakthroughs with DNA promise future parents the ability to choose their child's *gender*.

REVIEW Test 3

Vocabulary-Building Skills

A. Using the chart and the context of each sentence, select the word from the box that best fits the meaning of the sentence. Use each word once.

Prefix	Meaning	Root	Meaning	Suffix	Meaning
in-	into	*quir, quis*	question	*-tion*	action, state of, like, related to, being
				-ive	
				-or	one who

inquire	inquisition	inquisitive	inquisitor

1. You can *inquire* at the window about your food order.

2. The grand jury is conducting an *inquisitor* about the missing woman.

3. A 2-year-old child is naturally _curious_ about the world around her.

4. The defense attorney took on the role of _inquisitor_ in an attempt to prove that the witness was lying.

B. Look over the following words from *Merriam-Webster's Collegiate Dictionary, Eleventh Edition*. Then mark each statement **T** (true) or **F** (false), based on the entry.

> **IQ • ironness**
>
> **¹irk** \ˈərk\ *vt* [ME] (15c) : to make weary, irritated, or bored   *syn* see ANNOY
> **²irk** *n* (ca. 1570)   **1** : the fact of being annoying   **2** : a source of annoyance
> **irk·some** \ˈərk-səm\ *adj* (15c) : tending to irk : TEDIOUS <an ~ task> — **irk·some·ly** *adv* — **irk·some·ness** *n*

Source: Used by permission. From *Merriam-Webster's Collegiate® Dictionary, Eleventh Edition* © 2005 by Merriam-Webster, Incorporated (www.Merriam-Webster.com)

___T___ **5.** The word *irk* can be used as both a verb and a noun.

___F___ **6.** Another word for *irksome* is *tedious*.

___T___ **7.** The noun form of *irksome* is *irksomely*.

C. Look over the words from the glossary of the textbook *Psychology: The Brain, the Person, the World*. Based on the definition of each word and the context of the sentence, select the word that best fits the meaning of each sentence that follows the list.

Textbook
Skills

> **Glossary**
>
> **Social loafing** The tendency to work less hard when responsibility for the result is spread among a group's members.
> **Social phobia** A fear of public embarrassment and the desire to avoid social situations.
> **Social psychology** The study of how people think about other people, relationships, and groups.

—Adapted from Kosslyn & Rosenberg, *Psychology: The Brain, the Person, the World*, p. 691.

8. Randy is seldom selected by his peers for group projects; he is known for his _social loafing_.

9. Emma never leaves her apartment because of her *social phobia* .

10. Researchers who study how people flirt and make dates work in the field of *Psychology* .

REVIEW Test 4

Vocabulary-Building Skills

Read the passage. Then, using the glossary and the context of the sentences, answer the questions that follow it.

Glossary

catharsis release, relief

immune system the body's ability to fight off infections

nutrients vitamins and minerals found in food

opportunities occasions, events, chances

physiological related to the physical body

reduction a decrease in an amount

temporary short-term

torso chest, or trunk of the body

THE HEALING POWER OF HUMOR

[1]It may surprise you to learn that a good joke can do far more than just "tickle your funny bone." [2]In fact, studies have shown that humor and laughter can improve your physical and mental health. [3]The proven benefits of laughter include stress **reduction**, pain relief, an enhanced **immune system** and a healthier outlook on life.

[4]Laughter, like crying, is a form of **catharsis**. [5]It provides an outlet for you to relieve feelings of stress and anxiety. [6]Laughter can help "clear your head," helping you to look at a situation from a new angle.

[7]Studies show that laughter provides many **physiological** benefits. [8]It causes a **temporary** increase in your heart rate and blood pressure, which aids in the delivery of oxygen and **nutrients** to your entire body. [9]Laughter can also help relax tense muscles in your face, shoulders and **torso**, according to Allen Klein, author of *The Healing Power of Humor*. [10]And it exercises **abdominal** muscles.

[11]Laughter helps the body produce new immune cells faster. [12]Klein also believes that a boosted immune system will help you fight off many illnesses, including colds, flu and even cancer.

[13]Several studies have shown that exposing people to humorous experiences greatly improves their ability to deal with pain. [14]When you laugh, Klein suggests, your brain releases **endorphins**—the body's natural pain killers.

[15]To fully gain the benefits of humor, you need to seek **opportunities** to add humor to your life. [16]Go see a funny movie. [17]Watch your favorite sit-com; grab the funny pages out of the Sunday paper, or make funny faces in the mirror with your kids.

—"The Healing Power of Humor," *Living Healthy: Working Well, a Monthly Newsletter Distributed to State of California EAP Coordinators,* May 1999.

Read each of the sentences below and mark the statement that follows it **T** (True) or **F** (False).

1. The proven benefits of laughter include stress **reduction**, pain relief, an enhanced **immune system** and a healthier outlook on life. (*sentence 3*)

   ___T___ People who laugh often are happier and get sick less often.

2. Laughter, like crying, is a form of **catharsis**. (*sentence 4*)

   ___F___ Laughter offers a healing release from stress.

3–4. It causes a **temporary** increase in your heart rate and blood pressure, which aids in the delivery of oxygen and **nutrients** to your entire body. (*sentence 8*)

   ___T___ The term **temporary** means "long-term."

   ___T___ Nutrients are good for the body but not necessary for overall health.

5. Laughter can also help relax tense muscles in your face, shoulders and **torso**. (*sentence 9*)

   ___F___ Laughter seems to most benefit the upper body.

6. And it exercises **abdominal** muscles. (*sentence 10*)

   ___F___ Laughter affects the stomach and lower-back muscles.

7. When you laugh, Klein suggests, your brain releases **endorphins**—the body's natural pain killers. (*sentence 14*)

   ___F___ Laughter relieves pain, helping us to forget about it for a little while.

8. To fully gain the benefits of humor, you need to seek **opportunities** to add humor to your life. (*sentence 15*)

   ___T___ For most people, laughter does not come naturally.

Fill in each blank with a word from the box below. Use the definitions in the glossary to help you make your choice. Two words will not be used.

abdominal	catharsis	reduction	temporary

9. Yoga is an effective exercise program that strengthens the *abdominal* area.

10. After months of arguing with her parents, Heather's decision to move out of their house was a *temporary* ' for everyone involved.

SKILLED READER Scorecard

Vocabulary-Building Skills

Test	Number Correct		Points		Score
Review Test 1	_____	×	10	=	_____
Review Test 2	_____	×	10	=	_____
Review Test 3	_____	×	10	=	_____
Review Test 4	_____	×	10	=	_____
Review Test 5 (website)	_____	×	10	=	_____
Review Test 6 (website)	_____	×	10	=	_____

Enter your score on the Skilled Reader Scorecard: Chapter 3 Review Tests inside the back cover.

After Reading About Vocabulary Building Skills

Now that you have read and studied vocabulary-building skills, take time to reflect on what you have learned before you begin the mastery tests. Think about your learning and performance by answering the following questions. Write your answers in your notebook.

What did I learn about vocabulary-building skills?

What do I need to remember about vocabulary-building skills?

How has my knowledge base or prior knowledge about vocabulary-building skills changed?

More Review and Mastery Tests

For more practice, go to the book's website at http://www.ablongman.com/henry and click on *The Skilled Reader*. Then select "More Review and Mastery Tests." You will find the tests listed by chapter.

Name _Rory Lawrence_   Section _____

Date _4/ 8 2/0 9_   Score (number correct) _____ × 20 = _____ %

Read the following passage. Then, using the glossary and the context of the sentences, answer the questions that follow it.

Glossary

fault a fracture in a zone of rock

habitat territory, environment, living area

promontory peninsula, point

protuberances bulges, bumps

sonar sound

Huge California Surfing Waves Explained

[1]Researchers have mapped the seafloor off central California in unprecedented detail, revealing what produces the famed waves at a reef called Mavericks. [2]The towering waves are much prized by surfers.

[3]Advanced **sonar** equipment and above-ground light detection instruments helped produce detailed underwater images. [4]These images display the many **protuberances** and depressions marking the seafloor near the well-known surfing spot at Half Moon Bay.

[5]The newly collected data shows that the wave-making setup at Mavericks involves a portion of a rocky reef that protrudes above its surroundings while remaining under water. [6]As a wave approaches the shore and enters shallower water, it compresses and grows taller. [7]A ridge **promontory** also focuses wave energy and the wave rapidly increases in height, creating a monster.

[8]At the highest point of the protrusion, the wave becomes unstable and breaks. [9]Data collection was impossible in that location because the rough sea presented too much danger to the scientists.

[10]Scientists and others will use this data for a variety of purposes, including identifying hazards to navigation and classifying different **habitat** types. [11]The information will also help in locating biological hot spots, and studying the San Gregorio **fault**, a major active fault within the San Andreas Fault System.

[12]"This research is extremely valuable in identifying areas important to the California Marine Life Protection Act process and could simultaneously help to predict seismic hazards along California's coast," said Secretary for Resources Mike Chrisman, chair of the Ocean Protection Council.

—Adapted from "Huge California Surfing Waves Explained."
http://www.livescience.com/news/070417_maverick_waves.html.
Used by permission of Imaginova Corp.

Read each sentence, and mark the statement that follows it **T** (true) or **F** (false).

1. Advanced **sonar** equipment and above-ground light detection instruments helped produce detailed underwater images. (*sentence 3*)

   __T__ Sound bounces off of objects.

2. These images display the many **protuberances** and depressions marking the seafloor near the well-known surfing spot at Half Moon Bay. (*sentence 4*)

   __F__ An uneven seafloor creates larger waves.

3. A ridge **promontory** also focuses wave energy and the wave rapidly increases in height, creating a monster. (*sentence 7*)

   __F__ The shape of the sea shore does not affect the size of the waves.

4. Scientists and others will use this data for a variety of purposes, including identifying hazards to navigation and classifying different **habitat** types. (*sentence 10*)

   __T__ The ocean is an ideal habitat for people.

5. The information will also help in locating biological hot spots, and studying the San Gregorio **fault**, a major active fault within the San Andreas Fault System. (*sentence 11*)

   __T__ A fault is a type of underwater mountain.

MASTERY Test 2

Name *Daryl Lawrence* Section _____

Date *1/22/09* Score (number correct) _____ × 20 = _____ %

Read the following passage, adapted from the textbook *Social Psychology*. Then, using the glossary and the context of the sentences, answer the questions that follow it.

Intrinsic versus Extrinsic Motivation

Glossary

extrinsic motivation the desire to engage in an activity for outside rewards or pressures

intrinsic motivation the desire to engage in an activity for pleasure

overjustification effect placing too much emphasis on extrinsic reasons to explain behavior

performance-contingent rewards rewards given for how well a task is done

task-contingent rewards rewards given for performing a task, regardless of how well the task is done

[1]Say you love to play the piano. [2]We would say that your interest in playing the piano stems from **intrinsic motivation**. [3]Your reasons for engaging in the activity have to do with you— the enjoyment and pleasure you feel when playing the piano. [4]In other words, playing the piano is play, not work. [5]Now let's say your parents get the brilliant idea of rewarding you with money for playing the piano. [6]They figure this will make you practice even harder. [7]Your playing now stems from **extrinsic motivation** as well. [8]According to self-perception theory, extrinsic rewards can hurt intrinsic motivation. [9]Whereas before you played the piano because you love it, now you are playing it so that you'll get the reward. [10]What was once play is now work. [11]Replacing intrinsic motivation with extrinsic motivation makes most people lose interest in the activity they originally enjoyed. [12]This result is called the **overjustification effect**. [13]The results of overjustification studies are distressing, given the wide use of rewards and incentives by parents, educators, and employers. [14]However, certain types of rewards can have a positive impact. [15]So far we have been discussing **task-contingent rewards**. [16]In contrast, **performance-contingent rewards** are used to recognize how well people perform the task. [17]This type of reward is less likely to decrease interest in a task—and may even increase interest—because it conveys the message that you are good at a task.

—Adapted from Elliot, Aronson, Timothy D. Wilson, and Robin M. Akert. *Social Psychology*, 4th ed., Prentice Hall, 2002, pp. 155–157.

Read each sentence, and mark the statement that follows it **T** (true) or **F** (false).

1. We would say that your interest in playing the piano stems from **intrinsic motivation**. (*sentence 2*)

   _T_ Intrinsic motivations come from within a person.

2. Your playing now stems from **extrinsic motivation** as well. (*sentence 7*)

   _T_ An athlete competing for a trophy is an example of an extrinsic motivation.

3. The results of **overjustification** studies are distressing, given the wide use of rewards and incentives by parents, educators, and employers. (*sentence 13*)

   _F_ Overjustification is used by parents, educators, and employers to encourage hard work.

4. So far we have been discussing **task-contingent rewards**. (*sentence 15*)

   _F_ Getting extra credit for class attendance is an example of a task-contingent reward.

5. In contrast, **performance-contingent rewards** are used to recognize how well people perform the task. (*sentence 16*)

   _F_ Receiving a certificate for completing a training program is an example of performance-contingent reward.

Read the following passage. Then, using the glossary and the context of the sentences, answer the questions that follow it.

Pain

Glossary

impending looming, approaching, coming

inhibitory a person, thing, or substance that holds something back or restrains something

receptors receiver

stimulus cause, reason

transmit send out

[1]Despite the discomfort, even the agony, pain brings, the inability to feel pain is even worse in the long run than the inability to smell odors. [2]One researcher described children who could not feel pain normally. [3]As a result, they picked off their nostrils and bit off their fingers because they didn't notice what they were doing. [4]Pain serves to warn us of **impending** danger, and it is crucial to survival.

[5]The sensation of pain arises when three different kinds of nerves are stimulated. [6]These nerves differ in size and in the speed with which they **transmit** impulses. [7]Thus, we can feel double pain: the first phase, of sharp pain, occurs at the time of the injury; it is followed by a dull pain. [8]The two kinds of pain arise from different fibers sending their messages at different speeds.

[9]One of the ways we deal with pain is by producing substances in our brains, called endorphins, which have painkilling effects. [10]Some drugs, such as morphine, bind to the same **receptors** that accept endorphins. [11]This explains how those drugs can act as painkillers. [12]However, pain involves more than simple bottom-up processing. [13]Top-down processing can directly inhibit the inter-neurons that regulate the input of pain signals to the brain. [14]This gate control mechanism may explain how hypnosis can control pain. [15]Indeed, hypnosis can selectively alter our experience of the unpleasantness of pain without affecting how intense it feels. [16]Hypnosis thus may alter processing in only some of the brain areas that register pain. [17]**Inhibitory** impulses from the brain to neurons also send signals from the body. [18]Thus, pain is reduced by a *counter-irritant,* a painful **stimulus** elsewhere in the body. [19]Such effects may explain how acupuncture, the placing of small needles to treat pain, works. [20]People differ widely in the amount of pain they can stand.

—Adapted from Kosslyn, Stephen Michael. *Psychology: The Brain, The Person, The World.* Allyn & Bacon, 2001, p. 123.

125

Read the sentences, and mark the statements that follow them **T** (true) or **F** (false).

1. Pain serves to warn us of **impending** danger, and it is crucial to survival. (*sentence 4*)

   __F__ Pain signals a problem that could get worse if not corrected.

2. These nerves differ in size and in the speed with which they **transmit** impulses. (*sentence 6*)

   __F__ Nerves carry messages from the various parts of the body to the brain.

3. Some drugs, such as morphine, bind to the same **receptors** that accept endorphins. (*sentence 10*)

   __F__ Nerve endings are not receptors.

4. **Inhibitory** impulses from the brain to neurons also send signals from the body. (*sentence 17*)

   __T__ Acupuncture is a type of inhibitory impulse.

5. Thus, pain is reduced by a *counter-irritant,* a painful **stimulus** elsewhere in the body. (*sentence 18*)

   __F__ A stimulus is the result of pain.

Read the following passage, adapted from the textbook *Understanding Parenting*. Then, using the glossary and the context of the sentences, answer the questions that follow it.

Textbook Skills

Glossary

authority command, power

departure a going out, going away, separation

image-making making pictures in the mind, using the imagination

interdependent sharing a reliance on or trust in other people

interpretative explaining

nurturing supplying with nourishment, educating

[1]The main challenge of adulthood is learning to care for others and future generations. [2]Experts describe six stages that parents go through before, during and after they raise their children.

[3]During the first or **image-making** stage, expectant couples face several tasks; the major task is getting ready for birth and parenthood. [4]Before the birth of their child, all parents have to go on are "images." [5]These expectant parents imagine what their child and their new family will be like.

[6]The next stage is the **nurturing** stage. [7]During this stage, parents learn to love and accept the child. [8]This may seem like it should come naturally. [9]However, many parents struggle when the images they had before the birth of the child are different from the actual baby.

[10]The third or **authority** stage spans the preschool years. [11]During this stage, parents must learn how to assert their authority. [12]In the authority stage, parents are learning to use power. [13]Out of the use of power, self-concepts are being shaped—for both parent and child.

[14]The fourth or **interpretative** stage occurs during the elementary school years. [15]In this stage, parents explain and teach their children skills and values that help shape their self-image.

[16]The fifth or **interdependent** stage spans adolescence. [17]Authority and communication issues arise again. [18]As the child grows, the old issues must be updated to keep up with the changing needs of the child.

[19]The final or **departure** stage occurs when grown children leave home. [20]Parents are wise to prepare for a child's departure. [21]When the last child leaves home, the parents must redefine their own life's role. [22]This means that parents have to think differently about themselves as a couple and as individuals.

—Adapted from Jaffe, *Understanding Parenting*, 2nd ed., pp. 36–38.

Read each sentence, and mark the statement that follows it **T** (true) or **F** (false).

1. During the first or **image-making** stage, expectant couples face several tasks; the major task is getting ready for birth and parenthood. (*sentence 3*)

    __F__ Expectant couples think about the baby and the changes it will bring long before the baby is born.

2. The third or **authority** stage spans the preschool years. (*sentence 10*)

    __F__ Children fight their parents for control during the third stage of growth.

3. The fourth or **interpretative** stage occurs during the elementary school years. (*sentence 14*)

    __T__ In the fourth stage, the parents' main purpose is to teach their child.

4. The fifth or **interdependent** stage spans adolescence. (*sentence 16*)

    __F__ Parents and children rely on each other in the fifth stage.

5. The final or **departure** stage occurs when grown children leave home. (*sentence 19*)

    __T__ Parents should pack their children's belongings when the children leave home.

A. Look over the following excerpt from *Merriam-Webster's Collegiate Dictionary, Eleventh Edition*. Then mark the statement that follows it **T** (true) or **F** (false), based on the excerpt.

---

emissary • employment

emo·tive \i-'mō-tiv\ a*dj* (1830)   **1 :** of or relating to the emotions   **2 :** appealing to or expressing emotion <the ~ use of language> — **emo·tive·ly** *adv* — **emo·tiv·i·ty** \i-,mō-'ti-və-tē, ,ē-,mō-\ *n*

Source: Used by permission. From *Merriam-Webster's Collegiate® Dictionary, Eleventh Edition* © 2005 by Merriam-Webster, Incorporated (www.Merriam-Webster.com)

_____ **1.** The word *enabler* could be found on this page of the dictionary.

B. Using the chart and the context of each sentence, select the word from the box that best fits the meaning of the sentence. Use each word once.

Prefix	Meaning	Root	Meaning	Suffix	Meaning
a-	not, without	*path*	feeling	*-al*	of, like
sym-	together, with	*soror*	sister	*-ity*	quality, trait
		therm	heat	*-y*	quality, trait

apathy	sorority	sympathy	thermal

2. _Thermal_ underwear is an important part of one's wardrobe during the winter in Alaska.

3. A feeling of _sympathy_ may be one sign of a deep depression.

4. Joining a college _sorority_ offers many women an opportunity to feel connected to other women with similar interests.

5. Jamal cherished the _apathy_ of friends and family when recovering from his accident.

**Textbook
Skills**

C. Read the following passage, adapted from the textbook *Health Styles*. Then, using the glossary and the context of the sentences, answer the questions that follow it.

TOBACCO TAR

[1]**Tar** is the gummy mixture left over from burning tobacco. [2]It consists of more than two hundred chemicals and is the most **carcinogenic** substance in cigarettes. [3]Smoking damages the **cilia** in the **respiratory system**. [4]The cilia sweep debris, such as tar, out of the lungs. [5]With the cilia damaged, tar and other debris can easily enter the lungs and remain there. [6]One chemical in tar, benzopyrene, is one of the most toxic of all carcinogens. [7]Tar also affects the respiratory system by blocking the normal action of **mucous membranes**. [8]As a result, foreign materials are not screened from the lungs and irritants attack lung tissue. [9]A non-lethal example of what happens as a result of this damage is the hacking smoker's cough.

—Adapted from Pruitt & Stein, *Health Styles: Decisions for Living Well*, 2nd ed., p. 185.

Glossary

carcinogenic cancer-causing agent

cilia hairlike structures in the respiratory system

respiratory system the organ system in air-breathing animals that includes the lungs and exchanges gases with the environment; it brings in oxygen and removes carbon dioxide

tar a carcinogenic substance in tobacco; the gummy mixture left over from burning tobacco

Read each sentence, and mark the statement that follows it **T** (true) or **F** (false).

6. **Tar** is the gummy mixture left over from burning tobacco. (*sentence 1*)

_____F____ Tar is a substance found only in cigarettes.

7. It consists of more than two hundred chemicals and is the most **carcinogenic** substance in cigarettes. (*sentence 2*)

_____F____ Tar is a simple and harmless substance.

8–9. Smoking damages the **cilia** in the **respiratory system**. (*sentence 3*)

_____T____ The cilia are hairlike structures that help keep the lungs clean of debris.

_____T____ The respiratory system brings oxygen into the body and expels carbon dioxide from the body.

10. Tar also affects the respiratory system by blocking the normal action of **mucous membranes**. (*sentence 7*)

_____T____ The mucous membranes are also known as the lungs.

Name *Davy Lawrence* ___ Section _____

Date *11/22/09* ___ Score (number correct) _____ × 10 = _____ %

A. Look over the following excerpt from *Merriam-Webster's Collegiate Dictionary, Eleventh Edition.* Then mark each statement below it **T** (true) or **F** (false), based on the entry.

> **junior • justice**
>
> **ju·ror** \ˈju̇r-ər, ˈju̇r-ˌȯr\ *n* (14c)   **1 a :** a member of a jury   **b :** a person summoned to serve on a jury   **2 :** a person who takes an oath (as of allegiance)

Source: Used by permission. From *Merriam-Webster's Collegiate® Dictionary, Eleventh Edition* © 2005 by Merriam-Webster, Incorporated (www.Merriam-Webster.com)

VISUAL VOCABULARY

A _____ is being sworn in to serve in court.

a. jury
b. juror

_____ **1.** The word *juxtapose* could be found on this page of the dictionary.

_____ **2.** A juror must take an oath.

B. Using the chart and the context of each sentence, select the word from the box that best fits the meaning of the sentence. Use each word once.

Prefix	Meaning	Root	Meaning	Suffix	Meaning
dis-	apart, away	*pos, posit*	put, place	*-tion*	action, state
im-	in				

---

dispose	disposition	impose

3. The president promised not to ~~impose~~ any new taxes.

4. The ~~disposition~~ of the complicated lawsuit did not please everyone.

5. Medical workers must be very careful about how they ~~dispose~~ of needles, swabs, and other used supplies.

Textbook
Skills

C. Read the following passage, adapted from the textbook *The Media in Your Life.* Then, using the glossary and the context of the sentences, answer the questions that follow it.

Glossary

checkbook journalism paying a news source for information

mass media communication channels such as newspapers and television aimed at large groups of people

perks job benefits that are not part of salary, such as gifts or free meals and trips

[1]Until the 1980s, at least some people who worked in the **mass media** expected their low pay to be added to by **perks**, which are benefits such as gifts, free meals, and trips. [2]For example, sports reporters accepted free rides with teams, and movie critics accepted free movie passes. [3]These handouts to people in the media were attacked as corrupt. [4]Another closely watched use of money in the media is **checkbook journalism**. [5]Checkbook journalism is paying subjects or witnesses for information or interviews. [6]Barbara Walters paid Monica Lewinsky $150,000 for her March 3, 1999, interview on ABC.

—Adapted from Folkerts & Lacy, *The Media in Your Life: An Introduction to Mass Communication,* 2nd ed., p. 369.

Mark each statement **T** (true) or **F** (false).

___F___ **6.** The **mass media** direct information to large groups of people.

___T___ **7.** A **perk** is the money paid to a witness for information.

___T___ **8.** **Checkbook journalism** is the salary a reporter is paid.

___F___ **9.** Sports reporters' accepting free rides with teams is an example of a **perk**.

___T___ **10.** Barbara Walters's interview with Monica Lewinsky is an example of **checkbook journalism**.

VISUAL VOCABULARY

A feature of this truck is

its _____ cab.

   a. full
   b. extended

`EXPLANATION` As you read, it becomes clear that every statement in the paragraph has to do with a truck. In fact, the word "truck" is repeated several times. Of course, the paragraph isn't about just any truck; it discusses the one owned by the author's family, which happens to be a 2007 extended-cab Chevrolet. Therefore, if you guessed the topic of the paragraph to be "our truck," you were right.

To identify the topic of a paragraph, just ask yourself, "Who or what is the paragraph about?" You should be able to answer this question in just a few words.

PRACTICE 1

Read the following paragraph. Then write down the topic of the paragraph.

   Caffeine is a powerful drug. It is a mood-altering drug that makes one feel alert and full of energy. However, this powerful drug may raise heart rates, reduce fertility, and interfere with sleep. It is also known to cause withdrawal symptoms such as headaches and irritability. The powerful attraction of caffeine is seen in its widespread use. Some experts think that as much as 120,000 tons of caffeine are consumed a day. Tea, which contains caffeine, ranks second to water as the most common drink around the world.

Topic: The effects of *powerful drugs*

A topic is the general idea of a reading passage. Reading passages also include specific ideas.

General and Specific Ideas

The ability to identify the topic of a paragraph or passage is closely tied to the ability to see the differences between general ideas and specific ideas. In a reading passage, the **general idea** must be broad enough to include all the **specific ideas** that are used to explain or support it.

> A **general idea** is a broad subject that needs specific ideas to support or explain it.
> A **specific idea** is a point used to support or explain a general idea.

EXAMPLE   The following list is made up of one general idea and several specific ideas. Write the letter **G** in front of the general idea and the letter **S** in front of each specific idea.

S_ sunscreen   G_ towels   S_ items for the beach

S_ surfboard   S_ beach chairs   G_ beach umbrella

EXPLANATION   If you wrote **G** next to "items for the beach," you were correct, for it is the only idea general enough to include all the other ideas. Sunscreen, towels, surfboard, beach chairs, and beach umbrella are all examples of items someone might take to the beach. In a reading passage, each specific idea relates to and supports the general idea.

PRACTICE 2

A.   Each of the following items is made up of one general idea and four specific ideas. Write the letter **G** in front of the general idea and the letter **S** in front of each specific idea.

1. S_ hurricane   S_ rain   G_ wind   S_ flooding   S_ warnings
2. G_ hamburger   S_ lamb   G_ meats   G_ chicken   S_ turkey
3. G_ basketball   G_ sports   G_ soccer   S_ football   S_ baseball
4. G_ coins   S_ dimes   S_ nickels   S_ quarters   S_ pennies
5. S_ water   S_ soda   S_ coffee   G_ drinks   S_ wine
6. S_ peach   S_ apple   S_ fruit   S_ banana   S_ kiwi
7. S_ starfish   S_ sea life   G_ whale   S_ dolphin   S_ mackerel

8. _S_ emotions _A_ anger _G_ joy _S_ sadness _S_ love

9. _S_ chair _S_ couch _G_ furniture _S_ table _S_ bookshelf

10. _S_ Cadillac _S_ Camaro _G_ Mustang _G_ cars _S_ Malibu

B. For each of the following general ideas, list two additional specific ideas.

11. *General idea:* exercise

    Specific ideas: walking   *working out*   *running*

12. *General idea:* soft drinks

    Specific ideas: Pepsi   *Sprite*   *Fanta*

13. *General idea:* flowers

    Specific ideas: daisy   *rose*   *petunias*

14. *General idea:* hand

    Specific ideas: forefinger   *index finger*   *pinky.*

15. *General idea:* clothes

    Specific ideas: shirt   *~~Jan~~ Jeans*   *belts*

16. *General idea:* dogs

    Specific ideas: poodle   *pitbulls*   *german shepard*

17. *General idea:* fast-food restaurants

    Specific ideas: Burger King   *McDonalds*   *wendsy*

18. *General idea:* seasons

    Specific ideas: spring   *fall*   *winter.*

19. *General idea:* bodies of water

    Specific ideas: lakes   *pool*   *ocean*

20. *General idea:* extended family

    Specific ideas: cousin   *neise*   *nephew*

C. The following items are made up of specific ideas. Write a general idea that covers all the specific ideas. The first one is done as an example.

21. *Specific ideas:*   rake leaves   mow lawn   trim hedges   water garden

    General idea: *fixing your lawn* _____

22. *Specific ideas:*   strings   pick   frets   neck   bridge

    General idea: _____

VISUAL VOCABULARY

U2 lead guitarist Dave Evans achieves his trademark sound through digital delay effects. Dave Evans is playing

_____

   a. an electric guitar.
   b. a bridge.

---

23. *Specific ideas:*   stove   oven   grill   microwave

    General idea: *kitchen* _____

24. *Specific ideas:*   nail   print   cuticle   knuckle

    General idea: *Job essentials* _____

25. *Specific ideas:*   books   desks   students   teachers

    General idea: *School* _____

Identifying the Topic of a Paragraph

Remember that a broad subject needs specific ideas to support or explain it. However, no single paragraph can discuss all the specific ideas linked to a broad idea. So an author narrows the broad subject to a topic that needs fewer specific ideas to support it. The topic "fast-food restaurants" is an example of a general idea that has been narrowed. (See item 17 of Practice 2.) The very broad subject "restaurants" had been narrowed to "fast-food restaurants." In fact, you might have listed a very different set of specific ideas if the topic had remained as broad as "restaurants." The narrower topic of "fast-food restaurants" demanded a very specific list of ideas to support it. Study the diagram below for a better understanding of the flow from broad to specific ideas.

restaurant	fast-food restaurant	Burger King
broad, general subject	topic	narrow, specific idea

The challenge in reading a passage or paragraph is to pick the topic out of statements that range from broad and general to narrow and specific ideas.

EXAMPLE Read the following paragraph, and determine the topic.

> Hip-Hop is a form of popular music believed to have originated in the Bronx. Hip-Hop has four basic elements. Two main aspects of Hip-Hop are mc'ing, also known as rapping, and dj'ing. The other two elements are graffiti and breakdancing. Although Hip-Hop has evolved into big business, the music is often criticized for disrespecting women and glorifying violence. Hip-Hop has probably encountered more problems with censorship than any other form of popular music in recent years, due to the use of expletives.

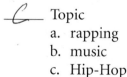 Topic
   a. rapping
   b. music
   c. Hip-Hop

EXPLANATION
"Rapping" (a) is too narrow, for the paragraph lists rapping as one of the traits of Hip-Hop music. "Music" (b) is too broad, for music includes all types from country to classical. "Hip-Hop" (c) is the topic of this paragraph.

PRACTICE 3

Each of the following paragraphs is followed by three ideas. One idea is too general to be the topic. Another idea is too specific. Identify the idea that correctly states the topic.

_c_ **1.**   Tiny killers lurk in some lakes during the summer months. Swimmers in these lakes are exposed to dangerous infections. One young boy inhaled a one-celled amoeba while he was swimming in the Conway chain of lakes northeast of Orlando, Florida. As a result, the boy became ill with a brain infection. This infection is not contagious but is often fatal. Within days, the boy died. Another young boy became critically ill due to swimming in a second Orlando lake. Bacteria entered his body through a cut on his leg. This infection causes death about 60 percent of the time.

—Associated Press, "Oviedo Boy Dies of Amoeba Infection," *The Ledger*, 27 July 2002: B5.

    a. swimming in lakes
    b. swimming in the Conway chain of lakes
    c. infections resulting from swimming in lakes

_b_ **2.**   Pain can be controlled by several methods. First, proper breathing can aid in pain control. For example, many women use breathing to manage pain during labor. Second, use of a focal point helps a person endure or even reduce pain. Often before an injection, a nurse will direct a patient to look at a picture or an object nearby. This keeps the patient from tensing up. A third method is, of course, the use of pain relievers. A large variety of medicines are available when the pain becomes unbearable.

    a. pain control through proper breathing
    b. pain control methods
    c. pain

_b_ **3.**   Dog bites are very common. One insurance expert states that of all injury claims filed, at least one-third are related to dog bites. Any dog may be capable of biting. Even the well-loved family dog can suddenly turn into a biter for no known reason. The most common breeds to bite are chows, cocker spaniels, pit bulls, and rottweilers. The most common victim is a child. Experts believe dogs go after children because of their size.

    a. dog bites
    b. dogs
    c. dog breeds that bite

Main Ideas

Daryl Lawrence 10/27-09

A skilled reader must be able to determine the author's main idea. The **main idea** of a paragraph is the author's controlling point about the topic.

Every piece of writing has a main idea. However, it is important to note here that some types of passages do not put the main idea directly into words. For example, novels, short stories, and poems do not directly state their main ideas. Chapter 10, *Implied Main Ideas,* teaches the skills needed to identify main ideas that are not stated.

Most of the paragraphs in college textbooks do state the author's main idea. In fact, the main idea is usually stated in a single sentence called the **topic sentence.**

To identify the main idea, ask yourself, "What is the author's controlling point about the topic?" You should be able to answer this question in one sentence.

To be sure you have selected the correct statement as the topic sentence, ask yourself, "Do all the specific details in the paragraph support this statement?"

> The **main idea** is the author's controlling point about the topic.
> The **topic sentence** is a single sentence in a paragraph that states the author's main idea.

A paragraph is like a well-planned house of ideas. The *topic* or general subject matter is the roof. The roof covers all the rooms of the house. The *main idea* is the frame of the house, and the supporting details are the different rooms. The following diagram shows these relationships:

Topic

Main Idea (stated in a topic sentence)

Supporting details	Supporting details	Supporting details

EXAMPLE   Here is a list that includes a topic, a main idea (stated in a topic sentence), and supporting details. Finish the following diagram by writing in the main idea.

Topic	Lack of sleep
Main idea (stated in *topic sentence*)	Lack of sleep can lead to serious health consequences and can jeopardize safety.
Supporting detail	Lack of sleep leads to an increase in body mass index.
Supporting detail	Lack of sleep increases risk of diabetes and heart problems.
Supporting detail	Lack of sleep increases risk of motor vehicle accidents

Topic: Lack of Sleep

Main Idea (stated in a topic sentence):

The lack of sleep

Supporting Details:

Leads to an increase in body mass index	Increases risk of diabetes and heart problems	Increases risk of motor vehicle accidents

EXPLANATION   If you wrote, "Lack of sleep can lead to serious health consequences and can jeopardize safety," you are correct. All the supporting details explain this main idea about lack of sleep. Remember: The main idea is general enough to cover all the supporting details and can be stated in one sentence (the topic sentence).

PRACTICE 4

A. Finish the following diagram by writing in the topic and main idea from the following paragraph.

- To find the **topic**, ask: "Who or what is the one thing the author is writing about in this paragraph?"

- To find the **main idea**, ask: "What is the controlling point the author is making about the topic?"

- To find the topic sentence, ask: "Does this sentence contain the topic and main idea, and does it cover all the other sentences in the paragraph?"

Many heroes are everyday people who simply rely on courage and hope. The father who gives one of his kidneys to his young daughter is just one instance of such a hero. Another inspiring example is the young person who refuses to let a friend drink and drive or the teacher who chooses to teach in a high-crime neighborhood. Even the young man who lost his arm in an accident yet learns to be a top-notch motorcycle technician is a living model of an everyday hero.

Topic: 1. _hero_

Main Idea (stated in a topic sentence):

2. _The main idea is about hero_

Supporting Details:

Father who gives a kidney to his young daughter	Young person who won't let a friend drive drunk	Young man who lost arm and learned to be a technician	Teacher in a high-crime area

B. Read the paragraph. Identify the topic and main idea by answering the questions that follow it.

^{1}Camping is a challenging activity that is also fun. ^{2}Setting up and living at the campsite often seems to be a test of patience. ^{3}Pitching the tent can be a tussle, threading poles through the canvas tent and sinking stakes. ^{4}In addition, the wildlife, from thieving raccoons to buzzing bugs, always seems to present curious problems to solve. ^{5}The fun is found in days warm enough for swimming, hiking, and canoeing and evenings cool enough for a roaring campfire. ^{6}For many campers, the most enjoyable times occur as darkness falls and everyone gathers around the fire. ^{7}Great tales and quiet secrets are told around a campfire.

_b_ 3. Which of the following best states the topic of the paragraph?
   a. raccoons   c. campsites
   b. camping   d. campers

_a_ 4. Identify the sentence that states the main idea in a topic sentence.
   a. sentence 1   c. sentence 3
   b. sentence 2   d. sentence 4

VISUAL VOCABULARY

These campers are

_____ a tent.

   a. sinking
   b. pitching

C. Read the paragraph. Identify the topic and main idea or controlling point by answering the questions that follow it.

> Road rage is a dangerous problem caused by fear and anger. The fast pace of our lives creates a strong sense of anxiety for many people. The person who is worried about getting somewhere on time may become frustrated and angry at slow-moving traffic. This anger sometimes intensifies if other drivers make careless mistakes, such as turning without signaling or stopping too quickly. The angry driver may try to get even by tailgating or passing and cutting in too quickly. Sometimes the angry driver even chooses to get out of the car for a face-to-face confrontation. Too many times, these kinds of situations have led to fistfights or shootings.

  5. What is the author's topic? _road rage_

  6. What is the author's main idea or controlling point? _that road rage is a dangerous problem_

Supporting Details

Most paragraphs have three essential parts:

- A topic (the general idea or subject)
- A main idea, often stated in a topic sentence (the author's controlling point about the topic)
- Supporting details (the specific ideas to support the main idea)

> **Supporting details** are specific ideas that *develop, explain, support,* or *illustrate* the main idea or controlling point.

Think again of the house of ideas that a writer builds. You will recall that the roof is the *general idea* that covers all the rooms' *specific ideas*. Think about all the different rooms of a house: kitchen, bedroom, bathroom, living room, and so on. Each room is a different part of the same house and serves a different purpose. Yet all the rooms are covered by the same roof.

The same is true for a paragraph. The supporting details of a paragraph are framed by the topic sentence and serve to explain or support the author's view of the topic.

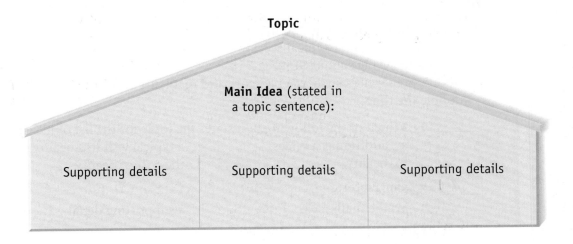

Now look again at the information about lack of sleep. First review the information; then study how it fits into the diagram on page 146.

Lack of sleep can lead to serious health consequences and can jeopardize safety. First, lack of sleep leads to an increase in body mass index. In addition, lack of sleep increases risk of diabetes and heart problems. Finally, lack of sleep increases risk of motor vehicle accidents.

As a skilled reader, you will see that every paragraph has a topic, a main idea or controlling point, and supporting details. It is much easier to tell the difference between these three parts of a paragraph once you understand how each part works.

Topic: Lack of Sleep

Main Idea (stated in
a topic sentence):

Lack of sleep can lead to serious health consequences and can
jeopardize safety.

Supporting Details:

Leads to an increase in body mass index	Increases risk of diabetes and heart problems	Increases risk of motor vehicle accidents

EXAMPLE   Read the following list of ideas. Answer the questions that follow.

A. Beauty takes effort, time, and money.
B. For many women, a typical weekly visit to a beauty salon can take three
   hours and average about $150.
C. Additional services such as a pedicure and manicure can triple the cost and
   double the time.

_____ **1.** Which of the following best states the topic for the list of ideas?
  a. additional services   c. a typical visit to a beauty salon
  b. beauty   d. the cost of beauty

 2. Sentence A states
  a. the main idea.   b. a supporting detail.

_____ **3.** Sentence B states
  a. the main idea.   b. a supporting detail.

_____ **4.** Sentence C states
  a. the main idea.   b. a supporting detail.

EXPLANATION   The topic of the ideas is (d) the cost of beauty. Notice that the
topic is very general and is stated in a phrase, not in a complete sentence.
Sentence A is the main idea stated in a topic sentence. Sentence B gives two details that support the main idea. Sentence C gives another supporting detail.

PRACTICE 5

A. Read each of the following groups of ideas. Answer the questions that follow
   each group.

Group 1

a. Effects of stress
b. Stress can cause loss of appetite and loss of sleep.
c. Many people toss and turn in bed for hours worrying about the mistakes they think they made that day.

 1. The first idea states
     a. the topic.   c. a supporting detail.
     b. the main idea.

 2. The second idea states
     a. the topic.   c. a supporting detail.
     b. the main idea.

 3. The third idea states
     a. the topic.   c. a supporting detail.
     b. the main idea.

Group 2

a. At the football game last weekend, the crowd around my 9-year-old daughter and me became drunk and used foul language.
b. Some people's behavior makes it impossible to enjoy attending live events.
c. Improper public behavior

_g_ **4.** The first idea states
     a. the topic.   c. a supporting detail.
     b. the main idea.

_a_ **5.** The second idea states
     a. the topic.   c. a supporting detail.
     b. the main idea.

_c_ **6.** The third idea states
     a. the topic.   c. a supporting detail.
     b. the main idea.

Group 3

a. Women must realize that drinking alcohol may raise their chances of developing breast cancer.
b. Alcohol and breast cancer
c. A woman who drinks four glasses of wine a week may be more likely to get breast cancer than a woman who does not drink alcohol.

_c_ **7.** The first idea states
   a. the topic.   c. a supporting detail.
   b. the main idea.

_b_ **8.** The second idea states
   a. the topic.   c. a supporting detail.
   b. the main idea.

_a_ **9.** The third idea states
   a. the topic.   c. a supporting detail.
   b. the main idea.

Group 4

a. The Public Broadcasting System (PBS)
b. For example, those people who love history enjoy the story of the Civil War as told through the actual photographs and letters of the soldiers who fought and died.
c. PBS offers high-quality programs for viewers of all interests.

_c_ **10.** The first idea states
   a. the topic.   c. a supporting detail.
   b. the main idea.

_c_ **11.** The second idea states
   a. the topic.   c. a supporting detail.
   b. the main idea.

_c_ **12.** The third idea states
   a. the topic.   c. a supporting detail.
   b. the main idea.

B. Read the paragraph. Identify the topic and main idea by answering the questions that follow it.

> [1]Coffee brings flavor and zest to life. [2]For countless people, coffee is the drink of choice. [3]First, coffee comes in a wide variety of flavors. [4]Some people drink only the heavy, thick Colombian brew; others love a sweeter French vanilla taste. [5]Still others love their coffee tinged with chocolate or mint or some other exotic flavor. [6]Second, even when coffee drinkers disagree on the choice of flavor, most agree on the need for its jolt of energy. [8]Nothing seems to open the eyes wider than coffee's caffeine.

_b_ **13.** Which of the following best states the topic of the paragraph?
   a. the attraction of coffee   c. the zest of coffee
   b. the taste of coffee

_5_ **14.** Which sentence states the author's main idea in a topic sentence?

Textbook Skills

Topics in Headings

Textbook authors often state the topic of a paragraph or passage in a heading. Identifying the topic in a heading makes it easier for you to see the main idea and supporting details. Remember, though, that headings and titles are *not* topic sentences.

EXAMPLE Read the following paragraph from the college communications textbook *Messages: Building Interpersonal Communication Skills*. Then answer the questions that follow it.

The Intimacy Stage

[1]At the intimacy stage of a relationship, you commit yourself deeply to the other person. [2]In fact, this person becomes your best or closest friend, lover, or companion. [3]Usually the intimacy stage divides itself quite neatly into two phases. [4]One phase is the interpersonal commitment phase. [5]In this phase, you commit yourselves to each other in a kind of private way. [6]The second phase is the social bonding phase. [7]In this phase, the commitment is made public—perhaps to family and friends, or perhaps to the public at large through formal marriage. [8]Here the two of you become a unit, a pair.

—DeVito, *Messages: Building Interpersonal Communication Skills*, 4th ed., p. 264.

1. The topic of the paragraph is *the intimacy stage*.

___a___ 2. Sentence 1 states
   a. the main idea.   b. a supporting detail.

___b___ 3. Sentence 2 states
   a. the main idea.   b. a supporting detail.

EXPLANATION The topic of the paragraph is *the intimacy stage;* it is stated in the heading. Sentence 1 is the main idea, and sentence 2 is a supporting detail. (In fact, in the passage, sentences 2–8 are all supporting details.)

PRACTICE 6

Read the following paragraph from a college science textbook. Then answer the questions that follow it.

Habitat

[1]The actual location or place where an organism lives is called its **habitat**. [2]Because habitat describes a location, we can define it on many levels. [3]Your habitat could be the country you live in, your state and city of residence, or the precise location of your home. [4]Depending on your activity, such as eating, your habitat could be your kitchen.

—Smith & Smith, *Elements of Ecology*, 4th ed., p. 16.

1. The topic of the passage is _habitat_.

_a_ 2. Sentence 1 states
   a. the main idea.   b. a supporting detail.

_a_ 3. Sentence 2 states
   a. the main idea.   b. a supporting detail.

_b_ 4. Sentence 3 states
   a. the main idea.   b. a supporting detail.

_a_ 5. Sentence 4 states
   a. the main idea.   b. a supporting detail.

Chapter Review

Test your understanding of what you have read in this chapter by filling in each blank with a word or phrase from the box. Each word is used once.

general idea	narrow	specific idea	topic	what
main	point	supporting	topic sentence	words

1. A _general idea_ is the general subject matter of a reading passage.
2. The topic can be stated in one word or just a few _words_.
3. A _point_ is a broad subject that needs specific ideas to support or explain it.
4. A _topic_ is a point used to support or explain a general idea.
5. The challenge for a skilled reader is to state the topic in a way that is neither too broad nor too _narrow_.
6. A _main_ idea is the author's controlling point about a topic.

7. A _supporting_ is a single sentence in a paragraph that states the author's main idea.

8. To find the topic, ask: "Who or _what_ is the passage about?"

9. To find the main idea, ask: "What is the author's controlling _topic idea_ about the topic?" _topic sentence_

10. _what_ details are specific ideas that develop, explain, support, or illustrate the controlling point.

Applications   10 - 29 - 09

Application 1: General and Specific Ideas

A. Each of the following items is made up of one general idea and four specific ideas. Write the letter **G** in front of the general idea in each item.

1. _G_court _G_hoop ___basketball game _G_foul _G_free throw
2. _G_tickets _G_movies _G_previews _G_popcorn ___movie theater
3. _G_Ellen DeGeneres _G_Stephen Colbert _G_Jon Stewart _G_Conan O'Brien ___comedians
4. ___nurse _G_exam room _G_exam table ___doctor's office _G_stethoscope
5. _G_keyboard ___computer _G_mouse _G_CD _G_software
6. ___shoes _G_sandals _G_loafers _G_high heels _G_running shoes

B. For each of the following general ideas, list two additional specific ideas.

7. *General idea*: female movie stars
   Specific ideas: Meg Ryan Carmen Electra Cameron Diaz

8. *General idea*: college courses
   Specific ideas: Freshman English math 101 reading 101

9. *General idea*: small kitchen appliances
   Specific ideas: blender fork spoon

10. *General idea*:   hair products

    Specific ideas: shampoo _____ _____

Application 2: Identifying Topics

Each paragraph is followed by three ideas. One idea is too general to be the topic. Another idea is too specific. Identify the idea that correctly states the topic.

Oprah Winfrey surmounted many barriers and became a great success. Oprah is an African American woman who was born in the South, out of wedlock and into poverty. Yet in 1998, America voted her one of the two most admired women in the country. By then, her talk show had earned 30 Daytime Emmy Awards. Later that same year, Oprah, only 44 years old, received a lifetime achievement award at the Emmys. Some 20 million people in the United States watch Oprah every day. And countless numbers of people from 132 other countries watch her afternoon show.

 1. The topic of the paragraph is
   a. Oprah Winfrey.
   b. Oprah Winfrey and her awards.
   c. Oprah Winfrey's overcoming barriers to become a great success.

Lower-back pain has several causes. First, weak stomach muscles can cause the lower back to ache. The muscles of the lower back and the stomach work together and need each other to support the body's frame. If the stomach muscles are weak, the lower back muscles feel the strain. Also, the lower back may hurt due to poor posture. Slouching the shoulders forward throws the whole back out of whack and places great pressure on the lower back. Finally, a common cause of lower-back pain is injury. Trying to lift heavy objects without proper support strains the lower-back muscles.

 2. The topic of the paragraph is
   a. lower-back pain caused by weak stomach muscles.
   b. lower-back pain.
   c. causes of lower-back pain.

Textbook
Skills

Loneliness puts a person at risk for other problems. Research shows that loneliness and poor health often go together. Older women who live alone on small pensions may find themselves in poor health. In addition, they are isolated from others and become lonely. Isolation and loneliness can lead to physical and mental breakdowns. These breakdowns can lead to more problems, such as increased risk of drug and alcohol abuse.

—Novak, *Issues in Aging: An Introduction to Gerontology*, p. 143.

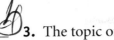

_____ **3.** The topic of the paragraph is
    a. risks associated with loneliness.
    b. loneliness.
    c. loneliness leading to increased risk of drug and alcohol abuse.

Textbook
Skills

    All life on Earth is carbon-based. What this means is that all living creatures are made up of complex molecules based on the framework of carbon atoms. The carbon atom is able to bond readily with other carbon atoms. As they bond, they form long, complex carbon-based molecules. The carbon needed to build these molecules comes from various sources. Humans, like all other animals, get their carbon by consuming plant and animal materials. However, the chief source of carbon is carbon dioxide in the atmosphere.

—Smith & Smith, *Elements of Ecology*, 4th ed., p. 21.

_____ **4.** The topic of the paragraph is
    a. life on earth.
    b. carbon-based life on earth.
    c. the carbon atom's ability to bond with other carbon atoms.

Application 3: Topics, Main Ideas, and Supporting Details

A. Read each of the following groups of ideas. Answer the questions that follow each group.

Group 1

    A. Two benefits of walking are stress reduction and weight loss.
    B. Benefits of walking
    C. Reduce stress by improving your body's overall health.
    D. Weight loss results from burning calories.

_____ **1.** The main idea is found in
    a. item A.   c. item C.
    b. item B.   d. item D.

Group 2

    A. When you try on new shoes, wear the socks you will wear with those shoes.
    B. Follow a couple of steps to get the best-fitting shoes.
    C. Shop at the end of the day when your feet are their largest.
    D. Shopping for shoes

_C_ **2.** The topic is found in
   a. item A.   c. item C.
   b. item B.   d. item D.

Group 3

A. An unusual talent and the drive to win make Michael Jordan an athlete to admire.
B. Few basketball players are as good as Michael; as Magic Johnson once said, "Really, there is Michael and then there's everyone else."
C. When Michael Jordan played, he was determined to win every time.
D. Michael Jordan's drive and talent

_b_ **3.** A supporting detail is found in
   a. item A.   c. item C.
   b. item B.   d. item D.

Group 4

A. Peer pressure can help stop school violence before it starts.
B. Peer pressure and school violence
C. A peer is a friend or fellow student.
D. A peer can listen or offer helpful advice.

_a_ **4.** The main idea is found in
   a. item A.   c. item C.
   b. item B.   d. item D.

B. Read the following paragraphs, and answer the questions that follow them.

[1]Chinatown is located in San Francisco, California. [2]And it is more than the noise of firecrackers, the scent of incense from temples, and the taste of Chinese food. [3]Chinatown is more than the exotic shops. [4]Chinatown is more than its glittering gold characters. [5]These are the things that tourists come to see and enjoy. [6]For the Chinese, Chinatown is a real community. [7]Chinatown is a neighborhood. [8]And as a neighborhood, it offers comfort, jobs, job training, and information about America. [9]Chinatown is a place where the Chinese can gather and talk with each other. [10]They can speak in their own language and act in keeping with their cultural traditions. [11]In Chinatown, the Chinese find emotional, economic, and social support.

—Adapted from Wong, Bernard. (1998) *Ethnicity and Entrepreneurship:*
The New Chinese Immigrants in the San Francisco
Bay Area. Boston: Allyn & Bacon. p. 26.

_____ **5.** What is the topic of the paragraph?

    a. Chinatown, San Francisco, California

    b. the Chinese

    c. a neighborhood

__C__ **6.** Which sentence states the author's main idea or controlling point?

[1]Have you ever noticed the dramatic effect of weather? [2]Weather seems to affect our moods. [3]An overcast sky and a cold, drizzly rain make us feel sad and quiet. [4]A cool, snappy breeze and a clear blue sky perk up our spirits and put a spring in our step. [5]Angry black clouds, zaps of lightning, and booms of thunder arouse fear in most of us. [6]Hot, humid summer days make some of us lazy and others of us irritable. [7]Brisk, cold air, snow-topped trees, and a warm fire give many of us a safe, cozy feeling.

_____ **7.** What is the topic of the paragraph?

    a. weather and our moods

    b. effect of weather

    c. an overcast sky

_____ **8.** Which sentence states the author's main idea or controlling point?

[1]People who wish to eat a meatless diet now find that grocery stores offer a variety of choices. [2]The frozen food department now stocks vegetarian hot dogs, veggie burgers, meatless tacos, and vegetarian lasagna. [3]The dairy shelves are full of soy-based spreads for toast and soy or rice milk for cereal and baking. [4]Of course, the fruit and vegetable bins have the standard offerings of apples, pears, bananas, oranges, and pineapples. [5]But they also now stock tofu. [6]Some grocery stores have even hired specialty chefs to make take-out sushi.

__C__ **9.** What is the topic of the passage?

    a. a meatless diet

    b. grocery stores

    c. the availability of vegetarian foods at grocery stores

_____ **10.** Which sentence states the author's main idea or controlling point?

REVIEW **Test 1**

General and Specific Ideas

A. Each of the following items is made up of one general idea and four specific ideas. Write the letter **G** in front of the general idea in each item.

1. —hot __temperatures —cold —warm —freezing
2. —remote control —surround sound —entertainment system —plasma screen
3. —wasp __insects —spider —ant —bee
4. — chapter —index —glossary __textbook —table of contents
5. __ rodents —mice —rats —gerbils —squirrels
6. —broccoli —carrots —squash —zucchini __vegetables
7. __sewing —thread —needle —cloth —pins
8. —fever —chills —nausea __flu symptoms —aching muscles
9. —joke __humor —cartoon —laughter —prank
10. —server —chef —entrée —menu __restaurant

B. The following items are made up of specific ideas. For each space, write a general idea that covers all the specific ideas.

11. *Specific ideas*: beef veal pork

    General idea: _____

12. *Specific ideas*: orange grapefruit tangerine

    General idea: _____

13. *Specific ideas*: weights treadmill personal trainer

    General idea: _____

14. *Specific ideas*: knuckle kneecap elbow

    General idea: _____

15. *Specific ideas*: surround sound big-screen TV DVD player

    General idea: _____

C. For each of the following general ideas, list two additional specific ideas.

16. *General idea:* allergy symptoms

    Specific ideas: runny nose _____ _____

17. *General idea:*   fire safety

    Specific ideas: fire extinguisher   _____   _____

18. *General idea:*   bees

    Specific ideas: stingers   _____   _____

19. *General idea:*   tobacco products

    Specific ideas: snuff   _____   _____

20. *General idea:*   résumé

    Specific ideas: job experience   _____   _____

REVIEW Test 2

Identifying the Topic of a Paragraph

A. Each of the following paragraphs is followed by three ideas. Identify the idea that correctly states the topic.

> Yosemite National Park is located in central California along the western edge of the Sierra Nevada mountain range. Yosemite offers beautiful views of deep valleys and spectacular mountains. At the center of the park is a valley 2,750 feet deep.

_____ 1. The topic of the paragraph is
   a. national parks.
   b. Yosemite National Park.
   c. beautiful views of deep valleys.

> The word *pueblo* is Spanish for "town." It is also the name of a group of Native American Indians. The Pueblos live in Arizona and New Mexico. Some of these Pueblo Indians still carry out age-old rituals and customs. The Pueblos were too out-of-the-way to be controlled by the government.

_____ 2. The topic of the paragraph is
   a. lack of control of the Pueblos.
   b. Native American Indians.
   c. Pueblo Indians.

> Charles "Chuck" Berry is an African American musician who greatly affected the development of rock music. Berry's rock music brought together blues and country music styles. His songs told stories about young love, fast cars, and disappointment, set to a catchy beat.

_____ **3.** The topic of the paragraph is
   a. a mixture of blues and country music styles.
   b. Chuck Berry and his music.
   c. rock music.

Brainwashing techniques force confessions of wrongdoing and replace lowered self-esteem with new beliefs. Confessions can be forced through lack of sleep and food. Kept awake for days without food, the person is told of his or her shortcomings and is forced to admit to them. The brainwashed person is also cut off from family and friends so that no one can contradict the new beliefs.

_____ **4.** The topic of the paragraph is
   a. two ways to brainwash a person.
   b. lack of sleep and food.
   c. brainwashing techniques.

B. In each pair, one idea is general and the other is specific. The general idea includes the specific idea. Do two things:

- Circle the idea in each pair that is *more general.*
- Then write one more specific idea that is covered by the general idea you circled.

5–6. light bulb	lamp	_____
7–8. money	dollar	_____
9–10. Johnny Depp	actors	_____

REVIEW **Test 3**

Topics, Main Ideas, and Supporting Details

A. Read the following paragraph from a communications textbook. Then fill in the house diagram with the topic, main idea, and supporting details from the passage.

Textbook
Skills

The Importance of Rules in a Family

Family rules are important for several reasons. First, rules define the family as a unit. Through rules, families establish roles for each member. Second, rules help members within the family relate to one another. Third, rules contribute to a family's sense of stability.

—Adapted from Galvin & Brommel, *Family Communication:
Cohesion and Change,* 5th ed., p. 88.

Topic: 1. _____

Main Idea (stated in
a topic sentence):

2. _____

Supporting   Details:

3. _____   **4.** _____   **5.** _____
    _____   _____   _____
    _____   _____   _____
    _____   _____   _____

B. Read the following paragraph from a college science textbook. Then answer the questions that follow it.

Reducing Fat in Your Diet

Textbook
Skills

[1]Three basic steps will help you reduce fat in your diet. [2]First, know what you are putting in your mouth; read food labels. [3]Second, choose lean meats, fish, or chicken. [4]Third, choose nonfat dairy products such as skim milk whenever possible.

—Adapted from Donatelle, *Access to Health*, 7th ed., pp. 229–30.

6. The topic of the paragraph is _____.

_____ **7.** Sentence 1 states
                a. the main idea.   b. a supporting detail.

_____ **8.** Sentence 2 states
                a. the main idea.   b. a supporting detail.

_____ **9.** Sentence 3 states
                a. the main idea.   b. a supporting detail.

_____ **10.** Sentence 4 states
                a. the main idea.   b. a supporting detail.

REVIEW **Test 4**

Topics and Main Ideas

The following paragraphs are adapted from an article by Tim Wendel called "Healing Harmonies." Read the paragraphs from the article, and answer the questions that follow each one.

[1]Music is good for us. [2]New studies point to the idea that music can change how our brains and bodies function. [3]Experts use music to battle cancer, stir memory in Alzheimer's patients, relieve stress, and boost test scores. [4]Doctors believe using music as a **therapy** (treatment) in hospitals and nursing homes makes the sick feel better and heal faster. [5]A growing number of nursing homes have hired music therapists to help older patients with physical and social skills. [6]As a result, some stroke patients have improved rapidly by listening to music as they exercise.

_____ 1. The word **therapy** in sentence 4 means
    a. sickness.
    b. music.
    c. treatment.
    d. distraction.

_____ 2. What is the topic of the paragraph?
    a. therapy to boost test scores
    b. music to battle cancer
    c. patients dancing to music
    d. positive effects of music

_____ 3. What is the main idea of the paragraph?
    a. sentence 2
    b. sentence 4
    c. sentence 1
    d. sentence 5

[7]Some experts found the sound of drums may influence how our bodies work. [8]Grateful Dead drummer Mickey Hart believes a simple drumbeat can stir long-forgotten memories. [9]He visits nursing homes, hands out drums, and leads residents in **impromptu,** or spur-of-the-moment, concerts. [10]One researcher states, "Deep in our long-term memory is this rehearsed music. [11]Here is where you remember the music played at your wedding, the music of your first love, that first dance. [12]Such things can still be remembered even in people with **progressive** (non-improving) diseases. [13]It can be a window to reach them."

_____ 4. The word **impromptu** in sentence 9 means
    a. planned far in advance.
    b. loud.
    c. fast-paced.
    d. occurring on the spur of the moment.

_____ 5. The word **progressive** in sentence 12 means
    a. serious.
    b. short-lived.
    c. improving.
    d. worsening.

_____ 6. What is the topic of the paragraph?
    a. music and memory
    b. the Grateful Dead
    c. music
    d. memory

_____ **7.** What is the main idea of the paragraph?
    a. sentence 7   c. sentence 12
    b. sentence 8   d. sentence 13

[14]Music is seen as **fodder** or food for the young, growing brain. [15]A small group of college students did better on certain tests after listening to Mozart. [16]As a result, many mothers played classical music to their babies in the womb. [17]Now newer studies focus on the benefit of music making instead of just listening to music. [18]One study found that 3- and 4-year-olds who were taught to play the piano scored higher in **abstract reasoning,** such as math and science than children who got computer instruction.

             —Tim Wendel, "Healing Harmonies," *USA Weekend Magazine,* 26–28 Oct. 2001,
             pp. 7–8. Copyright © 2001, *USA Today.* Reprinted by permission.

_____ **8.** The word **fodder** in sentence 14 means
    a. stress.   c. food.
    b. poison.   d. help.

_____ **9.** The term **abstract reasoning** in sentence 18 means
    a. problem solving.   c. college courses.
    b. hardly possible.   d. high school.

_____ **10.** What is the topic of the paragraph?
    a. music and the young brain   c. the young brain
    b. test scores   d. classical music

SKILLED READER Scorecard

Topics and Main Ideas

Test	Number Correct		Points		Score
Review Test 1	_____	×	5	=	_____
Review Test 2	_____	×	10	=	_____
Review Test 3	_____	×	10	=	_____
Review Test 4	_____	×	10	=	_____
Review Test 5 (website)	_____	×	20	=	_____
Review Test 6 (website)	_____	×	25	=	_____

Enter your score on the Skilled Reader Scorecard: Chapter 4 Review Tests inside the back cover.

After Reading About Topics and Main Ideas

Before you move on to the mastery tests on topics and main ideas, take time to reflect on your learning and performance by answering the following questions. Write your answers in your notebook.

What did I learn about topics and main ideas?

What do I need to remember about topics and main ideas?

How has my knowledge base or prior knowledge about topics and main ideas changed?

More Review and Mastery Tests

For more practice, go to the book's website at **http://www.ablongman.com/henry** and click on *The Skilled Reader*. Then select "More Review and Mastery Tests." You will find the tests listed by chapter.

A. Each of the following items is made up of one general idea and four specific ideas. Write the letter **G** in front of the general idea in each item.

1. ___Bart Simpson   ___Bugs Bunny   ___cartoon characters

___Daffy Duck   ___Scooby Doo

2. ___saddle   ___bridle   ___horseshoe   ___blacksmith   ___horses

3. ___notebooks   ___dictionary   ___school tools   ___textbooks

___highlighters

4. ___knee pads   ___roller skating   ___helmet   ___elbow pads   ___skates

5. ___ fishing   ___sinker   ___hook   ___bait   ___ pole

B. Read each of the following paragraphs. Answer the questions.

Textbook
Skills

Most experts now agree that global warming is occurring. And in response to its potential threat, a number of countries have made a commitment to reduce CO_2 emissions. However, some countries oppose taking strong action at this time for several reasons. First, a few experts think that the warming trend may be just a random change in temperature. Second, if the temperature increase is real, it has yet to be shown that it is caused by increased CO_2. Some people also believe that it would be difficult to cut CO_2 emissions without harming economic growth.

—Campbell, Reece, Taylor, and Simon. *Biology: Concepts and Connections*, 5th ed., Benjamin Cummings 2005. p. 122.

_____ **6.** The topic of the paragraph is
a. the Earth.   b. the Earth's warming trend.   c. increased CO_2.

Textbook
Skills

Handsome and outgoing, Franklin D. Roosevelt seemed to have a bright political future. Then disaster struck. In 1921, he was stricken with polio. It left him paralyzed from the waist down and in a wheelchair for the rest of his life. Instead of retiring, Roosevelt returned to public life. "If you had spent two years in bed trying to wiggle your toe," he later declared, "after that anything would seem easy."

—Martin et al., *America and Its Peoples: A Mosaic in the Making*, 3rd ed., p. 830.

165

_____ **7.** The topic of the paragraph is
   a. handsome Franklin D. Roosevelt.
   b. Franklin D. Roosevelt.
   c. Franklin D. Roosevelt and polio.

Textbook
Skills

    Emotions are the feelings you have. For example, you have feelings of anger, sorrow, guilt, depression, happiness and so on. *Emotional expression,* on the other hand, is the way you share these feelings. Experts do not agree over whether you can choose the emotions you feel. Some argue that you can; others argue you cannot. You are, however, clearly in control of the ways you express your emotions. You do not have to express what you feel.

        —Adapted from DeVito, *Messages: Building Interpersonal Communication Skills,* 4th ed., p. 176.

_____ **8.** The topic of the paragraph is
   a. emotional expression.
   b. emotions.
   c. anger, sorrow, guilt, depression, and happiness.

C. Read each of the following groups of ideas. Then answer the questions that follow.

Group 1

A. A day at Walt Disney World may cost a family a month's salary.
B. The ticket to get in for just one person for one day is $67.00.
C. A typical family may spend another couple of hundred dollars on food and souvenirs.
D. Walt Disney World

_____ **9.** The topic is found in
   a. item A.   c. item C.
   b. item B.   d. item D.

Group 2

A. Small learning groups
B. In small groups, students become responsible for their own learning.
C. In small groups, students learn to listen to one another to solve problems.
D. Small learning groups teach students to be responsible and work together.

_____ **10.** A supporting detail is found in
   a. item A.   c. item C.
   b. item B.   d. item D.

A. The following items are made up of specific ideas. In the given spaces, write a general idea that covers all the specific ideas.

   1. *Specific ideas*: 2 4 8 10 12

   General idea: _____

   2. *Specific ideas*: résumé   references   interview

   General idea: _____

   3. *Specific ideas*: toothbrush   dental floss   toothpaste

   General idea: _____

   4. *Specific ideas*: Justin Timberlake   Avril Lavigne   U2

   General idea: _____

   5. *Specific ideas*: producer   director   actor   script

   General idea: _____

   6. *Specific ideas*: ingrown toenails   athlete's foot   corns and bunions

   General idea: _____

B. Read each of the following paragraphs, then answer the questions.

Textbook
Skills

Television is central in our lives. Thus, a debate has raged for many years over the effects of viewing acts of violence on TV. Many worry about its effect on children and those who are emotionally unstable. About 3,000 studies have been carried out over three decades. Because of these studies, experts believe that a steady diet of TV violence can have an effect. The effect of TV violence is most noticed when there is also violence in the home and neighborhood.

—Adapted from Agee, Ault, & Emery, *Introduction to Mass Communications*, 12th ed., p. 85.

167

_____ **7.** The topic of the paragraph is
   a. about 3,000 studies carried out over three decades.
   b. television violence.
   c. the effects of television violence.

Textbook
Skills

Today's government is huge. And it has vast and powerful technologies. Social Security numbers, credit cards, driver's licenses, and school records are all stored on giant computers. The government has quick access to this data. In fact, it is very hard to hide from the police, the FBI, the Internal Revenue Service, or any other government agency. Thus government's power must be limited. The Bill of Rights sets limits on this power.

—Adapted from Edwards, Wattenberg, & Lineberry,
Government in America: People, Politics, and Policy,
5th ed., Brief Version, p. 128.

_____ **8.** The topic of the paragraph is
   a. government.
   b. government's power.
   c. the Bill of Rights.

C. Read each of the following groups of ideas. Then answer the questions.

Group 1

A. This remarkable woman invented a pushcart for street cleaners.
B. She also wrote articles and children's books.
C. Cynthia Westover, who lived from 1858 until 1931, showed that women could do whatever they set their minds to.
D. Women who achieve

_____ **9.** The main idea is found in
   a. item A.   c. item C.
   b. item B.   d. item D.

Group 2

A. Rescuers could not save the beached whales.
B. Rescuing beached whales
C. Dozen of the whales died.
D. Rescuers tried to push the whales back into deeper water.

_____ **10.** A supporting detail is found in
   a. item A.   c. item C.
   b. item B.   d. item D.

A. The following items are made up of specific ideas. Write a general idea that covers all the specific ideas.

1. *Specific ideas:* USA Today   New York Times   Washington Post

   General idea: _____

2. *Specific ideas:* mascara   eyeliner   lipstick   blush

   General idea: _____

3. *Specific ideas:* Marlboro   Virginia Slims   Camel   Parliament

   General idea: _____

4. *Specific ideas:* quarterback   running back   center   kicker

   General idea: _____

5. *Specific ideas:* sunny   partly cloudy   thunderstorms

   General idea: _____

6. *Specific ideas:* "Dilbert"   "Peanuts"   "Garfield"   "Blondie"

   General idea: _____

B. Read each of the following paragraphs. Then answer the questions.

   When Detail magazine's reporter Bart Blasengame, asked Justin Timberlake about his personal life, he attacked the gossip magazines that write about celebrities, "I despise what they do," he said about the celebrity gossip magazines, "They create soap operas out of people's lives." About how the gossip magazines obsess about Britney Spears and him, he said, "We had our thing, and it's over. They edit that stuff like MTV edits reality shows. It's a spin game, and I choose not to take part in it."

   —"Justin Timberlake: The new King of Pop wants to give his title back." *MEN.STYLE.COM/The Online Home of Details & GQ.* April 2007. <http://men.style.com/details/>

_____ **7.** The topic of the paragraph is
   a. gossip.
   b. Justin Timberlake's personal life.
   c. Justin Timberlake and celebrity gossip magazines.

Textbook
Skills

Earnings of physicians and surgeons are among the highest of any occupation. The average income of a physician varies by specialty. General practitioners earn an average of $156,000. Pediatricians earn around $161,000; psychiatrists average $174,000. Specialists in internal medicine earn $166,000 while the obstetric and gynecologists earn around $203,000. The highest earning doctors are the anesthesiologists at $321,000.

—Bureau of Labor Statistics, U.S. Department of Labor, *Occupational Outlook Handbook, 2006-07 Edition*, Physicians and Surgeons, on the Internet at http://www.bls.gov/oco/ocos074.htm (visited June 23, 2007).

_____ **8.** The topic of the paragraph is
   a. salaries.
   b. doctors' salaries.
   c. doctors' average income of $156,000.

Fiber is the part of plant food that the human system cannot digest. This plant bulk benefits a person by helping foods move through the digestive system. It also helps control weight by making one feel full without adding extra calories. Fiber is also known to reduce heart disease. Major sources of fiber such as oat bran, dried beans, fruits, and vegetables also offer other necessary vitamins and nutrients.

_____ **9.** The topic of the paragraph is
   a. fiber.
   b. major sources of fiber.
   c. the benefits of fiber.

C. Read the following group of ideas. Then answer the question.
   A. Poor posture
   B. Poor posture can lead to serious shoulder pain.
   C. Back and shoulder muscles work together.
   D. Weak back muscles cause shoulder muscles to work improperly.
   E. Over time, the shoulder muscles become sore and stiff.

_____ **10.** The main idea is found in
   a. item A.   c. item C.
   b. item B.   d. item D.

A. Read the following group of ideas. Then answer the questions.

   A. In addition, the Internet allows you to do research for school projects.

   B. The Internet can offer helpful resources.

   C. The Internet

   D. The Internet allows access to friends and family through e-mail and chat rooms.

_____ **1.** The topic is found in
   a. item A.   c. item C.
   b. item B.   d. item D.

_____ **2.** The main idea is found in
   a. item A.   c. item C.
   b. item B.   d. item D.

_____ **3.** A supporting detail is found in
   a. item A.   c. item C.
   b. item B.   d. item D.

_____ **4.** A supporting detail is found in
   a. item A.   c. item C.
   b. item B.   d. item D.

B. Read each paragraph. Then answer the questions that follow it.

[1]Legendary heroes fought courageously against slavery during the 19th century. [2]A runaway slave, Harriet Tubman was a courageous and selfless leader in this fight. [3]Tubman was born a slave in Dorchester County, Maryland, in 1821. [4]At the age of 25, fearing she was about to be sold, she ran away. [5]She made her escape to freedom by following the North Star. [6]During the 1850s, Tubman made twenty successful trips back to the South. [7]During these trips, she led more than 300 others to freedom by using a series of safe houses and routes known as the Underground Railroad. [8]She often forced panicked or exhausted runaways ahead by threatening them with a loaded pistol. [9]Tubman never lost one life. [10]She became known as the "Moses" of her people.

—Adapted from "Biographies," *Boston African American National Historic Site*. Homepage. 2001 June 3.

_____ **5.** Who or what is the topic of this paragraph?
   a. legendary heroes   c. Harriet Tubman
   b. a runaway slave   d. the Underground Railroad

_____ **6.** Which sentence states the main idea of this paragraph?
   a. sentence 1   c. sentence 3
   b. sentence 2   d. sentence 4

[1]Cherokee women had many rights and were highly valued by their communities. [2]Not only could they speak at their town's yearly Grand Council, but they had their own council, too. [3]A *ghigau*, or "Beloved Woman," led the women's council. [4]Also, the Cherokee woman chose her husband, and he was expected to build her a house or live with her in her mother's house. [5]Cherokee women owned the house, property, and children. [6]Women planted crops, tended livestock, made clothes and wove baskets. [7]Some women were even warriors.

_____ **7.** What is the topic of this paragraph?
   a. the "Beloved Woman"   c. Cherokee women
   b. Cherokee men   d. Cherokee children

_____ **8.** Which sentence states the main idea of the paragraph?
   a. sentence 6   c. sentence 4
   b. sentence 1   d. sentence 5

[1]One small room in the shuttle serves as the bathroom for astronauts in space. [2]The main item inside this 29-inch-wide area is the Waste Collection System, which is the Shuttle's toilet with all its accessories. [3]Its door is open, but two curtains, attached to the top and the side of the door, provide privacy. [4]Astronauts use two foot restraints and two body restraints (bars positioned over the thighs) to position and hold themselves on the commode's seat. [5]Body waste enters the commode through the 4-inch-diameter seat opening. [6]Then it is drawn in by air flowing through holes under the seat. [7]This downward rush of air substitutes for gravity in collecting and keeping the waste material in the commode. [8]The urinal is just a flexible hose with attachable funnels. [9]Each astronaut has a personal funnel. [10]The funnels are shaped differently for men and women. [11]The urinal can be used in a "standing" position or while the astronaut is "sitting" on the commode.

—Adapted from "Waste Collection System."
NASA. Homepage. 16 June 2001.

_____ **9.** What is the topic of this paragraph?
   a. the stress of being an astronaut
   b. traveling through space
   c. funnels and restraints
   d. the space shuttle's waste collection system

_____ **10.** Which sentence states the main idea of this paragraph?
   a. sentence 2   c. sentence 4
   b. sentence 10   d. sentence 9

MASTERY **Test 6**

A. The following item is made up of specific ideas. Write a general idea that covers all the specific ideas.

1. *Specific ideas*: marijuana   cocaine   heroin

   General idea: _____

B. Read the following paragraph and then answer the questions.

¹To make a small room in your home look larger, use tone-on-tone decor. ²Begin with a neutral base such as a tan or cream color for the walls. ³Cover the floor with a slightly darker shade of tan; and repeat the cream color on the furniture. ⁴Bring in some prints, but keep the patterns light and airy. ⁵Layer the walls, floors, and furniture with the same tones.

2. The topic of this paragraph is _____ .

_____ 3. Sentence 1 states
         a. the main idea.
         b. a supporting detail.

_____ 4. Sentence 2 states
         a. the main idea.
         b. a supporting detail.

C. Read the passage. Then answer the questions that follow it.

Muleteers

¹Most Americans think of mail carriers as drivers of little white Jeeps with the steering wheel on the "wrong" side of the car. ²While this description holds true for many, some people who deliver the mail do so in a way that is quite different from the Jeep and mailbag method. ³Supai, Arizona, home to the Havasupai Indians, has an unusual system. ⁴Since 1869, Supai has relied on mules for the delivery of its mail.

⁵The village of Supai is located in the Grand Canyon. ⁶The steep, rocky terrain makes it difficult to deliver the mail; it is not friendly to Jeeps. ⁷People travel by foot, horse, or helicopter. ⁸Obviously, the cost of using helicopters is expensive. ⁹Thus using helicopters or the Jeep and mailbags to get mail to the people is out of the question. ¹⁰So mail is delivered to Supai, Arizona by muleteers—drivers of postal mule trains.

¹¹Muleteers use ropes to tie packed boxes to the sides of mules. ¹²These packages include typical mail like cards and bills but also supplies such as water, bread, and even computers.

173

[13]Muleteers and their mules provide the citizens of Supai with the goods and communication they need. [14]In return, the demand for these services provides muleteers with an unusual workday.

—Adapted from Kemper, "Clippety-Clopping Along."
Smithsonian, Mar. 2001, pp. 38–40.

VISUAL VOCABULARY

Drivers of mule trains are called

_____.

a. Supai
b. muleteers

_____ **5.** What is the topic of the first paragraph (sentences 1–4)?
    a. muleteers   c. mail carriers
    b. the mountains   d. Arizona

_____ **6.** Which sentence states the main idea of the first paragraph?
    a. sentence 1   c. sentence 3
    b. sentence 2   d. sentence 4

_____ **7.** What is the topic of the second paragraph (sentences 5–10)?
    a. the village of Supai   c. muleteers
    b. traveling   d. problems caused by the terrain

_____ **8.** Which sentence states the main idea of the second paragraph?
    a. sentence 5   c. sentence 7
    b. sentence 6   d. sentence 8

_____ **9.** What is the topic of the third paragraph (sentences 11–14)?
    a. muleteers
    b. ropes to tie packed boxes
    c. supplies such as water, bread, and even computers
    d. mules

_____ **10.** Which sentence states the main idea of the third paragraph?
    a. sentence 11   c. sentence 13
    b. sentence 12   d. sentence 14

> Main idea: Topic sentence
> Supporting detail
> Supporting detail
> Supporting detail

EXAMPLE Read the following paragraph, and identify its topic sentence. In the space provided, write the number of the sentence you chose.

Domestic Violence

[1]Domestic violence arises from the need to control. [2]One person in the family wants to control another person. [3]Most people think that the abuser in a family is always the man. [4]More often than not, this is true. [5]Some men abuse others out of fear. [6]They fear losing control over their families; thus they use fear to make their families dependent on them. [7]However, some women become violent for the very same reason. [8]These women may act violently out of low self-esteem and anxiety. [9]They use violence to make an emotional connection or to force their partners into desired behaviors.

Topic sentence: _____

EXPLANATION The topic sentence of this paragraph is sentence 1: "Domestic violence arises from the need to control." All the other sentences explain violence as the need to control. Notice how the passage presents the general idea of domestic (family) violence. Next the details focus on men and then on women.

Topic Sentence Within a Paragraph

Topic sentences within a paragraph can be near the beginning or in the middle of the paragraph.

Near the Beginning

A paragraph does not always start with the topic sentence. Instead, it may begin with a sentence or two that give a general overview of the topic. These introductory sentences are used to get the reader interested in the topic. They also lead the reader to the topic sentence. Sometimes the introductory sentences tell how the ideas in one paragraph tie into the ideas that came before it. At other times, the introductory sentences give background information about the topic.

This flow of ideas is also an example of deductive thinking. The flow of ideas is from general ideas (the introduction) and main idea (topic sentence) to specific ideas (supporting details). Authors often rely on this flow of ideas to write human interest stories in magazines and newspapers. In addition, this flow is often used to write academic papers and speeches. The following diagram shows this flow from general to specific ideas:

Introductory sentence(s)
Main idea: Topic sentence
Supporting detail
Supporting detail
Supporting detail

EXAMPLE Read the following paragraph, and identify its topic sentence. Remember to ask, "Does this sentence cover all the ideas in the paragraph?"

[1]Bad habits are easy to form but hard to break. [2]Cursing is an example of a bad habit that is especially difficult for many to break. [3]However, strong will and self-awareness can break the habit of cursing. [4]First of all, a strong will is needed to stop the habit of swearing. [5]Many people yell out a profanity when they are under some kind of stress. [6]The stress may be caused by an argument or a stubbed toe. [7]Either case is likely to bring out a string of four-letter words. [8]Only a strong-willed person can choose another set of words in the moment of stress. [9]Next, self-awareness is needed to break this habit. [10]Often people who are in the habit of cursing do not listen to how they sound. [11]In fact, many times, they are not even aware of how often they swear or how many offensive words they use. [12]Thus to break this habit, a person needs to listen to what he or she is saying.

Topic sentence: _____

EXPLANATION Sentence 3 is the topic sentence of this paragraph. Sentence 1 offers a simple but true statement about the topic. The purpose of this sentence is to get the reader's attention. Sentence 2 introduces the topic. Sentences 4–12 are the supporting details that explain the topic sentence.

PRACTICE ▮

Identify the topic sentences of each of the following paragraphs. Remember to ask, "Does this sentence cover all the ideas in the paragraph?"

[1]Everyone wants a good friend. [2]The best way to get a friend is to be a friend. [3]However, few people know how to be a good friend. [4]Being a friend requires time, patience, and honesty. [5]First, being a friend takes time. [6]Even when a busy life means no free time, a friend finds time to run errands, go to a movie, or just hang out. [7]Even when money is tight, a friend gives when there is a need. [8]Second, being a friend demands patience. [9]Even when advice isn't wanted, a friend listens to unsolvable problems. [10]Finally, being a friend requires honesty. [11]When advice is wanted, a friend gently tells the truth.

1. Topic sentence: _____

[1]Binge eating may be a result of high stress. [2]Long workdays, important deadlines, and family demands take their toll. [3]Feelings of anxiety settle in the stomach. [4]That feeling of unease may be mistaken for hunger, and the eating begins. [5]Ice cream, cookies, and bread, for some reason, give comfort. [6]A full stomach slows the body down and may even cause sleepiness. [7]As the demands of a hectic lifestyle build, so does the urge to eat.

2. Topic sentence: _____

In the Middle

At times, an author will begin a paragraph with a few attention-grabbing details. These details are placed first to stir the reader's interest in the topic. The flow of ideas no longer follows the deductive pattern of thinking. The flow of ideas now moves from specific ideas (supporting details) to general ideas (the topic sentence) to specific ideas (additional supporting details). Creative essays and special-interest stories, in which authors strive to excite readers' interest, may take this approach. For example, often television news stories begin with shocking details to hook the viewer and prevent channel surfing. The following diagram shows this flow of ideas:

Supporting detail
Supporting detail
Main idea: Topic sentence
Supporting detail
Supporting detail

EXAMPLE   Read the following paragraph, and identify its topic sentence. Remember to ask, "Does this sentence cover all the ideas in the paragraph?"

¹A dozen bats made of black construction paper hung from the ceiling of the front porch. ²Four pumpkins with fierce faces of triangle eyes and jagged teeth glowed by the front door. ³Spindly cobwebs covered the bushes. ⁴Spooky music filled the air. ⁵A tall witch with green hair held out a piece of candy. ⁶But the children were too afraid to take the candy. ⁷One little girl dressed as a princess stood on the sidewalk and refused to go anywhere near the witch. ⁸A little boy dressed as Luke Skywalker screamed as his big brother dragged him up the steps. ⁹Two sisters, twin ballerinas, held hands as they started and stopped three times before they finally ran away.

Topic sentence: _____

EXPLANATION   Sentences 1, 2, 3, and 4 are all details that describe the spooky Halloween decorations. Sentence 5 describes a scary witch. Sentence 6 is the topic sentence. The reader is able to see why the children were afraid because of the opening details. The topic sentence also states that the children were too afraid to get their candy. Sentences 7–9 show the unwillingness of several children.

Topic Sentence at the End of a Paragraph

Sometimes an author waits until the end of the paragraph to state the main idea. This approach can be very effective, for it allows the details to build up to the main idea. This flow of ideas is known as inductive. The ideas move from specific (supporting details) to general (the topic sentence). When a topic sentence is at the end of a paragraph, it is usually a summary statement or a conclusion. Inductive thinking is used in math and science to build a theory or to explore how details connect with one other. In addition, inductive thinking is often used to argue a point. Politicians and advertisers use this approach. They want to convince people to agree with their ideas or to buy their products. If a politician begins with a main idea such as "Taxes must be raised," the audience may strongly disagree. Then the audience may not listen to the specific reasons why taxes must be raised. However, if the politician begins with the details and leads up to the main idea, people are more likely to listen. For example, people are more likely to agree that schools need to be improved. Once they hear the specific details, then they may agree to raise taxes. This flow from specific to general also works well in creative writing. Inductive thinking is the process of arriving at a general understanding based on specific details. The following diagram shows the ideas moving from specific to general:

EXAMPLE Read the following paragraph, and identify its topic sentence. Remember to ask, "Does this sentence cover all the ideas in the paragraph?"

¹Ashleigh had been trying to write her essay for three days. ²First, she tried to write about her summer vacation, but it seemed too boring. ³Next, she tried to write about breaking up with her boyfriend. ⁴She was able to write two full pages but knew she couldn't share the ideas with a teacher for a grade. ⁵Her third and final try brought nothing but a page full of doodles. ⁶Desperate, for the essay was due in the morning, Ashleigh turned on her computer. ⁷"Maybe I can find something to write about on the Internet," she said to herself. ⁸She typed in the words "essay ideas" and hit the search button. ⁹Several sites had essays already written for free. ¹⁰Quickly, she found an essay about soccer; she recopied it in her own handwriting, put her name on it, and turned it in. ¹¹By cheating, Ashleigh joined the ranks of countless other students who cheat themselves out of an education. ¹²Cheating can be easier than learning.

Topic sentence: _____

EXPLANATION Sentences 1–10 tell the story of Ashleigh struggling to do the assignment and then deciding to cheat. Sentence 11 makes a judgment about Ashleigh's actions and other students who choose to cheat. Sentence 12 is the topic sentence. It clearly states the point the author is making, and it sums up the details of the story. Starting the paragraph with the details of Ashleigh's story makes the idea much more interesting. Ending the paragraph with a main idea that draws a conclusion or makes a judgment is very powerful.

PRACTICE 2

Identify the topic sentence of each of the following paragraphs. Remember to ask, "Does this sentence cover all the ideas in the paragraph?"

September 11 Funds

[1]The American people gave large amounts of money to aid the victims of September 11, 2001. [2]Many people often wonder what happened to all that money. [3]The September 11th Fund collected $534 million. [4]These funds came from more than two million people. [5]It gave $528 million dollars to nearly 600 assistance programs. [6]The Salvation Army received $86 million and spent it all on 9/11 services. [7]The money was mainly used for practical items. [8]It paid for supplies for the rescue workers and volunteers who cleaned up Ground Zero. [9]Some of the supplies included food, steel-toed boots, socks, and eye drops. [10]Former President Bill Clinton and retired senator Bob Dole raised more than $125 million. [11]Their charity is the Families of Freedom Scholarship Fund. [12]This fund can aid the education of the children of victims through 2030. [13]The American Red Cross gained nearly a billion dollars in gifts. [14]And the Red Cross offered a wide variety of aid to those directly affected by the attacks. [15]Obviously, the generous donations from the public were well used.

1. **Topic sentence:** _____

[1]Joe Theisman, quarterback for the Washington Redskins, drew his arm back for one of his awesome passes. [2]Then two hard-charging defensive linemen hit him. [3]One hit him high; one hit him low. [4]The splintering snap of broken bone traveled with full force into living rooms across the country. [5]Joe Theisman was hurt, and hurt badly. [6]The television media turned an evening of football entertainment into a gruesome affair. [7]Theisman's injury took only a moment. [8]Yet the television media replayed the scene of Theisman's injury again and again, intensifying the horror and violence. [9]Only television could show the sickening, unnatural angle of his leg as it broke in slow motion. [10]Only television could repeat the horrible sound of bone snapping in two. [11]Only television could and did.

2. **Topic sentence:** _____

Topic Sentences at the Beginning and the End of a Paragraph

A paragraph may start and end by stating one main idea in two different sentences. Even though these two sentences state the same main idea, they word the idea in different ways. A topic sentence presents the main idea at or near the beginning of the paragraph. Then, at the end of the paragraph, the main idea is stated again, but with different words. The following diagram shows this flow of ideas.

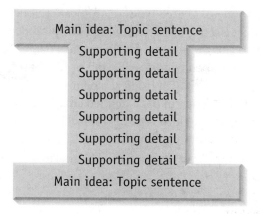

Main idea: Topic sentence
Supporting detail
Supporting detail
Supporting detail
Supporting detail
Supporting detail
Supporting detail
Main idea: Topic sentence

EXAMPLE Read the following paragraph, and identify its topic sentences. Remember to ask, "Do these sentences cover all the ideas in the paragraph?"

[1]Walking is a healthy, safe, and easy method of exercising. [2]Walking builds muscles in the legs, buttocks, torso, and arms. [3]The whole body is used when walking. [4]A brisk walk raises the heart rate, making the heart work harder, and become stronger. [5]Walking also helps keep weight within healthy guidelines. [6]Not only is walking healthy, but walking is also safe. [7]Unlike jogging, which can cause damage to ligaments and joints, walking is easy on the body. [8]Finally, walking is easy to do. [9]No special equipment, clothes, or training are needed. [10]All anyone needs for a good walk is desire and time. [11]Safe and easy, walking improves overall health.

Topic sentences: _____

EXPLANATION Sentences 1 and 11 both state the main idea of the paragraph: Walking is healthy, safe, and easy. Notice how the wording changes at the end of the paragraph. Repeating the main idea makes the point much stronger and more likely to be remembered. Remember: Even though the paragraph has two topic sentences, it only has *one* main idea.

PRACTICE 3

Identify the topic sentence(s) in each of the following paragraphs.

Types of Cyclones

[1]A hurricane is a type of tropical cyclone. [2]A tropical cyclone is the name for all circulating weather systems that turn counterclockwise in the Northern

Hemisphere. [3]Three types of tropical cyclones exist. [4]The first type of tropical cyclone is a tropical depression. [5]A tropical depression is an organized system of clouds and thunderstorms. [6]A tropical depression has a defined circulation, and it has sustained winds of 38 mph or less. [7]The second type of tropical cyclone is a tropical storm. [8]A tropical storm is an organized system of strong thunderstorms. [9]This storm has a defined circulation, and it has sustained winds of 39 to 73 mph. [10]The third type of tropical cyclone is a hurricane. [11]A hurricane has a well-defined circulation, and it has sustained winds of 74 mph or higher.

—Adapted from "Hurricane and Natural Disaster Brochures." National Weather Service. 31 August 2004.

1. Topic sentence(s): _____

Stress at Work

[1]Teresa shared the following information with a friend as they sat in her doctor's waiting room. [2]"In my new job, the computer routes the calls, and they never stop. [3]I even have to schedule my bathroom breaks. [4]All I hear the whole day are complaints from unhappy customers. [5]I try to be helpful and sympathetic, but I can't promise anything without getting my boss's approval. [6]Most of the time I'm caught between what the customer wants and company policy. [7]I'm not sure who I'm supposed to keep happy. [8]The other reps are so uptight and tense they don't even talk to one another. [9]We all go to our own little cubicles and stay there until quitting time. [10]To make matters worse, my mother's health is deteriorating. [11]If only I could use some of my sick time to look after her. [12]No wonder I'm in here with migraine headaches and high blood pressure. [13]A lot of the reps are seeing the employee assistance counselor and taking stress management classes, which seem to help. [14]But sooner or later, someone will have to make some changes in the way the place is run." [15]Teresa's story is unfortunate but not unusual. [16]Job stress has become a common and costly problem in the American workplace.

—Adapted from "Stress at Work." National Institute for Occupational Safety and Health. 7 January 1999.

2. Topic sentence(s): _____

Weather, Work, and Stress

[1]The hurricane had just left a messy trail a short two weeks earlier. [2]Now another hurricane threatens the area with 140 mph winds. [3]We all watch as the new storm moves steadily closer. [4]At work, we log online to Internet weather channels and gather in hallways to talk about our plans. [5]No one can concentrate on work; we all yearn to dash to our homes, gather our

belongings, secure our property, and flee. [6]Yet we feel obligated to wait until management gives the official release from work. [7]A hurricane causes great stress at the work place. [8]Most of us know that after the hurricane hits, we may not be able to return to work for days. [9]So we want to stay on the job as long as possible, hoping our businesses are still standing when we return. [10]Experience has taught us that we will lose electricity for days. [11]Incoming and outgoing mail will be delayed. [12]Cell phones won't work. [13]Tension and anxiety does not end with the storm. [14]In its path, a hurricane leaves a wake of on-the-job stress.

3. Topic sentence(s): _____

Choose the Colors of Health

[1]Eating 5 or more servings of colorful fruits and vegetables a day is an important part of a plan for healthier living. [2]Deeply hued fruits and vegetables provide a wide range of vitamins, minerals, fiber, and phytochemicals. [3]Your body needs each of these to maintain good health and energy levels. [4]Colorful fruits and vegetables protect against the effects of aging and reduce the risk of cancer and heart disease. [5]It's all about color—blue/purple, green, white, yellow/orange, and red: the power of colorful fruits and vegetables to promote good health. [6]So when you're grocery shopping, planning your meals, or dining out, think color. [7]Eat 5 or more servings of colorful fruits and vegetables a day and stay healthy.

—Adapted from "5 a Day, The Color Way." 5aday.org 1 Sept. 2004
http://www.5aday.com/html/colorway/colorway_home.php

4. Topic sentence(s): _____

Textbook
Skills

David Lawrence 11-8-10

The Central Idea and the Thesis Statement

Many paragraphs state the main idea in a topic sentence. Longer passages in articles, essays, and textbooks have **central ideas**, which can be thought of as the passage's main idea. Often the author will state the central idea in a single sentence called the **thesis statement**.

> The **central idea** is the main idea of a passage made up of two or more paragraphs.
> The **thesis statement** is a sentence that states a longer passage's central idea.

You identify the central idea of a longer passage the same way you identify the topic sentence of a paragraph. The thesis statement is one sentence that is general enough to include all the ideas in the passage. In longer reading selections, each paragraph will have a topic sentence in addition to the central idea.

EXAMPLE   Read the following passage. In the space provided, write the number of the sentence that states the central idea.

The Dangers of Marijuana Use

[1]Marijuana has significant short- and long-term effects. [2]The obvious short-term effects are increased heart rate, dry mouth, and dry, red eyes. [3]The red eyes result from the dilation, or widening, of the blood vessels in the eyes. [4]This dilation occurs throughout the body, increases the flow of blood, and causes a drop in blood pressure. [5]The drop in blood pressure makes some people dizzy. [6]Use of this drug also affects balance, coordination, and the ability to judge distances. [7]Research has shown that a majority of marijuana users failed roadside sobriety tests an hour and a half after smoking. [8]One study found that one-third of a group of reckless teenage drivers who had been tested for drugs on the scene had used marijuana.

[9]Marijuana may also have dangerous long-term effects. [10]First of all, marijuana smoke has over 150 ingredients that can cause cancer. [11]And smoking one marijuana joint is the same as smoking five tobacco cigarettes. [12]Thus five marijuana joints could do as much damage to the lungs as 25 cigarettes. [13]In addition, the marijuana smoke emits five times as much carbon monoxide into the blood and three times as much tar into the lungs. [14]Users may lower their immunity to diseases. [15]The body depends on white blood cells to fight off illness. [16]White blood cells attack and destroy germs and bacteria. [17]THC, a chemical found in marijuana, stops the growth of white blood cells. [18]Therefore, marijuana users are more prone to chest colds and coughs than nonusers. [19]Users are more likely to suffer from cancer of the throat, tongue, and sinuses.

Central idea: _____

EXPLANATION   The central idea of the passage is stated in sentence 1, "Marijuana has significant short- and long-term effects." The first paragraph discusses the drug's short-term effects, and the second paragraph discusses its long-term effects. Thus the first sentence is the only sentence broad enough to cover all the details in both paragraphs.

PRACTICE 4

Identify the central idea of the following passage.

Meet the Author: J. K. Rowling

[1]Harry Potter's magic has touched a huge audience of all ages all over the world. [2]In America, there are over 103 million books in print. [3]Each title has been #1 on the *New York Times, USA Today*, and *Wall Street Journal* best-seller lists.

[4]In 1998, *Harry Potter and the Sorcerer's Stone* was published in the United States, kicking off Harry-mania. [5]Suddenly, kids were reading again. [6]And their parents wanted to read the same books! [7]The second and third books were published in the spring and fall of 1999. [8]The sixth title, *Harry Potter and the Half-Blood Prince*, set a new world record for a first printing. [9]On July 16, 2005, 10.8 million copies hit stores. [10]*Harry Potter and the Deathly Hallows*, the seventh and final title in the series, went on sale July 21, 2007.

[11]Rowling first thought of Harry while riding a train back in 1990. [12]"Harry just strolled into my head fully formed." [13]She worked on the book for several years, finding quiet moments while her daughter napped. [14]Several publishers turned down the finished manuscript before one took interest.

[15]Warner Bros. enjoys certain rights in respect to all the Harry Potter books and has exercised its option to create films on all of those that have been published to date. [16]With over a quarter of a billion books sold, the books have been translated into 63 languages and distributed in over 200 countries. [17]All five books have appeared on bestseller lists in the United States, Britain, and around the globe. [18]J. K. Rowling has made reading fun for all ages.

—Adapted from "Meet the Author: J. K. Rowling."
From scholastic.com, April 25, 2007. Copyright © 2007 by
Scholastic Inc. Reprinted by permission.

Central idea: _____

Chapter Review

Test your understanding of what you have read in this chapter by filling in each blank with a word from the box. Use each word once.

central idea	general ideas	introductory	states	topic sentence
ending	interest	location	thesis statement	two

1. A ~~topic sentence~~ can be placed at or near the beginning of a paragraph, in the middle of a paragraph, or at the end of a paragraph.

2. One of the first things a skilled reader determines is the ~~location~~ of the topic sentence in a paragraph.

3. A topic sentence that begins a paragraph signals a move from ~~general idea~~ to specific ideas.

4. The topic sentence ~~state~~ the main idea of a paragraph.

5. A paragraph may begin with a sentence or two that give a general overview of the topic. These sentences are called ~~introductory~~ sentences.

6. At times, an author will begin a paragraph with a few attention-grabbing details. These details are placed first to stir the reader's ~~interest~~ in the topic.

7. ~~End~~ the paragraph with the topic sentence (main idea) can be very effective.

8. A paragraph may start and end by stating one main idea in ~~two~~ different topic sentences.

9. The ~~central idea~~ is the main idea of a passage made up of two or more paragraphs.

10. The ~~thesis statement~~ is a sentence that states a longer passage's central idea.

Applications

Application 1: Identifying the Topic Sentence

Identify the topic sentence in each paragraph. One paragraph will have two topic sentences: one at the beginning and one at the end.

1.   [1]Thirty minutes of walking three or four times a week can improve both fitness and attitude. [2]Walking tones muscles and strengthens the heart. [3]Well-developed muscles and a strong heart can lengthen a person's life. [4]Walking

also allows time for personal thoughts and works out stress. [5]Taking personal time and relieving stress lead to feelings of peace and well-being.

Topic sentence(s): _1_

2.   [1]AIDS is a devastating disease caused by the HIV virus. [2]So far, over a quarter of a million Americans have died from this disease. [3]The best safe-guard against getting AIDS is becoming educated about it. [4]Knowing how it is passed from one person to another is the first step. [5]One way HIV can be passed is by having sex with an infected person. [6]A second way it can be passed is by sharing a dirty needle, such as during heroin use.

Topic sentence(s): _3_

3.   [1]Rosa Parks was an African American woman who worked hard as a seamstress in a department store in the early 1960s. [2]One day, tired from work, she refused to give up her seat on a bus in Montgomery, Alabama, and became a national hero. [3]She was arrested and placed in jail for her refusal to move to the back of the bus, where African Americans were forced to sit in those days. [4]The way she was treated garnered national attention. [5]Some peo-ple say her refusal to give up her seat launched the civil rights movement. [6]Rosa Parks proved that one brave person can make a difference.

Topic sentence(s): _6_

4.   [1]Knowing the slang, or street words, used in the drug culture may help parents and teachers prevent the use of illegal drugs. [2]By learning the street language, adults show that they care enough to be involved. [3]It is also likely that young people will respect and listen to the advice of adults who know what they are talking about. [4]For example, "dope" used to be the name used for hard drugs like narcotics; now it refers to all drugs. [5]And a "dealer" usually only sells soft drugs like marijuana; a "pusher" sells hard drugs like heroin. [6]Knowing these terms gives adults a way to talk to young people about pre-venting drug use.

Topic sentence(s): _1 6_

Application 2: Identifying the Thesis Statement
Read the following passage, and identify the thesis statement.

Toys and Gender Roles
[1]Children will eagerly tell you about their favorite toy or about a "cool" new toy they would like to have. [2]Toys are without a doubt a major concern

Textbook
Skills

of most children because, as any child will tell you, they're fun. [3]However, toys not only entertain children; they also teach children. [4]Playing with toys teaches skills and allows children to try on different roles they may one day occupy as adults. [5]Some believe that there are significant differences between the toys girls and boys play with, and these different types of toys train girls and boys for separate roles as adults.

[6]More than twenty years ago, two researchers went into middle-class homes and studied the toys found in children's rooms. [7]Their comparison of the boys' and girls' rooms is a study of contrasts. [8]Girls' rooms contained a large number of dolls, dollhouses, and small appliances such as toy stoves. [9]In contrast, the boys' rooms contained military-type toys and athletic equipment. [10]Boys also had building and motor toys such as cars, trucks, and wagons. [11]In fact, boys had more toys overall, as well as more types of toys, including those considered educational. [12]The only items girls were as likely to have as boys were musical instruments and books.

—Adapted from Renzetti & Curran, *Women, Men, and Society,* 4th ed., p. 73.

Thesis statement: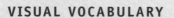

VISUAL VOCABULARY

A child learns adult
_____ through play.

a. roles
b. instruments

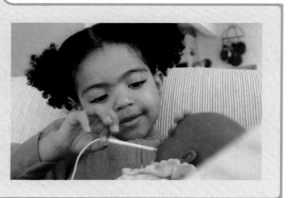

REVIEW Test 1

Identifying the Topic Sentence

Identify the topic sentence in each paragraph. One paragraph has two topic sentences: one at the beginning and one at the end.

1.   ¹Many of our cities have survived horrible natural disasters. ²One city that has faced and survived natural disaster is San Francisco, California. ³At 5:12 A.M. on April 18, 1906, a terrible earthquake shattered San Francisco. ⁴Fires broke out throughout the city due to broken gas pipes. ⁵Three thousand people were killed, and 200,000 were left homeless. ⁶In spite of the widespread damage, the city rebuilt.

Topic sentence(s): _____

2.   ¹In the past 200 years, bird and animal species have vanished from the earth as cities and towns have replaced the natural landscape. ²Only a small fraction of America's original forests remain. ³Sadly, more than the forest has been lost. ⁴Hunters killed off the last of the eastern bison in 1825 and the eastern elk in 1855. ⁵Millions of passenger pigeons once lived in the forest near the Great Plains. ⁶The last such pigeon died in a zoo in 1914. ⁷Many people have called these losses "progress."

Topic sentence(s): _____

3.   **A Mistake of Significance**
      ¹Don Imus was a shock jock. ²He manned the microphone of a nationally syndicated talk radio show for decades. ³He made a great living! ⁴Then in 2007 he made a joke that wasn't really funny. ⁵He used street slurs to describe the winning female basketball team from Rutgers University. ⁶The outcry against his use of "nappy headed 'hos" was swift and loud. ⁷Within a week, he was out of his job, dumped by CBS and MSNBC. ⁸He cried foul play. ⁹He pointed to the racial and sexist slurs used in Hip-Hop and Rap music by African Americans. ¹⁰Oprah held a town meeting on her daytime talk show. ¹¹She invited a panel from the music industry, including the rap artist Common and the Hip-Hop mogul Russell Simmons. ¹²They admitted that hate language toward women was a real problem in society. ¹³The mistake Don Imus made should teach us all a lesson about the power of words.

Topic sentence(s): _____

4.   **Boundaries**
      ¹Boundaries are the limits placed on behavior. ²Boundaries may be clear in some families and not as clear in others. ³**Rigid boundaries** are firmly set and difficult to break through. ⁴Rigid boundaries create a different situation than

Textbook
Skills

diffuse boundaries. [5]Diffuse boundaries change often and are easily crossed. [6]For instance, the mother and father in a family may set themselves apart from the rest of the family by making their bedroom off limits to other members of the family. [7]By doing this, they show that they expect to be respected as a couple. [8]In their case, the boundary or limit is rigid or clear. [9]Another couple may not have defined their boundary as a couple as clearly. [10]They may not have shown other members of the family that they must be respected as a couple. [11]Therefore, they may allow their children to interrupt their conversations and arguments. [12]In summary, boundaries affect the way a family functions.

—Adapted from Yerby, Buerkel-Rothfuss, & Bochner, *Understanding Family Communication*, 2nd ed., p. 62.

Topic sentence(s): _____

VISUAL VOCABULARY

The parents are setting _____ boundaries.

a. diffuse
b. rigid

REVIEW **Test 2**

Identifying the Topic Sentence

Identify the topic sentence for each paragraph. One paragraph has two topic sentences: one at the beginning and one at the end.

1.   [1]There is no such thing as a routine space flight, for the dangers are great. [2]Four flights have proved that the risks and tragedies of space flight are ever present. [3]A fire aboard the spacecraft *Apollo 1* on the ground in Cape

Kennedy, Florida, killed three astronauts in 1967. [4]On April 13, 1970, a major power failure crippled *Apollo 13*. [5]The astronauts had to use the frail lunar landing craft to get back to earth. [6]On January 28, 1986, the space shuttle *Challenger* exploded and killed all seven of its crew. [7]And on February 1, 2003, the space shuttle *Columbia* broke apart on its return to earth, costing another seven lives.

Topic sentence(s): _____

2.   [1]Ray Charles is a famous singer and musician who also happens to be blind. [2]As a young person, this remarkable man worked hard to overcome the constraints of his blindness. [3]Charles taught his ears to do what his eyes could not do. [4]He would stand in a hallway and throw a golf ball and listen to the sounds it made. [5]Then, as he listened, he would try to catch the ball as it came back to him. [6]By working hard, he learned how to live with being blind.

Topic sentence(s): _____

3.   [1]Reggae music is a complex mix of message and style. [2]Originating in Jamaica in the 1960s, reggae evolved from folk music that protested racism and corruption. [3]Reggae also has a religious side that is based on the Bible from the view of black culture. [4]Some critics say that the serious messages of reggae are easier to accept because of its powerful dance beat.

Topic sentence(s): _____

Textbook
Skills

4.   **The Role of Antioxidants**

[1]Although large doses of vitamins may be harmful, research has revealed a new role for some vitamins. [2]Some vitamins protect the body's cells by working as antioxidants. [3]Vitamins A, E, and C are a few of the vitamins that act as antioxidants. [4]Antioxidants stop a harmful kind of oxygen (called *oxygen free radicals*) from hurting the cells. [5]The body is always making free radicals. [6]If too many of these build up, diseases may occur. [7]Free radicals may be linked to cancer, lung disease, heart disease, and even the aging process. [8]Exercise may cause a rise in free radicals. [9]The question is, Do active people need to take in more antioxidants? [10]Some studies show that extra vitamin E may help fight against the damage caused by free radicals.

—Adapted from Powers & Dodd, *Total Fitness: Exercise, Nutrition, and Wellness*, 2nd ed., pp. 178–79.

Topic sentence(s): _____

REVIEW **Test 3**

Identifying the Topic Sentence

Identify the topic sentence for each paragraph. One or more paragraphs may have two topic sentences.

1.   [1]Many Americans who are overweight never lose weight because of fad diets and lack of exercise. [2]To lose weight, one must make two changes in lifestyle: eat healthful foods and exercise more. [3]When eating out, wise dieters order water instead of coffee or sodas and skip extras like bread and butter, appetizers, and alcoholic drinks. [4]Walking and biking on a regular basis can help most people lose one to two pounds a week. [5]In conclusion, if Americans would make two simple changes in lifestyle, fewer would be overweight.

   Topic sentence(s): _____

2.   [1]The improper handling of food causes millions of people to become sick, and thousands even die. [2]Simple steps in handling food can reduce the risk to your health. [3]First, be sure to wash your hands often with soap and water. [4]Next, add a little household bleach to the water when cleaning knives that have cut raw meat. [5]Finally, clean cutting boards by putting them in the dishwasher. [6]Remember these simple steps to protect your health as you prepare your food.

   Topic sentence(s): _____

Textbook
Skills

3.   [1]Flowers typically contain four types of modified leaves called floral organs: sepals, petals, stamens, and carpels. [2]Sepals, which enclose and protect the flower bud, are usually green and more leaflike than the other floral organs. [3]The petals are often colorful and advertise the flower to pollinators. [4]Stamens and carpels are the reproductive organs, containing the sperm and egg, respectively. [5]A stamen consists of a stalk (filament) tipped by an anther. [6]Within the anther are sacs in which meiosis occurs and in which pollen is produced. [7]Pollen grains house the cells that develop into sperm. [8]A carpel has a long slender neck (style) with a sticky stigma at its tip. [9]The stigma is the landing platform

for pollen. [10]The base of the carpel is the ovary, within which are ovules, each containing a developing egg and supporting cells.

—Campbell, Reece, Taylor, and Simon. *Biology: Concepts and Connections,* 5th ed. Benjamin Cummings 2008. p.636.

Topic sentence(s): _____

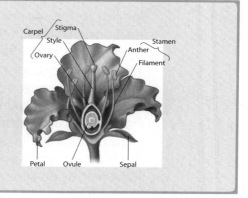

VISUAL VOCABULARY

_____ One part of the carpel of a flower is the

a. filament.
b. style.

Carpel · Stigma
Style
Ovary
Stamen
Anther
Filament

Petal   Ovule   Sepal

Textbook
Skills

4.

Basic Emotions

[1]Charles Darwin believed that we are born with many emotional behaviors—actions that come from emotions. [2]He noticed that people from many races and cultures use the same facial expressions to show the same emotions. [3]Likewise, blind people also use those very expressions, even if they never have had the chance to see the way others look. [4]Are we all born with a built-in set of emotions? [5]If so, these emotions would be a basic part of what we call "human nature." [6]Some experts believe that surprise, happiness, anger, fear, disgust, and sadness are basic emotions. [7]**Basic emotions** are those feelings that are innate (born within us) and shared by all humans. [8]Other experts list surprise, interest, joy, rage, fear, disgust, shame, and anguish. [9]The differences may be a simple matter of word choice. [10]Joy and happiness, for example, may be different words for the same emotion. [11]Although the exact number of basic emotions is debated, most agree that humans do have a set of built-in emotions.

—Adapted from Kosslyn & Rosenberg, *Psychology: The Brain, the Person, the World,* pp. 312–14.

Topic sentence(s): _____

REVIEW **Test 4**

Identifying Topic Sentences and the Central Idea

Read the passage; then answer the questions that follow it.

Textbook
Skills

Emotion: "I Feel; Therefore, I Am"

[1]After facing off a mugger, John felt an odd mixture of emotions as he hurried to the restaurant to meet Barbara. [2]He had no thought of what might happen later in the evening; his romantic after-dinner plans were no longer on his mind. [3]Instead, he was trembling with fear. [4]Now he felt nervous when he passed an alley, even though the mugger who attacked him was surely far away. [5]Also, he was surprised at the strength of his feelings when he was grabbed by the mugger and after the horrifying event was over. [6]When he saw Barbara, he was **overwhelmed** with intense feelings of warmth and relief.

[7]An emotion is a positive or negative effect of a seen or remembered object, event, or situation. [8]Emotions come with **subjective** (personal) feelings. [9]Emotions not only help guide us to move toward some things and move away from others, but they also give visible cues. [10]These cues help other people know key qualities of our thoughts and wishes.

[11]Understanding the difference between emotions is interesting, but it doesn't tell us what emotion is for or why an emotion arises when it does. [12]Why did John feel fear after the mugger had left? [13]Two major **theories** of emotion try to answer this question.

[14]Over 100 years ago, William James argued that you feel emotions after your body reacts. [15]For example, if you come across someone who begins acting like a mugger, James believes that you would first run and then feel afraid, not the other way around. [16]The emotion of fear arises because you sense your body as you flee. [17]You sense your heart speeding up and your breathing increase. [18]This theory says that emotions come from different sets of bodily reactions. [19]This theory is the "body-emotion theory."

[20]Walter Cannon did not agree with James's theory. [21]Instead, he claimed the brain itself is all that matters. [22]When you see a mugger, the brain gets the body ready to flee or fight *at the same time* as an emotion rises up. [23]This theory is the "brain-emotion theory."

—Adapted from Kosslyn & Rosenberg, *Psychology:
The Brain, the Person, the World,* pp. 315–16.

Vocabulary in Context

_____ **1.** What does **subjective** mean in sentence 8?
a. individual   c. intense
b. objective   d. physical

_____ **2.** What does **theories** mean in sentence 13?
a. types   c. ideas
b. nature   d. facts

Main Ideas

_____ **3.** Write the number of the sentence that is the topic sentence of the fourth paragraph (sentences 14–19).

_____ **4.** Write the number of the sentence that is the topic sentence of the fifth paragraph (sentences 20–23).

_____ **5.** Write the number of the sentence that states the central idea of the passage.

SKILLED READER Scorecard

Locating Stated Main Ideas

Test	Number Correct	Points	Score
Review Test 1	_____	× 25 =	_____
Review Test 2	_____	× 25 =	_____
Review Test 3	_____	× 25 =	_____
Review Test 4	_____	× 20 =	_____
Review Test 5 (website)	_____	× 25 =	_____
Review Test 6 (website)	_____	× 25 =	_____

Enter your score on the Skilled Reader Scorecard: Chapter 5 Review Tests inside the back cover.

After Reading About Locating Stated Main Ideas

Before you move on to the mastery tests on locating stated main ideas, take time to reflect on your learning and performance by answering the following questions. Write your answers in your notebook.

What did I learn about locating stated main ideas?

What do I need to remember about locating stated main ideas?

How has my knowledge base or prior knowledge about locating stated main ideas changed?

More Review and Mastery Tests

For more practice, go to the book's website at **http://www.ablongman.com/henry** and click on *The Skilled Reader*. Then select "More Review and Mastery Tests." You will find the tests listed by chapter.

Identify the topic sentence of each paragraph. One paragraph has two topic sentences.

1.   [1]Alzheimer's disease is a serious and growing problem for millions of the elderly. [2]In 2002, some 4 million Americans suffered from this dreadful disease. [3]Alzheimer's affects the brain as people age. [4]The disease causes a loss of memory, personality, and eventually all logical thought. [5]Unfortunately, this disease could affect 20 million Americans by the year 2050.

   Topic sentence(s): _____

2.   [1]Few of us become as skilled in our chosen field as Tiger Woods is in his. [2]This young man reached the top of his profession through determined hard work. [3]Not satisfied with his current skill level, Tiger spends hours after a day's play practicing his swings. [4]More of us should be as determined to succeed as Tiger Woods is.

   Topic sentence(s): _____

3.   [1]Today, students of all ages fill college classrooms. [2]In fact, 28 is the average age of a current community college student. [3]Many of these students are returning to the classroom after years on the job and away from the books. [4]Returning students often face many stresses. [5]The first problem many face is the college system. [6]Dealing with admissions and financial aid, transferring credits, and registering for classes can be an overwhelming process. [7]Once classes begin, these students often find balancing classwork, family life, and jobs challenging and tiring. [8]Finally, many of these older students feel the pressure to keep up with other college students. [9]Despite these challenges, returning students are often the most successful students in their classes.

   Topic sentence(s): _____

4.   [1]The West Nile virus is a deadly disease carried by mosquitoes that is fairly new to the United States. [2]Twenty-two people had died nationwide from the disease by the year 2002. [3]To avoid getting the virus, you can take several steps. [4]First, try to stay indoors at dawn and dusk; these are the times

of day that mosquitoes are most active. [5]Second, wear long-sleeved shirts, long pants, socks, and shoes when outside. [6]Third, use insect repellent. [7]Fourth, keep window and porch screens in good repair. [8]Fifth, do not allow mosquitoes to find breeding spots in standing pools of water. [9]Following these simple steps will reduce your risk of getting the West Nile virus.

Topic sentence(s): _____

The following selections have topic sentences that may appear at the beginning of, within, at the end of, or at two places in the paragraph. Write the number(s) of the topic sentence(s) of each paragraph in the space provided.

1.   [1]A simple smile has several benefits. [2]First, a smile brightens up your face and makes you much more attractive and approachable. [3]In fact, a smile puts others at ease and signals an openness to friendship. [4]During important moments in life, such as a job interview, a smile makes you look happy and self-confident. [5]It also leaves a good impression. [6]Finally, a smile is a great workout for the face: You exercise 16 muscles when you smile!

Topic sentence(s): _____

2.   [1]Depression can be bad for your heart and should not be ignored. [2]Recent studies indicate that people who are depressed are three times more likely to die of heart disease than those who are not depressed. [3]It seems that depression can raise the level of stress in the body. [4]And stress triggers an increase in heart rate and blood pressure. [5]In addition, if you are depressed, you are less likely to exercise or eat right than people who are not depressed. [6]Because depression can be harmful to your heart, it is important to pay attention to your emotional health.

Topic sentence(s): _____

3.   [1]Choosing a computer is a difficult task for many people. [2]Often the terms associated with computers make the task even more difficult. [3]Understanding three of these terms may make the choice a little easier. [4]First, RAM stands for random-access memory. [5]The more RAM a computer has, the more tasks the computer can do. [6]Second, the hard drive is the computer's storage space. [7]Files and programs are stored on the hard drive. [8]Third, the processor is the part of the computer that allows for speed in work. [9]A processor is usually measured in megahertz or gigahertz, and the faster the processor, the faster the computer will complete tasks like opening files and programs.

Topic sentence(s): _____

4.   [1]Lou is driving to work in his Mustang convertible with the top down. [2]It is a beautiful, crisp fall morning. [3]Suddenly, he is stricken with an intense and irrational sense of terror. [4]His heart races, he has trouble breathing, and he has a strong sense of impending doom. [5]He pulls over to the side of the road to try to calm down. [6]Even though nothing around him has changed, the feelings of anxiety only increase. [7]Lou is like millions of others who have experienced a panic attack. [8]A panic attack is an overwhelming fear that occurs without warning or reason.

Topic sentence(s): _____

MASTERY **Test 3**

Name _____ Section _____

Date _____ Score (number correct) _____ × 25 = _____%

The following selections have topic sentences that may appear at the beginning of, within, at the end of, or at two places in the paragraph. Write the number(s) of the topic sentence(s) of each paragraph in the space provided.

1. ¹Nothing in short-term memory lasts for long. ²In fact, for short-term memory to work, ideas need to be repeated often. ³Simply recite your list silently, over and over: "Software, books, Palm Pilot, tape, thumb tacks, stapler." ⁴Distractions of any kind can ruin an attempt at short-term memory. ⁵You've likely had a friend who, knowing you were trying to remember something, good-naturedly breaks in with unimportant ideas. ⁶Or your friend mixes up the order of items on your list. ⁷Such interruptions keep you from using your short-term memory; in fact, interference is the main factor affecting the rate of short-term memory loss.

—Adapted from Brownell, *Listening: Attitudes, Principles, and Skills*, 2nd ed., p. 149.

Topic sentence(s): _____

2.

Vocal Traits

¹There are four main vocal traits over which a speaker has considerable control. ²These traits are volume, pitch, quality, and rate. ³Because each element affects your response to a message, it is helpful to know how they are produced and their impact on your listening. ⁴**Volume** is related to breathing. ⁵The more deeply you breathe, the louder or stronger your voice. ⁶**Pitch** is used to express meaning. ⁷When your friend says one thing and means something else, it is due to the way he uttered the words. ⁸Sarcasm is a good example of pitch. ⁹When you breathe, the vocal cords vibrate. ¹⁰This vibration creates sound, and the rate of the sound creates the pitch. ¹¹**Quality** gives voice its unique traits, and emotions affect vocal quality. ¹²Voices are heard as harsh, nasal, breathy, hoarse, or squeaky. ¹³**Rate** is the speed at which you speak. ¹⁴Your rate can give clues about your mood or emotional state. ¹⁵Someone who is upset or excited speaks faster than the person who is tired or bored.

—Adapted from Brownell, *Listening: Attitudes, Principles, and Skills*, 2nd ed., pp. 199–201.

Topic sentence(s): _____

3.

Surrogate Motherhood

¹A surrogate mother is a woman who carries a baby to term for another person or couple. ²The surrogate mother gets a fee plus medical expenses. ³She then gives the baby to a married couple. ⁴Often the surrogate goes through a medical process that places the

father's sperm in her womb. [5]In this case, the surrogate mother is the physical mother of the baby. [6]In a different case, a surrogate mother may carry another woman's egg, which has been fertilized by the father or a donor. [7]Then, the surrogate mother is not biologically related to the baby she is carrying. [8]In the late 1980s, the surrogate mother of a baby called Baby M sued for custody. [9]She wanted the right to raise, or at least visit, the child she gave birth to. [10]In this case, the surrogate mother of Baby M was the physical mother of the baby and had other children of her own.

—Adapted from Ambert, *Families in the New Millennium,* pp. 110–11.

Topic sentence(s): _____

Textbook
Skills

4.   [1]Television is here to stay. [2]Over 99 percent of homes in the United States have TV sets. [3]A majority of homes have more than one set. [4]Most parents are probably not aware of how much time their children spend watching TV. [5]Keeping track of viewing time is probably a good first step. [6]If you judge that your children spend too much time viewing low-quality shows, consider setting time limits on their viewing. [7]Devices similar to credit cards are becoming available. [8]These devices limit children's television watching to an amount of time agreed on by parent and child. [9]Concerned parents should guide their children's choices of TV programs. [10]There are numbers of shows, especially on cable, that are just not suitable for children. [11]The new "V-chip" allows a parent to block violent shows.

—Adapted from Jaffe, *Understanding Parenting,* 2nd ed., p. 323.

Topic sentence(s): _____

VISUAL VOCABULARY

The new _____

allows a parent to block violent

shows.

   a. time limit
   b. V-chip

Daryl Lawrence

11-16-10

CHAPTER 6

Supporting Details

CHAPTER PREVIEW

Before Reading About Supporting Details
Questions for Locating Supporting Details
Major and Minor Details
Textbook Skills: Ideas from General to Specific: Creating a Summary

 ## Before Reading About Supporting Details

In Chapters 4 and 5, you learned several important ideas that will help you as you work through this chapter. Use the following questions to call up your prior knowledge about supporting details.

What is a main idea? (Refer to page 141.) *the athors conveying point about a topic.*

What are the three parts of most paragraphs? (Refer to page 144.) *a topic*, *Main idea*, and *supporting details*.

Define supporting details: (Refer to page 145.) *specfic ideas the develop, explain, support or illustrate the main idea.*

What are the different locations of topic sentences? (Refer to page 176.) *Beginning, middle, end*

211

What is a central idea? (Refer to page 185.) _____

_____ .

Questions for Locating Supporting Details

Look at the following main idea:

Main idea: Laughter speeds recovery from an illness and lengthens the life span.

This main idea raises two major questions: "How does laughter speed recovery?" and "How does laughter lengthen the life span?" Supporting details answer these questions, for the role of supporting details is to explain a main idea.

   Supporting details hold up a main idea by giving reasons, examples, steps, evidence, or any other kind of needed information.

> **Supporting details** explain, develop, and illustrate the main idea.

To identify supporting details, a skilled reader turns the main idea into a question. This question asks one of the reporter's questions: *Who, What, When, Where, Why,* or *How.* Supporting details answer the question, and the answer will yield a specific set of supporting details. For example, the question *why* is often answered by listing and explaining reasons or causes. The question *how* is answered by explaining a process. The answer to the question *when* is based on time order. An author strives to answer some or all of these questions with the details in the paragraph. You may want to try out several of the reporter's questions as you turn the main idea into a question. Experiment to discover which question is best answered by the details.

   Take the topic "the value of hard work." An author might choose to write about the people who have taught her the value of hard work. The main idea of such a paragraph might read as follows:

Main idea: Other people have taught me the value of hard work.

Using the word *who* turns the main idea into the following question: "Who has taught her the value of hard work?" Read the following paragraph for the answers to this question.

The Value of Hard Work
   [1]Other people have taught me the value of hard work. [2]First, my grandmother taught me the joy of hard work by her example. [3]The mother of a

farming family of nine children, she lovingly grew the vegetables, harvested the crops, and cooked three meals a day. [4]Her recipes for food and love still feed the family legacy. [5]Next, my sister taught me the importance of hard work by coaching me through high school. [6]When I wanted to goof off and ignore my studies, she coaxed me to study with her. [7]When I came across a discouraging problem, she helped me understand and praised my effort. [8]Finally, my first boss taught me the rewards of hard work. [9]He noticed my efforts by giving me a raise and offering me a college scholarship. [10]He said my willingness to work hard would take me far in life.

The supporting details for this main idea answer the question "who?" by listing three people who taught the author the value of hard work. Then the paragraph discusses what each person taught her. A simple outline chart shows the relationship between the main idea and its supporting details.

Topic: The Value of Hard Work

Main idea: Other people have taught me the value of hard work.
Question based on main idea:
Who has taught her the value of hard work?

Supporting detail:
1. Grandmother taught the joy of hard work.
Supporting detail:
2. Sister taught the importance of hard work.
Supporting detail:
3. First boss taught the rewards of hard work.

EXAMPLE   Read the following paragraph. Turn the main idea into a question. Then finish the simple outline that follows with a few words that state the three supporting details. The first detail has been filled in for you.

[1]Gossip is, by definition, harmful to people. [2]First, according to the dictionary, gossip entails spreading shocking facts or rumors about another person's personal life. [3]For example, Ruth saw John at a restaurant with someone who was not his wife. [4]Ruth then spread the rumor that John was cheating on his wife. [5]Second, no one trusts a gossiper; thus gossip hurts the person spreading the rumors. [6]In Ruth's case, it was later learned that John had been having dinner with his sister, who lives out of town. [7]The few people who

learned the truth decided never to trust Ruth again. [8]Those who believed the gossip knew that Ruth was willing to tell the worst about others. [9]Finally, gossip damages the reputation of the person who is the object of the gossip. [10]In John's case, many people believed and also spread the rumor about him, and as a result, his reputation was damaged. [11]Gossip hurt both John and Ruth.

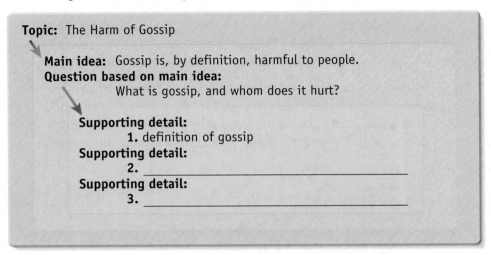

Topic: The Harm of Gossip

Main idea: Gossip is, by definition, harmful to people.
Question based on main idea:
            What is gossip, and whom does it hurt?

        Supporting detail:
            1. definition of gossip
        Supporting detail:
            2. _____
        Supporting detail:
            3. _____

EXPLANATION   The supporting details answer the question about the main idea in three parts: the definition of gossip, the person who gossips, and the person who is the object of the gossip. Thus the simple outline chart should look as follows:

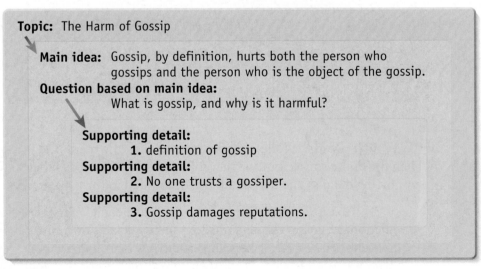

Topic: The Harm of Gossip

Main idea: Gossip, by definition, hurts both the person who
                gossips and the person who is the object of the gossip.
Question based on main idea:
            What is gossip, and why is it harmful?

        Supporting detail:
            1. definition of gossip
        Supporting detail:
            2. No one trusts a gossiper.
        Supporting detail:
            3. Gossip damages reputations.

PRACTICE **1**

Read the following paragraph. Turn the main idea into a question. Then use a few words to state two details that support the main idea.

Textbook
Skills

Before and After a Conflict

[1]You can make interpersonal conflict truly productive. [2]The following suggestions will help you use conflict to grow in your relationship. [3]First, before the conflict, try to arrange to fight in a safe private place. [4]Fighting in private allows you to be honest and avoid embarrassing your partner. [5]Also only choose to fight about problems you can solve. [6]Next, use after conflict strategies to ensure your relationship flourishes. [7]Establish a cooling-off period due to the need for extra space after a conflict. [8]Keep the conflict in perspective; don't make it bigger than it is. [9]Recognize unfair tactics and avoid them in the future. [10]Finally, show your positive feelings to demonstrate you are over the conflict.

—Adapted from DeVito, Joseph A. *Essentials of Human Communication,* 5th ed., Allyn & Bacon. 2005 p. 152.

Topic: Before and After a Conflict

Main idea: The following suggestions will help you use conflict to grow in your relationship.

Question based on main idea:
What are the suggestions that will help me before and after a conflict?

Supporting detail:
1. _____

Supporting detail:
2. _____

VISUAL VOCABULARY

The best synonym for interpersonal is

_____

a. social.
b. private.

Major and Minor Details

A supporting detail will always be one of two types:

> A **major detail** explains, develops, or supports the *main idea*.
> A **minor detail** explains, develops, or supports a *major detail*.

A **major detail** is directly tied to the main idea. Without the major details, the author's main idea would not be clear.

In contrast, a **minor detail** explains the major detail. The minor details could be left out, and the main idea would still be clear. Thus minor details are not as important as major details. Most often, minor details are used to add interest. To better understand the flow of ideas, study the chart:

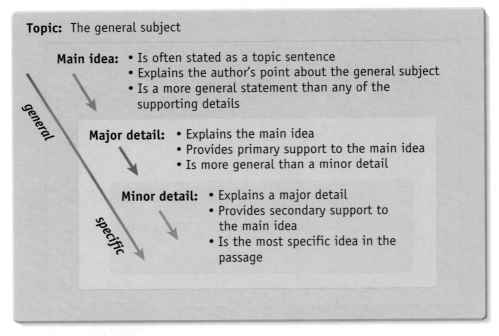

Topic: The general subject

Main idea: • Is often stated as a topic sentence
• Explains the author's point about the general subject
• Is a more general statement than any of the supporting details

Major detail: • Explains the main idea
• Provides primary support to the main idea
• Is more general than a minor detail

Minor detail: • Explains a major detail
• Provides secondary support to the main idea
• Is the most specific idea in the passage

general

specific

EXAMPLE   See if you can tell the difference between major and minor details. Read the following paragraph. The first sentence states the main idea. Turn the main idea into a question. Then complete the outline chart that follows.

The Three Stages of Alcoholism

¹Alcoholism can be divided into three stages. ²The first stage, *initiation*, happens as a harmless social event. ³For many young people, the initiation into alcoholism begins at weekend parties where beer is served as the drink of choice. ⁴Most think of these weekend binges as nothing more than fun. ⁵However, the

habit of seeking fun through drinking leads to the next phase. [6]The second stage is the *developing* phase of alcoholism. [7]A developing alcoholic turns to beer, wine, or hard liquor not only to have fun but also to relieve stress. [8]During this stage, few drinkers realize the extent of their problem and rarely find help until the final stage. [9]The last stage of alcoholism is the *chronic* stage. [10]This stage comes as the result of years of habitual drinking. [11]During this phase, the alcoholic will put family, job, property, and even safety at risk for the sake of a drink.

Topic: The Three Stages of Alcoholism

Main idea: Alcoholism can be divided into three stages.
Question based on main idea:

_____

Major supporting detail:
  1. _____

   Minor supporting details:
      a. _____
      b. _____
      c. leads to the next phase

Major supporting detail:
  2. _____

   Minor supporting details:
      a. _____
      b. _____

Major supporting detail:
  3. Last stage, the chronic phase

   Minor supporting details:
      a. result of years of habitual drinking
      b. _____

      _____

EXPLANATION The word *what* turns the topic sentence into a question that the major details answer. Compare your answers to the following outline chart:

Topic: The Three Stages of Alcoholism

Main idea: Alcoholism can be divided into three stages.
Question based on main idea:
        What are the three stages of alcoholism?

Major supporting detail:
        1. First stage, initiation, a harmless social event

    Minor supporting details:
            a. weekend parties where youth drink
            b. weekend binges seen as fun
            c. leads to the next phase

Major supporting detail:
        2. Second stage, developing alcoholism

    Minor supporting details:
            a. using alcohol to relieve stress
            b. few realize problem and rarely find help

Major supporting detail:
        3. Last stage, the chronic phase

    Minor supporting details:
            a. result of years of habitual drinking
            b. person puts family, job, property, and
                even safety at risk for a drink

PRACTICE 2

Read the following paragraph. The first sentence states the main idea. Turn the main idea into a question. Then complete the outline chart that follows.

Training Your Thoughts

[1]You can use three simple steps to train your mind to stop thinking negative thoughts. [2]First, recognize negative thoughts for what they are. [3]Negative thoughts may include phrases such as *I can't, I hate, this is stupid,* or *what a dumb question.* [4]Second, replace these negative thoughts with positive ones. [5]Select a few positive words and phrases that focus on the good things about life and yourself. [6]Replace *I can't* with *I can,* and instead of thinking how much you "hate" traffic and bad drivers, think up a list of things for which you are grateful. [7]Third, practice the

first two steps. [8]Negative thinking is a habit, and it takes practice to break its hold on you. [9]So you must be willing to practice replacing negative thoughts with positive ones. [10]You will be surprised how much better you feel.

Topic: Training Your Thoughts

Main idea: _____

_____

Major detail:

1. _____

Minor details:

a. _____

b. _____

c. _____

d. _____

Major detail:

2. _____

Minor details:

a. _____

_____

_____

b. _____

c. Instead of thinking how much you "hate" traffic and bad drivers, think up a list of things for which you are grateful.

Major detail:

3. _____

Minor details:

a. _____

_____

b. _____

_____

c. _____

_____

Ideas from General to Specific: Creating a Summary

Textbook authors often use headings that show the flow from general ideas to specific ideas. For example, textbook authors often use headings at the beginning of a passage. A heading at the beginning of a passage states the general topic. In addition, textbook authors also use headings within a passage to point out important ideas. In longer passages, headings signal the central idea of a section. In shorter passages, the headings may signal major supporting details. Usually, headings are in **bold** or *italic* type. A skilled reader can use headings, main ideas, and supporting details to create a summary of the text. Creating a summary is an effective activity to do after reading.

> A **summary** is a brief, clear restatement of the most important points of a paragraph or passage.

Annotating or marking your text during reading will help you create a summary after you read. First, locate and underline the main idea. Then, create a question based on the main idea. Write this question in the margin of your textbook. Next, as you read, assign a number or letter to each heading or detail that answers the question based on the main idea. Finally, to create a summary after you read, restate the ideas you marked in a few brief sentences. Often you will want to paraphrase or restate the ideas in your own words. You can use your annotations and summary to study the material. For example, cover up the passage. Next, use the question in the margin to test your memory of the material. Then, check your memory against your summary.

EXAMPLE   Read the following passage from the textbook *Communication@-Work*. Complete each activity as directed.

A.   As you read, annotate or mark the passage. Locate and underline the main idea. Write a question based on the main idea in the margin next to the passage. Number each detail that answers the question.

Use Academic Settings to Build Listening Strength

[1]Like training for athletic competition, listening training takes commitment, dedication, and endurance. [2]Ironically, some of the most effective behaviors are common sense, and yet they require the most effort.

[3]Use the following six practices to become an "Olympic listener."

- [4]Let the other person talk.
- [5]Ignore distractions.
- [6]Seek the speaker's picture.
- [7]Take time to listen.
- [8]Empathize with the speaker.
- [9]Note what you learn.

Get Active

[10]To become an Olympic listener, you must get active. [11]Be physically prepared to actively listen—rested, nourished, and alert. [12]For that "ears flapping forward" feeling, pretend that there will be a pop quiz at the end of class. [13]Don't let words flow through your ears and out through pens without registering the message in memory. [14]Instead of waiting to become interested, listen immediately and expect interesting ideas. [15]That is, *quit other tasks, quickly attend,* and quietly listen.

—Kelly, Marylin K. *Communication@Work.*
Allyn & Bacon 2006, pp. 97-98.

B. Note the flow of ideas. Fill in the blanks with the second major detail and its minor supporting details.

Topic: Use Academic Settings to Build Listening Strength

Main Idea: _____

_____

Second Major Detail:

Minor Details: _____

_____

_____

_____

_____

C. Create a summary. Paraphrase the ideas you marked as you read into a one- or two-sentence summary. Wording will vary.

_____

_____

EXPLANATION

A. You should have underlined sentence 1 "Like training for athletic competition, listening training takes commitment, dedication, and endurance." You should have a question based on the central idea similar to the following: "How do you build listening strength?" Finally, the sentences that answer the question based on the central idea are sentences 4 through 9, and sentence 15.

B. The flow of ideas is from general to specific. The author states the general topic in the heading. The thesis statement is at the beginning of the passage. The main idea explains how to build strong listening skills. The first major support asserts that six practices can build listening skills, and the minor supports state the six practices. The **second** major support states the need to be active to become an Olympic listener. The minor details give hints about how to quit other tasks, quickly attend, and quietly listen.

C. Compare the summary you created with the following wording: Listening training takes commitment, dedication, and endurance. You can become an Olympic listener, but you must practice six steps and be active throughout the process.

PRACTICE **3**

Textbook
Skills

Read the following passage, adapted from the textbook *The Dynamics of Drug Abuse.* As you read, complete each activity as directed.

A. As you read, annotate or mark the paragraph. Locate and underline the main idea. Write a question based on the main idea in the margin next to the passage. Number each detail that answers the question.

Drug Dependence

[1]Drug dependence is what most experts refer to as the final stage of drug use. [2]The onset of drug dependency is seen when users are no longer in control of their drug-taking behavior. [3]Three traits mark drug dependence:

[4]*Overwhelming need:* The user has a chemical need for the drug. [5]His or her strong desire to use means that efforts to stop are unsuccessful. [6]In addition, the user spends a great deal of time getting drugs.

[7]*Tolerance:* Larger doses are needed over time to produce the same original effect of a smaller dose. [8]The user becomes less responsive to the effects of the drug.

[9]*Withdrawal:* Withdrawal symptoms occur when drug use comes to an end. [10]Often withdrawal includes symptoms that are opposite to the effect produced by the drug. [11]For example, a person who has taken sleeping pills for a period of time and ends their use will feel unusually restless.

—Adapted from Fishbein & Pease, *The Dynamics of Drug Abuse,* pp. 64–67.

B. Note the flow from general to specific. Fill in the blanks with the main idea, the **second** major supporting detail, and its minor details from the passage.

Topic: Drug dependence

Topic sentence: _____

   Second major detail: _____

   Minor details: _____

_____

_____

C. Create a summary. Paraphrase the ideas you marked as you read into a one- or two-sentence summary.

_____

_____

_____

_____

Authors often use headings at the beginning and within a passage to show the relationship between the main idea, the major supporting details, and the minor supporting details in a paragraph or longer passage. Notice that when you pull these different parts out of the writing, you reduce the information to a few sentences or phrases. Reducing information, or **summarizing**, is an important reading and study skill.

Chapter Review

Test your understanding of what you have read in this chapter by filling in each blank with a word from the box. Use each word once.

after reading	minor detail	specific
annotating	paraphrase	summary
during reading	question	supporting details
major detail		

1. _____ explain, develop, support, or illustrate a main idea.

2. To locate supporting details, a skilled reader turns the main idea into a

_____ .

3. A _____ directly explains, develops, or illustrates the main idea.

4. A _____ explains, develops, or supports a major detail.

5. In a paragraph or longer passage, ideas usually flow from general to

_____ .

6. Creating a summary is an effective activity to do _____ .

7. A _____ is a brief, clear restatement of the most important points of a paragraph or longer passage.

8. Often you will want to _____ , or restate the ideas in your own words.

9–10. _____ or marking your text _____ will help you create a summary after you read.

Applications

Application 1: **Major Supporting Details**

Read the paragraph. Create a question based on the main idea. Then complete the outline and answer the questions following the paragraph.

Susan B. Anthony

[1]In the 1800s, women had very limited choices. [2]Women were not allowed to be well educated, own property, or vote. [3]Women were not paid the same wages a man was paid for the same work, and women were not allowed to speak at public gatherings. [4]Susan B. Anthony rose above these limits.

[5]First of all, Anthony became well educated. [6]She had been born to a Quaker father who saw to it that she had an excellent education. [7]He schooled her at home and later sent her to one of the few colleges that took women as students. [8]Next, Anthony became politically active. [9]Her father's passion against prohibition (banning the sale of alcohol) and slavery became her own issues. [10]Often arrested and harassed, she dedicated her life to the cause of women's rights. [11]Finally, she won new rights for women. [12]By the time she died in 1906, her efforts had made it possible for women to vote in four states.

Main idea: Susan B. Anthony rose above these limits.

Question based on main idea: _____

_____

1. Answers based on major supporting details:

    a. _____

    b. _____

    c. _____

2. What signal words introduce the first major detail? _____

3. What signal word introduces the third major detail? _____

Application 2: Main Idea and Supporting Details

Read the paragraph. Then complete the diagram with the question about the main idea and the missing supporting details from the paragraph.

Fire: A Deadly Weapon

[1]Fire has proved to be an effective, deadly, and unstoppable weapon of war. [2]For one thing, fire as a weapon of mass destruction was effectively used for the first time during World War II. [3]The Germans effectively destroyed Coventry, England, by dropping firebombs on the city. [4]The success of the German bombs triggered the worldwide use of bombs designed to start fires. [5]Moreover, fires started by bombing can turn into a deadly firestorm that burns like a furnace. [6]A firestorm results when several fires located close together break out at the same time. [7]The flames of these fires can create winds of 100 miles per hour that, like a furnace, draw them toward each other and upward. [8]Furthermore, the firestorm caused by bombing is mostly unstoppable. [9]The heat is so intense that nothing can survive. [10]Firefighters still have not found a way to effectively fight these deadly firestorms.

Topic: Fire as a Weapon

Main idea: Fire has proved to be an effective, deadly, and unstoppable weapon of war.

Question based on main idea:

_____

_____

Major supporting detail:

   1. _____

      Minor supporting details:
        a. German firebombs
        b. worldwide use of bombs

Major supporting detail:

   2. _____

      Minor supporting details:
        a. _____
        b. high winds and furnace heat

Major supporting detail:

   3. _____

      Minor supporting details:
        a. _____
        b. no way to fight them

Application 3: Central Idea and Supporting Details

A. As you read, annotate this passage from a college government textbook. Locate and underline the central idea. Write a question based on the central idea in the margin next to the passage. Number the five major details that answer the question.

Textbook
Skills

Why Is Voter Turnout So Low?

[1]The United States has one of the lowest voter turnout rates of any nation in the developed world. [2]Low voter turnout in the United States occurs for a number of reasons.

Question based on
the central idea:

_____

_____

_____

_____

_____

Difficulty of Registration. [3]Most people who are registered do vote. [4]However, a rather low number of adults take the time to register to vote. [5]Several reasons explain the low registration rates in the United States. [6]First, every other democracy in the world puts the burden to register on the government. [7]Yet, in the United States, the burden is on the person. [8]Thus, the time and effort to register is greater in the United States than it is in other countries. [9]Many nations automatically register all of their citizens to vote. [10]In contrast, people in the United States must remember on their own to register. [11]In addition, strict voter registration laws passed in the early part of the twentieth century caused a clear drop in voter turnout.

Difficulty of Absentee Voting. [12]Tough absentee ballot laws also lead to the low voter turn out in the United States. [13]In many states, for instance, citizens must apply in person for absentee ballots. [14]This condition creates a burden. [15]A voter's inability to be present in his or her home state is often the reason for absentee balloting in the first place.

Number of Elections. [16]A third reason for low voter turnout in this country is the sheer number and frequency of elections. [17]Few nations in the world match the number of elections held in the United States. [18]The separation of powers leads to the need for many layers of elections on the local, state, and national levels.

Voter Attitudes. [19]Voter attitudes are also key to turnout. [20]Some nations try to get around the effects of voter attitudes. [21]They force people to vote by law (Australia and Belgium). [22]Or they tax citizens who do not vote. [23]As a result, voter turnout rates in Australia and Belgium are often greater than 95 percent. [24]In the United States, some voters don't vote due to apathy. [25]Many others may be turned off by the quality of campaigns. [26]Campaigns seem to focus on petty issues and mudslinging more than ever. [27]Finally, more voters may now distrust the government. [28]More and more people state that they lack confidence in their leaders.

Weak Political Parties. [29]Political parties today are no longer as strong as they once were. [30]In the past, political parties rallied voters, made sure they were registered, and got them to the polls. [31]The parties once were grass-roots organizations. [32]They forged strong party-group links with their supporters. [33]Today these bonds have been stretched to the breaking point for many. [34]Now campaigns are focused on the candidate. [35]The growth of huge party systems has resulted in a more distant party. [36]Most people do not identify very strongly with these large, distant parties.

—Adapted from O'Connor and Sabato, *American Government: Continuity and Change*, 2000, pp. 496–98.

B. Create a summary of the passage you just read. Paraphrase the ideas you marked as you read into a one- or two-sentence summary. Wording of answers will vary.

_____

_____

_____

_____

_____

REVIEW **Test 1**

Main Ideas and Major Supporting Details

Read the paragraph. Complete the diagram by filling in the blanks with the topic, the main idea, a question based on the main idea, and two major supporting details from the paragraph.

Two Brave African-American Women

[1]African-American women have a tradition of independence and leadership dating back to the times of slavery. [2]In spite of great danger, black women took leading roles in the struggle for abolition. [3]Two strong leaders against slavery were Sojourner Truth and Harriet Tubman. [4]Sojourner Truth was a powerful speaker against slavery. [5]A heckler once called out, "Old woman . . . I don't care any more for your talk than I do for the bite of a flea." [6]Truth replied, "Perhaps not, but the good Lord willing, I'll keep you scratching." [7]Another strong leader, Harriet Tubman bravely attained her own freedom and then risked her life to lead many others to theirs. [8]Tubman declared, "I had a _right_ to liberty or death; if I could not have one I would have another." [9]Despite a reward of $40,000 for her capture, pistol-packing Tubman returned to the South many times. [10]She led more than 300 slaves to their freedom via the "Underground Railway." [11]She served with Union forces during the Civil War and acted as a scout behind enemy lines.

—Adapted from "Work Among Our Women." _The Progress of a People_. African-American Perspectives: Pamphlets from the Daniel A. P. Murray Collection, 1818–1907. American Memory. Library of Congress.

Topic: 1. _____

  ↓

  Main idea: 2. _____
_____

    Question based on main idea:
      3. _____
_____

        Major supporting detail:
         4. _____
_____

        Major supporting detail:
         5. _____
_____
_____

REVIEW Test 2

Main Ideas, Major and Minor Supporting Details

Read the paragraph from a college communications textbook. Answer the questions.

Textbook
Skills

Generic *Man*

[1]The National Council of Teachers of English (NCTE) offers guidelines for using nonsexist language. [2]One aspect of the guidelines speaks to the use of the generic *man*. [3]First, to use *man* to refer to both men and women can be thought of as sexist. [4]The word *man* refers most clearly to an adult male. [5]This use of *man* stresses "maleness" at the cost of "femaleness." [6]The terms *mankind* or the *common man* or even *caveman* also place a primary focus on adult males. [7]Second, gender-free terms can easily replace male-centered words. [8]For example, you can replace the word *mankind* with the words *humanity, people,* or *human beings.* [9]Instead of *common man,* you can say *the average person* or *ordinary people.* [10]Instead of *cavemen,* you can say *prehistoric people* or *cave dwellers.*

—Adapted from DeVito, Joseph A. *The Interpersonal Communication Book,* 11th ed., p. 156.

_____ **1.** Sentence 2 is a
        a. main idea.   c. minor supporting detail.
        b. major supporting detail.

_____ **2.** Sentence 3 is a
        a. main idea.   c. minor supporting detail.
        b. major supporting detail.

_____ **3.** Sentence 4 is a
        a. main idea.   c. minor supporting detail.
        b. major supporting detail.

_____ **4.** Sentence 7 is a
        a. main idea.   c. minor supporting detail.
        b. major supporting detail.

_____ **5.** Sentence 8 is a
        a. main idea.   c. minor supporting detail.
        b. major supporting detail.

REVIEW **Test 3**

Annotating a Text and Creating a Summary

Textbook
Skills

A. As you read, annotate this passage taken from a government website. (**1**) Locate and underline the central idea. (**2**) Write a question based on the central idea in the margin next to the passage. (**3–5**) Number the three major details that answer the question.

Question based on
the central idea: (**2**)

_____

_____

_____

_____

_____

The Symptoms of Attention
Deficit Hyperactivity Disorder

[1]Attention Deficit Hyperactivity Disorder (ADHD) occurs in some children in the preschool and early school years. [2]It is hard for these children to control their behavior or pay attention. [3]Children who have ADHD usually display one or more of the following traits.

Hyperactivity. [4]Children who are hyperactive always seem to be "on the go" or constantly in motion. [5]They dash around touching or playing with whatever is in sight, or they talk incessantly. [6]Sitting still at dinner or during a school lesson or story can be a difficult task. [7]They squirm and fidget in their seats or roam around the room. [8]Or they may wiggle their feet, touch everything, or noisily tap their pencil. [9]Hyperactive teenagers or adults may feel internally restless. [10]They often report needing to stay busy and may try to do several things at once.

Impulsivity. [11]Children who are impulsive seem unable to curb their immediate reactions. [12]They do not think before they act. [13]They will often blurt out inappropriate comments, display their emotions without restraint, and act without regard for the later consequences of their conduct. [14]It is hard for them to wait for things they want or to take their turn in games. [15]They may grab a toy from another child or hit when they're upset. [16]Even as teenagers or adults, they may impulsively choose to do things that have an immediate but small payoff. [17]They have trouble with activities that may take more effort yet provide much greater but delayed rewards.

Inattention. [18]Children who are inattentive have a hard time keeping their minds on any one thing. [19]They may get bored with a task after only a few minutes. [20]If they are doing something they really enjoy, they have no trouble paying attention. [21]But focusing deliberate, conscious attention to organizing and completing a task or learning something new is difficult. [22]Homework is difficult for these children. [23]They will forget to write down an assignment, or leave it at school. [24]They will forget to bring a book home, or they will bring the wrong one. [25]The homework, if finally finished, is full of errors and erasures. [26]Homework is often frustrating for both parent and child.

—Adapted from "Attention Deficit Hyperactivity Disorder (ADHD)." National Institute of Mental Health.

B. Paraphrase the ideas you marked as you read to complete the following summary. Wording of some answers may vary.

Children who have (**6**) _____ may have one or more of three (**7**) _____. First, (**8**) _____ _____ Second, (**9**) _____ _____. Third, (**10**) _____ _____.

REVIEW **Test 4**

Main Ideas and Major and Minor Supporting Details

Textbook
Skills

Before you read the following passage from a college communications textbook, skim the material and answer the Before Reading questions. Read the passage. Then answer the After Reading questions.

Vocabulary Preview

oration (1) speech

interred (1) buried

obvious (4) understandable, known

appreciation (17) approval, admiration, understanding

inferences (26) guesses, conclusions

communicate (29) to exchange ideas

relational (30) of or based on dealings with people

Surface and Depth Listening

[1]In Shakespeare's *Julius Caesar,* Marc Antony, in giving the funeral **oration** for Caesar, says: "I come to bury Caesar, not to praise him. / The evil that men do lives after them; / The good is oft **interred** with their bones." [2]And later: "For Brutus is an honourable man; / So are they all, all honourable men." [3]But Antony, as we know, did come to praise Caesar and to convince the crowd that Brutus was not an honorable man.

[4]In most messages there's an **obvious** meaning. [5]You arrive at this clear meaning from a **literal** reading of the words and sentences. [6]But there's often another level of meaning. [7]Sometimes, as in *Julius Caesar,* it's the opposite of the literal meaning. [8]At other times, it seems totally unrelated. [9]In reality, most messages have more than one level of meaning. [10]Consider some often heard messages. [11]Carol asks you how you like her new haircut. [12]On one level, the meaning is clear. [13]Do you like the haircut? [14]But there's also another, perhaps more important, level. [15]Carol is asking you to say something positive about her appearance. [16]The same is true for the parent who complains about working hard at the office or in the home. [17]The parent, on a deeper level, may be asking for an expression of **appreciation**. [18]The child who talks about the unfairness of the other children in the playground may be asking for comfort and love. [19]To grasp these other meanings you need to engage in depth listening.

[20]If you respond only to the surface-level message, you miss making meaningful contact with the other person's feelings and needs. [21]If you say to the parent, "You're always complaining. [22]I bet you really love working so hard," you fail to respond to his or her real need. [23]You have ignored his or her need for support and encouragement. [24]To adjust your surface and depth listening, think about the following guidelines:

^{25}*Focus on both verbal and nonverbal messages.* ^{26}Look for both **consistent** and inconsistent "packages" of messages. ^{27}Use these as guides for drawing **inferences** about the speaker's meaning. ^{28}Ask questions when in doubt. ^{29}Listen also to what is omitted. ^{30}Remember, speakers **communicate** by what they don't say as well as by what they do say.

^{31}*Listen for both content and* **relational** *messages.* ^{32}For example, take the student who always challenges the teacher. ^{33}On one level, this student may be disagreeing with the content. ^{34}Yet, on another level, the student may be confronting the teacher's authority. ^{35}The teacher needs to listen and respond to both types of messages.

^{36}*Make special note of statements that refer back to the speaker.* ^{37}People usually talk about themselves. ^{38}Whatever a person says is, in part, a result of who that person is. ^{39}So listen carefully to those personal messages.

^{40}*Don't ignore the literal meaning of a message in trying to find the hidden meaning.* ^{41}Balance your listening. ^{42}Reply to the different levels of meaning in the messages of others, just as you would like others to respond to you. ^{43}Be sensitive. ^{44}Listen carefully, but don't be too eager to uncover hidden messages.

—Adapted from DeVito, Joseph A. *The Interpersonal Communication Book*, 11th ed., pp. 111–112.

BEFORE READING

Vocabulary in Context

_____ **1.** In sentence 5 of the passage, the word **literal** means
  a. hidden.
  b. factual.
  c. natural.
  d. focused.

_____ **2.** In sentence 26 of the passage, the word **consistent** means
  a. conflicting.
  b. clear.
  c. subtle.
  d. reliable.

AFTER READING

Central Idea and Main Idea

_____ **3.** Which sentence states the central idea of the passage?
  a. Sentence 1
  b. Sentence 4
  c. Sentence 19
  d. Sentence 20

_____ **4.** Which sentence states the main idea of paragraph 3?
  a. Sentence 20
  b. Sentence 21
  c. Sentence 22
  d. Sentence 23

Supporting Details

_____   **5.** Sentence 32 is a _____ in its paragraph.
           a. major supporting detail   b. minor supporting detail

Supporting Details

_____   **6.** Sentence 34 is a _____ in its paragraph.
           a. major supporting detail   b. minor supporting detail

7–10. Complete the summary with information from the passage.

Listening at a **(7)** _____ level, a person reacts to a literal message.
(8) _____ listening responds to hidden meanings based on the
feelings and needs of the speaker. Several **(9)** _____ help one listen
on both levels. First, listen to messages that are verbal (what is said) and **(10)**
_____ (what is not said). Next, listen to messages about content
and relationships. Also, listen to statements that may be about the speaker.
Finally, don't ignore clear meanings in the hunt for hidden meanings.

Discussion Topics

   1. Men and women may listen differently. Is one gender more likely to listen
       at a surface level or a depth level? Why?
   2. In what ways do people express messages that are nonverbal (not stated)?
       Which is more powerful: the verbal message or the nonverbal message?
       Why?
   3. Which of the guidelines is most helpful? Why?

Writing Topics

   1. In a paragraph, describe a surface listener.
   2. In a paragraph, describe a depth listener.
   3. Write a letter to someone who is a surface listener. Explain how he or she
       can become a depth listener.

SKILLED READER *Scorecard*

Supporting Details

Test	Number Correct		Points		Score
Review Test 1	_____	×	20	=	_____
Review Test 2	_____	×	20	=	_____
Review Test 3	_____	×	10	=	_____
Review Test 4	_____	×	10	=	_____
Review Test 5 (website)	_____	×	20	=	_____
Review Test 6 (website)	_____	×	5	=	_____

Enter your scores on the Skilled Reader Scorecard: Chapter 6 Review Tests inside the back cover.

After Reading About Supporting Details

Before you move on to the mastery tests on supporting details, take time to reflect on your learning and performance by answering the following questions. Write your answers in your notebook.

What did I learn about supporting details?

What do I need to remember about supporting details?

How has my knowledge base or prior knowledge about supporting details changed?

More Review and Mastery Tests

For more practice, go to the book's website at **http://www.ablongman.com/henry** and click on *The Skilled Reader*. Then select "More Review and Mastery Tests." You will find the tests listed by chapter.

Name _____ Section _____

Date _____ Score (number correct) _____ × 20 = _____%

Read the paragraph, then complete the simple outline. In the chart below, fill in the blanks with the main idea, a question based on the main idea, and three major supporting details from the paragraph.

Textbook
Skills

Creative People Are Daring

[1]For the creative, thinking is an adventure. [2]Three traits reveal the daring nature of creative people. [3]First, creative people are fairly free of pre-set ideas and biased views. [4]Therefore, they are not as quick to accept existing views. [5]They are less narrow in their views. [6]And they are less likely to conform with the thinking of those around them. [7]Second, they are bold in their thinking. [8]They are willing to think about unpopular ideas. [9]They also consider seemingly unlikely possibilities. [10]Therefore, like Galileo and Columbus, Edison and the Wright brothers, they are more open than others to creative ideas. [11]Their daring has an additional benefit. [12]It makes them less prone to face-saving than others. [13]As a result, they are willing to face unpleasant experiences. [14]They apply their curiosity. [15]Then they learn from those experiences. [16]Thus, they are less likely than others to repeat the same failure over and over.

—Adapted from Ruggiero, *The Art of Thinking: A Guide to Critical and Creative Thought*, 7th ed., p. 84.

Topic: The Daring Nature of Creative People

Main idea: 1. _____
Question based on main idea:
     2. _____
          _____

     Major supporting detail:
          3. _____
               _____
     Major supporting detail:
          4. _____
     Major supporting detail:
          5. _____

Read the paragraph, then answer the questions.

How Do Hybrid Vehicles Work?

[1]Fuel economy is vital. [2]Fuel economy protects the environment; it reduces oil imports; it conserves fuel supplies for the future; and it saves money. [3]Three traits make a hybrid electric vehicle one of the best vehicles for fuel economy. [4]First, these smart vehicles join the best of internal combustion engines and electric motors. [5]In some hybrid vehicles, both the engine and the electric motor are joined to the wheels by the same transmission. [6]With the aid of the electric motor, the engine can be smaller. [7]Second, these vehicles are built to "think smart." [8]For example, smart power electronics decide when to use the motor and when to use the engine. [9]These smart vehicles also know when to store electricity in advanced batteries for future use. [10]The electric motor is used mostly for low-speed cruising. [11]The motor also supplies extra power for speeding up or hill climbing. [12]When braking or coasting to a stop, the hybrid also uses its motor. [13]The motor acts as a generator and creates electricity. [14]The electricity is then stored in its battery pack. [15]Finally, hybrid vehicles do not need to be plugged into an outside source of power. [16]Gasoline stored in a regular fuel tank supplies all the energy the hybrid vehicle needs. [17]Three hybrid vehicles are the Toyota Prius, Honda Insight, and the Honda Civic (hybrid).

—Adapted from "How Do Hybrid Vehicles Work? U.S. Department of Energy." 12 September 2004.

_____ **1.** Sentence 3 is a
    a. main idea.
    b. major supporting detail.
    c. minor supporting detail.

_____ **2.** Sentence 4 is a
    a. main idea.
    b. major supporting detail.
    c. minor supporting detail.

_____ **3.** Sentence 7 is a
    a. main idea.
    b. major supporting detail.
    c. minor supporting detail.

_____ **4.** Sentence 8 is a
      a. main idea.
      b. major supporting detail.
      c. minor supporting detail.

_____ **5.** Sentence 14 is a
      a. main idea.
      b. major supporting detail.
      c. minor supporting detail.

VISUAL VOCABULARY

Based on the photograph, the best definition for hybrid is

_____

a. the offspring of two different breeds.
b. formed or composed of different elements.

▲ Hybrid vehicles combine at least two different fuel sources for its energy source.

Read the paragraph, then answer the questions.

Space Fun

[1]Astronauts need a break from their busy schedules when they are orbiting Earth. [2]Days or even months of straight work cause stress among space workers. [3]Not only do astronauts have time to unwind, they also have many activities that help them relax and have fun. [4]First, free time is built into their routine. [5]They are given time every day to relax and exercise. [6]Like most people who work full time, they also get weekends off. [7]Second, space workers have a choice of fun and relaxing activities. [8]One popular pastime while orbiting the Earth is looking out the window. [9]Astronauts onboard the space shuttle can look out the cockpit windows. [10]They can watch the Earth below or the deep blackness of space. [11]Inside the International Space Station, crewmembers have many windows they can look out. [12]They often talk about their awe as they look at the Earth spin beneath them with its many shades and textures. [13]Stunning sunsets and sunrises occur every 45 minutes above the Earth's atmosphere. [14]In addition, space workers can watch movies, read books, play cards, and talk to their families. [15]They also have an exercise bike, a treadmill, and other equipment to keep their bodies in shape.

—Adapted from "Space Fun." NASA. 12 September 2004.

_____ **1.** Which sentence is the topic sentence of the paragraph?
  a. sentence 1
  b. sentence 2
  c. sentence 3

_____ **2.** Sentence 4 is a
  a. major supporting detail.
  b. minor supporting detail.

_____ **3.** Sentence 6 is a
  a. major supporting detail.
  b. minor supporting detail.

241

_____   **4.** Sentence 7 is a
            a.   major supporting detail.
            b.   minor supporting detail.

_____   **5.** Sentence 13 is a
            a.   major supporting detail.
            b.   minor supporting detail.

CHAPTER

7

Outlines and Concept Maps

CHAPTER PREVIEW

Before Reading About Outlines and Concept Maps
Outlines
Concept Maps
Textbook Skills: The Table of Contents in a Textbook

 Before Reading About Outlines and Concept Maps

In Chapter 6, you learned several important ideas that will help you effectively use outlines and concept maps. Review the diagram about the flow of ideas on page 216 in Chapter 6. Next, skim this chapter for key ideas in boxes about outlines, concept maps, and the table of contents in a textbook. Refer to the diagram and boxes and create at least three questions that you can answer as you read the chapter. Write your questions in the following spaces (record the page number for the key term in each question):

_____

_____ (page_____)?

_____

_____ (page_____)?

_____

_____ (page_____)?

    Compare the questions you created with the following questions. Then write the ones that seem most helpful in your notebook, leaving enough space between each question to record the answers as you read and study the chapter.

What words signal the topic sentence or central idea? What words signal each new idea in a passage? What is a concept map? Where are main ideas placed in an outline, concept map, and table of contents? Where are major supporting details placed in an outline, concept map, and table of contents? Where are minor supporting details placed in an outline, concept map, and table of contents? What is the difference between a formal outline and an informal outline?

Outlines

An outline shows how a paragraph or passage moves from a general idea to specific supporting details; thus it helps you make sense of the ways ideas relate to one another. A skilled reader uses an outline to see the relationships among the main idea, major supporting details, and minor supporting details.

> An **outline** shows the relationships among the main idea, major supporting details, and minor supporting details of a paragraph or passage.

An author often uses signal words and phrases to indicate that a supporting detail or a series of supporting details is coming. Signal words are sometimes called transitional words.

Signal words that indicate a series of details are frequently located in the stated main idea, so they can serve as a clue that the sentence is likely to be a topic sentence of a paragraph or the central idea of a passage.

Words That Signal the Topic Sentence or Central Idea		
a few causes	a few steps	several advantages
a few effects	a number of	several kinds of
a few factors	a series of	several steps
a few reasons	among the results	

Signal or transition words are also frequently used to introduce each new detail in a paragraph or passage.

Words That Signal Each New Detail in a Paragraph or Passage		
additionally	first of all	moreover
also	for example	next
another	furthermore	one
finally	in addition	second
first	last	third

EXAMPLE Read the following paragraph. Fill in the details to complete the outline. Then answer the questions that follow.

¹Jeremy tried a number of ways to get rid of his hiccups. ²First, he tried holding his breath and counting to 10 very slowly. ³However, he was never able to count any higher than 6 before an unstoppable string of hiccups would take over. ⁴Next, he tried breathing into a paper bag. ⁵While he was breathing out into the bag, the hiccups would erupt loudly and painfully. ⁶By this time, Jeremy's stomach had begun to hurt. ⁷Finally, he tried scaring his hiccups away. ⁸He asked his sister to help; several times she ran up behind him, when he least expected it, and screamed at the top of her voice. ⁹For a time, the scare tactic would seem to help, but then, without fail, the hiccups returned. ¹⁰Each time, they seemed louder and more frequent. ¹¹Jeremy suffered the whole day with his stubborn hiccups.

Main idea: Jeremy tried a number of ways to get rid of his hiccups.

Question: In what ways did Jeremy try to get rid of his hiccups?

1. **Major supporting details**

   a. _____

   _____

   b. _____

   _____

   c. _____

   _____

2. **Signal words for supporting details**

   a. What words in the main idea signal that a list of details will follow?

   _____

   b. What words introduce the three major details?

   Major detail 1: _____

   Major detail 2: _____

   Major detail 3: _____

EXPLANATION   Compare your answers with the following outline.

Main idea: Jeremy tried a number of ways to get rid of his hiccups.

Question: In what ways did Jeremy try to get rid of his hiccups?

1. **Major supporting details**

   a. tried holding his breath and counting to 10

   b. tried breathing into a paper bag

   c. tried scaring his hiccups away

2. **Signal words for supporting details**

   a. Signal words in the main idea: a number of

   b. Major detail 1: First

   Major detail 2: Next

   Major detail 3: Finally

Notice that even without the minor supporting details, the main idea and the major supporting details make sense. You do not need the minor details to understand the main point the author is trying to make. However, the minor details do make the passage more interesting to read and deepen the author's ideas.

The outlines you have worked with so far are informal outlines. Often, a traditional or formal outline is used to see the relationships between ideas in a longer passage of several paragraphs. A traditional outline uses the central idea as a heading and Roman numerals to indicate the topic sentence of each paragraph, capital letters to indicate the major details of each paragraph, and Arabic numbers to indicate the minor details of each paragraph. If you were to use a traditional outline to show the relationships among the main idea, the major supporting details, and the minor details in the paragraph about Jeremy, it would look like the following outline:

Main Idea: Jeremy tried a number of ways to get rid of his hiccups.

  I. He tried holding his breath.

     A. He was never able to count higher than 6.

     B. An unstoppable string of hiccups would take over.

 II. He tried breathing into a paper bag.

     A. While he was breathing out into the bag, the hiccups would erupt loudly and painfully.

B. Jeremy's stomach began to hurt.

III. He tried scaring his hiccups away.

A. He asked his sister to help.

B. She ran up behind him, when he least expected it, and screamed.

C. The scare tactic would seem to work.

D. The hiccups returned.

E. They seemed louder and more frequent.

F. Jeremy suffered the whole day.

PRACTICE 1

Read the following paragraph. Complete the outline with major details from the passage. Then answer the questions that follow.

The Wal-Mart Factor

[1]Wal-Mart has dramatically changed the retail business in several ways. [2]First, Wal-Mart sells items at much lower prices than malls and neighborhood shops can. [3]Wal-Mart is able to buy goods at lower cost by buying in bulk. [4]Then the company passes the lower prices on to the customer. [5]Second, Wal-Mart puts many neighborhood shops out of business. [6]Neighborhood shops just cannot match the lower prices, for a single owner doesn't have the money to buy in bulk. [7]Third, Wal-Mart builds large stores to house a wide variety of goods that includes everything from toys to furniture. [8]Neighborhood shops do not have the space to carry the variety of goods that Wal-Mart can stock. [9]Thus Wal-Mart has changed shopping into a money-saving one-stop shopping trip.

Main idea: Wal-Mart has dramatically changed the retail business in several ways.

Question: In what ways has Wal-Mart changed the retail business?

1. **Major supporting details:**

   a. _____

   b. Puts neighborhood shops out of business

   c. _____

VISUAL VOCABULARY

Wal-Mart sells a wide range of goods to _____ customers.

    a. wholesale
    b. retail

2. Signal words for supporting details:

a. What words in the topic sentence signal that a list of details will follow?

_____

b. What words introduce the three major details?

Major detail 1: _____

Major detail 2: _____

Major detail 3: _____

Concept Maps

An outline is one way to see the details in a paragraph or passage. Another way to see details is through the use of a concept map. A **concept map** is a diagram that shows the flow of ideas from the main idea to the supporting details. Think of what you already know about a map. Someone can tell you how to get somewhere, but it is much easier to understand the directions if you can see how each road connects to other roads by studying a map. Likewise, a concept map shows how ideas connect to one another.

A **concept map** is a diagram that shows the flow of ideas from the main idea to the supporting details.

To make a map, the skilled reader places the main idea in a box or circle as a heading and then places the major supporting details in boxes or circles beneath the main idea. Often arrows or lines are used to show the flow of ideas.

EXAMPLE Read the following paragraph. Then complete the concept map by adding the missing major supporting details from the paragraph.

[1]Instead of moping around without energy, overcome the "blahs" in two basic ways. [2]First, eat right. [3]A proper diet can help keep those lazy feelings of boredom away. [4]Avoid sweets, chips, and fast foods. [5]Instead eat a balanced diet from the four food groups to give your body the fuel it needs. [6]Second, get active. [7]Moderate exercise burns away that sluggish feeling. [8]Instead of relying totally on cars and elevators, walk and take the stairs.

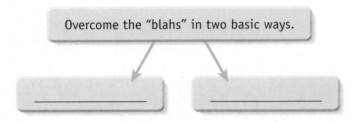

Overcome the "blahs" in two basic ways.

EXPLANATION The main idea is in the top box. The signal words *First* and *Second* indicate the major supporting details in the paragraph. Therefore, the missing details are "Eat right" and "Get active."

PRACTICE 2

Read each paragraph. Then complete the concept map for that paragraph.

American Idol

[1]*American Idol* is a one of a kind reality television show that turns contestants into stars. [2]The first winner of *American Idol*, Kelly Clarkson, has had an amazing career. [3]Kelly's first single, "A Moment Like This," set a record. [4]It shot from number 52 to number one on the Billboard singles chart in one week. [5]Her first album, *Thankful*, debuted at number one on

the Billboard. [6]Clarkson has won countless awards, including Grammy awards for Best Female Pop Vocal Performance and Best Pop Vocal Album. [7]The season two winner, Ruben Studdard, was dubbed the Velvet Teddy Bear, and his first album, *Soulful*, debuted at number one on the Billboard album. [8]Season three winner, Fantasia Barrino was a young, struggling single mom when she tried out for American Idol. [9]Her first single "I Believe" debuted at number one on the Billboard charts. [10]According to Billboard, she was the first new artist in history to debut a single at number one. [11]In 2005, Barrino released the book, *Life Is Not a Fairytale*, which revealed her struggles as a single teen mother and high school dropout. [12]She also revealed that she was functionally illiterate. [13]In 2006, she starred in a TV movie based on *Life Is Not a Fairytale*. [14]The fourth season's *American Idol* winner, Carrie Underwood's first song, "Inside Your Heaven," debuted as the best-selling song in the country. [15]Underwood also won the best female vocalist award at the 2006 CMA Awards. [16]*American Idol* serves up the American dream for its talented winners.

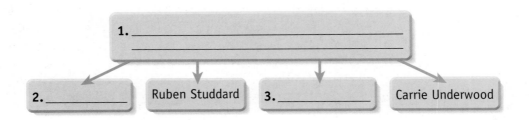

1. _____
   _____

2. _____   Ruben Studdard   3. _____   Carrie Underwood

A Piercing Problem

[1]One young woman's experience with piercing her tongue led to a series of alarming health problems. [2]First, an infection occurred within days of the piercing. [3]Her tongue became tender and swollen, and it oozed a foul-tasting discharge. [4]To get some relief, she removed the jewelry she had inserted. [5]Within days, the hole closed up. [6]Then she began to have severe headaches, trouble with balance, nausea, and vomiting. [7]These symptoms appeared almost a month after the piercing occurred. [8]Doctors discovered an abscess in her cerebellum, the part of the brain that controls coordination. [9]When they drained the abscess, they found four types of oral bacteria in the fluid. [10]The doctors believe that bacteria found in the mouth entered her bloodstream through her pierced tongue. [11]Once in the bloodstream, the bacteria made their way to her brain.

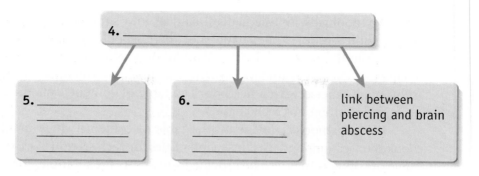

4. _____

5. _____   6. _____   link between piercing and brain abscess

Mattie's Heroic Story

[1]By 2001, Mattie Stepanek had become an 11-year-old national hero for several reasons. [2]First, Mattie showed great courage as he faced a horrible disease, muscular dystrophy. [3]Mattie had almost died more than once. [4]In fact, at one point, his mother said, "He lives on the edge; it could be one day or one year." [5]And Mattie lived each day in a wheelchair hooked to a ventilator that supplied him with oxygen. [6]Next, Mattie showed great talent. [7]He began writing poetry when he was three years old, and by 2004, five volumes of his poems had been published. [8]The titles are *Heartsongs, Journey Through Heartsongs, Hope Through Heartsongs, Celebrate Through Heartsongs,* and *Loving Through Heartsongs.* [9]Finally, Mattie showed great wisdom. [10]His message does not focus on his suffering; instead, he wants to bring peace and hope to the world. [11]His courage, talent, and wisdom landed him on shows like *Oprah* and *Good Morning, America.* Mattie Stepanek died at the age of 13 on June 22, 2004.

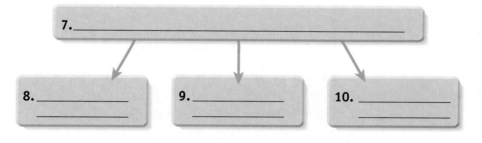

7. _____

8. _____   9. _____   10. _____

Textbook
Skills

The Table of Contents in a Textbook

The table of contents of a textbook is a special kind of outline that is based on topics and subtopics. A **topic** is the *general subject,* so a **subtopic** is a *smaller part* of the topic. The general subject of the textbook is stated in the textbook's title. For example, the title *Health in America: A Multicultural Perspective* tells us that the book is about health concerns from the view of different cultures.

Textbooks divide the general subject into smaller sections or subtopics. These subtopics form the chapters of the textbook. Because a textbook looks deeply into the general subject, a large amount of information is found in each chapter. A chapter is further divided into smaller parts or subtopics, and each subtopic is labeled with a heading. The table of contents lists the general subjects and subtopics of each chapter.

Most textbooks provide a brief table of contents which divides the textbook into sections and lists the chapter titles for each section. A separate detailed table of contents may also be provided which lists the subtopics for each chapter.

A skilled reader examines the table of contents of a textbook to understand how the author has organized the information and where specific information can be found.

EXAMPLE Survey, or look over, the following brief table of contents. Then answer the questions.

The Art of Being Human, 7th ed.

Brief Contents

Detailed Contents v
Preface xi

Part I
You and the Humanities 1
  1 The Art of Thinking Critically 3
  2 Apollonian Reason,
     Dionysian Intuition 41

Part II
Disciplines of the Humanities 69

  3 Myth 71
  4 Literature 103
  5 Art 139
  6 Music 199
  7 Theater 239
  8 The Musical Stage 289
  9 The Cinema 325
 10 Television 373

Part III
Themes in the Humanities 403
 11 Religion 405
 12 Morality 443
 13 Happiness 481
 14 Death Attitudes and
     Life Affirmation 507
 15 Controversy 539
 16 Freedom 571

1. What is the general topic of this textbook? _____

2. How many parts did the author use to divide the general topic? _____

3. How many chapters are in Part II? _____ What is the length of Chapter 3? _____ pages.

4. Write a one-sentence summary using the topic and subtopics for Part II.

_____

_____

EXPLANATION   The general topic of this textbook is stated in each of the part titles: the humanities. The book title also refers to the humanities. The author divides the general topic into three parts: "You and the Humanities," "Disciplines of the Humanities," and "Themes in the Humanities." Part II is divided into eight chapters. Knowing the length of each chapter helps you set aside the proper amount of time needed to read and study. For example, Chapter 3 is 32 pages in length. One way to get a general sense of the ideas in a chapter or part is by writing a summary. Compare your summary of Part II to the following: The disciplines of the humanities include myth, literature, art, music, theater, the musical stage, the cinema, and television.

PRACTICE 3

Study the following detailed table of contents for Chapter 4 of *The Art of Being Human*, 7th ed.

1. What is the topic of the chapter? _____

2. How many subtopics are listed for the section "Poetry"? _____

3. On what page does the discussion about modern poets begin? _____

4. What are the major supporting details of this chapter? _____

_____

Chapter Review

Test your understanding of what you have read in this chapter by filling in the blank with a word or term from the box. Use each word or term once.

concept map	outline	supporting detail
formal outline	signal words	

1. An _____ shows the relationships among the main idea, major supporting details, and minor supporting details.

2. An author often uses _____ such as *a few causes, a number of reasons, several steps,* or *several kinds of* to introduce a main idea.

3. An author often uses signal words such as *first, second, furthermore, moreover, next,* or *finally* to indicate that a _____ is coming.

4. A _____ uses Roman numerals to indicate the main idea, capital letters to indicate the major details, and Arabic numbers to indicate the minor details.

5. A _____ is a diagram that shows the flow of ideas from the main idea to the supporting details.

Applications

Textbook Skills

Application 1: Supporting Details and Outlines
Read the paragraph. Then complete the outline and answer the questions following the paragraph.

The Stages of Syphilis

[1]Though curable, syphilis is a serious and even deadly sexually transmitted disease. [2]Passed only through sexual contact, syphilis has three stages. [3]The first stage occurs ten days to three months after infection. [4]A small sore develops on the mouth, vagina, penis, or anus, where the bacteria that cause syphilis first entered the body. [5]The open, oozing sore is not painful. [6]The second stage begins within weeks or months after the sore goes away. [7]In this stage, the infected person breaks out in a rash and has flulike symptoms. [8]The rash may cover any or all of the body, including hands, feet, and groin. [9]One doctor called syphilis the "reptilian disease" because of the ugly black scabs that may form during this stage. [10]During both the first and second stages, syphilis is highly contagious. [11]After the second stage ends, the disease can lie hidden in the blood for as long as 40 years. [12]When it returns in its third stage, syphilis can be deadly. [13]It attacks organs and the nervous system. [14]It can cause a heart attack, paralysis, or even insanity. [15]Syphilis is curable in any of the three stages, yet whatever damage the disease has caused cannot be undone.

Main idea: Syphilis has three stages.

1. _____

    a. A small sore develops

    b. Open, oozing sores not painful

2. Second stage

    a. _____

    b. First and second stages highly contagious

    c. Hidden in the blood

3. _____

    a. Attacks organs and the nervous system

    b. Causes heart attack, paralysis, or even insanity

4. What signal word introduces the first major detail? _____

5. What signal word introduces the second major detail? _____

Application 2: Concept Maps and Signal Words

Read the following paragraph. Then complete the concept map with information from the paragraph and answer the questions.

Sitting Bull

[1]Sitting Bull was a notable Native American for two reasons. [2]First, Sitting Bull, leader of a Sioux tribe, won a key victory during one of the wars against the white man. [3]Sitting Bull brought together nearly 11,000 Sioux, Arapaho, and Cheyenne warriors at the Little Big Horn River in Montana. [4]In a bloody fight against the United States Army, Sitting Bull's warriors wiped out all of General Custer's 264 men. [5]Second, later in his life, Sitting Bull became a star in Buffalo Bill's Wild West Show. [6]Buffalo Bill's show included roundups, stagecoach robberies, and Indian fights. [7]Sitting Bull drew huge crowds, for many people were eager to see the famous Sioux warrior.

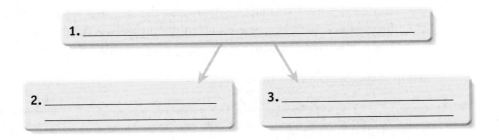

1. _____

2. _____   3. _____
   _____   _____

4. What signal word introduces the first major detail? _____

5. What signal word introduces the second major detail? _____

Application 3: A Textbook Table of Contents

Study the following detailed table of contents for Part I of *The Longman Handbook for Writers and Readers*. Then answer the questions.

1. What is the topic of Chapter 4? _____

2. How many subtopics are listed for Chapter 5? _____

3. On what page does the discussion about generating ideas begin? _____

   _____

4. What are the major supporting details of Chapter 2? _____

   _____

   _____

REVIEW **Test 1**

Outlines, Concept Maps, and Supporting Details

A. Read the paragraph. Then state a question based on the main idea, list the major supporting details from the paragraph, and answer the question.

Malcolm X

[1]Malcolm X has become a hero for several reasons. [2]First of all, he rose from humble but proud beginnings. [3]Born the seventh of 11 children to a Baptist minister, Malcolm X, whose name at birth was Malcolm Little, came from a modest background. [4]His father preached self-respect and black independence. [5]Next, Malcolm and his family faced many tragedies. [6]The local Ku Klux Klan, a hate group, ran the Little family out of Omaha, Nebraska. [7]When they moved to Lansing, Michigan, another hate group set fire to their home. [8]Malcolm's father rebuilt their home; the same men later murdered

him. [9]Six years old when his father died, Malcolm eventually dropped out of school and ended up serving time in prison. [10]Finally, he emerged as a national leader. [11]He became a Black Muslim, changed his last name from Little to X, and began to organize and educate African Americans.

Main idea: Malcolm X has become a hero for several reasons.

**Question based
on main idea:**   1. _____

Major supporting detail: 2. _____

Major supporting detail: 3. _____

Major supporting detail: 4. _____

5. What signal word introduces the last major detail? _____

B. Read the following paragraph. Then complete the concept map with information from the paragraph and answer the question.

Jeremy Getman

[1]Jeremy Getman's desire to kill his teenage peers represents the alarming social problem of teen-on-teen violence. [2]Jeremy's case demonstrates three aspects of this problem. [3]First, these violent teenagers seem to suffer from low self-esteem. [4]A very small number of teenage white males who did not seem to fit in at school or who may have had problems at home plotted revenge; they planned mass killings of their peers at school. [5]Jeremy, for example, saw himself as an outcast, saying, "Everyone hated me." [6]Second, these frustrated boys have access to weapons, and they are willing to use them. [7]Jeremy was caught with a duffel bag full of bombs and guns, and he admitted that he planned to shoot students and teachers and toss the bombs into crowds. [8]Finally, these violent youths may want to be stopped before they kill. [9]The potential killer usually offers hints about his plans before he carries them out. [10]Thankfully, Jeremy was stopped before he could hurt anyone because he passed a threatening note to a fellow student.

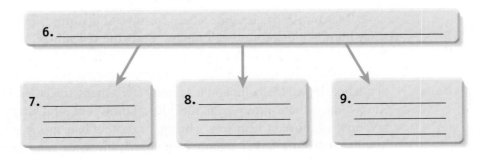

10. What signal word introduces the first major supporting detail? _____

_____

REVIEW **Test 2**

Supporting Details and Concept Maps

A. Read the following paragraph. Then complete the concept map by giving the main idea and the three major supporting details that are missing.

Stages of Grief

[1]Grief is a natural and healthy response to our loss of something or someone. [2]Elizabeth Kubler-Ross explains in her book *On Death and Dying* that grief occurs in stages, and understanding those stages helps us cope with our grief. [3]According to Kubler-Ross, grief has five stages. [4]The first stage of grief is *denial*. [5]At first, we tend to refuse to accept the reality of the loss. [6]Denial protects us from the shock of the loss until we are better able to cope. [7]The second stage is *anger*. [8]Anger results from feeling abandoned or helpless. [9]Sometimes resentment toward God or the one we lost takes first place in our emotions. [10] The third phase is the *bargaining* phase. [11]We may spend much time thinking about what we could have done differently to prevent the loss. [12]The fourth phase is *depression*. [13]Once we realize the depth of the loss, we often find we have trouble sleeping and concentrating. [14]Frequent crying jags and feelings of loneliness, emptiness, isolation, and self-pity often overtake us. [15]The fifth and final stage of grief is *acceptance*. [16]The sharp pain of grief lessens, and we begin to make plans for our future. [17]We learn to accept the new and different life that lies before us.

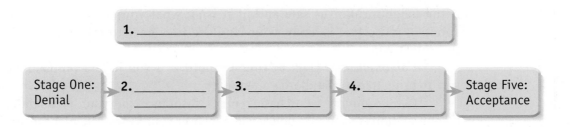

5. What signal words introduce the final major supporting detail? _____

_____

B. Read the following passage. Then complete the concept map using information from the passage.

Six Tips for Renters

[1]From finding the right place to beating out others who want the place to getting along with the landlord, renting can be tricky. [2]The following six tips should take some of the hassle out of finding and renting a home.

[3]*Be prepared!* [4]Bring the following papers with you when you meet prospective landlords, and you will have an edge over others: a filled-out rental application; written references from landlords, employers, friends, and colleagues; and a current copy of your credit report.

[5]*Read before signing!* [6]Carefully read the entire rental contract before you sign. [7]Your lease may have terms that you just can't live with; for example, there may be limits on the guests or pets you can have or on changes you can make in decorating. [8]Make sure you understand the security deposit refund policy.

[9]*Get everything in writing!* [10]Avoid quarrels with your landlord by getting everything in writing. [11]Keep copies of any correspondence, and follow up decisions made in person or over the phone with a letter. [12]For example, if you ask your landlord to make repairs, put your request in writing, and keep a copy for yourself. [13]If the landlord agrees verbally, send a letter to document your understanding.

[14]*Know your rights!* [15]You have the right to privacy. [16]A landlord must give you notice before entering your premises. [17]You have a right to a livable rental unit. [18]You have the right to heat, water, and electricity. [19]You have the right to live in a clean and safe building. [20]If your place is not properly kept up, you can keep part of the rent to pay for repairs, or you can move out without having to pay for future rent. [21]Ask if the neighborhood is safe and, if it isn't, what your landlord will do about it. [22]If crime is likely, your landlord may have to take some steps to protect you.

[23]*Communicate!* [24]Talk to your landlord. [25]If you have a problem, be sure to bring it to the landlord's attention.

[26]*Get insurance!* [27]Purchase renter's insurance for your belongings. [28]Your landlord's insurance policy will not cover your losses. [29]Renter's insurance typically costs $350 a year for a $50,000 policy that covers loss due to theft or damage caused by other people or natural disasters.

[30]Taking heed of these six tips should aid in the renting process.

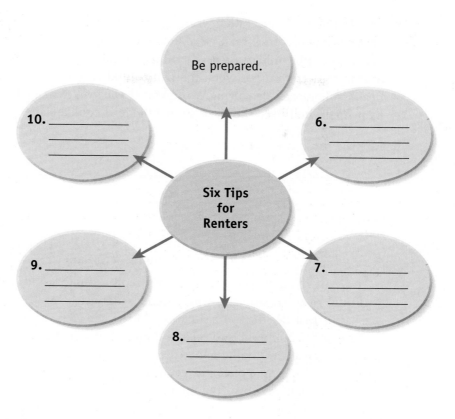

REVIEW Test 3

Major Supporting Details

Read each paragraph, and answer the questions that follow it.

Lies, Lies, Lies

[1]Even the best of us find ourselves telling a lie. [2]In fact, most of us have probably told at least one of three types of lies. [3]One kind of lie we tell is the "white lie." [4]We tell the white lie because we don't have faith in the person to whom we lie. [5]We do not believe that the person can bear to hear the truth, so we spare feelings by lying. [6]For example, when we tell a friend she looks good when she does not, we tell a white lie. [7]Another kind of lie we tell is the "face-saving lie." [8]The reason behind this lie is our need to look good to others and ourselves; low self-esteem leads us to think that others shouldn't know about our failure or that our best is not good enough. [9]In reality, when we tell a lie to make ourselves look good, we lie to ourselves, and we may begin to believe

our own lies. [10]Exaggerating work experience on a résumé is one example of a face-saving lie. [11]A third kind of lie is the "do-no-harm lie." [12]We tell this lie when the truth could cause devastating harm. [13]The need to tell this lie arises during those rare times when the truth could cost a life or damage mental health. [14]For example, during World War II, the lives of many Jews were saved by people who lied to the Nazis so that the Jews could escape.

What are the three types of lies we tell?

1. _____

2. _____

3. _____

The Warning Signs of Suicide

[1]Many of our young people are deeply troubled, and teenage suicide is on the rise. [2]To stop this tragic trend, we must be aware of the warning signs. [3]First, notice the teen's situation. [4]Stress can cause a young person with undeveloped coping skills to turn to thoughts of suicide. [5]The loss of a loved one, fear of academic failure, increased responsibilities, or a serious illness all cause stress. [6]Second, notice the teen's attitudes and emotions. [7]Inexperienced youth often fall victim to the intensity of their feelings. [8]Depression, guilt, rejection, and helplessness can seem never-ending, so suicide becomes a way to escape. [9]Finally, notice any changes in the teen's behavior. [10]An abrupt change in behavior offers a clear clue. [11]A suicidal teen may give away treasured belongings, withdraw from family and friends, have trouble sleeping, and slip in school performance.

What are the warning signs of teenage suicide?

4. _____

5. _____

6. _____

Three Benefits of Exercise

[1]Exercise benefits the aging mind, body, and spirit. [2]First, exercise helps the mind stay active longer. [3]Vigorous exercise three times a week lowers the risk of losing memory or developing Alzheimer's disease. [4]Even mild exercise helps the flow of blood to the brain. [5]The increase of blood flowing through the brain keeps brain cells alive and healthy. [6]Furthermore, exercise helps the

body work more effectively. [7]Exercise makes the immune system stronger, increases the appetite, and keeps muscles toned and strong. [8]Thus exercise will increase the chances of being healthy longer. [9]Finally, exercise helps the spirit. [10]Feeling and looking good add to a sense of well-being. [11]Remaining strong and independent makes life in the later years a true pleasure.

_____ **7.** Which sentence contains the main idea?

    a. sentence 1   c. sentence 3

    b. sentence 2   d. sentence 4

_____ **8.** Is sentence 5 a major detail or a minor detail?

    a. major detail

    b. minor detail

9. What signal word introduces the second major supporting detail? _____

_____

10. What signal word introduces the third major supporting detail? _____

_____

REVIEW Test 4

Supporting Details and Outlines

Before reading, skim the passage, and answer the Before Reading questions. Read the following passage, and answer the After Reading questions.

Vocabulary Preview

unfurls (2) opens up

hue (9) color, shade

origold (12) a color that has soft shades of orange, pink, and gold

marble (20) give a veined, spotty, or mottled look

silhouette (23) profile, outline

A Personal Journal

[1]In the struggle to stay in shape through daily walks and runs, I have discovered a beauty only to be found in nature. [2]In fact, twice a day, the sky **unfurls** a spectacle of **splendor**.

[3]First, the beauty of dawn makes a jog before daylight well worth the effort. [4]My daily run begins at 6:30 A.M. while the sky is still wrapped in the black of night. [5]On clear mornings, thousands of shimmering stars stud the darkness with a jeweled pattern. [6]On these mornings, the moon shows her many moods. [7]Sometimes she rides high as a silver smile; other times she hangs low and blushes with a coppery brilliance; sometimes she sits center sky, a full milky white globe, a glowing pearl. [8]Around 6:45 A.M., the sky

pulls up its dark hem, and first light begins to peek through at the **horizon**. [9]At first, a soft golden **hue** spreads across the edge of the earth where land and sky meet. [10]The velvet night begins to melt into morning's pale blue. [11]The night lights, the moon and the stars, slowly dim. [12]Soon ribbons of **origold** and pink thread through the trees and stretch across the sky. [13]As the sun's fiery head glides upward into sight, bright bands of orange and soft reds streak into the origold and pink ribbons. [14]The sky dances with a new day.

[15]Next, dusk holds a special charm that makes evening a beautiful time to enjoy my daily walk. [16]When the sun drops behind the treetops and the shadows stretch long across the lawn, the dazzle of the day's end is near, and my walk begins. [17]During the first 15 minutes, the sky's dome remains a pale blue. [18]At the same time, closer to earth, a brilliant white backlights the trees and tall buildings. [19]Rapidly, this bright white turns into shades of gold. [20]Across this background of white gold, veins of bronze, radiant pinks, and purples **mingled** with muted reds **marble** the sky. [21]Soon the sky turns a deep neon blue, and the moon and stars gleam softly. [22]Streetlights flicker on, and yellow lights from living rooms spill out of house windows. [23]The whole world moves in **silhouette**. [24]Finally, dusk ends as the sky throws her velvet black, star-studded cloak across the night.

BEFORE READING

Vocabulary in Context

_____   **1.** The word **splendor** in sentence 2 means
      a. brilliance.   c. hope.
      b. contrast.   d. joy.

_____   **2.** The word **horizon** in sentence 8 means
      a. future.   c. skyline.
      b. sliver.   d. bottom.

_____   **3.** The word **mingled** in sentence 20 means
      a. visited.   c. helped.
      b. mixed.   d. started.

AFTER READING

Main Ideas

_____   **4.** Which sentence best states the central idea of the selection?
      a. sentence 3   c. sentence 1
      b. sentence 2   d. sentence 15

_____   **5.** Which sentence contains the main idea of the third paragraph?

      a. sentence 15   c. sentence 17

      b. sentence 16   d. sentence 19

Supporting Details

6. Turn the main idea into a question: _____

_____

Now answer the question based on the main idea with the two major supporting details from the passage.

7. Major supporting detail:

_____

8. Major supporting detail:

_____

9. What signal word introduces the first major supporting detail? _____

10. What signal word introduces the second major supporting detail? _____

_____

SKILLED READER Scorecard

Outlines and Concept Maps

Test	Number Correct		Points		Score
Review Test 1	_____	×	10	=	_____
Review Test 2	_____	×	10	=	_____
Review Test 3	_____	×	10	=	_____
Review Test 4	_____	×	10	=	_____
Review Test 5 (website)	_____	×	10	=	_____
Review Test 6 (website)	_____	×	10	=	_____

Enter your scores on the Skilled Reader Scorecard: Chapter 7 Review Tests inside the back cover.

After Reading About Outlines and Concept Maps

Before you move on to the mastery tests on outlines and concept maps, take time to reflect on your learning and performance by answering the following questions. Write your answers in your notebook.

What did I learn about outlines and concept maps?

What do I need to remember about outlines and concept maps?

How has my knowledge base or prior knowledge about outlines and concept maps changed?

More Review and Mastery Tests

For more practice, go to the book's website at http://www.ablongman.com/henry and click on *The Skilled Reader*. Then select "More Review and Mastery Tests." You will find the tests listed by chapter.

A. Read the paragraph. The main idea is underlined. Complete the map by filling in the missing major and minor supporting details. You may use words and phrases instead of full sentences.

Four Major Biomes

[1]An ecosystem is made up of organisms living in a particular environment. [2]Major types of ecosystems that cover large regions are called *biomes*. [3]You can think of them as types of landscapes. [4]Most biomes are named for major physical or climatic features. [5]Four of the major biomes are tropical forests, savannas, deserts, and chaparrals. [6]First, tropical forests have layers of vegetation. [7]Trees in the canopy make up the topmost layer. [8]Another biome, savannas, are grasslands with scattered trees. [9]Third, deserts have sparse rainfall, and soil surface temperatures reach above 140° during the day. [10]Finally a fourth biome, chaparrals, occur in coastal areas with mild, rainy winters and long, hot, dry summers. [11]Dense, spiny, evergreen shrubs dominate a chaparral. [12]These four major biomes represent the great diversity of life on Earth.

—Adapted from Campbell, Neil A. and Jane
B. Reece. *Essential Biology*. Benjamin
Cummings, 2001., pp. 402–405.

1. _____

2. _____ 3. _____ 4. _____ 5. _____

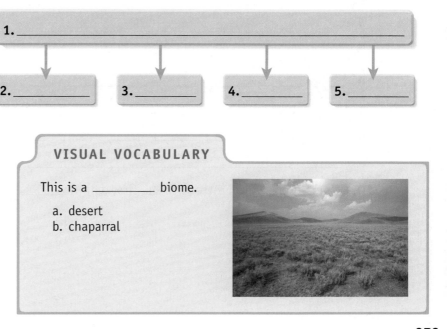

VISUAL VOCABULARY

This is a _____ biome.
a. desert
b. chaparral

B. Read the paragraph, and answer the questions that follow it.

Textbook
Skills

What Is Beauty?

[1]How are the women of the world defining beauty? [2]What do they really want to see as society continues to evolve? [3]A recent research study sponsored by Dove/Unilever company yields some interesting views of women about beauty. [4]For example, the study finds two-thirds of women strongly agree that physical attractiveness is about how one looks. [5]Yet, they also agree that beauty includes much more. [6]Women rate happiness, confidence, dignity, and humor as powerful components of beauty. [7]They also include the more traditional traits of physical appearance, body weight and shape, and even a sense of style. [8]The respondents also see beauty in many different forms. [9]According to the survey, beauty can be achieved through attitude, spirit, and other attributes that have nothing to do with physical appearance. [10]A woman can be beautiful at any age. [11]Finally, every woman has something about her that is beautiful.

—Adapted from "Only Two Percent of Women Describe
Themselves as Beautiful." Press Release by
Dove/Unilever of September 29, 2004.

What are some of the views of women about beauty?

6. _____

7. _____

_____

8. _____

_____

9. _____

_____

10. What signal words introduce the first detail? _____

Read the following paragraph. The main idea is underlined. Then complete the activities that follow the paragraph.

Kwanzaa: An African American Celebration

[1]Millions of African Americans celebrate Kwanzaa from December 26 until the first day of the new year. [2]Kwanzaa honors African roots, community, and family. [3]The holiday has two main goals. [4]First, the creator of the holiday, Ron Karenga, wanted American blacks to be proud of their African roots. [5]The word *Kwanzaa* is a term from Swahili (an East African language) that means "first" or "first fruits." [6]Many African villages set aside seven days of "first fruits" celebration to give thanks for a good harvest. [7]Just as the African holidays last seven days, so does Kwanzaa. [8]Second, each day of the holiday honors pride and service:

- [9]The first day teaches the value of unity. [10]African Americans come together in their family, community, nation, and race.
- [11]The second day is given to self-determination. [12]Self-determination teaches African Americans to know who they are and where they came from. [13]Then they can take control of their future.
- [14]The third day of Kwanzaa reminds people of collective work and responsibility. [15]By solving problems together, each and every person helps.
- [16]The fourth day teaches cooperative economics. [17]African American success comes by owning stores and businesses, and blacks must help one another succeed by shopping at these stores.
- [18]The fifth day teaches purpose. [19]The true purpose of each individual is to return black people to their greatness.

VISUAL VOCABULARY

The phrase "first fruits" in its original language comes from

_____.

   a. East Africa
   b. Kwanzaa

- [20]The sixth day teaches creativity. [21]Through creativity, humans can leave a place better than it was before.
- [22]The seventh day focuses on faith. [23]Kwanzaa teaches faith in black people: parents, teachers, and leaders. [24]Kwanzaa also teaches faith in the rightness and victory of the African American struggle.

Main idea: The holiday has two main goals.

Major supporting detail: _____

                                  _____

Minor supporting details: a.   _____

                                  _____

                             b.   Many African villages set aside seven days of "first fruits" celebrations to give thanks for a good harvest.
                             c.   Just as the African holidays last seven days, so does Kwanzaa.

Major supporting detail: _____

Minor supporting details: a.   The first day teaches the value of unity. Blacks come together in their family, community, nation, and race.

                             b.   _____
                                  Self-determination teaches African Americans to know who they are and where they came from. Then they can take control of their future.
                             c.   The third day of Kwanzaa reminds people of collective work and responsibility. By solving problems together, each and every person helps.
                             d.   The fourth day teaches cooperative economics. African American success comes by owning stores and businesses, and blacks must help one another succeed by shopping at these stores.
                             e.   The fifth day teaches purpose. The true purpose of each individual is to return black people to their greatness.
                             f.   The sixth day teaches creativity. Through creativity, humans can leave a place better than it was before.

                             g.   _____
                                  Kwanzaa teaches faith in black people: parents, teachers, and leaders. Kwanzaa also teaches faith in the rightness and victory of the African American struggle.

Read each textbook selection, and complete the activities that follow it.

Textbook
Skills

White Working-Class Families

[1]White working-class families are characterized by three factors: (1) the commitment to marry for love, not money; (2) the importance of extended kin; and (3) the separation of work and family. [2]First, working-class families marry for love. [3]In one research study, many blue-collar couples said they had married for love. [4]One young woman recalled, "We knew right away that we were in love. [5]We met at a school dance, and that was it." [6]The second trait of a working-class family is the reliance on extended kin. [7]These families rely on each other for meal sharing, baby-sitting, and small amounts of money. [8]Sometimes these extended kin relation-ships become a problem. [9]Many women complain about the struggle over who comes first, a man's wife or his mother. [10]For example, one woman said, "He used to stop off there at his mother's house on his way home from work, and that used to make me furious. [11]On top of that, they eat supper earlier than we do, so a lot of times, he'd eat with them. [12]Then he'd come home and I'd have a nice meal fixed, and he'd say he wasn't hungry. [13]Boy, did that make me mad." [14]The third trait of working-class families is the separation of work and family. [15]Blue-collar jobs do not include bringing work home. [16]And one's career does not carry over to one's identity in the way a middle-class professional's might.

—Adapted from Aulette, *Changing American Families*, pp. 121–22.

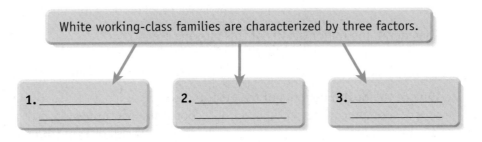

White working-class families are characterized by three factors.

1. _____
   _____

2. _____
   _____

3. _____
   _____

4. What signal words introduce the first major supporting detail? _____

5. What signal words introduce the last major supporting detail? _____

Textbook
Skills

Good Friends

[1]Good friends—they can make a boring day fun, a cold day warm, or a gut-wrenching worry disappear. [2]They can make us feel that we belong, that we matter, and that we have the strength to get through just about anything. [3]They can also make us angry, disappoint us, or se-riously jolt our own comfortable ideas about right and wrong. [4]No friendship is perfect, few are

fault-free, and most need careful attention if they are to remain stable over time. [5]Though we all know that friends enrich our lives, most people don't realize that real health benefits come from strong social bonds. [6]Social support has been shown to boost the immune system, improve the quality and possibly the length of life, and even reduce the risks of heart disease. [7]Good friends benefit us, so it is important to recognize the traits of a good friend. [8]Beyond the fact that two people are in a relationship as equals, friendships include the following traits.

- [9]*Enjoyment:* Friends enjoy each other's company most of the time. [10]Temporary states of anger, disappointment, or mutual annoyance may occur.
- [11]*Acceptance:* Friends accept each other as they are, without trying to change or make the other into a different person.
- [12]*Trust:* Friends share mutual trust. [13]Each assumes that the other will act in his or her friend's best interest.
- [14]*Respect:* Friends respect each other in the sense that each assumes that the other exercises good judgment in making life choices.
- [15]*Mutual assistance:* Friends are inclined to assist and support one another. [16]Specifically, they can count on each other in times of need, trouble, or personal distress.
- [17]*Confiding:* Friends share experiences and feelings with each other that they don't share with other people.
- [18]*Understanding:* Friends have a sense of what is important to each and why each behaves as he or she does. [19]Friends are not puzzled by each other's actions.
- [20]According to psychologist Dan McAdams, most of us are fortunate to develop one or two lasting friendships in a lifetime.

—Adapted from Donatelle, *Access to Health*, 7th ed., p. 131.

_____   **6.** In general, the major details of this passage are
      a. the reasons we make friends.   c. a study about how to make friends.
      b. the traits of good friends.   d. examples of problems with friends.

_____   **7.** One of the health benefits of friendship is to
      a. prevent cancer.   c. boost the immune system.
      b. shorten life.   d. reduce the risk of Lyme disease.

_____   **8.** "Friends are not puzzled by each other's actions" (sentence 19) is a
      a. major supporting detail.   b. minor supporting detail.

_____   **9.** According to the passage, friends
      a. feel free to play roles and wear masks.
      b. try to help each other become better people.
      c. never get angry at each other.
      d. share experiences and feelings with each other that they don't share with other people.

10. The answer to Question 9 can be found in sentence _____.

A. Read the passage, adapted from the college textbook *America and Its People.* Then answer the questions that follow it.

Textbook
Skills

Nancy Shippen

[1]Born in 1763, Nancy Shippen was to be admired for her beauty and her social graces rather than for her intellect. [2]She was an advantaged daughter in an upper-class family. [3]First and foremost, it was her duty to blossom into a charming woman. [4]Thus Nancy's schooling focused on skills that would please and entertain. [5]She learned how to dance, sing, play musical instruments, paint on fine china, and sew pretty pieces of needlework.

[6]In addition to being bound by duty, Nancy Shippen had two male tyrants in her life. [7]The first was her father, William, who in 1781 forced her to marry Henry Beekman Livingston, a man she did not love. [8]The man she did love wanted to know "for what reason in this free country a lady . . . must be married in a hurry and given up to a man she dislikes." [9]None of the Shippens answered him. [10]In truth, the answer was that Nancy legally belonged to her father until she became the property of her husband. [11]Her husband, Henry, was the second tyrant in her life. [12]The marriage was a disaster. [13]Henry was unfaithful. [14]Nancy took her baby daughter and moved back to her family. [15]She wanted full custody of the child, who by law was the property of her husband. [16]Henry made it clear that he would never give up his legal rights to his daughter, should Nancy embarrass him in public by seeking a divorce. [17]To keep her daughter, Nancy gave in. [18]Several years later, Henry changed his mind and arranged for a divorce, but by that time, Nancy's spirit was broken. [19]She lived unhappily, like a hermit, until her death in 1841. [20]The life of Nancy Shippen shows the fate that many women of her day faced.

—Adapted from Martin, et al., *America and Its Peoples:
A Mosaic in the Making,* 3rd ed., p. 184.

_____ **1.** Sentence 20 is
   a. the main idea.
   b. a major supporting detail.
   c. a minor supporting detail.

2. How does the life of Nancy Shippen show the fate that many women of her day faced?

   a. _____

   b. _____

_____ **3.** According to the passage, Henry Beekman Livingston was
         a. Nancy Shippen's loving son.
         b. Nancy Shippen's absent father.
         c. Nancy Shippen's tyrant husband.

_____ **4.** Sentence 5 is a
         a. major supporting detail.   b. minor supporting detail.

B. Read the paragraph, adapted from a health textbook. Create a map of the main idea and major supporting details by filling in the boxes. Then answer the questions that follow.

Textbook
Skills

Abetting Addiction

[1]The family and friends of an addict may suffer two main problems. [2]One major problem is codependency. [3]Codependence is a self-defeating relationship with the addict: A person is "addicted to the addict." [4]Codependence is not a single event but rather a pattern of behavior. [5]Codependents assume responsibility for meeting the needs of others. [6]Often the need to help others is so strong that they lose sight of their own needs. [7]Their need to help goes far beyond being kind to another person. [8]Codependents feel less than human if they fail to respond to the needs of someone else, even when their help was not sought. [9]A second main problem is the risk of becoming an enabler. [10]Enablers are people who protect addicts from the natural outcomes of their behaviors. [11]Without the benefit of having to deal with the effects of their addiction, addicts are unable to see the harm in their behavior. [12]Thus they continue the harmful behavior. [13]Codependents are the main enablers of their addicted loved ones. [14]But anyone who has contact with an addict can be an enabler and thus aid the addict in continuing the addiction. [15]Enablers are usually unaware that their behavior has this effect.

—Adapted from Donatelle, *Access to Health*, 7th ed., pp. 321–22.

5. _____

6. _____   **7.** _____

_____ **8.** According to the paragraph, enablers are "addicted to the addict."
         a. true   b. false

9. What signal words introduce the first supporting major detail? _____

_____

10. What signal words introduce the second major supporting detail? _____

_____

A. Read the paragraph, adapted from the college textbook *America and Its Peoples.* Then answer the questions that follow it.

Slave Life

Textbook
Skills

[1]It now seems clear that the life of a slave may have been even worse than the lives of the poorest, most downtrodden free laborers in the North and Europe. [2]In the nineteenth century, slaves remained much more likely than southern or northern whites to die prematurely, suffer malnutrition or dietary infections, or lose a child in infancy. [3]Three traits marked the life of slavery. [4]First, the slaves hardly ever varied their diet: They ate cornmeal, salt pork, and bacon. [5]Only rarely did slaves drink milk or eat fresh meat or vegetables. [6]This diet provided enough bulk calories so that slaves could work in the fields, but the diet did not supply nutritional needs. [7]Second, most slaves suffered poor health. [8]Plantation records reveal that over half of all slave babies died during their first year of life—a rate twice that of white babies. [9]Throughout their childhood, slaves were smaller than white children of the same age. [10]Moreover, most slaves only lived to be 21 or 22 years old. [11]Third, living conditions for the slaves were awful. [12]Lacking privies, slaves had to urinate and defecate in the cover of nearby bushes. [13]Chickens, dogs, and pigs lived next to the slave quarters. [14]Thus animal waste contaminated the area. [15]Slave quarters were cramped and crowded. [16]The typical cabin—a single room without a window—was about 10 feet by 10 feet to 21 feet by 21 feet. [17]These small cabins often held five, six, or more people.

—Adapted from Martin et al., *America and Its Peoples:*
A Mosaic in the Making, 3rd ed., p. 402.

_____ 1. The major supporting details of this paragraph are
   a. poor diet, poor health, and poor living conditions of slaves.
   b. examples from plantation records about slavery.
   c. descriptions of slaves.
   d. ways in which slave life improved in the nineteenth century.

_____ 2. How many major supporting details are contained in this passage?
   a. one   c. three
   b. two   d. four

3. What signal words introduce the major supporting details? _____

_____ 4. Sentence 3 is
   a. the main idea.   c. a minor supporting detail.
   b. a major supporting detail.

_____ 5. Sentence 13 is
   a. a major supporting detail.   c. the main idea.
   b. a minor supporting detail.

B. The following passage is from a science textbook. Remember, textbooks use **bold headings, subheadings,** and **bold print** to help you find the topics, main ideas, and supporting details.

Read the passage. Fill in the missing parts of the concept map with the ideas in bold print. Then answer the question that follows the map.

Textbook Skills

Some Basic Chemistry

[1]Taking any biological system apart, we always end up at the chemical level. [2]Let's now begin at this basic biological level by looking at the chemistry of life. [3]Imagination will help. [4]Try picturing yourself small enough to actually crawl into molecules and climb around on their atoms.

[5]Humans and other organisms and everything around them are all made of matter, the physical "stuff" of the universe. [6]Defined more formally, **matter** is anything that occupies space and has mass.

[7]Matter is composed of chemical elements. [8]A chemical **element** is a substance or matter that cannot be broken down into other matters. [9]There are 92 naturally occurring elements. [10]Examples of elements are gold, copper, carbon, and oxygen. [11]Each element has a symbol. [12]These symbols are made by taking the first letter or two of the English, Latin, or German name for each element. [13]For example, the symbol for gold, Au, is from the Latin word *aurum*; the symbol O stands for the English word *oxygen*. [14]Note that neither a rock nor a human body is an element. [15]Both rocks and humans can be decomposed—or broken down—into the many elements that make up "human matter" or "rock matter."

[16]Elements combine to form compounds. [17]A **compound** is two or more elements. [18]For example, table salt has equal parts of sodium and chlorine. [19]Most living creatures contain at least three or four different elements. [20]These elements are usually carbon, hydrogen, oxygen, and nitrogen.

—Adapted from Campbell & Reece, *Essential Biology,* p. 26.

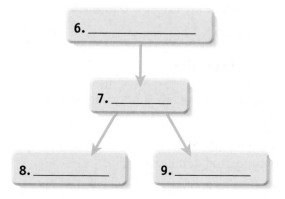

_____ **10.** According to the passage, a compound is made up of two or more elements.
    a. true   b. false

Name _____ Section _____

Date _____ Score (number correct) _____ × 20 = _____%

Read the paragraph, adapted from the textbook *Successful Nonverbal Communication*. Then answer the questions that follow it.

Textbook
Skills

Body Language

[1]Our bodies speak as loudly as our voices. [2]Bodily cues send messages about our openness, our likes and dislikes, and our sense of power. [3]First, openness is necessary to reach any kind of agreement. [4]Opening the hands, unbuttoning coats or loosening ties, and relaxing the body are all signs of openness. [5]In contrast, crossed arms and crossed legs are signs of being closed off, and the chances to reach agreement are slim. [6]Moreover, our bodies also let our likes and dislikes be known. [7]The need to be liked is common, and we tend to like those who like us. [8]Leaning forward, directly facing another person, keeping the body posture open, nodding the head, touching, smiling, and making eye contact are all signs of liking another person. [9]In contrast, not making eye contact, leaning away, and making an unpleasant face are signs of disliking another person. [10]In either case, we send out and pick up strong hints that affect our choices. [11]Finally, for many people, the need for power has a strong pull. [12]A relaxed body, precise gestures, steady and direct eye contact, touching, staring, and interrupting are all power cues. [13]In contrast, keeping the body tense, smiling too much, and making little or no eye contact signal weakness.

—Adapted from Leathers, *Successful Nonverbal
Communication: Principles and
Applications,* pp. 79–84.

_____ **1.** Sentence 2 is
     a. the main idea.
     b. a major supporting detail.
     c. a minor supporting detail.

_____ **2.** Sentence 6 is
     a. the main idea.
     b. a major supporting detail.
     c. a minor supporting detail.

_____ **3.** How many major supporting details does this paragraph give?
    a. one   c. three
    b. two   d. four

4. What signal words introduce the major supporting details? _____

_____

_____ **5.** According to the paragraph, which of the following are signs of openness?
    a. touching, staring, and interrupting (*sentence 12*)
    b. leaning forward, directly facing another person, keeping the body posture open, nodding the head, touching, smiling, and making eye contact (*sentence 8*)
    c. opening the hands, unbuttoning coats or loosening ties, and relaxing the body (*sentence 4*)

VISUAL VOCABULARY

This parent is displaying

_____

a. power cues.
b. weakness.

CHAPTER 8

Transitions and Thought Patterns

CHAPTER PREVIEW
Before Reading About Transitions and Thought Patterns
The Purpose of Transitions and Thought Patterns
Transition Words: Relationships Within a Sentence
Thought Patterns: Relationships Between Sentences
    The Time Order Pattern
    The Space Order Pattern
    The Listing Pattern
    The Classification Pattern
Textbook Skills: Transitions and Clear Information

Before Reading About Transitions and Thought Patterns

Refer to the chapter preview, and use the Reporter's Questions (such as What? and How?) to create at least three questions that you can answer as you study this chapter. Write your questions in the following spaces:

what are transitions ?

What are thought patterns ?

and how do they connect ?

Now take a few minutes to skim the chapter for ideas and terms that you have studied in previous chapters. List those ideas in the following spaces:

_____

_____

Compare the questions you created based on the chapter preview with the following questions. Then write the ones that seem the most helpful in your notebook, leaving enough space between each question to record the answers as you read and study the chapter.

What are transitions? What are thought patterns? What is the relationship between transition words and thought patterns? How do thought patterns use transition words?

On page 292, the terms *main idea, supporting details*, and *outlines* are discussed in relation to transitions and thought patterns. Consider the following study questions based on these ideas: How can transitions help me understand the author's main idea? How can transitions help me create an outline?

The Purpose of Transitions and Thought Patterns

Read the following set of ideas.

Overuse of painkillers can hurt you. *for example* , taking too much Tylenol over a long period of time can damage your liver.

What word or phrase makes the relationship between these two ideas clear?

 a. Also
 b. However
 c. For example

The phrase that makes the relationship between these two ideas clear is (c) *For example.* The first sentence offers a general idea. The second sentence offers an example for the general idea. The transition *for example* signals that Tylenol is an example of a painkiller that can hurt you if it is overused.

Transitions are key pattern words and phrases that signal the logical relationships within and between sentences. **Transitions** help you make sense of an author's idea in two basic ways. First, transitions join ideas within a sentence. Second, transitions establish **thought patterns** so readers can understand the logical flow of ideas between sentences.

> **Transitions** are words and phrases that signal thought patterns by showing the logical relationships within a sentence and between sentences.
> A **thought pattern** is established by using transitions to show the logical relationship between ideas in a paragraph or passage.

Transition Words: Relationships Within a Sentence

Transitions show how the ideas *within a sentence* are linked. Read the following sentences. Which words make the relationship of ideas within the sentence clear?

_____ **1.** "I love you, Ian, _*but*_____ you drive me crazy," Justine said.
    a. also   c. next
    b. but

_____ **2.** Danny's race car zoomed over the finish line _*while*_____ Rusty's car spun out of control and hit the wall.
    a. while   c. because
    b. for example

In the first sentence, the word that best states the relationship of ideas within the sentence is (b) *but.* The transition word *but* signals a contrast between the two ideas and helps us to understand that Justine loves Ian in spite of the fact that he drives her crazy. In the second sentence, the word that best states the relationship of ideas within the sentence is (a) *while.* The transition word *while* tells us when these two events occur in relationship to each other. Notice that these transition words link two ideas expressed in a single sentence. Transitions serve a vital role in building ideas within a sentence.

EXAMPLE   Complete the following ideas with a transition that shows the relationship within each sentence. Fill in each blank with a word from the box. Use each word once.

after	because	inside	such as

1. Every morning, I jog three miles _*after*_____ a ten-minute stretching routine.

2. The calm winds and blue skies _*inside*_____ the eye of a hurricane offer a peaceful lull between the violent storms in the hurricane's outer bands of rain and wind.

3. I quit drinking coffee _*because*_____ caffeine may speed up the aging process and cause weight gain.

4. Larissa has tried a variety of diet systems to lose weight _*such as*_____ Weight Watchers, Jenny Craig, the Atkins Diet, and even the Dr. Phil diet plan.

EXPLANATION

1. This sentence discusses two topics based on a time order relationship. The stretching routine happens first. Then *after* stretching, the writer jogs the three miles.

2. This sentence describes two traits of a hurricane based on space order (how the hurricane is arranged in space). The space order word *inside* signals where the calm winds, the blue sky, and the peaceful lull occur.

3. This sentence discusses three ideas: the author's decision to stop drinking coffee, aging, and weight gain. The ideas are linked to each other by a cause-and-effect relationship. Caffeine may cause early aging and weight gain. These possible effects of coffee caused the speaker to stop drinking coffee.

4. This sentence is about Larissa and the variety of weight loss systems she has tried. The transition *such as* signals a list of examples.

PRACTICE 1

Complete the following ideas with a transition that shows the relationship within each sentence. Fill in each blank with a word from the box. Use each word once.

because	even though	finally	in

1. After three follow-up phone calls, Nathan *finally* received the rebate the computer factory advertised.

2. Migraine headaches may occur *because* of certain foods, stress, or changes in weather, sleep patterns, or hormone levels.

3. To make sure that he could see the board and stay actively involved in class discussions, Andre claimed the center seat *in* the front row.

4. I don't want to go home *even though* I am extremely tired.

Transitions reveal a variety of relationships between ideas. Therefore, you must look carefully at the meaning of each transitional word or phrase. Sometimes the same words can serve as two different types of transitions, depending on how they are used. For example, the word *since* can reveal time order, or it can signal a cause. Notice the difference in the following two sentences.

Since *I got home from school, I have cleaned the apartment and completed my homework.*

Since *the baby is finally asleep, I am going to get some rest too.*

The relationship between the ideas in the first sentence is based on time order. The relationship between the ideas in the second sentence is based on cause and effect.

Some transition words have the same meaning. For example, *also, too,* and *furthermore* all signal the same relationship of addition or listing. Skilled readers look for signal words, study their meaning in context, and use them as keys to unlock the author's message.

Thought Patterns: Relationships Between Sentences

Not only do transitions reveal the relationship of ideas *within* a sentence, but they also show the relationship of ideas *between* sentences. Read the following sentence and choose the word that best states the relationship between the sentences.

> In a conversation, you receive feedback from yourself. You ___*also*___ receive feedback from others.

    a. in contrast   b. also   c. for example

VISUAL VOCABULARY

The best synonym for

feedback is ___*approval*___

  a. reaction.
  b. approval.

▲ Positive feedback tells the speaker he or she is doing well.

In this statement the word (b) *also* best signals the addition of the second idea. Transitions of **addition** signal that the writer is adding to an earlier thought. The writer presents an idea and then *adds* other ideas to deepen or clarify the first idea. Choice (a) *in contrast* signals a relationship based on contrast. Transitions of **contrast** indicate how two ideas differ. Choice (c) *for example* suggests a relationship based on examples. Transitions of **generalization and example** show that the first idea is a general statement and the second idea is an example of the first idea. Neither of these choices states the relationship of ideas in the two sentences.

In this chapter and Chapter 9, you will study the various ways in which authors use these and other transitions and thought patterns in paragraphs and passages. First, it is important to learn to read for the relationships **between** sentences.

EXAMPLE Complete each of the following items with a transition that makes the relationship between sentences clear. Fill in each blank with a word or phrase from the box. Use each word or phrase once.

another	as a result	first	for example

1. One basic human need is the need to be forgiven when we are sorry for

   our wrongs. _____ need is to forgive others who wrong us.

2. For your brain to function at its best, you should eat a variety of health-

   ful foods. _____, your diet should include eggs, wheat, salmon, green leafy vegetables, apples, bananas, lean meats, and plenty of water.

3. A significant number of citizens of this country do not register to vote.

   _____, they do not have a voice in the democratic process.

4. You can improve your vocabulary in a two-step process. _____, notice new and difficult words as you read; then look up these words in a dictionary.

EXPLANATION

1. The relationship between sentences is addition. The word *one* indicates that the first of two or more ideas is going to be discussed. The word *another* signals the addition of a second need.

2. The first sentence states a general idea. The phrase *for example* signals that specific examples will follow.

3. The fact stated in the second sentence occurs because of the fact stated in the first sentence. The phrase *as a result* states the cause-and-effect relationship between the sentences.

4. The relationship between these sentences is based on time order. The first sentence states the idea that vocabulary can be improved in two steps. The second sentence states the two steps. The transition word *first* signals the first step.

PRACTICE 2

Fill in each blank with a transition from the box that makes the relationship between sentences clear. Use each word or phrase once.

for example	however	now
then	since	still

Banning baseball caps during tests was obvious. Students were writing the answers under the brim. (**1**) _____, schools started banning cell phones, realizing students could text message the answers to each other. (**2**) _____, schools across the country are targeting digital media players as a potential cheating device. (**3**) _____, devices including iPods and Zunes can be hidden under clothing, with just an earbud and a wire snaking behind an ear and into a shirt collar to give them away, school officials say. "It doesn't take long to get out of the loop with teenagers," said Mountain View High School Principal Aaron Maybon. "They come up with new and creative ways to cheat pretty fast." Using the devices to cheat is hardly a new phenomenon, Kemp said. (**4**) _____, sometimes it takes awhile for teachers and administrators, who come from an older generation, to catch on to the various ways the technology can be used. Kelsey Nelson, a 17-year-old senior at the school, said she used to listen to music after completing her tests. (**5**) _____ the ban, she can no longer do so. (**6**) _____, she said, the ban has not stopped some students from using the devices.

—Adapted from Rebecca Boone, "Schools Banning iPods to Beat Cheaters," Associated Press, April 27, 2007. Copyright © 2007 by The Associated Press. All rights reserved. Reprinted with permission

You will recall that a paragraph is made up of a group of ideas. Major details support the main idea, and minor details support the major details. Transitions make the relationship between these three levels of ideas clear, smooth, and easy to follow.

Before beginning to write, an author must ask, "How should these ideas be organized so that the reader can follow and understand my point?" A **thought pattern** (also called a **pattern of organization**) allows the author to arrange the supporting details in a clear and smooth flow by using transition words.

> **Thought patterns** (or **patterns of organization**) are signaled by using transitions to show the logical relationship between ideas in a paragraph, passage, or textbook chapter.

Read the following heading taken from a college communications textbook:

Speaker Cues in Conversation

This heading clearly states the author's purpose: to explain the cues speakers use in conversations. Now read the following topic sentence about the topic "speaker cues in conversations."

A speaker controls the conversation with two cues.

A main idea (topic sentence) is made up of a topic and the author's controlling point about the topic. One way an author controls the topic is by using a specific thought pattern. This topic sentence clues the reader that the author is going to explain two cues a speaker uses to control conversation. A skilled reader can now skim ahead and look for the two cues. This sentence shows the close tie between an author's purpose, the topic, and the thought pattern, for this paragraph will list and explain the two cues. The thought pattern used here is listing. In this chapter we discuss four common thought patterns and the transition words and phrases used to signal each one:

- The time order pattern
- The space order pattern
- The listing pattern
- The classification pattern

Chapter 9 covers some additional common thought patterns.

The Time Order Pattern

The **time order** thought pattern generally shows a chain of events. The actions or events are listed in the order that they occur. This is called **chronological order**. Two types of chronological order are narration and process. An author uses narration to tell about the important events in the life of a famous person or during a significant event in history. The narration time order is also used to organize a piece of fiction. The second type of time or chronological order is process. Authors use process to give directions to a task using time order. In summary, there are two basic uses of time order: (1) narration: a chain of events and (2) process: steps, stages, or directions.

Narration: A Chain of Events

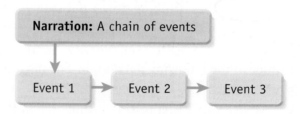

Transitions of **time** signal that the writer is describing when something occurred and in what order. The writer presents an event and then shows when each of the additional details or events flowed from the first event. Thus the details follow a logical order based on time.

Transitions Used in Narration: A Chain of Events				
after	eventually	later	over time	then
afterward	finally	meanwhile	previously	ultimately
as	first	next	second	until
before	in the end	now	since	when
currently	last	often	soon	while
during				

Harriet Tubman, a runaway slave, led hundreds of slaves to freedom over the course of 10 years; later, during the Civil War, she was a spy for the federal forces in South Carolina as well as a nurse.

Notice that this sentence narrates a chain of events in the life of Harriet Tubman. Transition words and phrases (*over the course, later, during*) tell when each event occurred.

EXAMPLES   Determine a logical order for the following three sentences. Write **1** by the sentence that should come first, **2** by the sentence that should come second, and **3** by the sentence that should come last. Circle the narration transition words.

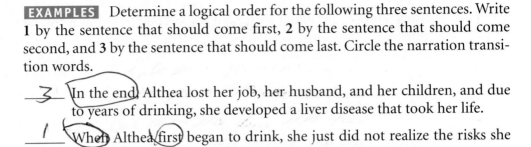

___3___   In the end, Althea lost her job, her husband, and her children, and due to years of drinking, she developed a liver disease that took her life.

___1___   When Althea first began to drink, she just did not realize the risks she faced.

___2___   Over time, her drinking slowly but surely took total control of her life.

EXPLANATIONS   Compare your answers to the sentences arranged in the proper order in the following paragraph. The narration transition words are in **bold** print.

> **When** Althea **first** began to drink, she just did not realize the risks she faced. **Over time,** her drinking slowly but surely took total control of her life. **In the end,** Althea lost her job, her husband, and her children, and due to years of drinking, she developed a liver disease that took her life.

PRACTICE 3

Determine a logical order for the following four sentences. Write **1** by the sentence that should come first, **2** by the sentence that should come second, **3** by the sentence that should come third, and **4** by the sentence that should come fourth. Circle the time transition words.

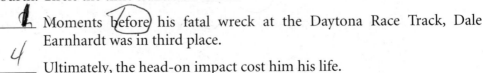

___1___   Moments before his fatal wreck at the Daytona Race Track, Dale Earnhardt was in third place.

___4___   Ultimately, the head-on impact cost him his life.

___2___   At that time, he was moving up and down the track to keep the cars behind him from passing.

___3___   Then, suddenly, on the fourth turn, his car shot straight up the bank and into the wall.

Process: Steps, Stages, or Directions

The time order pattern for steps, stages, or directions shows actions that can be repeated at any time with similar results. This pattern is used to give directions.

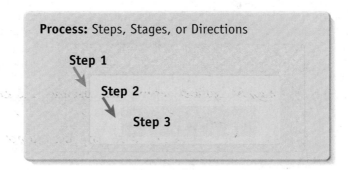

Read the following topic sentences. Circle the words that signal process time order.

1. Follow five simple steps to create an online identity and password for your email account.

2. Alcoholism is a cycle of self-destruction.

3. Learning occurs in several phases.

Sentence 1 uses the words *steps* and *create* to introduce a series of directions for the reader to follow. Sentence 2 signals that alcoholism occurs in phases with the use of the word *cycle*. Sentence 3 uses the process signal word *phases* combined with the action verb *occurs* to convey the time order of learning. In paragraphs developing these topic sentences, transitions of time order will likely signal the supporting details.

Transitions Used in the Process: Steps, Stages, or Directions				
after	during	later	previously	ultimately
afterward	eventually	meanwhile	second	until
as	finally	next	since	when
before	first	now	soon	while
currently	last	often	then	

EXAMPLE   The paragraph that follows uses the time order pattern of process to organize its ideas. Complete the list of steps that follows it by giving the missing details in their proper order. Circle the process transition words.

How to Change a Tire

To change a tire safely, first, be sure your car is on level ground. Next, place the car jack under the frame of the car near the tire that needs to be changed. Then, before you use the jack to lift the wheel off the ground, loosen the lug nuts on the tire one-half turn.

How to Change a Tire

Step 1: *first, be sure your car is on level ground*

Step 2: *Next, place the car jack under the frame of the car near the tire that needs to be change*

Step 3: *you use the jack to lift the wheel off the ground*

Step 4: *loosen the lug nuts on the tire one-half turn*

EXPLANATION Compare your answers to the following:

Step 1: Be sure your car is on level ground.

Step 2: Place the jack under the frame of the car near the tire that needs to be changed.

Step 3: Loosen the lug nuts on the tire one-half turn.

Step 4: Use the jack to lift the wheel off the ground.

PRACTICE 4

The following paragraph uses the time order thought pattern. Complete the list of steps that follows it by giving the missing details in their proper order. Circle the process transition words.

Tattoo Care

[1]Tattoos require proper care. [2]First, ask your artist for care tips, and follow those steps carefully. [3]When the tattoo is brand new, leave the bandage on for two to ten hours. [4]Next, using only your hands, wash your tattoo with mild soap twice a day. [5]After you wash, pat it dry with a clean towel. [6]During the first several days, apply a thin coat of an antibacterial ointment. [7]After several days, use a lotion after you wash. [8]No matter what, do not scratch! [9]When your tattoo itches, tap it lightly. [10]No matter what, do not pick at your tattoo! [11]When it peels, apply lotion and leave it alone. [12]Once your tattoo heals completely, use sunblock when outdoors. [13]Finally, have an artist touch up your tattoo every few years to keep it fresh and beautiful.

Steps to Care for Your Tattoo

1. Ask the artist for care tips.

2. Leave the bandage on for two to ten hours.

3. Wash the tattoo with hands and mild soap.

4. _____

5. _____

6. Use lotion.

7. Do not scratch; tap lightly.

8. _____

9. _____

10. _____

11. Touch it up every few years.

The Space Order Pattern

The **space order pattern** allows authors to describe a person, place, or thing based on its location or the way it is arranged in space. In the space order pattern, also known as spatial order, the writer often uses descriptive details to help readers create vivid mental pictures of what the writer is describing. An author may choose to describe an object from top to bottom, from bottom to top, from right to left, from left to right, from near to far, from far to near, from inside to outside, or from outside to inside.

> **Space Order: Descriptive Details**
>
> Descriptive detail 1 ➡ Descriptive detail 2 ➡ Descriptive detail 3

Transition words of **space order** signal that the details follow a logical order based on two elements: (1) how the object, place, or person is arranged in space, and (2) the starting point from which the author chooses to begin the description.

Transition Words Used in the Space Order Pattern						
above	at the side	below	center	front	middle	there
across	at the top	beneath	close to	here	nearby	under
adjacent	back	beside	down	in	next to	underneath
around	back up	beyond	far away	inside	outside	within
at the bottom	behind	by	farther	left	right	

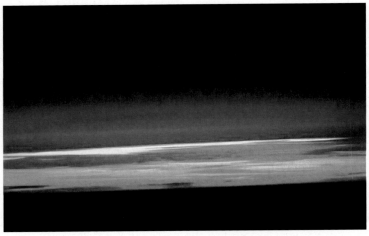

—Image courtesy of Earth Sciences and Image Analysis Laboratory,
NASA Johnson Space Center. (ISS001:421:24)
http://eol.jsc.nasa.gov.

EXAMPLE   Study the picture. Then fill in each blank with the best word based on space order.

around	bottom	on	side
at	from	over	

Some of the most breathtaking views of Earth taken (**1**) _____ space are those that capture our planet's limb. When viewed from the (**2**) _____, the Earth looks like a flat circle, and the atmosphere appears like a halo (**3**) _____ it. This glowing halo is known as the limb. This image shows the Earth's limb captured by astronauts (**4**) _____ the International Space Station. This picture is a view of the limb at sunset. The surface of the Earth appears as a dark area (**5**) _____ the (**6**) _____ with the blackness of outer space draped (**7**) _____ the limb.

EXPLANATION   Compare your answers to the completed paragraph.

Earth's Limb

Some of the most breathtaking views of Earth taken from space are those that capture our planet's limb. When viewed from the side, the Earth looks like a flat circle, and the atmosphere appears like a halo around it. This glowing halo is known as the limb. This image shows the Earth's limb captured by astronauts on the International Space Station. This picture is a view of the limb at sunset. The surface of the Earth appears as a dark area at the bottom with the blackness of outer space draped over the limb.

PRACTICE 5

Fill in each blank in the paragraph with the best word based on space order.

Mangrove Trees

Mangroves are one of Florida's true natives. They thrive (**1**) _____ salty environments because they are able to obtain fresh-water (**2**) _____ saltwater. Different species do this in a variety of ways. Some secrete excess salt (**3**) _____ their leaves while others block absorption of salt (**4**) _____ their roots.

—"Mangroves." Florida Keys National Marine
Sanctuary. 23 September 2004.

The Listing Pattern

Often authors want to list a series or set of reasons, details, or points that support the main idea. Transitions of addition, such as *and, also,* and *furthermore,* are generally used to indicate a **listing pattern**.

Listing Pattern
Idea 1
Idea 2
Idea 3

Many people use the Internet to pay bills *and* shop for goods. *In addition,* people turn to the Internet as a source of information.

Notice that in these sentences, two transitions signal the addition of ideas: *and* and *in addition.* Transitions of addition signal that the writer is adding another idea to an earlier thought.

Addition Transitions Used in the Listing Pattern				
also	final	for one thing	last	one
and	finally	furthermore	moreover	second
another	first	in addition	next	third
besides	first of all			

EXAMPLES   Refer to the box of addition transitions used in the listing pattern. Complete the following paragraph with transitions that show the appropriate relationship between sentences.

Latinos have excelled as television hosts and news commentators. _____, Geraldo Rivera is one of the most recognized faces in the media. He has worked as a reporter for WABC-TV, chief reporter on *20/20.* He has hosted his own national daytime talk show, *The Geraldo Rivera Show,* and now appears as a correspondent for the Fox News Channel. _____ successful correspondent is Elizabeth Vargas. She worked as a substitute anchor with NBC before joining ABC News' *Good Morning America.* She has been its news anchor since 1996. _____, Giselle Fernandez covered international news stories and major events for CBS and NBC. She has earned five Emmys for her outstanding work.

EXPLANATIONS   Compare your answers to the following paragraph. The addition transition words are in **bold** print.

Latinos have excelled as television hosts and news commentators. **First,** Geraldo Rivera is one of the most recognized faces in the media. He has worked as a reporter for WABC-TV, chief reporter on *20/20.* He has hosted his own national daytime talk show, *The Geraldo Rivera Show,* and now appears as a correspondent for the Fox News Channel. **Another** successful correspondent is Elizabeth Vargas. She worked as a substitute anchor with NBC before joining ABC News' *Good Morning America*. She has been its news anchor since 1996. **Finally**, Giselle Fernandez covered international news stories and major events for CBS and NBC. She has earned five Emmys for her outstanding work.

This paragraph began with a general idea, followed by two major supporting details. Each detail required a transition to show addition.

PRACTICE 6

This paragraph uses the listing thought pattern. Complete the chart that follows it by giving the missing details in their proper order. Circle the addition transition words in the paragraph.

[1]How many times have you heard the warning "You can't judge a book by its cover?" [2]This saying is so overused that it has become just another one of thousands of clichés, and many clichés don't make a lick of sense. [3]Some of the silliest clichés refer to animals. [4]First, bugs are quite popular in senseless clichés. [5]"Snug as a bug in a rug" is supposed to express comfort, and "Don't let the bedbugs bite" is a way of saying, "Sleep well." [6]In addition, "crazy as a June bug" means crazy, but just how crazy is a June bug? [7]Bulls are also used in some pretty silly clichés. [8]To begin with, a "cock and bull story" is an untrue story, and "to shoot the bull" is to get together and talk. [9]Finally, the saying "like a bull in a china shop" refers to someone who is vigorous but clumsy. [10]When would anyone let a bull in a china shop? [11]It makes you wonder how these sayings got started.

Silly Animal Clichés

Bug clichés	Bull clichés
1. Snug as a bug in a rug	1. Cock and bull story
2. _____	2. _____
3. _____	3. _____

The Classification Pattern

Authors use the **classification pattern** to sort ideas into smaller groups and describe the traits of each group. Each smaller group, called a **subgroup,** is based on shared traits or characteristics. The author lists each subgroup and describes its traits.

Because groups and subgroups are listed, transitions of addition are used in this thought pattern. These transitions are coupled with words that indicate classes or groups. Examples of classification signal words are *first type, second kind,* and *another group.*

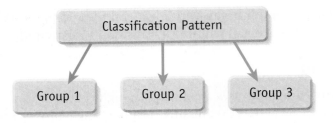

Transitions Used in the Classification Pattern	
another (group, kind, type)	first (group, kind, type)
categories	order
characteristics	second (group, kind, type)
class	traits

EXAMPLE   Determine a logical order for the following three sentences. Write **1** by the sentence that should come first, **2** by the sentence that should come second, and **3** by the sentence that should come last. Circle the addition and classification words.

_____ The second type of access is high-speed broadband through the TV cable line or high-speed DSL through fiber optic phone lines.

_____ The first type of access to the Internet is the old-fashioned phone line, which is quite slow.

_____ Internet users have two types of access choices for surfing the Web.

EXPLANATION   Compare your answers to the sentences arranged in the proper order in the following paragraph. The classification words are in **bold** print.

Internet users have **two types** of access choices for surfing the Web. The **first type** of access to the Internet is the old-fashioned phone line, which is quite slow. The **second type** of access is high-speed broadband through the TV cable line or high-speed DSL through fiber optic phone lines.

In the paragraph, transitions of addition combine with the classification signal word *type.* In this case, *first* and *second* set the order of discussion for the types listed.

PRACTICE 7

This paragraph uses the classification thought pattern. Complete the concept map that follows it by giving the missing details in their proper order. Circle the classification and addition transition words in the paragraph.

Offensive Players

^{1}Several types of players make up the offense of a football team. ^{2}The offense is the unit of the team that moves the ball up the field to score points. ^{3}The first type is the center. ^{4}The center takes his place at the center of the offensive line. ^{5}As the first player to touch the football, he bends over the ball as it lies on the ground and snaps it to the quarterback. ^{6}The second type of player is the quarterback; he takes the ball from the center and can either pass, run, or hand the ball off to another player. ^{7}Most often, he works hard to get the ball into the hands of his offensive teammates. ^{8}Since he is the driving force of the offensive line, he is protected by the other players. ^{9}The third type of player on the offense is the guard. ^{10}There are two guards, one on either side of the center; their job is to keep the other team's players away from the quarterback so he can have time to pass or run with the ball. ^{11}The fourth type of offensive player is the tackle. ^{12}Tackles are two players who line up next to the guards. ^{13}Their main job is not really to tackle but to block for the quarterback or for any offensive player who has the ball. ^{14}A fifth type of offensive lineman is the tight end. ^{15}The two tight ends line up on each end of the offensive line. ^{16}A tight end not only blocks for other offensive players, but also is allowed to catch passes thrown by the quarterback. ^{17}A sixth type of offensive lineman is the wide receiver. ^{18}Wide receivers are placed on either side of the offensive line. ^{19}Wide receivers run down the field to catch the football when the quarterback throws to them and then run as far as they can without being tackled. ^{20}The final type of offensive player is the running back. ^{21}The two running backs line up in the back of the offensive line and carry the ball on most running plays; they are also allowed to receive catches. ^{22}When all eleven offensive players do each of their jobs well, football is exciting to watch.

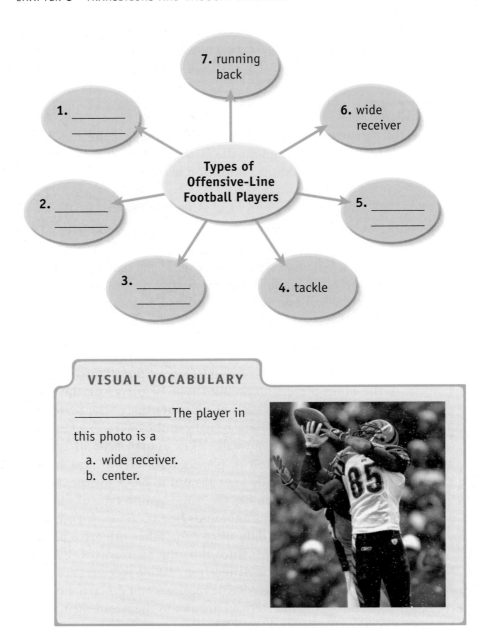

Types of Offensive-Line Football Players

7. running back

1. _____ _____

6. wide receiver

2. _____ _____

5. _____ _____

3. _____ _____

4. tackle

VISUAL VOCABULARY

_____The player in this photo is a

a. wide receiver.
b. center.

Textbook Skills

Transitions and Clear Information

Textbook authors try to make information very clear and understandable. Often they use transitions to make relationships between ideas clear.

EXAMPLES Read each of the following paragraphs, taken from college history, science, and social science textbooks. Circle the transitions used in each paragraph. Then identify the type of organizational thought pattern used in each paragraph.

William Bradford, the First Pilgrim

Throughout his life, William Bradford (1590–1657) was a humble man. Early in life, he dedicated his life to serving the will of God. When he was a baby on a farm in England, his father died. After his mother remarried, his grandfather raised him to become a farmer. By the age of 12, William was an eager reader and focused his studies on the Bible. To his family's shame, he soon started worshiping with separatists in a nearby town. Later, in 1608, he was among the first Pilgrims who went to Holland in search of religious freedom.

—Adapted from Martin et al., *America and Its Peoples: A Mosaic in the Making*, 3rd ed., p. 49.

_____ **1.** The thought pattern of the paragraph is
   a. time order.
   b. classification.
   c. listing.

Two Types of Carbohydrates

There are two major types of carbohydrates: **simple sugars** and **complex carbohydrates**. The first type, simple sugars, is found mainly in fruits. The second type, complex carbohydrates, is found in several kinds of foods. One kind of complex carbohydrate is made up of grains and cereals. Another kind includes vegetables and fruits. Dark green leafy vegetables and yellow fruits and vegetables like carrots and yams are in this group. Most of us do not get enough complex carbohydrates in our diets. A typical diet contains large amounts of simple sugars.

—Donatelle, *Access to Health*, 7th ed., p. 226.

_____ **2.** The thought pattern of the paragraph is
   a. time order.
   b. classification.
   c. listing.

How to Stay Young

Leroy "Satchel" Paige was the oldest baseball player, age 59. He pitched three scoreless innings in 1965 for the Kansas City Athletics. When asked about the secret of a good old age, Paige gave six rules for staying young. "First, avoid fried meats which angry up the blood. Second, if your stomach disputes you, lie down and pacify it with cool thoughts. Third, keep the juices flowing by jangling around gently as you move. Fourth, go very lightly on the vices, such as carrying on in society. The social ramble ain't restful. Fifth, avoid running at all times. And sixth, don't look back. Something might be gaining on you."

—Novak, *Issues in Aging: An Introduction to Gerontology,* p. 15.

_____ **3.** The thought pattern of the paragraph is
    a. time order.
    b. classification.
    c. listing.

EXPLANATIONS   Compare your answers to the ones that follow:

The paragraph in example 1 uses time order to relay biographical information about an historical figure, William Bradford. Notice the use of time order transitions such as "throughout," "when," and "later."

The paragraph in example 2 uses the classification thought pattern. The title uses one of the classification signal words, which is "types." The purpose of the paragraph is to describe the different types and traits of carbohydrates. Some of the classification transition phrases used include "the first type," "another type," and "group."

The paragraph in example 3 uses the listing pattern to offer advice about staying young. The author suggests behaviors, but these behaviors do not have to be completed in a certain order or in a specific time frame, so the pattern of organization is not time order.

PRACTICE **8**

Textbook
Skills

Read the following paragraph from a college communications textbook. Circle the transitions. Then identify the type of organizational thought pattern used in the paragraph.

Types of Media

The mass media fall broadly into two groups with certain traits in common but with unlike physical features. The first group is print. Print includes newspapers, magazines, newsletters, and books. Their words create images in the mind as well as give information. The second type is made up of electronics and film. This group includes radio, recordings, television, still and motion pictures, and video. These media create images by using the senses of seeing and hearing.

—Agee, Ault, & Emery, *Introduction to Mass Communications*, 12th ed., p. 6.

_____ The thought pattern of the paragraph is
    a. time order.
    b. classification.
    c. listing.

Chapter Review

Test your understanding of what you have read in this chapter by filling in each blank with a word or phrase from the box.

adjacent	listing	thought pattern	transitions
classification	space order	time order	when
first type	steps		

1. _____ are words and phrases that signal thought patterns by showing the logical relationship within a sentence and between sentences.

2. A _____ is established by using transitions to show the logical relationship between ideas in a paragraph or passage.

3. Narration and process are two uses of the _____ thought pattern.

4. Transitions of time signal that the writer is describing _____ something occurred.

5. In addition to showing a chain of events, the time order pattern is used to show _____, stages, or directions that can be repeated at any time with similar results.

6. Transitions of addition, such as *and*, *also*, and *furthermore*, are generally used to indicate a _____ pattern.

7. Authors use the _____ pattern to sort ideas into smaller groups and describe the traits of each group.

8. Examples of classification signal words are _____, *second kind,* or *another group.*

9. The _____ pattern allows authors to describe a person, place, or thing based on its location or the way it is arranged in space.

10. Some of the words used to establish the space order pattern include _____, *below,* and *underneath.*

Applications

Application 1: Identifying Transitions

Fill in each blank with a word or phrase from the box. Use each answer once.

also	and	eventually	in addition	next

1. Jonathan Moore is a good father. He is taking a full load of classes, works two jobs, _____ still manages to make all of his son's football games.

2. As toddlers, people fight to do things for themselves and begin to love the word *mine.* The _____ time they struggle with the same need for control and self-identity is when they are teenagers.

3. The fire ant is thought of as a painful pest, but some ants _____ eat insects and are used as helpful protectors of crops.

4. Cell phones and beepers are two ways that workers stay closely connected to their customers and bosses; _____, e-mail has helped make the workday much more productive.

5. For a long time, Sarah believed that John Powers was the ideal man; _____, she found out that he was greedy and self-centered.

Application 2: Identifying Transitions

Fill in each blank with one of the words from the box. Use each word once.

another	besides	first	into	third

1. One way to overcome boredom is by turning on the television. _____ way is to read a good book.

2. _____ taking time to housebreak a dog to the outdoors, dog owners sometimes paper-train their pets.

3. While the family was away on vacation, a burglar broke _____ their house and carted off their televisions and sound systems.

4–5. Hurricanes have three phases. The _____ phase is the front of the storm; the second phase is the calm eye, and the _____ phase is the back of the storm.

Application 3: Identifying Thought Patterns

Identify the thought pattern suggested by each of the following topic sentences.

_____ **1.** Three kinds of parenting styles show a wide range of behaviors.
   a. classification   b. time order

_____ **2.** A few simple steps can cut your cost of living and save you money.
   a. classification   b. time order

_____ **3.** There are several reasons to include low-impact exercises in your daily routine.
   a. listing   b. classification

_____ **4.** Mike Tyson rose from the streets to become a prize-winning boxer.
   a. time order   b. listing

_____ **5.** Drivers should sit 10 to 12 inches from the steering wheel to allow the air bag to inflate toward the chest and away from the face and neck.
   a. space order   b. classification

_____ **6.** The body of an insect has three distinct parts.
      a. listing   b. time order

_____ **7.** Five simple steps can lead to effective communication.
      a. time order   b. listing

_____ **8.** The Trail of Tears, the forced removal of Cherokees, began in Tennessee, Georgia, and North Carolina and ended in Oklahoma.
      a. space order   b. time order

_____ **9.** Certain characteristics usually lead to student success in college.
      a. classification   b. time order

_____ **10.** Understanding how the circulatory system works is a basic required unit of study in medical training programs.
      a. listing   b. time order

REVIEW Test 1

Transition Words

Match each of the thought patterns to the appropriate group of transition words. Thought patterns will be used more than once.

a. time order   _____ **1.** one kind, several groups, another type

b. space order   _____ **2.** first, second, third, fourth

c. listing   _____ **3.** before, after, while, during

d. classification   _____ **4.** in, on, next to, over

                                 _____ **5.** presently, as, ultimately

                                 _____ **6.** in addition, as well, besides

                                 _____ **7.** characteristics, traits, order

                                 _____ **8.** below, nearby, within

                                 _____ **9.** here, there

                                 _____ **10.** and, also, for one thing

REVIEW Test 2

Transition Words

Read the passage. Some of the transition words are in bold print. Identify the relationship between ideas signaled by each transition word by filling in the blanks that follow the paragraph.

Capillary Action and the Physical Nature of Water

[1]Capillary action is important for moving water (and all of the things that are dissolved in it) around. [2]It is defined as the movement of water **within** the spaces of a porous material. [3]Capillary action is due to the forces of adhesion, cohesion, **and** surface tension.

[4]Capillary action occurs because water is sticky. [5]Water molecules stick to each other. [6]They also stick to other substances, such as glass, cloth, organic tissues, and soil. [7]Dip a paper towel into a glass of water and the water will "climb" onto the paper towel. [8]In fact, it will keep going up the towel **until** the pull of gravity is too much for it to overcome. [9]**When** you spill a glass of juice (which is, of course, mostly water) on the kitchen table you rush to get a paper towel to wipe it up. [10]**First**, surface tension keeps the liquid in a nice puddle on the table. [11]**Next,** when you put the paper towel **onto** your mess the liquid attaches itself to the paper fibers.

[12]Plants and trees couldn't thrive without capillary action. [13]Plants put down roots into the soil. [14]Roots are capable of carrying water from the soil **up** into the plant. [15]Water, which contains dissolved nutrients, gets inside the roots and starts climbing up the plant tissue. [16]**As** the first water molecule starts climbing, it pulls along the water molecule **next** to it. [17]The second water molecule then drags up the water molecule **beside** it, and so on.

—Adapted from "Capillary Action." *Water Science for Schools*. USGS 27 September 2004. http://ga.water.usgs.gov/edu/waterproperties.html

Addition	Space (spatial) Order	Time Order
1. _____	2. _____	7. _____
	3. _____	8. _____
	4. _____	9. _____
	5. _____	10. _____
	6. _____	

REVIEW Test 3

Transition Words

Textbook
Skills

Fill in each blank with a transition word from the box. Use each transition word once.

after	finally	first	second	third

Steps to Stop Sexual Harassment

Sexual harassment is defined as any form of unwanted sexual attention. Most companies now have sexual harassment policies in place. If you feel you are being harassed, there are several steps you can take. _____, ask the harasser to stop. Be clear and direct. This may be the first time the person has ever been told such behavior is wrong. _____, record the event. Having a record of exactly what occurred (and when and where) will be helpful in making your case. _____, complain to a higher authority. Talk to your manager about what happened. _____, remember that you have not done anything wrong. You will likely feel awful _____ being harassed. However, you should feel proud that you are not keeping silent.

—Donatelle, *Access to Health*, 7th ed., pp. 109–10.

REVIEW Test 4

Transition Words and Thought Patterns

Before you read, skim the following essay from the Biography Resource Center, an online reference. Answer the Before Reading questions. Then read the essay, and answer the After Reading questions.

Oprah Winfrey: A Notable Success

[1]Thought of as the "Queen of Talk" since the mid-1980s, she is the first African American woman to host a national weekday talk show. [2]In addition,

she is one of the richest and most powerful African American women in America. [3]Oprah Winfrey's life story makes her success **notable**.

Humble Beginnings. [4]Winfrey was born January 29, 1954, on a farm in Kosciusko, Mississippi. [5]She is the product of a brief meeting between 20-year-old Vernon Winfrey and 18-year-old Vernita Lee. [6]Since her father was in the service when she was born and her mother was eager to leave Mississippi, Winfrey lived on the farm with her maternal grandparents until the age of six. [7]Her father apparently learned of her birth when he received a printed baby announcement in the mail with a scribbled note: "Send clothes!" [8]As a young child, she was raised in the rural tradition, and she received whippings and harsh **chastisement** as punishment for wrongdoing. [9]At the age of six, she moved to Milwaukee to live with her mother, who was working as a housecleaner.

An Imaginative Child. [10]Rarely at home because of work demands, Vernita had a difficult time providing for the emotional needs of the intelligent, high-spirited Winfrey. [11]Several sources have relayed the creative ways Winfrey tried to get her mother's attention. [12]Once, her mother refused to buy her a new pair of eyeglasses—claiming that she couldn't afford them. [13]Winfrey then staged a fake burglary at her home. [14]She said that she had been knocked unconscious, and during the ordeal her glasses had broken. [15]Another time, she ran away from home. [16]While on the streets, she approached Aretha Franklin's limousine and convinced the singer that she was an abandoned child. [17]Franklin is said to have given her $100. [18]Winfrey's last antic involved her frantic attempt to keep an unhousebroken puppy. [19]She created a tale about the brave puppy fending off robbers. [20]She even added a bit of realism to the "scene" by tossing her mother's jewelry out of the window.

Molested as a Child. [21]At the age of nine, and for several years thereafter, Winfrey was sexually abused by a teenaged cousin and then by other male relatives and friends. [22]She spoke openly about this on her talk show in 1991. [23]At that time, she offered support and showed **empathy** to guests and viewers who had gone through similar painful experiences. [24]In an article for *Essence* she admitted that she couldn't free herself of the "shame" she felt until 1990, when she finally admitted, "I was not responsible for the abuse." [25]The molestation Winfrey experienced in Milwaukee ended when, at the age of 14, she went to live with her father in Nashville.

"Saved" by Father. [26]While under the care of her father, she flourished and honed many of her communication skills. [27]Winfrey credits her father, and the time she spent with him and his wife Zelma, for "saving" her. [28]He functioned as a strict and constant presence in her life. [29]She told Jill Nelson in an interview for *Washington Post Magazine,* "If I hadn't been sent to my father, I would have gone in another direction. [30]I could have made a good criminal. [31]I would have used these same instincts differently." [32]Winfrey's life under her father's care was purposeful and disciplined.

      Spectacular Success. [33]In January 1984, Winfrey took over the ailing television talk show *AM Chicago.* [34]She instantly turned it into a smash hit. [35]Her earthy and down-home style won her large audiences. [36]In September of 1986, the *Oprah Winfrey Show* made its national debut. [37]Within five months, it was the third-highest-rated show on television, behind the game shows *Wheel of Fortune* and *Jeopardy!* [38]In addition, her show was ranked the number-one talk show. [39]At that time, her show reached between 9 and 10 million people in 192 cities on a daily basis. [40]Since then, Winfrey and her show have received many Daytime Emmy awards. [41]Winfrey's talent and energy have brought her success in other areas as well. [42]For one thing, she is _____ a successful publisher. [43]In 2001, *Book* magazine named her among the ten most powerful people in publishing.

—From *American Decades on CD,* for Windows, 1st edition.
Reprinted with permission of Gale, a division of Thomson
Learning: www.thomsonrights.com Fax 800-730-2215.

BEFORE READING

Vocabulary in Context

_____   **1.** The word **notable** in sentence 3 means
     a. major.   c. surprising.
     b. minor.   d. expected.

_____   **2.** The word **chastisement** in sentence 8 means
     a. foods.   c. chores.
     b. scoldings.   d. praise.

_____   **3.** The word **empathy** in sentence 23 means
     a. disbelief.   c. understanding.
     b. shock.   d. disgust.

Concept Maps

Finish the concept map by filling in the missing idea with information from the passage.

The story of Oprah Winfrey's success makes her life notable.

| Humble Beginnings | An Imaginative Child | Molested as a Child | 4. _____ _____ _____ | Spectacular Success |

AFTER READING

Central Idea and Main Idea

_____ **5.** What is the central idea or thesis statement of the essay?
   a. Oprah Winfrey is a successful African American woman.
   b. Oprah Winfrey has suffered during her life.
   c. Oprah Winfrey's life and success are notable.
   d. Oprah Winfrey is a rich and powerful woman.

Supporting Details

_____ **6.** Sentences 12–14 are what type of supporting detail?
   a. major supporting detail
   b. minor supporting detail

Transitions and Thought Patterns

_____ **7.** What is the thought pattern suggested by sentence 3?
   a. time order   c. classification
   b. space order

_____ **8.** What is the relationship between sentences 1 and 2?
   a. time order   c. classification
   b. addition

_____ **9.** The word **while** in sentence 26 is a transition that shows
   a. time order.   c. classification.
   b. addition.

_____ **10.** Choose the best transition word(s) for the blank in sentence 42.
   a. now   c. first
   b. a type of   d. finally

Discussion Questions

1. In what ways do you think childhood experiences affect people?

2. How has society changed since Oprah was entering the workforce in the 1960s and 1970s?

3. Is Oprah a good role model? Why or why not?

Writing Topics

1. Write a paragraph about someone you know who is successful.

2. Define success and give examples in a paragraph.

3. Describe in a paragraph or two some of the barriers people overcome to be successful.

SKILLED READER Scorecard

Transitions and Thought Patterns

Test	Number Correct		Points		Score
Review Test 1	_____	×	10	=	_____
Review Test 2	_____	×	10	=	_____
Review Test 3	_____	×	20	=	_____
Review Test 4	_____	×	10	=	_____
Review Test 5 (website)	_____	×	10	=	_____
Review Test 6 (website)	_____	×	10	=	_____

Enter your scores on the Skilled Reader Scorecard: Chapter 8 Review Tests inside the back cover.

After Reading About Transitions and Thought Patterns

Before you move on to the mastery tests on transitions and thought patterns, take time to reflect on your learning and performance by answering the following questions. Write your answers in your notebook.

What did I learn about transitions and thought patterns?

What do I need to remember about transitions and thought patterns?

How has my knowledge base or prior knowledge about transitions and thought patterns changed?

More Review and Mastery Tests

For more practice, go to the book's website at **http://www.ablongman.com/henry** and click on *The Skilled Reader*. Then select "More Review and Mastery Tests." You will find the tests listed by chapter.

Read the paragraph. Some of the transition words are in bold print. Identify the relationship between ideas signaled by each transition word by filling in the blanks that follow the paragraph.

One Unsafe Place in a Tornado

[1]Stopping **under** a bridge to take shelter from a tornado is a very dangerous idea, for several reasons. [2]**First,** deadly flying debris can still be blasted into the spaces **between** the bridge and the grade. [3]Flying debris can impale any people hiding **there.** [4]**Second,** even when they strongly grip the girders (if they exist), people may be blown loose, out from under the bridge and into the open. [5]People can even be pulled well up **into** the tornado itself. [6]Chances for survival are not good **when** that happens. [7]**Third,** the bridge itself may fail. [8]It may peel apart and create large flying objects, or even collapse down onto people underneath. [9]The structural integrity of many bridges in tornado winds is unknown—even for those that look sturdy. [10]**Finally,** whether or not the tornado hits, parking on traffic lanes is illegal and dangerous to yourself and others. [11]You could create a potentially deadly hazard for others, who may plow into your vehicle at full highway speeds in the rain, hail, or dust. [12]**Also,** parking on traffic lanes can trap people in the storm's path against their will or block emergency vehicles from saving lives.

—Adapted from Edwards, Roger. *The Online Tornado FAQ: Frequently Asked Questions about Tornados.* National Weather Service Storm Prediction Center. 27 September 2004. http://spc.noaa.gov/faq/tornado/#f-scale1.

Space (spatial) Order	Addition	Time Order
1. _____	5. _____	10. _____
2. _____	6. _____	
3. _____	7. _____	
4. _____	8. _____	
	9. _____	

A. Read the paragraph, and answer the questions that follow it.

The Five Phases of Conversation

[1]When experts discuss conversation, they divide the process into stages. [2]The **first** step is the opening or greeting that starts the conversation. [3]A message such as "Hello, this is Joe" establishes a connection between two people. [4]Openings can **also** be a nonverbal gesture such as a smile or kiss. [5]At the **second** step, you usually provide some kind of feedforward. [6]This step gives the other person a general idea about the topic of conversation. [7]"I'm really depressed and need to talk" is an example of feedforward that also sets the tone of the conversation. [8]The third step is the "business," the focus of the conversation. [9]All conversations are goal directed. [10]That is, you converse to fulfill one or several general purposes: to learn, influence, play, or help. [11]This is the longest part of the conversation. [12]The fourth step is feedback, the reverse of the second step. [13]Here you signal that the business is completed: "So you want to send Jack a get-well card?" [14]Of course the other person may not agree that the business has been completed and may counter with "But what hospital is he in?" [15]When this happens, you normally go back a step and complete the business. [16]The _____ and fifth step is the closing, the goodbye, which often reveals how satisfied the persons were with the conversation: "I hope you'll call soon" or "Don't call us, we'll call you." [17]When closings are vague, conversation becomes awkward; you're not sure if you should say goodbye or if you should wait for something else to be said.

—Adapted from DeVito, Joseph A. *The Interpersonal Communication Book*, 11th ed., Allyn & Bacon 2007. pp. 194–196.

VISUAL VOCABULARY

The situation in the photograph shows the

_____ phase of a conversation.

a. opening
b. feedforward
c. business
d. feedback
e. closing

_____ 1. The word **first** in sentence 2 is a transition that shows
   a. addition.
   b. time order.
   c. classification.

_____ 2. **Also** in sentence 4 shows
   a. addition.
   b. time order.
   c. classification.

_____ 3. **Second** in sentence 5 shows
   a. time order.
   b. classification.
   c. addition.

_____ 4. The best transition word for the blank in sentence 16 is
   a. since.
   b. later.
   c. final.

_____ 5. The thought pattern for this paragraph is
   a. classification.
   b. listing.
   c. time order.

B. Fill in the blanks in the paragraph with transition words from the box. Use each expression once.

another type	kinds	one type	these kinds	two kinds

Laws That Protect Children

Unwanted infants are protected by (**6**) _____ of laws. Both (**7**) _____ deal with parents who are unable to cope with the pressures of parenthood. (**8**) _____ of law punishes neglect. Several states, such as Georgia and Massachusetts, will put parents in jail for several years if they leave or abandon a child. (**9**) _____ of law rewards parents for handing their unwanted children over to authorities. A number of states, such as South Carolina and California, have "safe haven" laws. (**10**) _____ of laws allow parents to leave the unwanted child at a church or hospital without being charged with a crime. These laws are supposed to lead to better treatment for the unwanted children.

The following paragraphs come from the college textbook *Family Communication: Cohesion and Change*. Fill in the blanks with the transition words from the box above each paragraph. Use each word once.

and	then	when

Textbook
Skills

I guess you could say I've had three "moms" and two and a half "dads." My parents divorced (**1**) _____ my twin brother and I were about 3 years old. My dad remarried (**2**) _____, after having two more sons, got divorced again. (**3**) _____ he remarried, and now I have a baby sister young enough to be my daughter. My mom remarried and got divorced again when we were about 7. The "half-father" that we had was a man who lived with us for 10 years who recently moved out on my mother's request. The reason my brother and I are still sane is because Mom and Dad have always remained friends. We were never treated like pawns in the middle of a battle.

—Adapted from Galvin & Brommel, *Family Communication:
Cohesion and Change,* 5th ed., p. 2.

after	and	often

Textbook
Skills

(**4**) _____ 26 years of marriage, my parents seem to have an incredibly close relationship that I haven't seen in many other people. They (**5**) _____ hold hands. They share common interests in music (**6**) _____ theater. They just can't get enough of each other, but each has special friends and interests, which balances their intensity. Life hasn't been all that easy for them, either, yet each has helped the other cope.

—Adapted from Galvin & Brommel, *Family Communication:
Cohesion and Change,* 5th ed., p. 134.

additional	first	next	one

Textbook
Skills

Families have distinct styles of decision making. There is uniqueness in each family's problem-solving style. The reasons for these differences vary from family to family. (**7**) _____ reason for a family's decision style is learned behavior. (**8**) _____ reasons include a shared view of the world, expectations of roles, and the structure of the family. The (**9**) _____ style, "I win; you lose," uses the lower level of reasoning for decisions and focuses on self-interest. The (**10**) _____ style, decision by rules, uses tradition and obedience to rules. The third style is based on values of right and wrong.

—Adapted from Galvin & Brommel, *Family Communication: Cohesion and Change,* 5th ed., p. 208.

Name _____ Section _____

Date _____ Score (number correct) _____ × 10 = _____ %

A. The following topic sentences are taken from a college science textbook. Identify the thought pattern for each one.

Textbook
Skills

_____ **1.** There are two types of reproduction: asexual and sexual.
    a. classification   b. time order

_____ **2.** The formation of soil begins with the weathering of rocks and their minerals.
    a. classification   b. time order

_____ **3.** Animals can be divided into three groups, according to the way they maintain temperature.
    a. classification   b. time order

_____ **4.** In the United States in the early 1900s, a number of individuals began to make serious efforts to halt the destruction of wildlife.
    a. classification   b. listing

_____ **5.** There are two significant sources of atmospheric oxygen.
    a. time order   b. listing

B. Read the paragraph, and answer the questions that follow it.

Textbook
Skills

[1]Geologists define three major types of rock. [2]The first type, igneous rocks, are formed by the cooling of volcanic flows. [3]The makeup of these rocks depends on the rate and temperature at which they form. [4]The second type, sedimentary rocks, are formed from deposits of mineral (sediments). [5]The makeup of sedimentary rocks depends on the type of sediment from which they are formed. [6]Some sediments are of biological origin; for example, shells of sea life may fall **to** the ocean floor. [7]The third type, metamorphic rocks, are either igneous or sedimentary rock that have been changed by heat and the pressure of overlying rock.

—Adapted from Smith & Smith, *Elements of Ecology*, 4th ed., p. 97.

_____ **6.** What thought pattern is suggested by the topic sentence (sentence 1)?
    a. classification   b. time order

_____ **7.** What relationship is suggested by the word **to** in sentence 6?
    a. space order   b. classification

C. Complete the following list with information from the passage in part B.

Three Types of Rock

First type: **8.** _____

Second type: **9.** _____

Third type: **10.** _____

VISUAL VOCABULARY

Three types of rock are igneous, metamorphic, and _____, pictured here.

A. Read the following passages from the college textbook *The Dynamics of Drug Abuse,* and fill in the blanks with the correct transition word from the box. Use each word once.

also	first	onto
and	into	then

Textbook
Skills

To obtain the full effects of cocaine, users generally inject or inhale the drug. As in South America, coca leaves may (**1**) _____ be chewed or sucked so that the cocaine is absorbed slowly (**2**) _____ the body. When cocaine is taken by mouth, digestion slows down (**3**) _____ weakens the effects of the drug. Social cocaine users, including those who are known as "chippers" (sometime users), will inhale cocaine in its powder form. (**4**) _____, the powder is poured (**5**) _____ a smooth, flat surface, such as a mirror; next, it is shaped into thin lines that are (**6**) _____ inhaled. The nasal membranes are so absorbent that the cocaine reaches the brain quickly.

—Adapted from Fishbein & Pease, *The Dynamics of Drug Abuse,* pp. 162–63.

B. Read each set of sentences, and answer the questions that follow it.

The first step of treatment for drug addiction is to detoxify the drug addict. The _____ step is to assist the person through the withdrawal stage.

—Fishbein & Pease, p. 162.

_____ **7.** The best transition word for the sentence is
   a. second.
   b. previous.
   c. third.

_____ **8.** The relationship of the ideas between the two sentences is one of
   a. listing.
   b. time order.

Taking cocaine leads to increased heart rate, high blood pressure, and increased energy. _____, high doses of cocaine result in anxiety and psychotic behavior.

—Fishbein & Pease, p. 259.

_____ **9.** The best transition word to complete the idea is
   a. Instead.
   b. Next.
   c. In addition.

_____ **10.** The relationship of ideas between the two sentences is one of
   a. classification.
   b. time order.
   c. listing.

A. Read the following paragraph from the textbook *American Government: Continuity and Change*, and fill in the blanks with the correct transitions from the box. Use each expression once.

also	and	first	in addition	into

Textbook
Skills

The 1850s: Changing Times

By 1850, much was changing in America. (**1**) _____, people were on the move. The Gold Rush had spurred westward migration. Cities grew as people were lured from their farms. Railroads and the telegraph increased mobility and communication. (**2**) _____, immigrants flooded (**3**) _____ the United States. Second, reformers called for change. The women's movement gained strength, (**4**) _____ slavery continued to tear the nation apart. Harriet Beecher Stowe's novel *Uncle Tom's Cabin* showed the evils of slavery. Its picture of a slave family torn apart (**5**) _____ tore apart the nation. *Uncle Tom's Cabin* sold more than 300,000 copies in a single year. Abraham Lincoln called Stowe "the little woman who started the big war."

—O'Connor & Sabato, *American Government: Continuity and Change*, p. 179.

B. Read each of the following topic sentences taken from textbooks. Identify the thought pattern each one suggests.

_____ **6.** Stress has three types of symptoms.
    a. time order
    b. classification

_____ **7.** Vision can be divided into three main phases.
    a. time order
    b. classification

_____ **8.** There are a number of reasons that explain why we don't listen.
    a. time order
    b. listing

_____ **9.** Animals can be divided into three groups based on physical traits.
    a. space order
    b. classification

_____ **10.** Monument Valley sits in the northwest section of the Navajo Nation, whose territory is spread throughout the states of Arizona, New Mexico, and Utah.
    a. space order
    b. classification

More Thought Patterns

 ## Before Reading About More Thought Patterns

In Chapter 8, you learned two important ideas that will help you as you work through this chapter. Use the following questions to call up your prior knowledge about transitions and thought patterns.

What are transitions? (Refer to page 286.) _____

_____

_____

What are thought patterns? (Refer to page 286.) _____

_____

_____

Transitions and thought patterns show the relationships between ideas in sentences, paragraphs, and passages. You have studied four common types: time order, space order, listing, and classification. In this chapter, we will explore some other common thought patterns:

- the comparison-and-contrast pattern
- the cause-and-effect pattern
- the generalization-and-example pattern

The Comparison-and-Contrast Patterns

Many ideas become clearer when they are thought of in relation to one another. For example, comparing the prices different grocery stores charge makes us smarter shoppers. Likewise, noting the difference between loving and selfish behavior helps us choose partners in life. The comparison-and-contrast patterns enable us to see these relationships. This section discusses comparison and contrast, both individually and in combination.

The Comparison Pattern

Comparison points out the ways in which two or more ideas are alike. Sample signal words are *similar, like,* and *just as.*

Words and Phrases of Comparison				
alike	equally	in the same way	likewise	similar
as	in a similar fashion	just as	resemble	similarity
as well as	in a similar manner	just like	same	similarly
both	in like manner	like		

Here are some examples:

Our brains are capable of storing and getting information into and out of our memory. *Similarly,* computers have a memory bank in which they can store and get information.

Like a deer frozen in the headlights of a car, Justin could not move.

Conan O'Brien opens his late-night show with a stand-up comedy routine. *Likewise,* Jimmy Kimmel begins his show with his own five minutes of comedy.

PRACTICE ■1

Complete the following ideas with transitions that show comparison. Fill in each blank with a word or phrase from the "Words and Phrases of Comparison" box. Use each choice only once.

1. My little dog snorts and smacks when she eats; she sounds

_____ a pig.

2. Hypnotism works _____ nicotine chewing gum or patches to help some people quit smoking.

3. A cool autumn morning causes my steps to quicken and my spirit to rise, and a hot summer afternoon makes me lazy and irritable.

_____, music affects my moods.

4. _____ a pond of water that never moves can become choked with algae, a person who never reads strangles creative and critical thought.

5. The desert grasslands that stretch from Texas to Mexico are

_____ in many ways to the shortgrass plains in the Black Hills of South Dakota.

When comparison is used to organize an entire paragraph, the pattern looks like this:

Comparison Pattern		
Idea 1		**Idea 2**
Idea 1	*is like*	Idea 2
Idea 1	*is like*	Idea 2
Idea 1	*is like*	Idea 2

EXAMPLE Determine a logical order for the following three sentences. Write **1** by the sentence that should come first, **2** by the sentence that should come second, and **3** by the sentence that should come last. Then complete the chart based on the information in the paragraph.

_____ And just as universities offer chances for students to learn leadership skills through honor and service clubs, community colleges also have both honor and service clubs.

_____ Universities and community colleges offer some of the same academic experiences.

_____ Like universities, community colleges offer all the basic courses needed during the first two years of study.

Similarities Between Universities and Community Colleges

Universities	Community Colleges
1. basic courses	basic courses
2. honor and service clubs	_____

EXPLANATION   Here are the sentences arranged in the proper order. The organization and transition words are in **bold** print.

Universities and community colleges offer some of the **same** academic experiences. **Like** universities, community colleges offer all the basic courses needed during the first two years of study. **And just as** universities offer chances for students to learn leadership skills through honor and service clubs, community colleges also have both honor and service clubs.

To fill the blank, you should indicate that community colleges have honor and service clubs.

The Contrast Pattern

Contrast points out the ways in which two or more ideas are different. Sample signal words are *different*, *but*, and *yet*.

Words and Phrases of Contrast			
although	different	in spite of	rather than
as opposed to	different from	instead	still
at the same time	differently	nevertheless	to the contrary
but	even though	on the contrary	whereas
conversely	however	on the one hand	while
despite	in contrast	on the other hand	yet
difference			

Here are some examples:

Most television programs are geared for mindless enjoyment, *yet* good shows full of interesting information are becoming more common.

Janet and Rob reduced the amount of starchy foods they ate and began exercising three times a week. *Nevertheless,* they both gained 5 pounds in the next two months.

Despite having gone to the grocery store twice in the past three days, I need to go again today.

PRACTICE 2

Complete the sentences with transitions that show contrast. Fill in each blank with a word or phrase from the "Words and Phrases of Contrast" box. Use each choice only once.

1. Mark Twain's novel *Huckleberry Finn* has often been banned from school libraries, _____ it remains popular with millions of young readers.

2. _____ Alkmal and Syreta have been married for over 30 years, they act like newlyweds.

3. Former president Bill Clinton is known for his effective leadership skills; _____, he is remembered as a deeply flawed man who needlessly put his presidency at risk.

4. _____ the risk for multiple births, many women who cannot become pregnant without medical help choose to take fertility drugs.

5. Resist honking your horn or cursing at annoying drivers; _____, give them room, leave them alone, and be thankful for your own driving skills.

When contrast is used to organize an entire paragraph, the pattern looks like this:

Contrast Pattern		
Idea 1		**Idea 2**
Idea 1	*differs from*	Idea 2
Idea 1	*differs from*	Idea 2
Idea 1	*differs from*	Idea 2

EXAMPLE   Determine a logical order for the following three sentences. Write **1** by the sentence that should come first, **2** by the sentence that should come second, and **3** by the sentence that should come last. Then complete the chart based on the information in the paragraph.

_____ On the other hand, beaches on the west coast have no waves, but they do have plenty of shells for collecting.

_____ Florida beaches on the east and west coasts differ.

_____ On the one hand, beaches on the east coast offer large enough waves for surfing and body boarding, yet they have very few shells.

Differences Between East and West Coast Florida Beaches

West Coast	East Coast
1. no waves	_____
2. _____	very few shells

EXPLANATION   Here are the sentences arranged in the proper order. The transition words are in **bold** print.

> Florida beaches on the east and west coasts **differ. On the one hand,** beaches on the east coast offer large enough waves for surfing and body boarding, **yet** they have very few shells. **On the other hand,** beaches on the west coast have no waves, **but** they do have plenty of shells for collecting.

To complete the chart, you should indicate that the east coast has waves for surfing and body boarding and the west coast has plenty of shells for collecting.

The Comparison-and-Contrast Pattern

The **comparison-and-contrast pattern** shows how two things are similar, how they are different, or both.

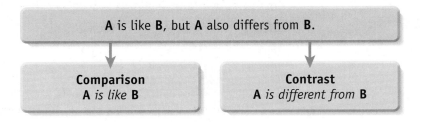

Fast-food restaurants McDonald's and Subway are *similar* to each other, *but* not as much as one might think. The two fast-food chains do share obvious *similarities*. They *both* offer quick meals at low cost. They *both* also offer the choice of eat-in or take-out. *However,* there are striking *differences* between the two. McDonald's offers a menu that is filled with foods high in calories and fats, such as hamburgers and French fries. *Unlike* McDonald's fried hamburgers, Subway offers a very different and much healthier choice in lean meats such as turkey and chicken. Subway also *differs* from McDonald's by not offering the option of a drive-through window.

In the paragraph, the two things being compared and contrasted are the fast-food restaurants McDonald's and Subway. The author offers two similarities: quick, low-cost meals and the choice to eat in or take out. The author also offers two differences: the health factor in food choices and the lack of a drive-through window at Subway.

EXAMPLE Determine a logical order for the following three sentences. Write **1** by the sentence that should come first, **2** by the sentence that should come second, and **3** by the sentence that should come last.

_____ Both high school and college are important places of learning.

_____ Although high school and college seem similar, they differ in one major way.

_____ However, unlike high school, students attend college by their own choice.

EXPLANATION Here are the sentences arranged in the proper order. The transition words are in **bold** print.

Although high school and college seem **similar**, they **differ** in one major way. **Both** high school and college are important places of learning. **However, unlike** high school, students attend college by their own choice.

EXAMPLE Read the following paragraph adapted from a college communications textbook. Circle the comparison-and-contrast words, and answer the questions that follow the paragraph.

In the face of a mistake, one can offer either a good excuse or a bad excuse. Although good excuses and bad excuses share some similarities, their differences have deep meaning. Both good and bad excuses make it possible

Textbook
Skills

to take risks and be a part of an activity that may bring failure. They are also similar in their attempt to put a failure in the best possible light. Despite their similarities, good and bad excuses differ greatly in their effect. A good excuse helps one get out of a problem, while a bad excuse only makes matters worse. Good excuses avoid blaming others, especially those one works with; in contrast, a bad excuse avoids taking responsibility and blames others unfairly.

—Adapted from DeVito, *Messages: Building Interpersonal Communication Skills*, 4th ed., p. 214.

1. What are the two ideas being compared and contrasted? _____

   _____

2. List four different comparison and contrast words or expressions used in

   the paragraph. _____

   _____

EXPLANATION   The paragraph compares and contrasts good excuses and bad excuses. Nine different comparison and contrast words are used: *although, similarities, differences, both, similar, despite, differ, while,* and *in contrast.*

PRACTICE 3

The following paragraphs use comparison and contrast. Read each paragraph, and answer the questions that follow it.

Humans are similar to apes in several ways. First, humans and apes both have grasping hands with opposable thumbs, and both have fingernails. These traits allow both of them to hold objects and use tools. A second similarity that humans and apes share is the tendency to have single births. Usually mothers give birth to one offspring at a time. In addition, both have binocular vision, which gives the ability to judge depth. Both have sets of eyes that sit in the front of the face and look forward. Finally, both have very large forebrains.

_____ 1. What thought pattern is used in this passage?
   a. comparison
   b. contrast
   c. both

2. What two ideas are being compared or contrasted? _____ and

   _____

Several distinct symptoms mark the difference between the common cold and the flu. The first difference is in the onset of the illness. Whereas a cold starts slowly, the flu begins very suddenly. Second, although the body aches a little with a cold, the aching is more intense with the flu, as if a person has suffered a beating. Third, with a cold, a person puts up with much sneezing and nose dripping; however, with the flu, there is little sneezing or dripping. In addition, a cold is usually marked by a mild rise in body temperature to 100°F, in contrast to the flu's high fever of 103° to 104°F. Finally, a person with a cold can continue with everyday life, whereas a person with the flu feels exhausted for days or weeks and must rest in bed.

_____ **3.** What thought pattern is used in this passage?
   a. comparison
   b. contrast
   c. both

4. What two ideas are being compared or contrasted? _____

and _____

The Cause-and-Effect Pattern

Sometimes an author talks about *why* something happened or *what* results came from an event. A **cause** states why something happens. An **effect** states a result or outcome. Sample signal words include *because* and *consequently*.

Cause-and-Effect Words			
accordingly	because of	leads to	so
as a result	consequently	results in	therefore
because	if . . . then	since	thus

Here are some examples:

George had run up his credit card bill to its limit. *As a result,* his monthly payments only covered the interest the bank charged.

Because peer pressure can be one of the greatest influences on a young person's life, we must teach our children to choose their friends wisely.

Dustin was always late for work, spent most of his time gossiping, and kept his home stocked with supplies from the office. *Consequently,* he was fired.

PRACTICE 4

Complete each sentence with a cause-and-effect word or phrase from the "Cause-and-Effect Words" box. Use each choice only once.

because	because of	leads to	result in	therefore

1. The bubonic plague is a horrible disease that _____ high fevers, muscle pain, vomiting, and delirium.

2. During the 14th century, _____ the bubonic plague, one third to one half of all the people in Europe died.

3. Lightning strikes may _____ more deaths than tornadoes and hurricanes.

4. _____ President John F. Kennedy backed the space program with great resolve, the space launch building located in Florida was re-named after him.

5. Opponents of the death penalty say that it is cruel, does not stop crime, and can result in innocent people being sentenced to die; _____, they sometimes hold candlelight vigils to protest an execution.

VISUAL VOCABULARY

Opponents of the death penalty do not believe it _____ lower crime rates.

a. results in
b. compares to

The writer using cause and effect introduces an idea or event and then provides supporting details to show how that event *results in* or *leads to* another event. Many times, the second event comes about because of the first event. Thus the first idea is the cause and the following ideas are the effects. If more than two ideas are discussed, the added ideas may show a chain reaction.

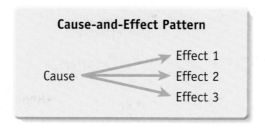

For example, read the following topic sentence:

Too much stress may lead to fatigue and anxiety.

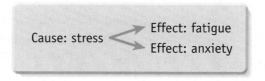

Often an author will begin with an effect and then give the causes.

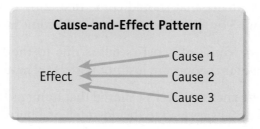

For example, read the following topic sentence:

The bone disease osteoporosis may be the result of poor diet and genetics.

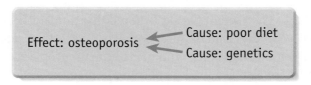

Sometimes the author may wish to emphasize a chain reaction.

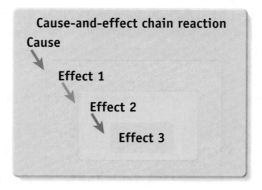

For example, read the following topic sentence.

Children spend more time using technology, and thus less time exercising; the less they exercise, the more likely they are to be overweight.

> **Cause-and-effect chain reaction**
> Cause: Children spend more time using technology. →
> Effect: Children spend less time exercising. →
> Effect: Children become overweight.

EXAMPLE   Determine a logical order for the following three sentences. Write **1** by the sentence that should come first, **2** by the sentence that should come second, and **3** by the sentence that should come last.

_____ One cause of a hero's fall is due to the limits that come with being human; people are just not perfect by nature.

_____ The ancient Greeks believed that humans have two kinds of flaws; these flaws always lead to the downfall of a hero.

_____ A hero also faces failure because of extreme pride.

EXPLANATION   Here are the sentences arranged in the proper order. The transition words are in **bold** print.

> The ancient Greeks believed that humans have two kinds of flaws; these flaws always **lead to** the downfall of a hero. **One cause** of a hero's fall is **due to** the limits that come with being human; people are just not perfect by nature. A hero **also** faces failure **because of** extreme pride.

In this paragraph, two addition words combine with the cause-and-effect signal words. In this case, *one* and *also* indicate the order in which these causes are discussed.

PRACTICE 5

This paragraph uses the cause-and-effect pattern of organization. Read the paragraph, and answer the questions that follow it.

Textbook
Skills

There are several reasons for your self-concept. One is the image others have of you. If those you love and respect think highly of you, you will see a positive self-image reflected in their behaviors. Another cause of self-concept comes from social comparisons. Comparing your test scores to your classmates' is a good example of a social comparison; if you do better than your peers, then you will most likely have a positive view of your abilities. Cultural teachings are another explanation for your self-concept. Parents, teachers, and the media instill a belief about success; when you fit in with these beliefs, you are likely to see yourself as successful.

—Adapted from DeVito, *Messages: Building Interpersonal Communication Skills*, 4th ed., pp. 38–40.

1. What are the three causes discussed in the paragraph?

a. _____

b. _____

c. _____

2. What is the effect of these causes? _____

3. What are the cause-and-effect signal words used in the paragraph?

a. _____

b. _____

c. _____

The Generalization-and-Example Pattern

Going to a movie can be expensive. Two tickets may cost $16.

The first sentence is a general statement. This sentence suggests that it is only the high cost of tickets that makes going to a movie expensive. But expensive popcorn, candy, and drinks also help make moviegoing costly. Adding an **example word** makes it clear that the cost of tickets is only one part of the expense.

Going to a movie can be expensive. *For example,* two tickets may cost $16.

In the generalization-and-example thought pattern, the author makes a general statement and then offers an example or a series of examples to clarify the generalization.

The Generalization-and-Example Pattern	

Statement of a general idea
    Example
    Example	

Example words signal that a writer is giving an instance of a general idea.

EXAMPLE Read each of the following items and fill in the blanks with an appropriate example word or phrase.

Words and Phrases That Introduce Examples			
as an illustration for example	for instance including	once such as	to illustrate typically

1. Many classes teach worthwhile skills. _____, math teaches problem-solving skills.

2. Green plants living indoors help keep the air clean. _____, the corn plant absorbs many household chemicals.

3. More and more people have technology in the home, _____ a computer with access to the Internet, microwave ovens, remote controlled televisions, and cell phones.

EXPLANATION Many words and phrases that introduce examples are easily interchanged. In the first two examples, you could have used any of these phrases: *for example, for instance, as an illustration,* or *to illustrate.* They all are similar in meaning. In the third example, the use of the transition phrase *such as* signals a list. Even though transition words have similar meanings, authors carefully choose transitions based on style and meaning.

PRACTICE 6

Complete each selection with an example word. Fill in each blank with a word or phrase from the "Words and Phrases That Introduce Examples" box. Use each choice only once.

1. Some popular video games send the message that killing is fun.

   _____, the ads for the video game Carmageddon state that playing the game is "as easy as killing babies with axes."

2. The Chrysler 300M is a sports luxury car that comes with extra options,

   _____ front seats that heat up and an Infinity sound system.

3. To compete in the sport of basketball, a player needs many skills,

   _____ quick thinking, running speed, jumping power, and sharp aim.

4. Kim is always willing to help others; _____ she cooked and delivered meals every night to a family for two weeks while the mother was in the hospital.

5. During deep breathing exercises, it is important to relax every part of the

   body; _____, loosening up a clenched jaw helps the whole body relax.

Textbook Skills: The Definition Pattern

Textbooks are full of new words and special terms. Even if the word is common, it can take on a special meaning in a specific course. To help students understand the ideas, authors often include a definition of the new or special term. Then, to make sure the meaning of the word or concept is clear, the author will also give examples.

Textbook
Skills

Self-disclosure is a type of communication in which you reveal information about yourself. *For example,* slips of the tongue and gestures may send self-disclosing messages. Self-disclosure may also include your reactions to the feelings of others, *as* when you tell your friend you are sorry she was fired.

—DeVito, *Messages: Building Interpersonal Communication Skills,* 4th ed., p. 45.

In this paragraph, the term *self-disclosure* is defined in the first sentence. Then the author gives two examples to make the term clear to the reader.

> **Definition Pattern**
>
> Term and definition
> Example
> Example

- The **definition** explains the meaning of new, difficult, or special terms. Definitions include words like *is* and *means:* "Self-disclosure *is* a type of communication in which you reveal information about yourself."
- The **examples** follow a definition to show how the word is used or applied in the content course. Examples are signaled by words like *for example* and *such as:* "For example, slips of the tongue and gestures may send self-disclosing messages."

EXAMPLE 1   Determine a logical order for the following three sentences. Write **1** by the sentence that should come first, **2** by the sentence that should come second, and **3** by the sentence that should come last. Then read the explanation.

_____ For example, a person may repress or forget painful childhood memories.

_____ Repression is the mind's power to block fearful thoughts, impulses, and memories.

_____ Forgetting a dental appointment may also be an example of repression.

EXPLANATION   Here are the sentences arranged in the proper order. The organization and transition words are in **bold** print.

> Repression **is** the mind's power to block fearful thoughts, impulses, and memories. **For example**, a person may repress or forget painful childhood memories. Forgetting a dental appointment may **also** be an **example** of repression.

In this paragraph, the first sentence defines *repression*. The second and third sentences offer two examples of repression.

EXAMPLE 2   Annotate the paragraph: circle the term being defined and its definition. Underline the signal word for the example and the example. Answer the questions that follow.

[1]In the 1970s and 1980s, movies began to advertise through product placement. [2]Product placement is the act of charging a fee to place a product in a movie in a way that attracts attention. [3]For example, Starbuck's Coffee

Textbook
Skills

had to pay a product placement fee to have its logo appear in Mike Myers's 1999 film *Austin Powers: The Spy Who Shagged Me.*

> —Adapted from Folkerts & Lacy, *The Media In Your Life: An*
> *Introduction to Mass Communication*, 2nd ed., p. 43.

1. What is the example that illustrates the term being defined? _____

_____

2. Which words signal the example? _____

EXPLANATION   When you annotate your text, you highlight the most important information for easy review. To make the most of your annotations, only underline key words in the examples. Compare your annotations to the following:

> [1]In the 1970s and 1980s, movies began to advertise through product placement. [2]Product placement is the act of charging a fee to place a product in a movie in a way that attracts attention. [3]For example, Starbuck's Coffee had to pay a product placement fee to have its logo appear in Mike Myers's 1999 film *Austin Powers: The Spy Who Shagged Me.*

Circling and underlining key ideas creates an opportunity for a quick review of the material. The answer to the questions are as follows:

1. The example is Starbuck's Coffee.

2. The signal words that introduce the example are *for example.*

PRACTICE 7

This paragraph uses the definition thought pattern. Annotate the paragraph: circle the terms being defined and their definitions. Underline the signal words for the examples and the examples. Then complete the concept map that follows it by filling in the missing details in the proper order.

Figures of Speech

[1]Although many of us may think that only great writers use vivid language, our everyday speech is full of colorful words and phrases. [2]This colorful speech is often poetic. [3]One figure of speech we use to create dramatic mental pictures is the *simile* (SIM-uh-lee). [4]A **simile** is an indirect comparison that uses the word *like* or *as.* [5]For example, some of us may have heard the expression "He eats like a pig." [6]Another figure of speech is *synecdoche* (sin-EK-doe-kee). [7]**Synecdoche** is using a part of something to stand for the whole. [8]For example, many of us have heard the expression "Ask for her hand in marriage," which uses the woman's hand to represent her as a whole person.

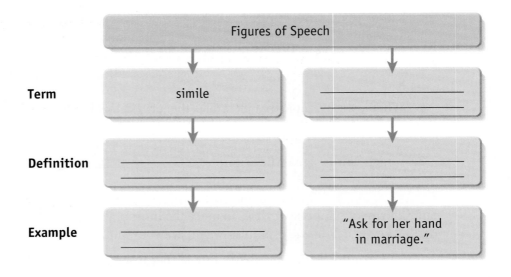

Figures of Speech

Term   simile   _____
_____

Definition   _____
_____   _____
_____

Example   _____
_____   "Ask for her hand
in marriage."

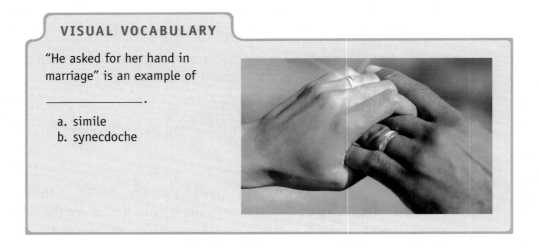

VISUAL VOCABULARY

"He asked for her hand in
marriage" is an example of

_____.

   a. simile
   b. synecdoche

Textbook
Skills

A Final Note: Thought Patterns and Textbooks

Textbook authors rely heavily on the use of transitions and thought patterns to make information clear and easy to understand.

EXAMPLES   The following topic sentences have been taken from college textbooks. Identify the thought pattern that each topic sentence suggests.

_____ **1.** People often develop poor listening skills for several reasons.
   a. cause and effect
   b. comparison and contrast
   c. definition

_____ **2.** Symmetry is the balanced arrangement of body parts around a center point.
   a. cause and effect
   b. comparison and contrast
   c. definition

_____ **3.** Unlike the South, the North's economy thrived during the Civil War.
   a. cause and effect
   b. comparison and contrast
   c. definition

EXPLANATIONS   Topic sentence 1, from a psychology textbook, suggests (a) cause and effect. Topic sentence 2, from a biology textbook, suggests (c) definition. Topic sentence 3, from a history textbook, suggests (b) comparison and contrast.

PRACTICE 8

Textbook
Skills

The following topic sentences have been taken from college textbooks. Identify the thought pattern that each topic sentence suggests. (The type of textbook is identified after each topic sentence.)

_____ **1.** Sandy and muddy shores appear empty of life at low tide, in contrast to the abundant life found on rocky shores. (_ecology_)
   a. cause and effect
   b. comparison and contrast
   c. generalization and example

_____ **2.** Unlike European railroads, the American railway system grew without government regulation or planning. (_history_)
   a. cause and effect
   b. comparison and contrast
   c. generalization and example

_____ **3.** Sickle cell disease is a blood disease. (_health_)
   a. cause and effect
   b. comparison and contrast
   c. definition

_____ **4.** Beethoven created program music, which is music that tells a story or describes a setting. (*humanities*)
   a. cause and effect
   b. comparison and contrast
   c. definition

_____ **5.** A family's image of itself affects the way it works. (*social science*)
   a. cause and effect
   b. comparison and contrast
   c. definition

Chapter Review

Test your understanding of what you have read in this chapter by filling in each blank with a word or phrase from the box. One answer is used twice.

alike	comparison	effect
cause	contrast	example
cause and effect	definition	examples

1. Comparison points out the ways two or more ideas are _____.

2. _____ points out the ways two or more ideas are different.

3. The words *like, similarly,* and *likewise* show the _____ pattern.

4. A _____ states why something happens.

5. An _____ states a result or outcome.

6. An author will often begin with the _____ and then give the effects.

7. The phrases *as a result, leads to,* and *therefore* show the pattern of _____.

8. _____ words signal that a writer is giving an instance of a general idea to clarify a point.

9. _____ explains the meaning of new, difficult, or special terms.

10. _____ follow a definition to show how the word is used or applied.

Applications

Application 1: **Using Example and Definition Patterns**

A. The following paragraph uses the generalization-and-example thought pattern. In the spaces provided, write the main idea and its example.

Shoppers' Choice

Most shoppers in America have an unbelievable number of choices. Just study the toothpaste aisle in a grocery store or drugstore as an example. First of all, there must be at least a dozen name brands of toothpaste. The best known include *Arm and Hammer, Crest, Colgate,* and *Aim.* Second, each of these brands offers another dozen choices, for each major brand offers a toothpaste to attack every imaginable problem. Labels shout that the toothpaste contains baking soda, mouthwash, cavity fighters, fluoride, and many other ingredients, singly or in combination. Choices fill several shelves, and this is just the toothpaste aisle!

1. Main idea: _____

_____

2. Example: _____

B. The following paragraph contains a definition and one example. In the spaces provided, write the term, its definition, and the example.

Survivor's Guilt

A person who survives a life-threatening event may experience survivor's guilt, the feeling that it is wrong to have survived. *Survivor's guilt* is made up of many feelings, including shame, confusion, and depression. For example, many of those who lived through the concentration camps of the Holocaust reported struggling with survivor's guilt. They could not come to grips with the fact that they had survived when so many of their family and friends were horribly killed.

3. Term: _____

4. Definition: _____

5. Example: _____

Application 2: **Using the Contrast Pattern**

The following paragraph uses the contrast thought pattern. Complete the idea map that follows the paragraph.

Native American Culture

Native American culture differs from the values and behaviors of mainstream American culture. The Native American way of life values the group more than the individual. However, the mainstream way of life values the individual more than the group. This contrast in values is seen in the role of the family. The extended family is the center of Native American life. (An extended family is made up of grandparents, aunts, uncles, cousins, nieces, and nephews.) In contrast, the nuclear family is the center of mainstream culture. (A nuclear family is made up of the mother, father, and children.) Native Americans behave differently than mainstream Americans. For example, Native Americans rely on and help others. In contrast, mainstream Americans rely on and look out for themselves. Native Americans respect humility. So they do not make direct eye contact. Mainstream Americans respect self-confidence. So they expect direct eye contact. In general, Native Americans cooperate with others to achieve a goal. Mainstream Americans compete with others to achieve a goal.

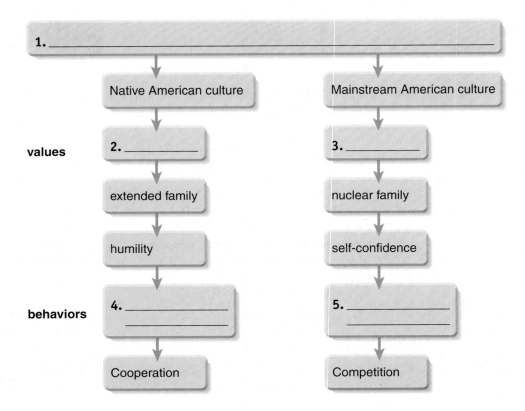

Application 3: Using the Cause-and-Effect Pattern

The following sentences use the cause-and-effect thought pattern. Identify the cause and effect for each item.

1. The pollen from the springtime blossoms led to a severe eye infection in our cat.

   Cause: _____

   Effect: _____

2. Recent research suggests that a glass of red wine every day may prevent heart disease.

   Cause: _____

   Effect: _____

3. Good communication skills result in strong relationships at home and at work.

   Cause: _____

   Effect: _____

4. Anorexia can result in death.

   Cause: _____

   Effect: _____

5. Strong stomach muscles result in good posture.

   Cause: _____

   Effect: _____

REVIEW Test 1

Transitions and Thought Patterns

A. Read the following paragraph, and answer the questions that follow it.

Training for Success

[1]On the first day of classes at American Motors Institute, the teacher began with a warning. [2]"If you aren't serious about learning the trade, don't show up here tomorrow." [3]He then went over the entire six-month course of study, and he didn't make it sound easy. [4]He told the students that they would be expected to work on machines eight hours a day to learn the trade.

⁵They would also have to read and study written materials every night.

⁶_____, he did encourage them with the news that the program is known for high job placement with good salaries.

> **1.** Fill in the blank in sentence 6 with a transition word or phrase that makes sense. _____

> _____ **2.** The relationship between sentence 5 and sentence 6 is one of
> a. generalization and example.   c. cause and effect.
> b. comparison and contrast.

B. Read each paragraph, and answer the questions that follow it.

Latino Music

Music sensations like Selena, Jennifer Lopez, and Ricky Martin have brought the diversity of Latino music into the mainstream. Latino music has several different sounds. Contrasting the musical influences on salsa and Tejano music is interesting. Salsa first began in New York City in the 1970s and blends Afro-Cuban and Puerto Rican music with rock and jazz. Salsa grew out of several types of dance rhythms such as the rhumba and the cha-cha. The use of claves, congos, horns, and guitars give salsa its dance rhythms. In contrast is the Latino sound of Tejano, which is Texan with Mexican roots. This music first came about in the early 1900s from the rhythms of the waltz and the polka. The use of the accordion, drums, the bajo sexto (a 12-stringed Spanish guitar), and the keyboard give Tejano its Tex-Mex sound.

VISUAL VOCABULARY

The _____ music played by this band grew out of dance rhythms such as the rhumba and the cha-cha.

a. salsa
b. Tejano

_____ **3.** The thought pattern for this paragraph is
   a. generalization and example.   c. cause and effect.
   b. comparison and contrast.

Give two transition words or phrases from the paragraph:

4. _____

Yin and Yang

The Chinese use the terms *yin* and *yang* to define the balance in life. Yin is the feminine and passive side of nature. For example, the cold of winter, the darkness of night, the wetness of water, the moon, and death belong to yin. Yang is the masculine and active side of nature. For example, the heat of summer, the light of day, the energy of fire, the sun, and life belong to yang. For balance to occur, yin and yang come together and complete each other. One cannot exist without the other.

_____ **5.** The thought pattern for this paragraph is
   a. process.   c. cause and effect.
   b. definition.

6. Give one transition word or phrase from the paragraph:

_____

Philosophy

Philosophy is the study of thought or a search for meaning. For example, the mind-body philosophy came about mainly through the work of a man named René Descartes. Descartes was born in France in 1596. During his lifetime, many people were challenging widely accepted ideas. In response, Descartes created a method of logical thought for reaching the truth. He began with the idea "I think; therefore, I am." Then he divided a human into two parts: mind and body. The mind is the thinking being, and the body is only an extension of the mind. Next, he reasoned that the thinking part, the "I" of "I am," could outlive the body.

_____ **7.** The thought pattern for this paragraph is
   a. definition.   c. cause and effect.
   b. comparison and contrast.

8. Give one transition word or phrase from the paragraph:

_____

The Driverless Car of the Future

Cars of the future will be much different from cars of today. One difference is that in-car navigation systems, in only a few cars today, will be commonplace in the future. All cars will have a computer in the dashboard that stores maps, gets information from satellites in space, gives directions, and sends signals to rescuers if the driver is lost or hurt. Another difference will be the role of the driver; an automated highway may take the tasks of steering, speeding up, slowing down, and braking away from the driver. The cars that use these highways will have computers that pick up signals from magnets built into the road.

_____ **9.** The thought pattern for this paragraph is
      a. generalization and example.
      b. cause and effect.
      c. comparison and contrast.

10. Give one transition word or phrase from the paragraph:

_____

REVIEW **Test 2**

Topic Sentences and Thought Patterns

Read each of the following topic sentences. Then write the letter of the thought pattern that each topic sentence suggests.

_____ **1.** Like African Americans, most Mexican Americans benefited from the New Deal.
      a. generalization and example   c. cause and effect
      b. comparison

_____ **2.** Addiction to prescribed drugs is very similar to addiction to illegal drugs.
      a. cause and effect   c. generalization and example
      b. comparison

_____ **3.** Energy can only be described by the effect it has on matter.
      a. generalization and example   c. cause and effect
      b. contrast

_____ **4.** Today, political videos aim to produce very specific reactions in voters.
      a. generalization and example   c. comparison
      b. cause and effect

_____ **5.** Self-affirming statements include phrases such as "I can do it" and "I can and I will succeed."
   a. generalization and example   c. cause and effect
   b. contrast

_____ **6.** Toddlers and teenagers may face some of the same stresses as they try to separate from their parents.
   a. comparison   c. classification
   b. generalization and example

_____ **7.** The way that people thought about and treated children in the 19th century stands in sharp contrast to their current treatment.
   a. cause and effect   c. contrast
   b. definition

_____ **8.** Psychology is the science of mental processes and behavior; let's look at the key words in this definition.
   a. comparison   c. definition
   b. cause and effect

_____ **9.** Ambulances rushing to the rescue can lead to deadly results.
   a. cause and effect   c. definition
   b. contrast

_____ **10.** The human body responds to stressful events by making extra energy available; for example, ordinary people have lifted cars off bodies trapped under them.
   a. comparison   c. generalization and example
   b. cause and effect

REVIEW Test 3

Transitions and Thought Patterns

Read each group of transition words and phrases, and identify the thought pattern that each group suggests.

_____ **1.** On the one hand, on the other hand, likewise, however
   a. comparison and contrast   c. time order
   b. cause and effect

_____ **2.** Is, means, for example, such as
   a. process   c. cause and effect
   b. definition

_____ **3.** Leads to, results in, therefore, thus, reasons
     a. comparison and contrast   c. cause and effect
     b. example

_____ **4.** Accordingly, consequently, because, if . . . then
     a. summary   c. cause and effect
     b. comparison and contrast

_____ **5.** Differs from, instead, rather than, to the contrary
     a. time order   c. generalization and example
     b. comparison and contrast

REVIEW Test 4

Transition Words and Phrases and Thought Patterns

Before you read, skim the passage and answer the Before Reading questions. Read the essay. Then answer the After Reading questions.

[1]Some experts believe that birth order—the family position into which we are born—leads to many of our other traits. [2]Whether we are the oldest, the youngest, or the middle child, the order in which we are born can influence both the kinds of goals we set and the ways in which we relate to other people. [3]Understanding the effect of birth order may help us better understand others and ourselves.

[4]Being born first often results in leadership skills. [5]Only children are also included in this group. [6]Firstborns are often competitive, hardworking, and high-achieving. [7]Consequently, high numbers of firstborns earn degrees in higher education and become leaders in large corporations. [8]People in this group often **strive** for perfection. [9]They tend to be responsible, organized, and strong-minded.

[10]Middle children, by contrast, are often known as peacemakers. [11]They can see both sides of an issue and find the places where people can agree. [12]Middle children are good managers and leaders. [13]People in this group are often flexible, sociable, and generous. [14]They are often **tactful** even though they can be competitive. [15]Being the middle child results in a person who is balanced and skilled at getting along with others.

[16]Because of their position in the family, youngest children often love to be around people. [17]The baby of the family is likely to be outgoing and fun-loving. [18]Youngest children are direct and honest. [19]Many youngest children become highly successful salespeople as a result of their ability to motivate others. [20]In summary, birth order seems to have a strong effect on a person's nature.

BEFORE READING
Vocabulary in Context

_____ **1.** The word **strive** in sentence 8 means
    a. fight back.
    b. look around.
    c. work to achieve.
    d. go on.

_____ **2.** The best synonym for the word **tactful** in sentence 14 is
    a. rude.
    b. considerate.
    c. true.
    d. forceful.

AFTER READING
Concept Maps

Complete the concept map by filling in information from the essay.

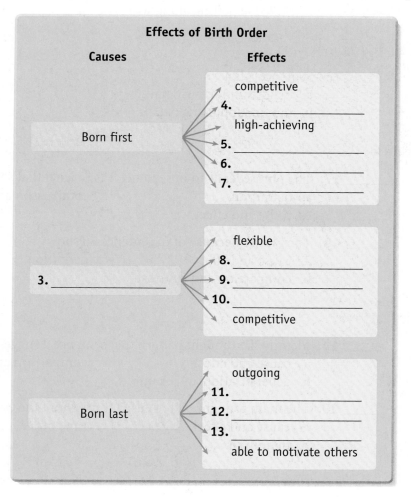

Effects of Birth Order

Causes   **Effects**

Born first

    competitive
4. _____
    high-achieving
5. _____
6. _____
7. _____

3. _____

    flexible
8. _____
9. _____
10. _____
    competitive

Born last

    outgoing
11. _____
12. _____
13. _____
    able to motivate others

Central Idea and Main Idea

_____ **14.** What is the central idea or thesis statement of the essay?
a. Birth order is the single most important influence on our lives.
b. Birth order determines our success or failure.
c. Each birth order has its own problems.
d. Understanding the effect of birth order will help us understand ourselves.

_____ **15.** What is the best statement of the main idea for the third paragraph (sentences 10–15)?
a. The second group is the middle child.
b. Middle children are peacemakers.
c. Being a middle child leads to being pulled in different directions.
d. Being a middle child results in a person who is balanced and skilled at getting along with others.

Supporting Details

_____ **16.** Sentence 5 is a
a. major supporting detail.
b. minor supporting detail.

Transitions

_____ **17.** The phrase **leads to** in sentence 1 is a signal that shows
a. definition.   c. comparison and contrast
b. cause and effect.

_____ **18.** The phrase **because of** in sentence 16 shows
a. cause and effect.   c. definition.
b. comparison and contrast.

Thought Patterns

_____ **19.** Identify the thought pattern that sentence 3 suggests.
a. cause and effect   c. comparison and contrast
b. generalization and example

_____ **20.** The main thought pattern used throughout the essay is
a. cause and effect.   c. time order.
b. definition.

Discussion Questions

1. Why would birth order produce specific traits in people?

2. What conflicts might come about between people because of birth order?

3. What are some of the drawbacks of being a firstborn, middle, or youngest child?

Writing Topics

1. In a paragraph, discuss the ways in which your birth order has influenced you.

2. Identify and give at least three examples of the birth order traits of someone in your family.

3. Identify and discuss the effects of birth order on someone famous.

SKILLED READER Scorecard

More Thought Patterns

Test	Number Correct		Points		Score
Review Test 1	_____	×	10	=	_____
Review Test 2	_____	×	10	=	_____
Review Test 3	_____	×	20	=	_____
Review Test 4	_____	×	5	=	_____
Review Test 5 (website)	_____	×	10	=	_____
Review Test 6 (website)	_____	×	10	=	_____

Enter your scores on the Skilled Reader Scorecard: Chapter 9 Review Tests inside the back cover.

After Reading About More Thought Patterns

Before you move on to the mastery tests on more thought patterns, take time to reflect on your learning and performance by answering the following questions. Write your answers in your notebook.

What did I learn about more thought patterns?

What do I need to remember about more thought patterns?

How has my knowledge base or prior knowledge about more thought patterns changed?

More Review and Mastery Tests

For more practice, go to the book's website at **http://www.ablongman.com/henry** and click on *The Skilled Reader*. Then select "More Review and Mastery Tests." You will find the tests listed by chapter.

Read each paragraph, and answer the questions that follow it.

The Hmong

The Hmong are a group of people originally from China whose struggle to keep their culture and freedom has affected them deeply. In the early 1900s, many Hmong fled China because the government wanted to do away with Hmong traditions. When they fled China, many settled in the highland areas of Laos and Vietnam. During the Vietnam War in the 1960s and 1970s, thousands of Hmong died because they sided with the United States. After the war, the Hmong fled once more, this time to Thailand, where they waited in refugee camps until they could come to America.

_____ **1.** The main thought pattern is
   a. cause and effect.
   b. comparison and contrast.
   c. generalization and example.

2. What is one transition word that signals the main thought pattern?

_____

**What's the Difference: Immigrant,
Refugee, Illegal Alien?**

To properly respond to the complex issue of immigration, we must understand the differences between an immigrant, a refugee, and an illegal alien. Immigrants are persons who choose to leave their country of origin for any number of reasons. Usually, immigrants are looking for better jobs and may live where they please as long as they abide by the laws of the land. By contrast, refugees are persons who fled their country of origin due to fear of persecution. Usually, refugees must leave behind their personal possessions and fortunes, and many are forced to live in refugee camps for years. An illegal alien is an individual who enters a country without proper documentation or permission. Usually, illegal aliens are desperate to reunite with family or to escape war or poverty, and some unwillingly become illegal aliens due to slavery and prostitution.

_____ **3.** The thought pattern is
a. comparison and contrast.
b. summary.
c. cause and effect.

What two words or phrases signal the thought pattern?

4. _____

5. _____

A. Read the paragraph. Then answer the questions and complete the list that follow it.

Textbook
Skills

Double Life

In Greek, the word *amphibious* means "living a double life." Most members of this class **Amphibia** exhibit a mixture of aquatic and terrestrial adaptations. Most species are tied to water because their eggs lack shells and dry out quickly in the air. For example the frog spends much if its time on land, but it lays its eggs in water. An egg develops into a larva called a tadpole. A tadpole is a legless, aquatic algae-eater with gills and a long finned tail. In changing into a frog, the tadpole undergoes a radical metamorphosis. When a young frog crawls onto shore and begins life as a terrestrial insect-eater, it has four legs, air-breathing lungs instead of gills, and no tail. Because of this change, many amphibians truly live a double life.

—Campbell, Reece, Taylor, and Simon. *Biology: Concepts & Connections*, 5th ed., Benjamin Cummings, 2008, p.389.

VISUAL VOCABULARY

Terrestrial means

_____

a. living in water.
b. living on land.

▲ A frog crawls onto the shore and begins life as a terrestrial insect-eater.

_____ **1.** The thought pattern is
   a. cause and effect.
   b. definition.
   c. comparison and contrast.

What two words or phrases signal the thought pattern?

2. _____

3. _____

Complete the following study notes with details from the paragraph:

Term: Amphibious   **Definition:** Living a double life

Term: Amphibia   **Definition: (4)** _____

_____

Term: aquatic   **Definition:** refers to water

Term: terrestrial   **Definition:** refers to land

Term: metamorphosis   **Definition:** radical change

Summary: Amphibians live a double life. They have adapted to living in water and on land. For example, a tadpole is an aquatic larva that metamorphoses into a **(5)** _____ frog.

B. Read the paragraph. Then answer the questions and complete the concept map that follow it.

Listening Skills

The difference between good and poor listening skills may mean the difference between success and failure. Poor listeners often do not hear what is being said. They are sidetracked by other tasks such as watching TV or daydreaming, and they miss needed information. Often they misunderstand what they do hear. Missing information leads to mistakes, problems, and failure. In contrast, good listeners hear what is being said, and they understand what they hear. They focus on ideas and ask questions when needed. They gather information. Listening helps a person avoid mistakes, solve problems, and achieve success.

_____ **6.** The thought pattern is
     a. generalization and example.
     b. cause and effect.
     c. comparison and contrast.

7. What word or phrase signals the paragraph's thought pattern?

_____

Complete the following chart using information from the passage.

Topic: The difference between poor and good listening skills

	Poor Listeners		**Good Listeners**
Listening:	**8.** _____	*differs from*	focused
Contrasts:	misunderstanding	*differs from*	**9.** _____
	misses information	*differs from*	gathers information
	makes mistakes	*differs from*	solves problems
	failure	*differs from*	**10.** _____

Read each paragraph. Then answer the questions and complete the activities that follow it.

Textbook
Skills

What Is Veganism?

Veganism covers far more than just diet. Veganism is a way of living that avoids all forms of cruelty to any animal; vegans avoid eating all meat, fish, or fowl, as well as any other foods of animal origin such as butter, milk, yogurt, honey, eggs, gelatin, or lard, and any prepared foods that contain these items. This belief system values animal life. For example, vegans are outraged by the way commercial dairy farms treat their cows. According to vegans, the milking cow is kept pregnant so she will produce milk, and vegans say she lives the majority of her life hooked to a milking machine.

—Adapted from Stepaniak, "What Is Veganism?" *Vegan Vittles.* Farm Sanctuary. Online. 8 Sept. 2002.

VISUAL VOCABULARY

Vegans are _____ by the treatment of cows.

a. encouraged
b. outraged

_____ **1.** The thought pattern is
   a. comparison and contrast.   c. definition.
   b. cause and effect.

What two words or phrases signal the paragraph's thought pattern?

2. _____

3. _____

Complete the following outline using information from the paragraph.

Main idea: Veganism covers far more than just diet.

A. Definition

    4. _____

- Avoid eating meat, fish, or fowl; other foods of animal origin; and prepared foods that contain these items
- Value animal life

B. Examples

    5. _____

- Spend life hooked to milking machine

Health Care in North America

Although similar in many ways, the United States and Canada differ significantly in their health care systems. These two countries are very similar in their standard of living. Both have thriving economies. Both have their share of people who range from poor to wealthy. Major store and food chains have outlets in both places. Stores such as Sears and Wal-Mart and fast-food chains like Arby's and McDonald's are found in both countries. However, Canada and the United States differ in the way they deliver health care. In Canada, health care is supported by taxes, and nobody has to pay directly for services. Medicare, not the patient, pays all doctor visits, treatments, and surgeries. Even the poor have access to good health care. In contrast, in the United States, the patient pays for health care. Of course, health insurance helps, but the patient must pay for the insurance. Those who cannot pay are often left untreated.

_____ **6.** The thought pattern is
    a. generalization and example. c. comparison and contrast.
    b. cause and effect.

What four words or phrases signal the paragraph's thought pattern?

    7. _____

    8. _____

    9. _____

    10. _____

A. Write the numbers **1** through **6** in the spaces provided to show the correct order of the ideas.

Textbook
Skills

_____ **1.** The third factor is the lack of shelters or safe houses; many have no place to go.

_____ **2.** One attitude that leads victims to stay is the fear that the abuser will kill them if they do leave.

_____ **3.** Five factors result in many abuse victims' staying with their abusers.

_____ **4.** A fourth cause of victims' staying is their lack of money.

_____ **5.** Finally, the attitude that "this is a private matter" keeps many victims from seeking help.

_____ **6.** Another cause for staying is that they have been cut off from family and friends.

—Adapted from Mignon, Larson, & Holmes, *Family Abuse: Consequences, Theories, and Responses,* p. 38.

B. Read the paragraph, and answer the questions that follow it.

Textbook
Skills

Managing Stress

Millions of people suffer from stress-related problems. Become an active stress manager instead of a passive stress victim. Active stress managers think about and plan for the future. In contrast, passive stress victims leave things to chance. Managers save time and energy for the unexpected. However, victims try to cram in everything at the last minute. Finally, stress managers have a plan to reduce stress. To the contrary, stress victims let problems pile up.

—Adapted from Brownell, *Listening: Attitudes, Principles, and Skills,* 2nd ed., pp. 159–60.

_____ **7.** The thought pattern is
   a. listing.
   b. contrast and comparison.
   c. generalization and example.

371

8. What is one word or phrase that signals the paragraph's thought pattern?

_____

C. Read the paragraph, and answer the questions that follow it.

Causes of Cancer

Cancer in humans has several major causes. A leading cause seems to be related to diet. In fact, according to some experts, diet leads to a third to one-half of all cancers. For example, overcooking and charcoal grilling have been linked to cancer as well as high-fat and low-fiber diets. Even the chemicals in some molds are known as cancer-causing agents. The second leading cause of cancer is tobacco products; they account for as much as one-third of all cases. Tobacco use results in cancer of the mouth, throat, lungs, kidneys, and bladder. A less common cause of cancer is a virus. A small number of viruses have been linked with cancer. The hepatitis B and Epstein-Barr viruses are two examples of cancer-causing viruses.

—Adapted from Ward, _The Cancer Handbook: A Guide for the_
Nonspecialist. Ohio State University Press, 1995.

_____ **9.** The thought pattern is
    a. generalization and example.
    b. cause and effect.
    c. comparison and contrast.

10. What is one word or phrase that signals the paragraph's thought pattern?

_____

Read the paragraph. Then answer the questions and complete the concept map that follow it.

Types of Abuse

Textbook
Skills

There are a number of differences between physical and sexual abuse. Typically, sexual abuse is mostly mentally harmful, while physical abuse is physically harmful. Society takes a strong stand against sexual abuse, yet violence is much more accepted. Health care workers tend to react differently to sexual and physical abuse as well. Sexual abuse does not get the same attention that physical abuse gets from doctors. Doctors are trained to deal with physical problems, but sexual abuse may not have any physical signs.

—Adapted from Mignon, Larson, & Holmes, *Family Abuse: Consequences, Theories, and Responses*, pp. 78–79.

_____ **1.** The thought pattern is
   a. cause and effect.
   b. generalization and example.
   c. comparison and contrast.

2. What is one word or phrase that signals the paragraph's thought pattern?

_____

Complete the following chart with ideas from the passage:

Main idea: 3. _____

_____

		Sexual Abuse	**Physical Abuse**
Harm	4. _____	5. _____
Society's outlook	6. _____	7. _____
8. _____	9. _____	10. _____

A. Read the following passage from a psychology textbook. Answer the questions, and finish the outline that follows them.

Textbook
Skills

Definition and Causes of Stress

¹**Stress** is the general term describing the psychological and bodily response to an event. ²A **stressor** is a stimulus that throws the body out of balance. ³Stressors can be acute or chronic.

⁴The **stress response** causes physical changes in the nervous systems that get the body ready for physical effort and repair of injury. ⁵These effects include changes in the heart and breathing rates and the release of natural chemicals throughout the body. ⁶These changes occur during the **alarm stage** of the event. ⁷If the stressor continues, the body tries to adapt or resist. ⁸During the **exhaustion phase**, the stress response can cause damage and lead to stress-related diseases.

⁹Certain factors are likely to lead to a stress response. ¹⁰First, a sense of lack of control causes stress. ¹¹For example, jobs that do not allow a worker to have control over how the work is done and work that is too challenging or not challenging all cause stress. ¹²Another cause of stress is environmental factors such as noise and crowding. ¹³Finally, daily hassles and conflict result in stress.

—Adapted from Kosslyn & Rosenberg, *Psychology: The Brain, The Person, The World,* p. 432.

_____ **1.** The thought pattern of the first paragraph (sentences 1–3) is
   a. cause and effect.
   b. comparison and contrast.
   c. definition.

_____ **2.** The thought pattern of the second paragraph (sentences 4–8) is
   a. cause and effect.
   b. comparison and contrast.
   c. definition.

_____ **3.** The main thought pattern of the third paragraph (sentences 9–13) is
   a. cause and effect.
   b. comparison and contrast.
   c. definition.

B. What are three words that suggest the thought pattern used in the second paragraph (sentences 4–8)?

4. _____

5. _____

6. _____

C. Fill in the concept map using information from the passage.

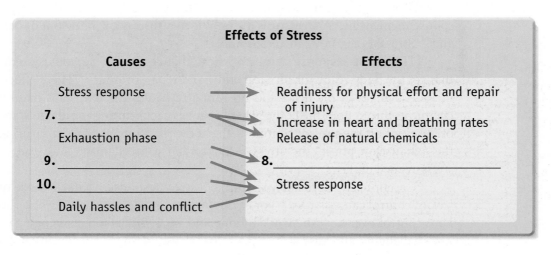

Effects of Stress

Causes	**Effects**
Stress response	Readiness for physical effort and repair of injury
7. _____	Increase in heart and breathing rates
Exhaustion phase	Release of natural chemicals
9. _____	8._____
10. _____	Stress response
Daily hassles and conflict	

CHAPTER

10

Daryl Lawrence   10/03/09

Implied
Main Ideas

CHAPTER PREVIEW

Before Reading About Implied Main Ideas
An Introduction to Implied Main Ideas
Studying Supporting Details to Identify and State the Topic
Using Topics, Supporting Details, and Thought Patterns to
    Determine the Implied Main Idea
Annotating the Paragraph to Determine the Implied Main Idea
Creating a One-Sentence Summary from Supporting Details
Textbook Skills: Pictures as Details

Before Reading About Implied Main Ideas

Take a moment to study the chapter preview. Underline key words that refer to
ideas you have already studied in previous chapters. Each of these key words
represents a great deal of knowledge upon which you will build as you learn
about implied main ideas. These key terms have been listed below. In the given
spaces, write what you already know about each one:

- Main ideas: _Is basically what descrube what_
  the paragraph is really about
- Supporting details: _Are information that help_
  the audiens understand the passage
  or story.

- Thought patterns: _____

_____

_____

- A summary: _A brief paragraph of what the passage is about_
- Annotating: _to make or note a comment_

Compare what you wrote with the following paragraph, which summarizes this vital prior knowledge:

> Main ideas are stated in a topic sentence. A topic sentence includes a topic and the author's controlling point. Supporting details explain the main idea. There are two types of supporting details. Major supporting details directly explain the topic sentence (or thesis statement), and minor supporting details explain the major supporting details. Authors use transitions to create thought patterns. Thought patterns organize details. Some examples are time order, cause and effect, and comparison and contrast. A summary condenses a paragraph or passage to its main idea. Annotating is marking or highlighting ideas in the paragraph, and helps create a summary.

Recopy the list in your notebook; leave several blank lines between each idea. As you work through this chapter, record how you apply each idea in the list to the new information you learn about implied main ideas and implied central ideas.

An Introduction to Implied Main Ideas

Often an author will create a paragraph that does not include a topic sentence or a stated main idea. Even though the main idea is not stated in a single sentence, the paragraph still has a main idea. In these cases, the details clearly suggest or **imply** the author's main idea. When the main idea is not stated, you must figure out the author's point based on the facts, examples, descriptions, and explanations given. Learning how to develop a main idea based on the details will help you develop several skills. You will learn how to study information, value the meaning of supporting details, and use your own words to express an implied main idea.

> An **implied main idea** is a main idea that is not stated directly but is strongly suggested by the supporting details in the passage.

Many different types of reading materials use implied main ideas. For example, you will often need to formulate the implied main idea when you read literature. Short stories, novels, poems, and plays rely heavily on vivid details to suggest the author's point. In addition, many paragraphs in college textbooks do not provide a topic sentence. In these paragraphs, the author uses supporting details to imply the main idea.

When a main idea is not stated but **implied**, you must figure out the main idea on your own. For example, read the following paragraph.

> [1]Employees with burnout feel tired all the time, and they often show symptoms of depression. [2]The likelihood of burnout is increased if they feel trapped in the job. [3]Burnout can also occur if the job demands an overload of work. [4]Ongoing lack of social support, rigid rules, and unkind bosses also lead to burnout.

Did you notice that every sentence in this paragraph is a supporting detail? In the paragraph, no single sentence covers all the other ideas. Ask the following questions to figure out the implied main idea:

Questions for Determining the Implied Main Idea

1. What is the topic, or subject, of the paragraph?
2. What are the major supporting details?
3. What is the author's controlling point?

Apply these three questions to the paragraph you just read by writing your responses to each question in the blanks.

1. What is the topic of the paragraph? *implied main ideas*

   Each of the sentences in the paragraph uses the word *burnout*.

2. What are the major supporting details? List four supporting details:

   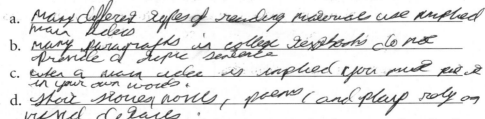

   a. *Many different types of reading materials use implied main ideas*

   b. *many paragraphs in college textbooks do not provide a topic sentence*

   c. *when a main idea is implied you must put it in your own words.*

   d. *short stories, novels, poems, and plays rely on vivid details.*

   All the examples listed deal with burnout at work. The supporting details make up a list of a few causes of burnout at work.

3. What is the author's controlling point? *That implying*
main ideas is a key to sucess

By identifying the topic and supporting details used, it is easy to find the main idea of this paragraph.

EXAMPLE Read the following paragraph. Then answer the questions that follow it.

[1]Glen painfully jogged 3 of the 6 miles he runs every morning. [2]For several weeks, his right knee had become increasingly sore. [3]Suddenly, he yelped in pain and came to a full stop. [4]He tried to take a step, but the sharp pain in his knee made it impossible. [5]He had to sit helplessly on the curb while his wife ran back to their house to get the car. [6]At the doctor's office, Glen learned that a small piece of bone had broken off right above the kneecap. [7]The doctor said that over time, the punishing impact of running had cut off blood to the bone, making it weak. [8]Like many runners, Glen had to face surgery and give up running.

_C_ **1.** The topic of this paragraph is
    a. exercising.
    b. Glen's knee surgery.
    c. Glen's injury from running.
    d. the pain Glen experienced.

_b_ **2.** The supporting details include
    a. a list of reasons why people shouldn't run.
    b. one runner's story about a serious and painful injury.

_b_ **3.** The implied main idea for this paragraph is
    a. Running can cause a broken bone.
    b. Running can have serious and painful effects.
    c. Glen's injury occurred over time.
    d. People should not run for exercise.

EXPLANATION

1. The topic of the paragraph is (c) "Glen's injury from running." Choice (a) is too broad; the paragraph focuses on a running injury and does not mention other kinds of exercise. Choice (b) is too specific because only one sentence deals with Glen's surgery. Choice (d) is too general because many sentences describe Glen's pain, but sentences 5, 6, and 7 do not mention pain.

2. The supporting details include (b) "one runner's story about a serious and painful injury."

3. The implied main idea for the paragraph is (b) "Running can have serious and painful effects." The last sentence (8) gives a good clue to the author's main point. "Like many runners" suggests that the author used Glen's story as an example of how serious and painful running injuries can be. Choice (a) is too specific in that a broken bone is only one kind of injury that runners may experience. Choice (c) is also too specific; it is a supporting detail. Choice (d) is too general because not all runners suffer serious and painful injuries.

Searching for an implied main idea is much like a treasure hunt. You must carefully read the clues provided by the author. This kind of careful reading is a skill that improves dramatically with practice. The following examples and practices are designed to strengthen this important skill.

Studying Supporting Details to Identify and State the Topic

A topic is a general subject to which specific details belong. Thus, specific details suggest a specific topic. You can study the details to determine the topic that the details develop.

Following is a list of specific details. Read the list. Then determine the topic that best covers all the specific details.

Specific details: brushes, chalk, pens, inks, paints

 The **topic** is
   a. art.
   b. art supplies.
   c. painting supplies.

The topic of art includes many ideas that are not listed here. So (a) is too general. Item (c) is too specific, for it does not cover chalk, pens, and inks. Thus (b) is the correct choice, for all the specific details belong to the topic of art supplies. Look for the flow of ideas from general to specific. The flow of ideas will help you find the topic for a specific set of details. For example, study the following diagram. The diagram shows the flow from general to specific ideas.

art	art supplies	painting supplies	paint brushes
broad, general topic	more specific topic than "art"	more specific topic than "art supplies"	more specific topic than "painting supplies"

In the diagram, the topics become more and more specific. And each specific topic suggests a specific set of supporting details. The following diagram shows the flow of ideas. The diagram shows how ideas move from a general topic to a more specific topic, to a specific set of supporting details.

art	art supplies	painting supplies	paint brushes
drawing painting sculpting	brushes chalk pens inks paints	brushes paints	oil paint brushes watercolor brushes

Each topic generates a unique list of details. The topic "art supplies" is the only topic that matches this list of details: brushes, chalk, pens, inks, and paints. To identify topics suggested by specific details ask the following questions:

Is this topic *too specific?* Does it cover *all* the given details?

Is this topic *too general?* Does it suggest *more* details than the ones that are given?

Once you identify the topic based on a set of details, these questions will also help you state the topic. Following is a list of specific details. Study the details. Determine the topic based on the details. Then state the topic by filling in the blank with your own words.

Specific details: lightning strikes, tornadoes, hurricanes, floods, mudslides

Topic: _Natural disasters_

This list of details is a list of events that occur in nature. Wording may vary, but one possible way to state this topic is "acts of nature." You must be able to study a set of specific details and find your own accurate label for the topic.

EXAMPLES

A. Read the following lists of specific details. In the space provided, write the letter of the best topic for each list.

Specific details: Wendy's, Taco Bell, McDonald's, Burger King

___b___ **1.** The **topic** is
 a. fast food.
 b. fast-food restaurants.
 c. fast-food restaurants that sell hamburgers.

Specific details: toothbrush, toothpaste, dental floss, mouthwash

___a___ **2.** The **topic** is
 a. items for cleaning the teeth and mouth.
 b. items for brushing teeth.
 c. items for flossing teeth.

B. Read the following list of specific details. Then write a word or phrase that best states the topic. Remember: not too specific; not too general; find that perfect fit!

Specific details: printer, monitor, keyboard, mouse, processor

Topic: *Computers* _____

EXPLANATIONS

A.   **1.** Item (a) is too broad. "Fast food" covers specific details not listed. Item (c) is too narrow, for Taco Bell does not sell hamburgers. So (b) is correct. All the places listed are fast-food restaurants.

   2. Item (b) is too narrow. "Items for brushing teeth" does not include dental floss or mouthwash. Item (c) is also too narrow, because toothbrushes, toothpaste, and mouthwash are not used to floss teeth. So (a) is correct, for it includes all the items in the list.

B. Each of these objects is a specific part of a personal computer. Thus a personal computer is the topic suggested by the details.

PRACTICE 1

A. Read each group of specific details. In the space provided, write the letter of the best topic for each group.

Specific details: beds, a couch, easy chairs, a dining table, televisions

  1. The **topic** is
 a. furniture.
 b. furniture for a house.
 c. furniture for a living room.

Specific details: Georgia, Alabama, Mississippi

___*c*___ **2.** The **topic** is
     a. geographical regions.
     b. states in the United States of America.
     c. southern states in the United States of America.

Specific details: pancakes, waffles, eggs, salad, roasted pork, green beans, carrot cake

___*a*___ **3.** The **topic** is
     a. foods.
     b. foods found on a menu.
     c. foods found on a restaurant dinner menu.

Specific details: Mountain Dew, Coca-Cola, Pepsi, Dr Pepper

___*b*___ **4.** The **topic** is
     a. drinks.
     b. soft drinks.
     c. soft drinks with caffeine.

Specific details: driving too slowly, tailgating, leaving a turn signal on for miles and miles, cutting in too close while changing lanes

___*b*___ **5.** The **topic** is
     a. driving.
     b. driving habits.
     c. annoying driving habits.

Specific details: marijuana, alcohol, cocaine, heroin

___*c*___ **6.** The **topic** is
     a. drugs.
     b. illegal drugs.
     c. legal drugs.

Specific details: trucks, vans, minivans, sport utility vehicles

___*b*___ **7.** The **topic** is
     a. cars.
     b. vehicles.
     c. vehicles used for sports.

Specific details: whole-wheat muffins, rye bread, brown rice casserole

___*b*___ **8.** The **topic** is
   a. food.
   b. foods made from grains.
   c. breads.

Specific details: CD player; tape deck; AM/FM radio; speakers in the car's dash, both front doors, and the rear window

___*b*___ **9.** The **topic** is
   a. equipment.
   b. sound equipment.
   c. sound equipment for a car.

Specific details: pit bulls, German shepherds, rottweilers

___*a*___ **10.** The **topic** is
   a. animals.
   b. dogs often used as guard dogs.
   c. dogs.

B. Read each group of specific details. Then, in the space provided, using your own words, write the topic for the group. (Clues are given for Questions 1–5.)

1. **Topic:** types of ___*Math*___ questions

   Specific details: multiple-choice, matching, fill-in-the-blank

2. **Topic:** recent ___*presidents*___ of the United States

   Specific details: Ronald Reagan, George H. W. Bush, Bill Clinton, George W. Bush

3. **Topic:** items served at a ___*sea-food*___ restaurant

   Specific details: shrimp, lobster, crab cakes, fried catfish, broiled trout

4. **Topic:** types of ___*money*___

   Specific details: sales, property, state, federal income

5. **Topic:** types of ___*emotion*___

   Specific details: love, hate, jealousy, anger, sorrow

6. **Topic:** ___*Shows*___

   Specific details: *Scrubs, George Lopez, The Office*

7. Topic: _light_

Specific details: sun, fire, candle, lamp

8. Topic: _Church_

Specific details: church, mosque, synagogue, temple

9. Topic: _mail_

Specific details: letter, postcard, E-mail

10. Topic: _Caution signs_

Specific details: STOP, YIELD, SOFT SHOULDER, SLIPPERY WHEN WET

Using Topics, Supporting Details, and Thought Patterns to Determine the Implied Main Idea

Remember that an implied topic is suggested by a set of specific details. Similarly, specific details given in a series of sentences suggest the **implied main idea**. The implied main idea cannot be so general that it suggests details not given; nor can it be so specific that some of the given details are not covered. Instead, the implied main idea must cover *all* the details given.

The skill of identifying a stated main idea will also help you grasp the implied main idea. You learned in Chapter 4 that the stated main idea (the topic sentence) has two parts. A main idea is made up of the topic and the author's controlling point about the topic. One trait of the controlling point is the author's opinion or bias. A second trait is the author's thought pattern. Consider, for example, the topic sentence "Running can have serious and painful effects." The topic of this sentence is "running." The words "serious and painful" state the author's opinion (bias). And the word "effects" states the thought pattern. When you read material that implies the main idea, you should mentally create a topic sentence based on the details in the material.

EXAMPLE Read the following list of supporting details. Circle the topic as it recurs throughout the list of details. Underline transition words and biased words. Then choose the statement that best expresses the author's controlling point about the topic.

The sun and its atmosphere consist of several distinct zones or layers.

The sun consists of three layers.

From inside out, the three zones of the sun are the core; the radiative zone; and the convection zone.

Surrounding the sun, its atmosphere is also made up of three zones: the photosphere, the chromosphere, and the corona.

Beyond the corona is the solar wind.

—Adapted from NASA. "Hinode Mission to the Sun." Photo Gallery. 27 March 07. <http://www.nasa.gov/mission_pages/solar-b/photos07-031.html>.

 The implied main idea is

    a. The sun consists of several zones or layers.

    b. The sun's atmosphere consists of several zones or layers.

    c. The sun and its atmosphere consist of several distinct zones or layers.

    d. The sun is a beautiful ball of gas.

VISUAL VOCABULARY

The sun's _____ is made up of the photosphere, chromosphere, and corona.

    a. interior

    b. atmosphere

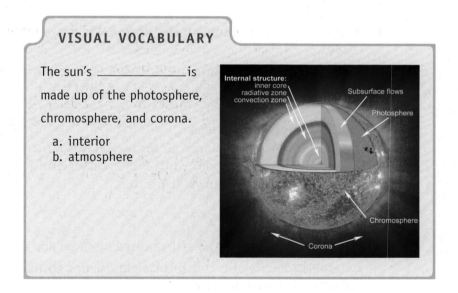

EXPLANATION The topic that recurs throughout the list is the *sun and its atmosphere*. The transition words include *from inside out, surrounding,* and *beyond*. These transitions suggest the spatial (space) order thought pattern. The author's purpose is to inform the audience about the structure of the sun based on scientific facts, so the author uses only one bias word: *distinct*. This word asserts the belief that each layer is clearly physically separate from the next. Although this is an expert opinion based on research and logic, no one has actually seen inside the sun's interior to verify that layers are clearly distinct. In fact, the most basic difference among most layers is the temperature. The sentence that best combines the topic, the thought pattern, and the author's purpose is (c) "The sun and its atmosphere consist of several distinct zones or layers." Choices (a) "The sun consists of several zones or layers" and (b) "The sun's atmosphere consists of several zones or layers" are both too narrow. Choice (d) is too broad.

PRACTICE 2

Read each group of information. Circle the topic and underline words that reveal the author's bias and thought pattern. Then choose the best statement of the implied main idea.

Group 1

- First, emergency rooms treated over 8,000 fireworks injuries in the year 2001.
- Second, fireworks injuries include blindness, scarring, and amputation.
- Third, fireworks are made of gunpowder.

 The **implied main idea** is
   a. Fireworks are dangerous for several reasons.
   b. Fireworks are fun because they are dangerous.
   c. Fireworks are fun yet dangerous.

Group 2

- First, aerobic exercise gives the heart a workout and aids overall health.
- Aerobic exercise also controls weight, shapes up the body, and improves flexibility.
- Second, exercising with weights builds muscles.
- Weight-bearing exercise boosts bone density and stops the loss of muscle.

 The **implied main idea** is
   a. There are many benefits to exercising.
   b. Aerobic exercise is a great way to get in shape.
   c. Aerobics and weightlifting are two beneficial kinds of exercise.

Group 3

- The first trait of a problem gambler is the uncontrollable urge to gamble.
- The second trait of a problem gambler is the likelihood of committing fraud and theft to keep on gambling.
- The third trait of a problem gambler is an obsession with gambling.
- The fourth trait of a problem gambler is the habit of reliving a past gamble or planning a future one.
- A final trait is that tolerance for gambling changes as the problem gambler needs to risk more money to feel the excitement of the bet.

 The **implied main idea** is
    a. Gambling is difficult to control.
    b. A problem gambler can be recognized by several traits.
    c. The problem gambler will steal to gamble.

Group 4

- Regular seat belts leave the driver's head free to snap around with great force.
- In contrast, the HANS is a type of head and seat restraint used by race car drivers.
- The HANS uses a collar system made of carbon fiber and Kevlar.
- Kevlar is a synthetic material used in bulletproof vests.
- The device is worn on the upper body under the shoulder straps.
- It is connected to the helmet by two flexible straps.
- Unlike regular seat belts, the HANS device keeps the driver's head from violent movement.

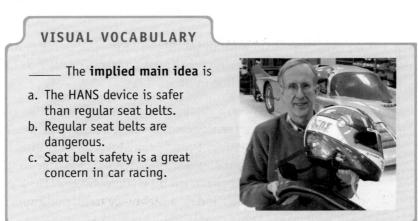

VISUAL VOCABULARY

_____ The **implied main idea** is
a. The HANS device is safer than regular seat belts.
b. Regular seat belts are dangerous.
c. Seat belt safety is a great concern in car racing.

Group 5

- Human hair extensions are often used to make beautiful braids and weaves.
- The extensions must be lightweight and thin.
- The hair extensions should match the color of the middle or end of the natural hair because natural hair is much darker at the roots.
- Braided hair should be washed between rows and at the scalp every few days.
- Going to sleep with a wet or damp weave will turn it into a tangled mess.
- Braided and weaved hair should be misted with water daily to keep the braid pattern even and neat.

_b_   The **implied main idea** is
   a. Braids and weaves are beautiful.
   b. Hair extensions must be carefully chosen.
   c. Proper selection and care of braids and weaves will make these beautiful hairstyles last longer.

Annotating the Paragraph to Determine the Implied Main Idea

So far, you have found the implied main idea from the specific details in a group of sentences. In this next step, the sentences will form a paragraph, but the skill of determining the implied main idea is exactly the same. The implied main idea of a paragraph must not be too general or too specific. In the last section, you learned to annotate or mark ideas. You circled the topic and underlined words that revealed the author's thought pattern and bias. Annotating a paragraph in the same way is a helpful tool in determining its implied main idea.

EXAMPLE   Read and annotate the following paragraph. Circle the topic and underline words that reveal thought patterns and bias. Then choose the best statement of the implied main idea.

[1]Argus was a mythical giant guard with 100 eyes. [2]According to the Greek myth, Argus was created by Hera, queen of the Greek gods, to keep her husband, Zeus, away from his mistress. [3]It was difficult to slip past Argus's hundred eyes, but another god, Hermes, was able to lull Argus to sleep with music and then behead him. [4]Myth has it that Hera put Argus's eyes on the tail of a peacock. [5]Today, a highly watchful and prepared person can be described as "Argus-eyed."

_C_   The **implied main idea** is

a. Greek myths have had a powerful impact on our society.

b. Argus was a tragic Greek character.

c. The story of Argus is one example of current sayings that came from Greek myths.

EXPLANATION   *Argus* is the obvious topic of this paragraph. However, several clues point to a more general topic. For example, the words *mythical, Greek myth,* and *myth* appear often enough to suggest that Greek myths are also part of the topic. In addition, sentence 5 suggests that the story of Argus, one of many Greek myths, has had an effect on us *today*. However, the first choice is too broad. There are many other ways in which Greek myths have affected our society. This paragraph just gives one specific way. The second choice is too narrow. Argus is just an example of the implied main idea. The correct answer is (c), for it includes the idea in sentence 5.

PRACTICE 3

Read and annotate the following paragraphs. Then choose the best statement of the implied main idea for each paragraph.

_C_   **1.**   ¹They are considered extravagant toys for adults. ²When the economy is good, more people buy them. ³In Europe, they are known as cabriolets. ⁴In the United States, they are known as convertibles or ragtops. ⁵The most popular model is the Ford Mustang, although Chrysler and Mitsubishi also have a hard time keeping their convertibles in stock. ⁶And now that these cars come equipped with increased safety features like air bags and stability control, more people are buying convertibles.

a. The Ford Mustang is a popular convertible.

b. Convertibles are popular luxury cars.

c. More people are buying convertibles.

_a_   **2.**   ¹The members of today's gangs are younger and more active than gang members in the 1970s. ²Gangs now rise up in wealthier and more suburban communities than they used to. ³Gangs are more likely to include girls and people of different races. ⁴The use of drugs and alcohol has increased in today's gangs, and so has violence. ⁵In fact, many newer gangs show no regard for human life and cause senseless deaths. ⁶Some make large amounts of money from prostitution and the sale of illegal drugs. [7]These new gangs use cell phones, beepers, automatic weapons, and guerrilla warfare tactics.

a. Gangs are violent.
b. Today, gangs rise up in wealthier and more suburban communities.
c. Today's gangs are different from gangs of the past.

<u>b</u>   **3.**   [1]One aspect of self-concept is self-image. [2]*Self-image* is the sort of person you believe yourself to be. [3]It is made up of physical and attitudinal descriptions of the self and the roles you play. [4]Another aspect of self-concept is self-esteem. [5]*Self-esteem* is a measure of the value you place on the images you have of yourself. [6]It includes your attitudes and feelings about yourself. [7]It is your judgment of how you are doing in life compared to how you think you should be doing. [8]A number of social forces come together to help create and feed your self-concept.

—Adapted from Gamble, Teri Kwal and Michael W. Gamble.
The Gender Communication Connection.
Houghton Mifflin 2003, p. 44.

a. The self-concept is sometimes broken in two components: self-image and self-esteem.
b. Self-image is an important aspect of self-concept.
c. Self-concept is the result of many forces.

<u>a</u>   **4.**   [1]Most Chinese immigrants entered California through the port of San Francisco. [2]They came by the thousands looking for better jobs and freedom from oppression. [3]Sadly, Chinese settlers faced bigotry immediately upon arrival in California. [4]In the 1850s, the United States reserved the right of citizenship for white immigrants to this country. [5]Thus, Chinese immigrants lived at the whim of local governments. [6]Some were allowed to become citizens, but most were not. [7]Without this right, they had difficulty earning a living. [8]For example, they were unable to own land or file mining claims. [9]Also in the 1850s, California passed a law taxing all foreign miners. [10]And in 1885, the citizens of Tucson, Arizona, created a petition to force Chinese to live in Chinatowns. [11]During this time, many Chinese chose to live in Chinatowns. [12]One Chinatown grew

in the middle of San Francisco. [13]They called it *Dai Fou* or "Big City." [14]It remains one of the largest Chinatowns in the country.

—Adapted from "Topical Overview: Essays & Galleries: Chinese and Westward Expansion." Special presentation. *The Chinese in California, 1850-1925. American Memory.* Lib. of Congress. 28 March 2003. 12 July 2007. <http://memory.loc.gov/ammem/award99/cubhtml/theme1.html>.

a. Thousands of Chinese immigrated into San Francisco.
b. Chinese Americans fled China due to bigotry.
c. Chinese Americans faced many obstacles when they immigrated to America during the nineteenth century.

VISUAL VOCABULARY

A _____ is a formal request to an authority for a benefit, right, or action.

a. law
b. petition

---

 5. [1]When offering praise to someone, it is best to avoid statements that sound judgmental. [2]Instead, describe what you see, hear, or feel. [3]For example, when your child brings you a piece of artwork, avoid saying, "You are so talented." [4]Instead say, "Your use of yellow in the sun and flowers reminds me of a warm summer day." [5]If correction is needed, try to avoid criticizing. [6]Instead, suggest what needs to be done. [7]For example, as you read your child's essay, avoid saying, "You have made careless spelling mistakes." [8]Instead suggest, "Be sure to check your spelling. I see you have confused *there* with *their*."

a. Praise and correction are often needed.
b. Praise should not sound judgmental.
c. When giving praise and correction, one should avoid judgments and suggest solutions.

Creating a One-Sentence Summary from Supporting Details

In this chapter so far, you have developed the skill of figuring out main ideas that are not directly stated. This ability to reason from specific details to main ideas will serve you well throughout college.

One further step will also prove helpful in your reading and studying: the ability to state the implied main idea in your own words. The statement you come up with must be a complete sentence. It must not be too specific, for it must cover all the details in the paragraph, and it must not be too general or go beyond the supporting details.

The one-sentence statement of the implied main idea is a one-sentence summary of all the details given in the paragraph. This summary states the topic and the author's controlling point about the topic. Remember, the controlling point has two traits. First, the controlling point is made up of the author's opinion about the topic. Second, the controlling point often states the author's thought pattern. You have learned to annotate the topic, thought pattern, and biased details. Once you have marked these ideas in the paragraph, you can then blend them into a one-sentence summary. This one-sentence summary states the implied main idea in your own words.

EXAMPLE   Read and annotate the following paragraph. Circle the topic as it recurs throughout the paragraph. Underline words that reveal the author's thought pattern and bias. Use your own words to state the implied main idea.

[1]According to government figures, over 16,000 gangs are active in this country, and at least half a million gang members commit more than 600,000 crimes each year. [2]Many members are young people who come from unhappy homes. [3]They feel neglected or are abused by their parents. [4]In addition, their parents may be gang members themselves. [5]Also, gang members often have a history of poor performance in school, and they have trouble making and keeping friends. [6]Sometimes they feel threatened by peers or the violence in their neighborhoods. [7]Others live in poor neighborhoods with few resources.

Implied main idea: *That gangs are very inappropriate for students to join*

EXPLANATION   To come up with the implied main idea, it is important to review all the supporting details. The first sentence points out that half a million young people join gangs and commit crimes. Sentences 2–6 give the reasons they join these gangs. You should have annotated the following words. The words *gangs, members,* and *gang members* should have been circled as the topic. The words *more, unhappy, neglected, abused, often, poor, trouble, threatened,* and *few* should have been underlined as biased words. The words *come from* signal the cause-and-effect thought pattern. The transitions *in addition, also, often,* and *sometimes* add to the list of reasons that young people join gangs. The following statement puts those ideas into one sentence: *Young people become gang members for many reasons.*

PRACTICE 4

Read the following paragraphs. Circle the topic as it recurs throughout the paragraph. Underline words that reveal the author's thought pattern and bias. Use your own words to state the implied main idea for each paragraph.

1.   [1]No one knows for sure how Valentine's Day came to be. [2]In ancient Rome, Juno, queen of the Roman gods and goddesses, was also the goddess of women and marriage. [3]February 14 was set aside as a holiday to honor Juno. [4]On the following day, February 15, the Feast of Lupercalia began. [5]It was customary to keep young boys and girls apart as they were growing up. [6]However, on the night before the festival of Lupercalia, the names of Roman girls were written on slips of paper and placed in jars. [7]Each young man would draw a girl's name from the jar; then for the rest of the festival, they would be partners. [8]Sometimes the couple would stay a pair for the year. [9]And often they fell in love and got married when they were grown.

Implied main idea: *how valentines day came*

2.   [1]On February 21, 2002, the following headlines were printed on pages 8–9 of the *USA Today* newspaper. [2]The first one stated, "Proving liability for events so far in the past could be tough." [3]Another said, "Insurance firms issued slave policies." [4]A third declared, "Several media companies owned newspapers that were essential to the slave industry." [5]A fourth stated, "Brown Bros: Loans gave planters cash to buy slaves." [6]A fifth claimed, "Lehman Bros: 1 brother owned 7 slaves in 1860." [7]A sixth said, "Railroads: Slaves 'formed the backbone of the South's railway labor force.'" [8]A seventh headline read, "We're still living with the vestiges of slavery." [9]An eighth offered, "FleetBoston: Traced to slave-trading merchant." [10]And the ninth headline claimed, "West Point Stevens: Textile firm linked to rough 'Negro cloth' slaves had to wear."

—Adapted from Cox, "Activists Challenge Corporations That They Say Are Tied to Slavery," *USA Today,* 21 Feb. 2002, pp. 1A, 9A. Copyright © 2002, *USA Today.* Reprinted with permission.

Implied main idea: *The different insurances*

Textbook
Skills

3. [1]More than 2 million Native Americans live in the United States. [2]More than one-third live on reservations, on lands placed in trust for them, or in other areas set aside as Native American. [3]One of every three lives in poverty. [4]Sixteen percent of Native American homes do not have a telephone. This number is alarming when compared to the fact that 6 percent of non–Native American homes do not have phones. [5]In some places, the state of affairs is much worse. [6]For example, on the Navaho Reservation, phone lines are available to less than 20 percent of the people; this means that 80 percent of the Navahos cannot have telephone service. [7]On reservations where phones are offered, the average person pays $100 for basic monthly service. [8]Calls off the reservation are billed as long distance. Thus, an average phone bill can soar quickly past $200 a month.

—Adapted from Folkerts & Lacy, *The Media in Your Life: An Introduction to Mass Media,* 2nd ed., p. 288.

Implied main idea: *More than 2 million native americans live in the united States*

4. [1]Wisconsin has over 15,000 inland lakes, 43,000 miles of rivers, and 650 miles of Great Lakes shoreline. [2]In addition to the inland lakes, parts of Lake Michigan and Lake Superior lie within Wisconsin's boundaries. [3]These Great Lakes are two of the largest freshwater lakes in the world, and they add nearly 6 million acres of water to Wisconsin. [4]Thus boating is a major part of life in Wisconsin's great outdoors. [5]The state also has nearly 500 public golf courses, ranking it among the top states for its ratio of golfers to courses. [6]Late summer and fall are some of the best times of the year to play Wisconsin's golf courses. [7]Finally, winter brings snow and the joys of skiing and snowboarding.

Implied main idea: *The lake and rivers in Wisconsin*

5. [1]Speeding is a factor in almost one-third of all crashes involving young drivers. [2]For example, on his way to the beach, which was 90 miles from his house, Marcus averaged around 80 mph instead of the posted 65 mph speed limit. [3]When confronted with a car going the limit in front of him, Marcus hugged the car's bumper. [4]Often he passed other cars when he did not have the room to do so by flooring the gas pedal. [5]His girlfriend constantly asked him to slow down and to stop tailgating. [6]Marcus replied, "Don't worry; I know what I am doing." [7]Suddenly, Marcus noticed the traffic in front of him

had slowed significantly. [8]He tried to brake, but the pressure of the brakes at high speed spun his car out of his lane and off the road.

Implied main idea: *how deadly speeding can be*

Textbook
Skills

Pictures as Details

Textbook authors often use pictures, drawings, or graphs to make the relationship between the main ideas and supporting details clear.

EXAMPLE   Study the figure, and read the caption beside it. Put the main idea suggested by the details into a sentence.

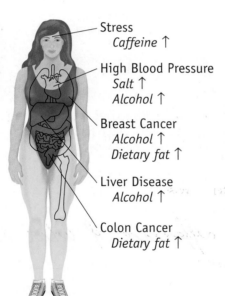

Stress
Caffeine ↑

High Blood Pressure
Salt ↑
Alcohol ↑

Breast Cancer
Alcohol ↑
Dietary fat ↑

Liver Disease
Alcohol ↑

Colon Cancer
Dietary fat ↑

◄ Possible health problems linked to poor diet habits. The upward arrow indicates excessive intake.

Source: From Melvin H. Williams, *Nutrition for Fitness and Sport,* 4th ed., p.174. Copyright© 1995 by The McGraw-Hill Companies. Reproduced with permission of The McGraw-Hill Companies.

Implied main idea: *The possible health problems*

EXPLANATION   The figure clearly shows that taking in too much caffeine, salt, alcohol, and fat leads to stress, high blood pressure, breast cancer, liver disease, and colon cancer. Thus the implied main idea is "Poor eating habits can lead to serious health problems."

PRACTICE 5

Study the photographs, and read the caption. Put the main idea suggested by the details into a sentence.

▲ Which version of the picture do you find more attractive? If you are male, you probably find the one with the larger pupils (left) "more feminine," "soft," or "pretty," whereas the one with the small pupils (right) may appear "hard," "selfish," or "cold" (Hess, 1975).

—From Kosslyn & Rosenberg, *Psychology*, p. 95.

Implied main idea: *the difference of what men find attractive*

Chapter Review

Test your understanding of what you have read in this chapter by filling in each blank with a word from the box. Use each word once.

controlling point	implied	specific	supporting details	topic

1. A main idea that is not stated directly but is strongly suggested by the supporting details in the passage is a(n) _implied_ main idea.

2. The first question to ask to find the implied main idea is: What is the _topic_ of the passage?

3. The second question to ask to find the implied main idea is: What are the major _supporting details_?

4. The third question to ask to find the implied main idea is: What is the _controlling point_ the author is trying to get across?

5. Implied main ideas must be neither too general nor too _specific_.

Applications

Application 1: Determine the Topic

Read each group of specific details. In the space provided, write the letter of the best topic for each group.

Specific details: osprey, eagles, falcons, vultures

 1. The **implied topic** is
   a. birds.
   b. birds of prey.
   c. winged creatures.

Specific details: shells, driftwood, seaweed, sea turtles, sand

 2. The **implied topic** is
   a. nature.
   b. wildlife at the beach.
   c. nature at the beach.

Specific details: credit card, debit card, money order, check

 3. The **implied topic** is
   a. ways to spend money.
   b. money.
   c. ways to use credit to spend money.

Specific details: greenish black clouds, a loud roaring noise, whirling wind, flying debris

_b_   **4.** The **implied topic** is
    a. dangerous weather.   c. traits of a tornado.
    b. sounds of a tornado.

Application 2: **Identify and State Topics**

Read each group of specific details. Then use your own words to state the topic.

   1. **Specific details:** tennis shoes, walking shoes, running shoes

      Topic: _sport shoes_

   2. **Specific details:** uncles, aunts, cousins, nephews, grandparents

      Topic: _relatives_

   3. **Specific details:** popcorn, pretzels, potato chips, crackers

      Topic: _snacks_

   4. **Specific details:** fire extinguishers, smoke alarms, escape plan

      Topic: _fire escaping plan_

Application 3: **Study to Determine the Implied Main Idea**

Read the following lists of information. Annotate the text using circles and underlines. Then choose the best statement of the implied main idea for each list.

_a_   **1.** Some parents and politicians think that video games encourage violent behavior in young people.

      For example, Doom 3, Crime Life: Gang Wars, and Killer 7, violent, shoot-'em-up games full of blood and gore, may make some young people more aggressive.

      These games seem to send the message that violence is fun and does not have serious effects.

      In addition, certain television shows have raised the same concerns.

      During the first six seasons of _South Park_, one of the show's main characters was killed off in each episode, only to come back in the next episode.

   a. Video games lead to murder.
   b. Hollywood has a negative effect on young people.
   c. Violence in the media may have a negative effect on some young people.

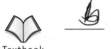

Textbook
Skills

 2. Every year, nearly half a million Americans are newly diagnosed with skin cancer.

   Skin cancer is mainly found in people who are most often exposed to the sun.

   Ultraviolet rays from the sun often are the cause.

   Repeated exposure to the sun has an increased effect.

   —Nakamura, *Health in America: A Multicultural Perspective,* p. 189.

   a. Skin cancer is a growing problem.
   b. Exposure to the sun causes skin cancer.
   c. Everyone is in danger of getting skin cancer.

Application 4: Study to Determine the Implied Main Idea in a Paragraph

Read the following paragraphs. Annotate the text using circles and underlines. Then choose the best statement of the implied main idea for each paragraph.

Elvis

   [1]A young Tennessee truck driver who made his first amateur record in 1954, Elvis Presley was first heard on a Memphis radio station and quickly became an international rock-and-roll superstar. [2]By the time he died in 1977, at 42 years of age, Presley had become a legend. [3]He left an estate of $15 million from the sales of more than 500 million records. [4]His death touched off mass mourning. [5]More than a generation later, Presley remains a cult hero, and sales of his records continue to be high. [6]Thousands of visitors tour his mansion in Memphis, spending large sums on Elvis ashtrays, scarves, and other trinkets. [7]A U.S. postage stamp was issued in his honor. [8]Elvis imitators abound.

1. The best statement of the **implied main idea** of the paragraph is

   a. Elvis Presley died before his time.
   b. Elvis Presley was a rich and successful performer who is still admired.
   c. Elvis Presley was a rock-and-roll superstar.

Home Video Voyeurism

[1]The dictionary defines a *voyeur* as a "prying observer." [2]A voyeur enjoys watching someone else in action. [3]The explosion of the Internet has created a new pastime for millions of people worldwide: voyeurism. [4]With a computer and an Internet server, we can now peek into the lives of anyone who wishes to put his or her most private acts in front of a camera. [5]For example, in 1996, a young woman who called herself Jenny Cam launched home video voyeurism. [6]She published images of herself doing absolutely everything. [7]Since then, the Internet has been offering thousands of sites that make the most private deeds accessible to anyone who cares to watch.

2. The best statement of the **implied main idea** for the paragraph is

  a. Millions of people are involved in voyeurism.
  b. Voyeurism is a popular pastime on the Internet.
  c. Jenny Cam publishes private acts worldwide.

Application 5: Create One-Sentence Summaries

Read the following paragraphs. Annotate the text. Use your own words to state the implied main idea for each paragraph.

Going Public

[1]By law, people who want to make their private lives public have every right to do so. [2]However, it is illegal to videotape or record another person's image without that person's consent. [3]A camera hidden by a landlord for the purpose of taping the tenant's private life is illegal. [4]Recording is a crime if its purpose is sexual arousal. [5]In these cases, the crime could be a misdemeanor, and the guilty party could be fined as much as $2,000 in some states. [6]If, however, the recording is distributed to others without the agreement of the subject, the crime becomes a felony. [7]The guilty party could serve up to five years in jail and be fined up to $5,000.

1. Write a one-sentence summary that states the **implied main idea** for the paragraph:

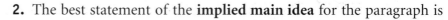

how people want to make there private lives public

Cramming

[1]Like many high school students, 16-year-old Sandy pulled a "late-nighter." [2]As usual, she had not studied ahead of time for her history midterm, scheduled for first period the next day. [3]So she stayed up cramming and listening

to music until 3 A.M. [4]She had gotten no more than two hours' sleep when her alarm rang. [5]During the exam, she was so tired that she became confused and forgot most of what she had studied the night before. [6]Like many of her peers who pull late-night cram sessions, Sandy failed her exam.

2. Write a one-sentence summary that states the **implied main idea** for the paragraph:

_____

REVIEW Test 1

Determining Topics from Specific Details

A. Read each group of specific details. In the space provided, write the letter of the best topic for each group.

Specific details: athletic socks, athletic shoes, athletic shorts, tank top, sweat towel, weights, treadmill

VISUAL VOCABULARY

__C__ 1. The **topic** is

a. items found in a locker room at a gym.
b. items of clothing.
c. items needed to work out at the gym.

Specific details: haircut, massage, facial, manicure

__C__ 2. The **topic** is
a. beauty.
b. services provided by a hairstylist.
c. services provided at a salon or spa.

Specific details: pimples, whiteheads, blackheads, acne

   _b_   **3.** The **topic** is
- a. diseases.
- b. skin problems.
- c. cleanliness.

Specific details: lasagna, spaghetti, ravioli

   _C_   **4.** The **topic** is
- a. sausage dishes.
- b. meat dishes.
- c. pasta dishes.

Specific details: paper, pen, pencil, calendar, textbook

   _a_   **5.** The **topic** is
- a. items needed for class.
- b. items needed for work.
- c. items needed for drawing.

Specific details: chrysanthemums, geraniums, begonias, impatiens

   _C_   **6.** The **topic** is
- a. trees.
- b. flowering plants.
- c. dried flowers.

Specific details: ice cream, cake with candles, balloons, presents, noisemakers

   _a_   **7.** The **topic** is
- a. a birthday party.
- b. a party.
- c. a social event.

Specific details: Tic-Tacs, Certs, Altoids, Dentyne

   _b_   **8.** The **topic** is
- a. breath mints.
- b. mints and gum often used to fight bad breath.
- c. candy.

B. Read the following lists of information. Then check off the best statement of the implied main idea for each list. (Hint: Annotate the text.)

List A

    Sarah is mother to two preschool children.

    She works full time at a minimum-wage job and goes to school part time to earn a nursing degree.

    Between family and work demands, Sarah finds that she is not able to take classes when most are offered.

Online computer courses through her local community college allow Sarah to work on her degree from home.

____C____ **9.** The **implied main idea** for this list is
   a. Single mothers face many challenges.
   b. Regularly scheduled classes are hard for some students to attend.
   c. Online college courses allow Sarah to pursue her education.

List B

Donna and Jason thought they would be lost without their children.

The day their youngest daughter, Jill, drove out of the driveway and headed off to college seemed like one of the saddest days of their lives.

Within the first few weeks, Donna and Jason found the house strangely quiet and peaceful.

Though they missed seeing Jill every day, they found that they had more time for each other and became closer as a couple.

____a____ **10.** The **implied main idea** for this list is
   a. Many people dread the empty nest when the children all leave home.
   b. Donna and Jason found that their marriage became stronger when the children left home.
   c. Children leaving home is a fact of life.

REVIEW **Test 2**

Studying Details to State the Topic

A. Read each group of specific details. Then use your own words to state the topic for each group.

1. **Specific details:** gift wrap, bow, ribbon, card

   Topic: _gifts_

2. **Specific details:** raisins, apples, bananas, pears

   Topic: _fruits_

3. **Specific details:** answering machine, fax machine, copier-printer, telephone, computer

   Topic: _office accessories_

4. **Specific details:** table of contents, index, glossary, chapter headings

   Topic: _textbook or book_

5. **Specific details:** oil, oil filter, dipstick, drip pan

   Topic: _oil change in a vehicle_

6. **Specific details:** daydreaming, talking when the teacher talks, sleeping, cracking jokes

   Topic: _disrupting the class_

7. **Specific details:** Army, Navy, Marines, Air Force

   Topic: _the workforce_

8. **Specific details:** custard, jelly, apple pie filling, peanut butter, marshmallow, fruit puree

   Topic: _snacks_

B. Read the following lists of information. Then choose the best statement of the implied main idea for each list. (Hint: Annotate the text.)

   _a_   **9.** In most public schools, a small group of kids who could be called the "rulers" occupied the top of the social ladder.

The largest peer group was made up of the "regular" kids. They were not wildly popular, but they were not outcasts either.

At the bottom of the social ladder in public schools were the "rejects."

These may at one time have been either rulers or regulars, but for some reason, they lost favor.

The **implied main idea** for this list is

a. People struggle to fit in.
b. Most students in public schools likely belonged to one of three peer groups.
c. In most public schools, the group of kids who could be called the "rulers" occupied the top of the social ladder.

___c___ **10.** Signs of pauses and uneven pressure in handwriting may be the result of pain.

The handwriting of stroke victims is often weak and slants downward.

Downward slopes in handwriting may also indicate depression.

Upward slopes in handwriting may show hopefulness.

The **implied main idea** for this list is

a. Physical problems and mental states may be revealed by handwriting.
b. Handwriting reveals emotions.
c. Handwriting provides interesting information.

REVIEW **Test 3**

Determining the Implied Main Idea

A. Read the following paragraphs. Then choose the best statement of the implied main idea for each paragraph. (Hint: Annotate the text.)

___c___ **1.** ^{1}Andrea was frustrated. ^{2}When she arrived at work, her phone was blinking with three messages from unhappy customers. ^{3}At midmorning, she discovered that the assistant store manager had not completed an order in time for the big sale that was to begin the next day. ^{4}Then the home office called to announce a surprise audit and demanded a monthly sales report by the end of the day. ^{5}The last blow came when two key workers on the afternoon shift called in sick. [6]Andrea's head throbbed. [7]She felt like screaming at someone or hitting something. [8]So she left work three hours early.

The **implied main idea** for the paragraph is

a. All managers face stress.
b. Andrea walked off the job.
c. High work stress can lead to worker absenteeism.

___C___ **2.**   [1]Steven drove around aimlessly trying to gain control of his anger. [2]He noticed the entrance to River End Park, and he pulled in. [3]He parked under a tree facing the Tomoka River and rolled down his car windows. [4]A gentle breeze brought the smell of water and freshly mowed grass into the car. [5]A few thin, white clouds slowly moved across a deep blue sky. [6]The sun glistened on the water's surface. [7]The soft sounds of small waves lapping against the pier drifted into range. [8]Slowly, he began to relax. [9]An osprey flew low above the water in search of a catch. [10]The sound of a small boat puttered in the distance. [11]Steven breathed deeply and lingered by the river for a little while. [12]Finally, he felt ready to go back home and make up with his wife.

The **implied main idea** for the paragraph is

a. Driving is good for stress.
b. Nature has a positive impact on Steven's emotions.
c. Anger can be controlled only by noticing nature.

B. Read the following paragraphs. Using your own words, write a one-sentence summary that states the implied main idea for each paragraph. (Hint: Annotate the text.)

3.   [1]Many men are choosing to stay home and let their wives support the family. [2]According to government records, the number of men working or looking for work fell to a record low in the early part of 2002. [3]The number of men who now choose not to work may be as high as one in ten. [4]One reason may be because of the growing success of women in the workforce. [5]Second, men are leaving the workforce because companies are eliminating their jobs. [6]Finally, technology has replaced many of the hard-labor jobs. [7]Jobs that call for strength and muscle no longer exist in the numbers that they once did.

The **implied main idea** for the paragraph is

Many men are choosing to stay home and let their wives support family

4. [1]They were the kids who just didn't fit in. [2]Perhaps they looked or dressed in an offbeat or creative fashion. [3]Sometimes physical traits, such as severe acne or obesity, marked them as undesirable. [4]Too often, gifted youngsters who loved to study and learn found themselves at odds with most of their peers. [5]Interestingly, not fitting in is most often a short-term problem. [6]Multimillionaire computer wizard Bill Gates is a good example. [7]In a graduation speech he once gave, he said, "Be nice to the geeks; they will be your boss one day."

The **implied main idea** for the paragraph is

How kids that didn't fit in with everyone else

5. [1]A local youth baseball, football, or soccer league may charge as much as $50 for registration and a shirt. [2]Shoes, gloves, and protective gear can run as high as $150. [3]In addition, parents are often expected to bring refreshments once or twice during the season, which can add an extra $40 in expenses. [4]Then there is the cost of transportation. [5]The total cost can run over $200, and that is just for one child. [6]Some parents simply cannot afford the cost.

The **implied main idea** for the paragraph is

How young baseball, football and soccer leagues are expensive.

REVIEW **Test 4**

Implied Main Ideas

Before you read, skim the passage and answer the Before Reading questions. Read the essay. Then answer the After Reading questions.

Power Plays

[1]Power plays are patterns of communication that take unfair advantage of another person. [2]Power plays aim to rob us of our right to make our own choices. [3]Power plays bully through **intimidation** and call for specific responses. [4]For example, in the power play *Nobody Upstairs*, another person will not recognize your request, no matter how or how many times you make it.

Textbook
Skills

⁵One common form of this power play is the refusal to take no for an answer. ⁶Sometimes *Nobody Upstairs* takes the form of pleading ignorance of unspoken rules. ⁷These common rules include knocking when you enter someone's room or asking permission before opening another person's mail or wallet. ⁸This person says, "I didn't know you didn't want me to look in your wallet" or "Do you want me to knock the next time I come into your room?"

⁹Another power play is *You Owe Me*. ¹⁰Here others do something for you and then demand something in return. ¹¹They remind you of what they did for you and use this to get you to do what they want. ¹²In the *You've Got to Be Kidding* power play, one person attacks the other by saying "you've got to be kidding" or some similar phrase: "You can't be serious," "You can't mean that," "You didn't say what I thought you said, did you?" ¹³The purpose here is to show utter disbelief in the other's statement. ¹⁴This disbelief is supposed to make the statement and the person seem stupid.

¹⁵These power plays are just examples. ¹⁶There are, of course, many others that you've no doubt encountered on occasion. ¹⁷What do you do when you see such a power play? ¹⁸One common response is to ignore the power play and allow the other person to take control. ¹⁹Another response is to treat the power play as just one incident and object to it. ²⁰For example, you might say, "Please don't come into my room without knocking first" or "Please don't look in my wallet without asking me first."

²¹In a **cooperative** response, you state your feelings, describe the behavior that you don't like, and state a response you both can live with. ²²A cooperative response to *Nobody Upstairs* might go something like this: "I'm angry [statement of feelings] that you keep opening my mail. ²³You have opened my mail four times this past week alone [description of behavior]. ²⁴I want you to allow me to open my own mail. ²⁵If there is anything in it that concerns you, I will let you know" [statement of cooperative response].

—DeVito, *Messages: Building Interpersonal Communication Skills*, 4th ed., pp. 333–34.

BEFORE READING

Vocabulary in Context

_C___ **1.** The word **intimidation** in sentence 3 means
  a. lies.   c. threats.
  b. anger.   d. love.

_A___ **2.** The word **cooperative** in sentence 21 means
  a. one-sided.   c. caring.
  b. for shared benefit.   d. angry.

AFTER READING

Concept Maps

3. Complete the concept map by filling in the missing item with information from the passage.

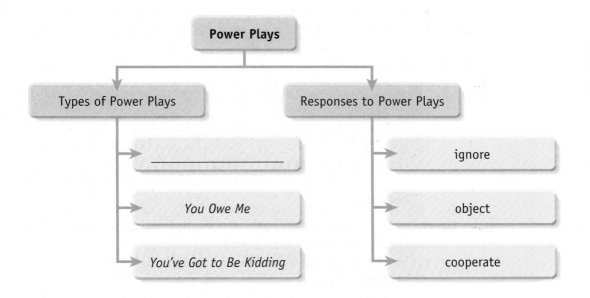

Central Idea and Main Idea

_____d_____ **4.** What is the central idea of the passage?
   a. sentence 1
   b. sentence 2
   c. sentence 3
   d. sentence 15

Supporting Details

_____a_____ **5.** Sentence 5 is a
   a. major supporting detail.   b. minor supporting detail.

If you were to outline the fifth paragraph (sentences 21–25), you would list three items under the heading "Cooperative Response." The first would be "State your feelings." What would the other two be?

6. <u>understanding</u>
7. <u>conclusion</u> ✓

Transitions and Thought Patterns

_d_ **8.** What is the relationship between sentences 18 and 19?
  a. cause and effect
  c. comparison and contrast
  b. time order
  d. generalization and example

Implied Main Idea

_b_ **9.** What is the best statement of the implied main idea for the second paragraph (sentences 4–8)?
  a. Walking into someone's room without asking is unfair.
  b. Someone playing *Nobody Upstairs* will not take no for an answer.
  c. One type of power play is called *Nobody Upstairs*.
  d. A person playing *Nobody Upstairs* pleads ignorance of unspoken rules.

_c_ **10.** What is the best statement of the implied main idea for the third paragraph (sentences 9–14)?
  a. *You Owe Me* and *You've Got to Be Kidding* are two additional examples of power plays.
  b. In *You Owe Me*, a person demands something in return for a favor.
  c. A person playing *You've Got to Be Kidding* tries to make the other person seem stupid.
  d. Power plays attack other people.

Discussion Questions

1. What other types of power plays have you seen?

2. What is your typical reaction to power plays?

Writing Topics

1. In a paragraph or more, describe your own experience with power plays.

2. Why do people need to use power plays? Write a paragraph to explain the possible reasons.

3. Write a paragraph to discuss why power plays are so effective.

SKILLED READER *Scorecard*

Implied Main Ideas

Test	Number Correct		Points		Score
Review Test 1	_____	×	10	=	_____
Review Test 2	_____	×	10	=	_____
Review Test 3	_____	×	20	=	_____
Review Test 4	_____	×	10	=	_____
Review Test 5 (website)	_____	×	10	=	_____
Review Test 6 (website)	_____	×	10	=	_____

Enter your scores on the Skilled Reader Scorecard: Chapter 10 Review Tests inside the back cover.

After Reading About Implied Main Ideas

Before you move on to the mastery tests on implied main ideas, take time to reflect on your learning and performance by answering the following questions. Write your answers in your notebook.

> What did I learn about implied main ideas?
>
> What do I need to remember about implied main ideas?
>
> How has my knowledge base or prior knowledge about implied main ideas changed?

More Review and Mastery Tests

For more practice, go to the book's website at **http://www.ablongman.com/henry** and click on *The Skilled Reader*. Then select "More Review and Mastery Tests." You will find the tests listed by chapter.

Name _Daryl Lawrens_ Section _____

Date _11/09/09_ Score (number correct) _____ × 20 = _____ %

A. Read each group of specific details. Then choose the best topic for each group.

Specific details: crossword puzzles, dictionary, thesaurus, Scrabble

_C_ **1.** The **topic** is
- a. games.
- b. reference tools.
- c. resources to build word skills.

Specific details: Honda Accord, Chrysler Super Bee, Toyota Camry, Dodge Neon, Chevrolet Sting Ray

_a_ **2.** The **topic** is
- a. names of cars.
- b. names of wildlife.
- c. names of trucks.

B. Read the following lists of information. Then choose the best statement of the implied main idea for each list.

_b_ **3.** Comfortable chairs make it easy to linger over coffee and dessert.

Good food is presented with elegance.

Fresh flowers on the table add a special touch.

Linen tablecloths and napkins, soft lighting, and excellent service round out the fine dining experience.

The **implied main idea** for this list is
- a. Atmosphere and good food are important in fine dining.
- b. Places of fine dining use cloth table linens.
- c. Fine dining is fun.

_c_ **4.** Hypnosis is often used to help hard-core smokers kick their habit.

Nicotine chewing gum also helps many people quit smoking.

A number of smokers have found relief in nicotine patches.

Good old-fashioned willpower is often needed.

The **implied main idea** for this list is

a. Giving up smoking is hard for many people.
b. Smoking becomes a habit because of a lack of willpower.
c. Several methods can help smokers quit smoking.

C. Read the following paragraph. Then choose the best statement of its implied main idea.

_____ **5.** [1]Basketball is fast-paced and requires the body to run, turn, twist, pass, jump, aim, and shoot, all at high speeds and for long periods of time. [2]Football is a slower-moving game and brings together a team of players who have specialized skills. [3]Each type of player requires a different kind of physical skill. [4]Quarterbacks must be able to aim, throw, run short distances, and fall without getting hurt. [5]Centers must be able to hand off the ball, block, and tackle. [6]Running backs must be able to run, jump, catch, and fall without getting hurt. [7]Golf moves slowly and requires the ability to concentrate, aim, swing, putt, and walk.

The **implied main idea** for the paragraph is

a. Different sports move at different paces and require different sets of skills.
b. Football is more complicated than other sports.
c. People who participate in sports have amazing athletic abilities.

A. Read each group of specific details. Then choose the best topic for each group.

Specific details: toys, elves, reindeer, decorated tree

___c___ **1.** The **topic** is
a. winter.
b. Christmas.
c. Santa Claus.

Specific details: runny nose, itchy eyes, aching joints, chills, fever

___c___ **2.** The **topic** is
a. death.
b. surgery.
c. flu.

B. Read the following lists of information. Then choose the best statement of the implied main idea for each list.

___b___ **3.** In the first half of the 1900s, most women in the United States expected to marry and have children.

Few women even dreamed of establishing careers outside the home.

Those who did work outside the home most often became secretaries, teachers, or nurses.

Rare was the woman who headed a business or became a doctor.

In fact, higher education was a privilege extended mostly to men.

The **implied main idea** for this list is

a. Most women were unhappy in the early 1900s.
b. Men had more rights than women did in the 1900s.
c. Women had few choices in the early 1900s.

___a___ **4.** Setting a realistic goal is the first step.

Losing one to two pounds a week is realistic.

You should lower your intake of fatty foods and carbohydrates.

You must exercise for 20 minutes at least three times a week.

417

The **implied main idea** for this list is

a. Weight loss takes time.
b. Realistic weight loss requires diet and exercise.
c. Exercise is important for weight loss.

C. Read the following paragraph. Then choose the best statement of its implied main idea.

_a_ **5.**   [1]The lunch crowd at Billy's Tap Room in Ormond Beach, Florida, is largely made up of Ormond's own. [2]Town leaders and longtime residents use Billy's as a favorite place for lunchtime gatherings. [3]Special events such as business meetings, bridal showers, and anniversary parties are held in a room reserved for larger gatherings. [4]The evening crowd usually comes in two shifts. [5]The before-dark group is usually an older crowd; these include people who don't like to drive at night or who hate to wait for a table. [6]The after-dark crowd is made up of professionals; these people are looking for a quality reward at the end of a hard workday.

The **implied main idea** for the paragraph is

a. Billy's Tap Room creates a good atmosphere for its customers.
b. Several types of crowds support Billy's Tap Room.
c. Billy's Tap Room is busy in the evenings.

A. Read each group of specific details. In the space provided, use your own words to write the best statement of the topic for each group.

1. Specific details: iced tea, wine, water, soft drinks, milk

   Topic: *drinks*

2. Specific details: pacifier, bottles, diapers, bib, crib, walker

   Topic: *baby accessories*

3. Specific details: associate of arts, bachelor of arts, master of arts

   Topic: *degrees*

4. Specific details: sweaty palms, pounding heart, shaky voice, trembling knees and hands

   Topic: *love*

B. Read the following paragraph. Then choose the best statement of its implied main idea.

c **5.** [1]When world champion Michelle Kwan skated her short program during the 2002 Olympics, her scores placed her first. [2]Little attention was given to relatively unknown Sarah Hughes. [3]After her short program, Hughes placed fourth. [4]In the final long skate program, Hughes skated a difficult program beautifully. [5]Kwan's long program was less difficult, and she even slipped and almost fell. [6]Only 16 years old, Sarah Hughes had won the Gold medal and out-skated the world champion, Michelle Kwan.

The **implied main idea** for the paragraph is

a. Michelle Kwan lost the 2002 Olympic gold medal in figure skating.
b. Michelle Kwan was expected to win.
c. Newcomer Sarah Hughes won a surprise victory over Michelle Kwan at the 2002 Olympics.

419

A. Read each group of specific details. Then use your own words to state the topic of each group.

1. **Specific details:** toothpaste, deodorant, toothbrush, floss, shampoo, fingernail clippers, makeup

   Topic: _bathroom accessories_

2. **Specific details:** spatulas, wooden spoons, knives, measuring cups, measuring spoons

   Topic: _kitchen utensils_

3. **Specific details:** Jenny Craig, Weight Watchers, the Atkins Plan

   Topic: _Movies_

B. Read the following paragraphs. Then choose the best statement of the implied main idea for each paragraph.

_C_ **4.**   **Yesterday's Homemaking**

[1]Many of our great-grandmothers learned to cook on a wood-stove and draw water out of a well. [2]To fix a meal, many had to kill the chicken or clean the fish. [3]They also had to pick the vegetables from the family garden. [4]Women worked hard in the hot months canning food for the winter months. [5]Without running water, laundry and bathing called for heating water on the woodstove or over open fires. [6]Large families were common, and laundry was done on washboards or with wringer washers. [7]Ironing clothes meant heating a heavy wedge of iron with an attached handle on the woodstove or in the fireplace.

The **implied main idea** for the paragraph is

a. Homemaking tasks at one time demanded much physical labor.
b. Homemaking led to early death for women.
c. Homemaking meant tending the family's livestock.

Wind and Waves

Textbook
Skills

[1]The drag caused by the friction of the wind on the surface of smooth water ripples the water. [2]As the wind continues to blow, it applies more pressure to the steep side of the ripple, and wave size begins to grow. [3]As the wind becomes stronger, short, choppy waves of all sizes appear; and as these waves absorb more energy, they continue to grow. [4]When the waves reach a point at which the energy supplied by the wind is equal to the energy lost by breaking waves, they become whitecaps. [5]Up to a certain point, the stronger the wind, the higher the waves.

—Smith & Smith, *Elements of Ecology*, 4th ed., p. 489.

_____   **5.** The **implied main idea** for the paragraph is

    a. A strong wind means high waves.
    b. Wind creates waves.
    c. Wind creates friction.

A. Read each group of specific details. Use your own words to state the topic for each group.

Textbook
Skills

1. Specific details: toast, eggs, jelly, hash browns, pancakes, cereal

Topic: *breakfast*

2. Specific details: moss, birds, squirrels, bark, leaves

Topic: *wildlife*

3. Specific details: north, south, east, west

Topic: *compass*

B. Read the following paragraphs. Using your own words, write a one-sentence summary that states the implied main idea for each paragraph.

4. *Seventeen* **Readers**

Textbook
Skills

[1]*Seventeen* magazine caters to teenage females. [2]Every few years, the magazine's audience "ages out," and *Seventeen* has to find new readers. [3]The magazine does not target a set of specific women, but rather an age group. [4]And the wants and needs of this age group are always changing. [5]Since readers change, so do the topics that grab their interest. [6]Today's *Seventeen* includes stories that were not considered interesting or proper 10 or 20 years ago. [7]Chances are that gun violence in the schools and beepers for staying in touch would not have concerned an editor in the 1970s or 1980s. [8]Even if your older sister or aunt read *Seventeen* when she was a high school student, she most likely read a very different magazine than teenagers read today.

—Adapted from Folkerts & Lacy, *The Media in Your Life: An Introduction to Mass Media*, 2nd ed., pp. 132–33.

Implied main idea: *How Seventeen magazine caters to teenagers*

423

5.   **Layers of the Rain Forest**

[1]The uppermost layer of a tropical rain forest is made up of emergent trees. [2]These trees are over 40 to 80 meters and have deep crowns that billow above the rest of the forest. [3]Their canopy is uneven. [4]The second layer is made up of mop-crowned trees, and their canopy is also uneven. [5]It is hard to tell these two layers apart from each other and together they form one unbroken canopy. [6]The third level of a tropical rain forest is the lowest level of trees. [7]These trees have conelike crowns, and their canopy is unbroken, deep, and well defined. [8]The fourth layer, usually poorly developed in deep shade, is made up of shrubs, young trees, tall herbs, and ferns. [9]The fifth level is the ground layer of tree seedlings and low-growing plants and ferns.

—Adapted from Smith & Smith, *Elements of Ecology,* 4th ed., pp. 444–45.

VISUAL VOCABULARY

Figure 31.3 Vertical stratification of a tropical rain forest.

▲ Vertical Stratification of a Tropical Rain Forest

Source: Smith & Smith, *Elements of Ecology,* 4th ed. Update. Benjamin Cummings, 2000, p. 444. Reprinted by permission of Pearson Education, Inc., Glenview, IL.

Implied main idea: *There are alot of layers of rain forest*

The fifth and lowest level of a rain forest is the ___*b*___

a. ground layer.
b. shrubs and saplings.

Name _____ Section _____

Date _____ **Score** (number correct) _____ × 20 = _____%

A. Read each group of specific details. Then use your own words to state the topic of each group.

1. **Specific details:** time-outs, spankings, taking away privileges

    Topic: _punishment_ _____

2. **Specific details:** speaking, listening, reading, writing

    Topic: _classes_ _____

3. **Specific details:** California, Oregon, Nevada, Utah

    Topic: _States_ _____

4. **Specific details:** pupil, cornea, retina, iris, aqueous humor

    Topic: _expression_ _____

B. Read the following passage. Using your own words, write a one-sentence summary that states the implied central idea.

5.   **Support for My Mother**

Textbook
Skills

¹In the spring of 1991, my mother fell as she walked down the steps outside her doctor's office. ²She had broken her hip many years before and walked with an uneven gait. ³When she lost her balance on the steps, she feared that she had broken her hip again. ⁴An ambulance took her to a nearby hospital for X-rays. ⁵The doctors there thought she had a hairline fracture in her hip. ⁶She couldn't walk well enough to be on her own at her apartment, so the hospital discharged her to a nursing home.

⁷I lived about 2,000 miles away at the time and arrived in town after my mother had settled into the home. ⁸My sister and I knew that she could only stay in the nursing home for a short time under Medicare. ⁹The costs would start to mount after that. ¹⁰So we created a discharge plan that would allow my mother to move into her own apartment after a short stay with my sister.

[11]To carry out this plan, we had to find the health care and social supports she needed to live on her own. [12]I had to get back to work and my family. [13]I felt unsure we could get my mother the support she needed.

—Novak, *Issues in Aging: An Introduction to Gerontology*, pp. 182–83.

Implied central idea: _How to support your mother._

Inferences   *Daryl Lawrence*
11/05/09

CHAPTER PREVIEW

Before Reading About Inferences

Study the chapter preview and underline words that relate to ideas you have already studied or know about. Did you underline the following terms: *facts, prior knowledge,* and *bias?* What you already know about these topics will help you learn about inferences. Use the blanks that follow to write a one- or two-sentence summary about each topic:

Facts: *are true and important information about the topic.*

Prior knowledge: *Is grasping and know about a certain topic.*

Bias: *Is often prejudge the outlook.*

Now, skim the chapter to find three additional topics that you have already studied.

List those topics (be sure to see page 434): _____

_____

Copy the following study outline in your notebook. Leave ample blank space between each topic. Use your own words to fill in the outline with information about each topic as you study about inferences:

Reading Skills Needed to Make VALID Inferences:

    I. Verify Facts

   II. Assess Prior Knowledge

  III. Learn from the Text

        a. Context Clues

        b. Thought Patterns

        c. Implied Main Ideas

  IV. Investigate for Bias

   V. Detect Contradictions

Inferences: Educated Guesses

Read the following short paragraph.

Katherine Collier was running late for class again. She knew all the good parking spaces in the student lots would be taken, so she turned in to the faculty parking lot that was always half empty. She located a parking space directly in front of the math building where her first-period class was on the ground floor. Since she had a very brief walk to class, she took the time to back into the parking space so that campus security could not easily see the parking sticker that indicated she was in the wrong lot. When she came back to her car after class, she was not surprised to see the yellow ticket under her windshield wipers. She was not even surprised that the ticket stated she was being charged $50 for this third violation.

Which of the following statements might be true based on the ideas in the passage?

_____ Katherine Collier is a teacher.

_____ Katherine Collier is a student.

_____ Katherine Collier expected to get a ticket.

Congratulations! You have just made a set of educated guesses or **inferences** about the paragraph. An author suggests or **implies** an idea, and the reader uses the facts and background knowledge to come to a conclusion and make an **inference** about what the author means.

In the paragraph about Katherine Collier, the second and third statements are clearly based on the information in the passage. However, the first statement is not backed by the supporting details. The facts that she receives a ticket for parking in the faculty parking lot and that her car has a sticker indicating she is in the wrong lot suggest that she is a student, not a teacher. The facts that she was not surprised and had received two previous tickets suggest that she expected to get this ticket, too.

What Is a Valid Inference?

We use the skill of making inferences countless times every day. For example, when we see gray clouds, we infer rain is coming, and a slammed door may imply anger.

> An **inference** is an unstated idea that is suggested by the facts or details in a passage.

Study the photo, and answer the question accompanying it.

VISUAL VOCABULARY

What emotions are shown in this photo? _____
_____.

If you wrote *happiness, joy, relief, pride*, or another positive emotion, you made a valid inference based on the clues given in the family's facial expressions and the details of the situation. A **valid inference** is a thoughtful judgment based on details and evidence. For example, if you are bitten by an insect such as a spider or tick, you must pay careful attention to the effects of the bite. Some bites lead to serious, long-term diseases. Lyme disease is one example of the harmful effects of a tick bite. Lyme disease requires immediate medical attention. Many other bites can easily be treated at home. The decision to go to a doctor (or not) is based on making valid inferences. If you or someone you know has been bitten, you must make a set of wise decisions based on the evidence. The most effective inferences are based on the details given.

> A **valid inference** is a logical conclusion based on evidence.

The ability to make a valid inference is a vital life skill. Making valid inferences aids us in our efforts to care for our families, succeed in our jobs, and even guard our health.

EXAMPLE Read the following paragraph. Write the letter **V** beside the *two* valid inferences. Remember that valid inferences are firmly supported by the details in the passage.

Only in the fifth grade, Roxanne already stood a full head and shoulders above most of her peers, including the boys. Constant exposure to the chlorine in the family swimming pool had given her hair a distinct greenish tint. In addition, she had to wear both orthodontic braces and thick eyeglasses. When Josh saw her on the first day of school, he immediately began harassing her. His favorite taunt to her was the nickname "The Goofy Green Giant." The nickname caught on, and soon Roxanne was the most talked-about girl in school, even though few knew her real name.

_____ **1.** Roxanne is tall for her age.

__V__ **2.** Roxanne was not well liked by the other kids her age.

_____ **3.** Josh's nickname for Roxanne is based on her looks.

__V__ **4.** Roxanne is not a pretty girl.

EXPLANATION Statements 1 and 3 are valid inferences. Both are firmly based on the information in the paragraph. The expression "stood a full head and shoulders above most of her peers" implies that Roxanne is tall for her age. The nickname "Goofy Green Giant" is a negative label based on the physical descriptions of Roxanne.

PRACTICE 1

Each paragraph is followed by three inferences. Only one inference is valid. In the space provided, write the letter of the inference that is most clearly supported by the paragraph.

_____ *c* **1.**   Jamul and Shanice sat across from each other in a corner booth in the restaurant. For most of the meal, Jamul did not smile, and despite Shanice's efforts to make conversation, he barely spoke to her. Halfway through the meal, Jamul threw down his napkin and walked away without a backward look.

    a.   Jamul and Shanice are related to each other.
    b.   Jamul and Shanice are angry at each other.
    c.   Jamul is unhappy with Shanice.

_____ *b* **2.**   Yvonne was traveling on Interstate 95 in her Honda Accord. Suddenly, she heard a strange flapping noise, and the car started listing or pulling to the right. She immediately found it difficult to steer as the car shifted from its usual easy smoothness into an uneven ride, as if the right front of the car were lower than the other side. Yvonne finally managed to pull safely to the side of the interstate.

    a.   Yvonne is a poor driver.
    b.   Yvonne has a flat tire.
    c.   Yvonne ran out of gas.

_____ *c* **3.**   Glenn was playing with his 5-year-old son Rob by tossing him into the air and then catching him. Suddenly, Glenn lost his balance and failed to catch the little boy. Rob landed with a thud several yards away. He immediately began crying and refused to stand up. He said his right leg hurt too much. Glenn carried his son inside and rocked him to sleep. Later that evening, Rob still couldn't put any weight on the leg. In addition, the lower leg around the shin was tender to the touch and a little swollen.

    a.   Rob is trying to get attention.
    b.   Glenn is an abusive father.
    c.   Rob's leg is probably broken.

Making VALID Inferences and Avoiding Invalid Conclusions

As skilled readers, our main goal is to find out what the author is stating or implying. Valid inferences come from orderly thinking. Skilled readers learn to use a VALID thinking process to make valid inferences. The VALID approach avoids drawing false inferences or coming to **invalid conclusions.**

> An **invalid conclusion** is a false inference that is not based on the details, facts, or reasonable thinking.

The VALID approach consists of 5 steps in thinking:

Step 1: **V**erify and value the facts.

Step 2: **A**ssess prior knowledge.

Step 3: **L**earn from the text.

Step 4: **I**nvestigate for bias.

Step 5: **D**etect contradictions.

Step 1: Verify and Value the Facts

Develop a devotion to finding and examining the facts. Valid inferences are firmly based on the facts. However, authors often mix fact with opinion. Facts are details that can be verified. Opinions are stated with biased words. A skilled reader first separates facts from opinion. Then, a skilled reader takes a close look at the facts. Once you verify the facts, you can decide if you agree or disagree with an opinion.

Read the following sentence. Answer the questions that follow it.

> Katherine Collier should break her disrespectful habit of being late to all her classes.

What are the facts in this sentence that can be verified? _She has a habit of being late to her classes_

What are the biased words that reveal an opinion? _Should_ _of being_

This sentence blends fact and opinion. We can check with the registrar or the class rolls to verify that Collier is a student. We can also contact each of her teachers and verify the number of times she has been late to all of her classes. The biased words of opinion are *should* and *disrespectful.* Once we verify the facts, we can then decide whether we agree with the opinion. Often the opinion is an interpretation of the facts. Some readers come to an invalid conclusion or opinion from a misunderstanding of the facts.

At times, authors use false information for their own purposes. Just as authors may make this kind of mistake, readers may, too. Readers may draw false inferences by mixing the author's fact with their own opinions, or by misreading the facts. It is very important to find, verify, and stick to factual details.

EXAMPLE Read the following paragraph. Write **V** next to the *two* inferences supported by the facts in the paragraph.

Textbook
Skills

The state and federal governments set the ages at which you could get your driver's license, drink alcohol, and vote. Before you could get a job, the federal government had to give you a Social Security number. And you have been paying Social Security taxes every month in which you have been employed. If you worked a low-paying job, your starting wages were set by state and federal minimum-wage laws.

—Adapted from Edwards, Wattenberg, & Lineberry, *Government in
America: People, Politics, and Policy,* 5th ed., Brief Version, p. 1.

_____✓_____ **1.** The state and federal governments are unfair.

_____✓_____ **2.** The state and federal governments affect daily life.

_____ **3.** Governments have influence over people.

EXPLANATION The last two statements are valid inferences based on the facts. However, there is no hint or clue that the state or federal governments are unfair. Skilled readers draw conclusions that are supported by the facts.

Step 2: Assess Prior Knowledge

Once you are sure of the facts, the next step is to draw on your prior knowledge and use your sense of logic. What you have already learned and experienced can help you make valid inferences.

EXAMPLE Study the photo. Write **V** beside the *two* inferences supported by the details in the picture.

VISUAL VOCABULARY

_____ 1. A synonym for *cosmopolitan* is crowded.

_____ 2. A synonym for *cosmopolitan* is sophisticated.

_____ 3. Times Square is a place to get ripped off or robbed.

_____ 4. Times Square offers a wide variety of experiences.

▲Times Square in New York City has a cosmopolitan appeal.

EXPLANATION Based on the details in the photo, the valid inferences are 2 and 4.

Step 3: Learn from the Text

When you verify and value facts, you are learning from the text. A valid inference is always based on what is stated or implied by the details in the text; in contrast, an invalid inference goes beyond the evidence. Thus, to make a valid inference, you must learn to rely on the information in the text. Many of the skills you have studied from previous chapters work together to enable you to learn from the text. For example, context clues unlock the meaning of an author's use of vocabulary. Becoming aware of thought patterns teaches you to look for the logical relationship between ideas. Learning about stated and implied main ideas teaches you to study supporting details. (In fact, you use inference skills to find the implied main idea.) In addition, you often use inference skills to grasp the author's opinion. As you apply these skills to your reading process, you are carefully listening to what the author has to say. You are learning from the text. Once you learn from the text, only then can you make a valid inference. The following examples show you how you learn from the text.

EXAMPLE 1 Read the following set of details. Answer the questions that follow.

Janet's sense of smell told her that Todd had been with another woman, for he **reeked** of cheap perfume.

_c_   **1.** The best *synonym* of the word **reeked** is
       a. stank.   c. glowed.
       b. wafted.

_b_   **2.** What is the primary relationship of ideas within the sentence?
       a. time order
       b. generalization and example
       c. cause and effect

_c_   **3.** Which of the following details are facts?
       a. Janet smelled perfume on Todd.
       b. Todd reeked with perfume.

_c_   **4.** Choose the main idea statement that best matches the supporting details in the sentence.
       a. Todd is in trouble.
       b. Todd is an immoral person who cannot be trusted.
       c. Janet suspects Todd of being with another woman.

_a_   **5.** Which of the following states a valid inference?
       a. Todd is having an affair with another woman.
       b. Todd carried a scent of perfume on his person.
       c. Janet has a keen sense of smell.
       d. Todd smelled good.

EXPLANATION

1. The synonym of *reeked* is implied by the details in the sentence. Based on the context clues "smell" and "cheap" you can infer the synonym of the word is (a) *stank*.

2. The relationship of ideas within the sentence is (c) cause and effect based on the transition *for*.

3. The fact is (a) *Janet smelled perfume on Todd*. The word *reeked* is a biased word that reveals an opinion. So (b) *Todd reeked of perfume* is an interpretation of the facts.

4. The main idea statement that best matches the supporting details in the sentence is (c). Choices (a) and (b) use the biased words "trouble," "immoral," and "not . . . trusted." These biased words are interpretations that go beyond the facts.

5. Based on what we have learned from analyzing the text, the valid inference is (b) *Todd carried a scent of perfume on his person*. Choices (a) and (d) are

invalid conclusions because they go beyond the details in the text. Choice (c) is an invalid conclusion because *reeked* suggests anyone could have smelled the perfume.

EXAMPLE 2   Read the following paragraph from a college psychology textbook. Answer the questions.

Textbook
Skills

Trial-and-Error Learning

¹Edward L. Thorndike, a psychologist, created a puzzle box, a cage with a latched door that a cat could open by pressing on a pedal inside the cage. ²Food, such as fish, was placed outside the cage door in the cat's sight. ³The cat tried many behaviors to get out of the box to the fish, but only pressing the pedal would work. ⁴Finally, the cat pressed the pedal, and the door opened. ⁵When the cat was put back in the box, it pressed the pedal more quickly, improving each time. ⁶Thorndike called this type of learning "trial-and-error learning."

—Kosslyn & Rosenberg, *Psychology: The Brain,
The Person, The World*, pp. 177–178.

_____ **1.** Based on the general context, a *psychologist*
    a. mainly works with animals.
    b. studies thoughts and behaviors.
    c. is college educated.

_____ **2.** What is the relationship of ideas within sentence 6?
    a. spatial order
    b. time order
    c. classification

_____ **3.** What is the primary thought pattern of sentences 2–5?
    a. spatial order
    b. time order
    c. classification

_____ **4.** The details of the paragraph are mostly
    a. facts.
    b. opinions.

_____ **5.** Which sentence states the main idea?
    a. Sentence 1
    b. Sentence 2
    c. Sentence 6

_____ **6.** Which of the following states a valid inference based on the details in the paragraph?

    a. Cats are slow learners.

    b. An action that brings a positive result is likely to be repeated.

    c. Animals are extremely intelligent.

EXPLANATION

1. Based on the general context, a *psychologist* (b) *studies thoughts and behaviors.*

2. The relationship of ideas within sentence 6 is (c) *classification.*

3. The primary thought pattern of sentences 2–5 is (b) *time order.* These sentences stated the *steps* the cat took *during* trial-and-error learning.

4. The details are mostly (a) *facts.* The paragraph describes a series of actions that were taken. The authors do not offer their opinion about these events.

5. The sentence that states the main idea is (c) *sentence 6.*

6. Based on what is learned from the text, the valid inference is (b) *An action that brings a positive result is likely to be repeated.* This inference is a generalization based on the example of the cat's learning process.

Step 4: Investigate for Bias

One of the most important steps in making a valid inference is confronting your biases. Each of us possesses strong personal views that influence the way we process information. Often our personal views are based on prior experiences. For example, if we have had a negative prior experience with a used car salesperson, we may become suspicious and stereotype all used car salespeople as dishonest. Sometimes, our biases are based on the way in which we were raised. Some people register as Democrats or Republicans and vote for only Democratic or Republican candidates simply because their parents were members of either the Democratic or Republican party.

To make a valid inference, we must look for bias in our response to information. Our bias can shape our reading of the author's meaning. To investigate for bias, note biased words and replace them with factual details as you form your conclusions.

EXAMPLE 1 Read the following paragraph. Investigate the list of inferences that follows for bias. Underline the biased words. Write **V** in the blank if the inference is valid or **I** if the inference is invalid due to bias.

Panhandling on the Internet

[1]After an 18-month wild buying spree of merchandise with brand names such as Gucci and Prada, Karyn Bosnak found herself out of a job and more than $20,000 in debt. [2]Then the 29-year-old spotted an odd request on a sign in a supermarket "Wanted $7,000 To Pay Off Debt." [3]It made perfect sense. [4]The television producer offered a similar appeal to a much wider audience: the World Wide Web. [5]Now more than 3½ months after launching www.savekaryn.com, Bosnak has gotten more than $13,000 from hundreds of donors worldwide. [6]Coupled with the online auction of the high-ticket items that drove her into debt, plus earnings from a new job, she finally broke even.

—Adapted from Alpert, "Panhandling Moves into the Internet
Age," *Daytona Beach News-Journal*, 11 Nov. 2002. 2A.

_____ **1.** Panhandling is a shameful way to get money.

_____ **2.** Panhandling is asking for money as opposed to earning money.

_____ **3.** Karyn Bosnak is an effective manager of her finances.

_____ **4.** Karyn Bosnak is dishonest.

_____ **5.** Karyn Bosnak made unwise decisions that led to her debt.

EXPLANATION Items 2 and 5 are (**V**) valid inferences that can be drawn based on information from the paragraph. Sentence 2 avoids the use of biased language. Although sentence 5 does include the biased word "unwise," based on the general context, "unwise" is a valid inference. Bosnak's debt is the result of unwise decisions. Item 1 is an (**I**) invalid inference. The biased word *shameful* is an opinion not supported by the details. Some readers may think Bosnak was wise to ask for money via the Internet. The decision helped her get out of debt. Item 3 is an (**I**) invalid inference. The word *effective* is a biased word that does not accurately describe someone who was $20,000 in debt from shopping. Item 4 is an (**I**) invalid inference. The paragraph does not contain any details to support this inference.

EXAMPLE 2 Read the following paragraph. Investigate the list of inferences that follow for bias. Underline the biased words. Write **V** in the blank if the inference is valid or **I** if the inference is invalid due to bias.

The Power of Self-Talk

[1]Disparaging statements such as "I'm a failure" or "I'm foolish" or "I'm stupid" are destructive. [2]These statements imply that failure, foolishness, and stupidity are in you and will always be in you. [3]Instead, use statements that

Textbook
Skills

refer to the here and now. [4]In addition, describe actions and reasons for your feelings. [5]Such statements might look like this:

[6]"I feel like a failure right now; I've erased this computer file three times today."

[7]"I felt foolish when I couldn't think of that formula."

[8]"I feel stupid when you point out my grammatical errors."

—Adapted from DeVito, *Messages: Building Interpersonal Communication Skills*, 4th ed., p. 187.

V

_____ **1.** The word *disparaging* means "degrading" or "devaluing."

__*I*___ **2.** Once we fail, we are most likely always going to fail.

__*I*___ **3.** We often believe the statements we make about ourselves.

__*V*___ **4.** You should keep criticisms about yourself general.

EXPLANATION   Items 1 and 3 are (**V**) valid inferences based on the details in the paragraph. Item 1 states the correct meaning of the word *disparaging* based on the general context of the passage. Item 3 states the implied main idea of the passage. Items 2 and 4 are (**I**) invalid inferences. In sentence 2, the biased words *most likely always* and *fail* are not supported by the details in the passage. Sentence 4 is an opinion that contradicts the details stated in sentences 5–7.

Step 5: Detect Contradictions

Have you ever misjudged a situation or formed a wrong first impression? For example, have you ever assumed a person was conceited or rude only to find out later that he or she was acutely shy? You may find a better explanation for a set of facts than the first one that comes to mind. The skilled reader hunts for the most reasonable explanation. The best way to do this is to consider other explanations that could logically contradict your first impression.

EXAMPLE 1   Read the following list, which describes the behaviors of a young person. Then, in the blank, write as many explanations for the behaviors as you can think of.

Making careless errors

Not sitting still

Talking excessively

Always interrupting

Being forgetful

making careless mistakes is definitely describing a young person. when you are younger you basically do what you think is cool so you can fit in.

EXPLANATION Some readers may think this list described a rebellious or disrespectful child. It is actually a list of symptoms for attention deficit hyperactivity disorder (ADHD). This disorder affects almost 5 percent of all children. Often those who have ADHD face difficulties in their school and social lives. Without thinking about other possible views, anyone can easily jump to a wrong conclusion. Skilled readers consider all the facts and all the possible explanations for those facts. Skilled readers look for contradictions.

EXAMPLE 2 Study the photo. Using inference skills, answer the question accompanying it.

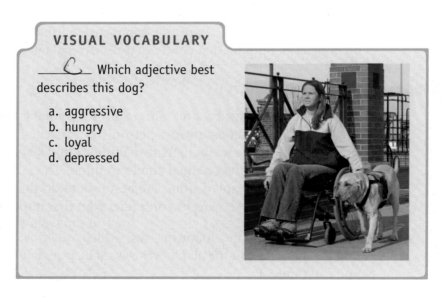

VISUAL VOCABULARY

____C____ Which adjective best describes this dog?

a. aggressive
b. hungry
c. loyal
d. depressed

EXPLANATION Several clues point to (c) in the photo: The dog is a guide dog, trained to be loyal, and the care the dog is taking to lead its owner implies its loyalty.

Use these five steps to think your way through to VALID conclusions based on sound inferences: (1) verify and value the facts, (2) assess prior knowledge, (3) learn from the text, (4) investigate for bias, and (5) detect contradictions.

PRACTICE 2

A. Read the following paragraph. Identify the facts. Check those facts against your own experience and understanding. Write **V** for valid beside *two* inferences supported by the facts in the paragraph.

Textbook
Skills

[1]Sandra Rosado had known poverty most of her young life, but she was determined to go to college. [2]She saved every dollar she could from her part-time job after school. [3]Sandra seemed well on her way to providing for herself rather than ending up on welfare like her mother. [4]When welfare officials found out about Sandra's $4,900 bank account, they told her mother that the family was no longer eligible for aid. [5]Without means to support her eight children, Mrs. Rosado asked whether there wasn't some way to get around the problem. [6]The easiest way, she was told, was simply for Sandra to spend the money quickly. [7]Thus, rather than spending her money on a college education, Sandra ended up buying clothes, jewelry, shoes, and perfume.

—Adapted from Edwards, Wattenberg, & Lineberry, *Government in America: People, Politics, and Policy*, 5th ed., p. 33.

___V___ Sandra made unwise decisions.

_____ It is difficult to break the cycle of poverty.

_____ The government encourages the poor to spend their money to support
         V   themselves instead of saving their money.

_____ Poor people choose to be poor.

B. Write **V** next to a valid inference you can make about this "Peanuts" cartoon featuring Charlie Brown and Linus.

VISUAL VOCABULARY

_____ It's important to hold
   V   opinions.

_____ Opinions should be
        based on facts.

_____ Never changing an
        opinion once you have
        it makes you strong.

▲Peanuts reprinted by permission
of United Features Syndicate, Inc.

Inferences and Photos

Textbook authors often include photographs or other visual cues to aid your understanding of the main point of a passage or section in the text. A skilled reader will study these pictures and visual aids to make inferences about the author's main idea. Read the following paragraph, taken from a college communications textbook. Study the picture, and then answer the questions.

Facial Expressions

[1]The face is a source of information to those around us. [2]For example, a criminal lawyer pays close attention to the face and eyes of future clients for clues to their possible guilt or innocence. [3]Think of all the things your face can say about you without saying a word. [4]Things such as wrinkles, baldness, and coloring comment not only on your age but also on the kind of life you lead. [5]For example, we suspect that people with dark tans spend a good deal of time outdoors. [6]Facial expressions that reveal emotion can speak for you before you ever open your mouth.

—Adapted from Barker & Gaut,
Communication, 8th ed., p. 58.

1. Complete the following caption for the photograph based on the details in the picture. Study the paragraph above for clues.

   ◄ Faces tell us about the _feelings_ of others.

___b___ 2. The facial expression of the boy in the picture shows
   a. anger.
   b. sadness.
   c. joy.

___a___ 3. The best statement of the author's implied main idea is
   a. The face is one of our main communication tools.
   b. The color of our skin reveals information about us.
   c. Our faces betray us.

Chapter Review

Test your understanding of what you have read in this chapter by filling in each blank with a word from the box. One word will be used twice.

assess	bias	context	inference

1. An _____*bias*_____ is an unstated idea that is suggested by the facts or details in a passage.

2. An author implies an idea, and a reader makes an ___*context*___ about the author's meaning.

3. Using _*context*_ clues to understand the meaning of a word is one example of making an inference.

4–5. Complete the list of the five steps for making a valid inference:

Step 1:   Verify and value the facts.

Step 2:   _*Understand*_ prior knowledge.

Step 3:   Learn from the text.

Step 4:   Investigate for _*inference*_

Step 5:   Detect contradictions.

Applications

Application 1: Making Inferences

Read the paragraph; then answer the questions that follow it.

Manners in America

[1]Several years ago, *A Status Report on Rudeness in America* revealed some interesting details about American manners. [2]Nearly 8 out of 10 surveyed worried about the increasing lack of respect and courtesy in America. [3]Most people agreed that they have to deal with people daily who treat them with **contempt**. [4]Almost half of all shoppers said they have walked out of stores because of poor service. [5]Over half of all drivers complained about hostile and reckless drivers. [6]Many people complained about the public use of swear words. [7]Still others resent those who hold loud cell phone conversations in public places. [8]Finally, most admitted that they too have been rude. [9]Everyone agreed that people used to be nicer to one another.

_____C____ **1.** Based on context clues, we can infer that the word **contempt** in sentence 3 means
   a. love.   c. boredom.
   b. disrespect.

_____a____ **2.** Based on the details of the paragraph, we can conclude that its implied main idea is
   a. Americans have become more rude.
   b. Americans are under too much stress.
   c. Americans have worse manners than people from other countries.
   d. Americans' rudeness is going to lead to violence.

Application 2: Making Inferences

Read the following list of facts, and write **V** beside *two* inferences based on the details in the list.

- Joan of Arc was only 17 years old when she led the French army to victory over the English.
- Marie Curie was an important scientist who won the Nobel Prize in chemistry and in physics.
- Margaret Thatcher became prime minister of Britain.
- Sally Ride traveled into space on the space shuttle.
- Two women writers, Pearl Buck and Toni Morrison, have won the Nobel Prize for literature.

_____V____ **1.** Women have made important contributions to history, science, and literature.

_____ **2.** These women chose careers over family life.

_____V____ **3.** The Nobel Prize is given in several different fields.

_____ **4.** These women succeeded because of the fight for women's rights.

Application 3: Making Inferences

Read the paragraph; then answer the questions that follow it.

Mass Arrests After Murder

[1]In the summer of 1942, the body of José Díaz was found in the waters of Sleepy Lagoon in Los Angeles. [2]During the search for the killers, police

arrested nearly 300 young Mexican American gang members. ³Twenty-two of these were put on trial for the murder. ⁴**Prejudice** against Mexican Americans played a major role in the trial, and 17 were found guilty. ⁵Even though there was no real proof and there were no witnesses, the defendants were convicted of a wide range of crimes, from assault to murder. ⁶A higher court over-turned the jury's rulings. ⁷A riot broke out in response. ⁸The military was called in, and many Mexican Americans were hurt. ⁹The police efforts to get rid of the Mexican American gangs in Los Angeles failed. ¹⁰The gangs formed again, for the young people felt the need to protect themselves.

_____ **1.** Based on context clues, we can infer that the word **prejudice** in sentence 4 means
    a. bias.   c. power.
    b. bravery.

_____ **2.** The implied main idea for the paragraph is
    a. The police used the murder of José Díaz to try to wipe out Mexican American gangs in Los Angeles.
    b. Mexican American gangs in Los Angeles were responsible for the murder of José Díaz.
    c. Mexican Americans hate the police.

REVIEW **Test 1**

Making Inferences

A. Read the following three amendments, or changes, that have been added to the Constitution of the United States. Write **V** beside *two* inferences that are based on the information in them.

Amendment 15 (Passed March 30, 1870): The right of citizens of the United States to vote shall not be denied or abridged by the United States or by any State on account of race, color, or previous condition of servitude.

Amendment 19 (Passed August 18, 1920): The right of citizens of the United States to vote shall not be denied or abridged by the United States or by any State on account of sex.

Amendment 26 (Passed July 1, 1971): The right of citizens of the United States, who are eighteen years of age or older, to vote shall not be denied or abridged by the United States or by any State on account of age.

_____ Former American slaves were allowed to vote long before American women could vote.

___✓___ Age, race, and gender were once barriers to voting in the United States.

_____ Age, race, and gender no longer affect one's right to vote in the United States.

___✓___ The Constitution of the United States can never be changed.

B. Read the paragraph. Write **V** beside *one* inference that is based on the information in it. Then answer the question.

Textbook
Skills

[1]When friends with women, men benefit from the access to more emotional support than they are likely to feel with their male friends. [2]Being friends with women allows men to spend more time in conversation, to be freer about their emotions and feelings, and to expand emotionally. [3]When with women friends, men do more talking and sharing of each other's problems. [4]Men are also more comfortable disclosing to women friends than to other men. [5]When talking about themselves to female friends, men tend to confide more about their weaknesses. [6]However, they do include and enhance their strengths. [7]Men who are used to challenging each other believe that they do not have to compete with female friends. [8]Men rate their friendships with women as more enjoyable and higher in overall quality than their male friendships.

—Adapted from Gamble, Teri Kwal and Michael W. Gamble. *The Gender Communication Connection*. Houghton Mifflin 2003, pp. 155–156.

___✓___ Men are better friends than women.

___✓___ Men do not often talk with other men about their feelings or emotions.

_____ Men do not grow emotionally unless they have a female friend.

_____ Which of the following statements is the best implied main idea of the paragraph?

    a. Forming friendships with females offers men several benefits.
    b. Women are more supportive than men.
    c. Men trust women.

REVIEW Test 2

Making Inferences

A. Read the paragraph. Write **V** beside *two* inferences that are based on the information in it.

Cable TV Companies in the City

[1]Every three years, the city council looks at the local cable TV companies and grants them the right to do business within the city limits. [2]During this review, new cable TV companies are allowed to bid for access. [3]The council also looks at the current company's rates and services. [4]The idea is to be sure that fair prices are charged for good service. [5]No new cable TV companies have been approved in many years. [6]The current cable TV company, which is the only company allowed access, pays a hefty fee to the city every year.

✓ ____ The city council can help ensure fair prices for access to cable.

____ The review process is fair and open.

____ The cable company and the city council have made a deal with each other.

✓ ____ The current cable company charges fair rates.

B. Read the paragraph. Write **V** beside *one* inference that is based on the information in the paragraph. Then answer the question.

Textbook
Skills

[1]Karen Quinlan was an active twenty-one-year-old when disaster struck. [2]She lapsed into a coma in the early morning hours of April 15, 1975, after drinking a few gin-and-tonics and possibly taking some drugs as well. [3]On the night before, Karen went with several friends to a roadside tavern. [4]They were to celebrate a friend's birthday. [5]She was seen "popping some pills," reportedly Quaaludes, earlier in the day. [6]And that evening, she had several drinks before even reaching the bar. [7]Karen "started to nod out" after only one drink at the tavern. [8]So she was driven home. [9]By the time they arrived, Karen had passed out entirely. [10]A few minutes later, the driver realized that she had stopped breathing. [11]He began to give her resuscitation. [12]An ambulance was called and Karen was carried off unconscious to the hospital, never to wake again. [13]Karen spent several years in a coma. [14]Meanwhile, her parents fought to discontinue the life support system that forced air into he

lungs through an incision in her throat. [15]Karen remained in a "persistent vegetative state" until her death.

—Adapted from Fishbein, Diana H. and Susan E. Pease. *The Dynamics of Drug Abuse*. Allyn & Bacon, 1996, p. 239.

_____ Karen Quinlan was an alcoholic.

___✓___ Karen Quinlan's friends were partly responsible for her tragedy.

_____ Karen Quinlan's tragedy was avoidable.

_____ Which of the following statements is the best implied main idea of the paragraph?

    a. The Karen Quinlan case shows the harmful effects of taking a mixture of Quaaludes and alcohol.

    b. Karen Quinlan had the right to die.

    c. People shouldn't let others drive while under the influence of alcohol or drugs.

REVIEW Test 3

Making Inferences

A. Read the paragraph. Write **V** beside *three* inferences that are supported by the ideas in it.

Weathering a Tornado

[1]Living in "Tornado Alley," I had seen my share of storms, but nothing had prepared me for that day in Texas. [2]The violent afternoon thunderstorm had ended quickly. [3]A sudden and strange quiet sent chills up my back. [4]I glanced around the wide-open spaces of my farm and then looked up. [5]The sky had turned a sickly greenish black. [6]The clouds were moving quickly and rotating to a corner in the western sky. [7]A thin black funnel appeared. [8]I stood rooted in fear, listening to a sound like a waterfall. [9]Within minutes, the funnel had grown into a wide shaft of swirling black death. [10]Debris began falling from the sky. [11]I ran and flung myself in the gully at the edge of the yard. [12]As I lay in that ditch, a loud roar like jet engines filled the air, and wind and rubble whipped every inch of me. [13]The funnel froze in place for what seemed like forever, and I prayed to live. [14]After just a few minutes, it passed, so I lifted my head and watched the

now white swirling mass of wind and debris head east toward town. ¹⁵Only after the monster was no longer in sight did I climb out of my ditch. ¹⁶The tornado had missed the house, but it had gouged a trench the length of the entire yard 3 feet deep. ¹⁷It had also flipped the family van upside down.

_____✓_ A sky that is greenish black is a tornado warning sign.

_____ Tornadoes have a roaring sound.

_____✓_ Tornadoes do not occur in Texas.

_____ Tornadoes stay in one place for hours.

_____ Tornadoes can do significant damage.

_____✓_ Tornadoes mostly destroy mobile homes.

B. Study the map. Write **V** beside *one* inference that is based on the information in the map.

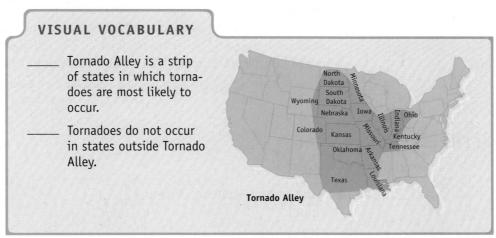

VISUAL VOCABULARY

_____ Tornado Alley is a strip of states in which tornadoes are most likely to occur.

_____ Tornadoes do not occur in states outside Tornado Alley.

Tornado Alley

—Map of Tornado Alley reprinted from www.tornadochaser.net.
Reprinted by permission of Tim Baker.

REVIEW **Test 4**

Making Inferences

Textbook Skills

Before you read, skim the passage from a college textbook. Next answer the Before Reading questions. Read the passage. Then answer the After Reading questions that follow it.

Vocabulary Preview

notable (2) outstanding, famous, important

rallied (4) brought together, united

protest (11) challenge, object to, disagree with

inferior (12) less than

Two Famous Black Journalists

[1]Two men figure strongly in the growth of the black press during the nineteenth and early twentieth centuries: Frederick Douglass and W. E. B. Du Bois. [2]Frederick Douglass was the **notable** ex-slave who founded *The North Star* in 1847. [3]He became an **icon** of hope for blacks in his day. [4]He **rallied** the public against slavery. [5]His essays and speeches helped white men and women see the hardship of slavery through black eyes. [6]Around 3,000 people in the United States and Europe read *The North Star*. [7]Many readers were influential people. [8]After the Civil War, Douglass edited magazines for 15 years. [9]He also wrote three **autobiographies** retelling the events of his amazing life and career.

[10]In 1910, W. E. B. Du Bois founded *The Crisis*. [11]This new paper was the **protest** voice of the National Association for the Advancement of Colored People (NAACP). [12]"Mentally the Negro is **inferior** to the white," said the 1911 *Encyclopaedia Britannica*. [13]First, Du Bois knew, beliefs like this had to be changed. [14]Then the bias against blacks in education, housing, and social status could be defeated. [15]Under his leadership, *The Crisis* grew to have more than 100,000 readers. [16]He retired as editor in 1934.

—Agee, Ault, & Emery, *Introduction to Mass Communications*, 12th ed., p. 126.

BEFORE READING

Vocabulary in Context

_____ **1.** The word **icon** in sentence 3 means
a. symbol.   c. topic.
b. threat.

_____ **2.** The word **autobiographies** in sentence 9 means that Douglass wrote
a. books about the Civil War.   c. articles for newspapers.
b. books about himself.

AFTER READING

Concept Maps

Finish the concept map with information from the passage.

Two Famous Black Journalists

3. _____   **4.** _____

Nineteenth century   Twentieth century

Founded *The North Star*   **5.** _____

3,000 readers   100,000 readers

Fought against slavery   Fought against bias

Worked as an editor   Worked as an editor

Main Idea

_____   **6.** Choose the best statement of the implied main idea of the second paragraph (sentences 2–9).
- a. Frederick Douglass started his own newspaper.
- b. Frederick Douglass was a successful white writer.
- c. Frederick Douglass was an influential journalist.

Supporting Details

_____   **7.** Sentence 15 is a
- a. major supporting detail.
- b. minor supporting detail.

Transitions

_____   **8.** The relationship between the ideas in sentences 13 and 14 is one of
- a. classification.   c. contrast.
- b. time order.

Thought Patterns

_____   **9.** The thought pattern used in this passage is
- a. time order.   c. definition.
- b. classification.

Inferences

10. Write **V** beside the inference that is based on the information in the passage.

_____ Frederick Douglass and W. E. B. Du Bois have much in common.

_____ W. E. B. Du Bois was more successful than Frederick Douglass.

Discussion Questions

1. What were some of the barriers that both Douglass and Du Bois faced?

2. In what ways have things changed for African Americans from the 19th century to the 21st?

3. What stories of hardship do you think Frederick Douglass might have shared with white men and women in his speeches about slavery?

4. What is important about the 1911 entry in the *Encyclopaedia Britannica* about the Negro?

Writing Topics

1. What are three or four ways reading and writing benefit society? Write a paragraph to explain your thinking.

2. Discuss the importance of newspapers. How important are they, and why? Write a paragraph or more.

3. How do people struggle for equality? Write a paragraph on the topic, drawing on any prior knowledge you may have.

SKILLED READER Scorecard

Inferences

Test	Number Correct		Points		Score
Review Test 1	_____	×	25	=	_____
Review Test 2	_____	×	25	=	_____
Review Test 3	_____	×	25	=	_____
Review Test 4	_____	×	10	=	_____
Review Test 5 (website)	_____	×	20	=	_____
Review Test 6 (website)	_____	×	25	=	_____

Enter your score on the Skilled Reader Scorecard: Chapter 11 Review Tests inside the back cover.

After Reading About Inferences

Before you move on to the mastery tests on inferences, take time to reflect on your learning and performance by answering the following questions. Write your answers in your notebook.

What did I learn about inferences?

What do I need to remember about inferences?

How has my knowledge base or prior knowledge about inferences changed?

More Review and Mastery Tests

For more practice, go to the book's website at **http://www.ablongman.com/henry** and click on *The Skilled Reader*. Then select "More Review and Mastery Tests." You will find the tests listed by chapter.

Name _D̶w̶g̶e̶ L̶u̶u̶r̶e̶n̶c̶e̶_____ Section _____

Date _1̶1̶ ̶1̶0̶ ̶0̶9̶_ Score (number correct) _____ × 10 = _____ %

A. Read the following short article published in *USA Today*. Write **V** beside *five* inferences supported by the ideas in the article.

From Death Row to Freedom for the 200th Time

[1]Jerry Miller is a former army cook who spent nearly 25 years behind bars. [2]He became the nation's 200th person freed from prison or death row through DNA testing. [3]The first DNA acquittal in the U.S. took place in 1989. [4]Thirteen years later, the number of freed inmates reached 100. [5]And just five years after that, the number doubled. [6]"Five years ago, people said that the number (of exonerations) was going to dry up because there just weren't many wrongful convictions. [7]But clearly, there are plenty of innocent persons still in prison. [8]There's no way you can look at this data without believing that," said Barry Scheck. [9]He is a co-founder of the New York-based *Innocence Project*. [10]The organization assisted Miller and helps other prisoners prove their innocence through DNA evidence. [11]Right after Miller's release, the Innocence Project launched "200 Exonerated, Too Many Wrongfully Convicted," a month-long national campaign.

—Adapted from "200th Prisoner Cleared Through DNA Testing."
USA Today, April 23, 2007, and Innocence Project Press Release,
April 23, 2007. *Death Penalty Information Center.*
<http://www.deathpenaltyinfo.org/newsanddev.php?scid=6>.

___✓___ DNA provides important information.

_____ DNA can prove that a person is innocent of a crime.

___✓___ DNA can prove that a person is guilty of a crime.

___✓___ Jerry Miller was guilty of the crime.

___✓___ Jerry Miller was innocent of the crime.

___✓___ Jerry Miller's conviction was overturned.

___✓___ Jerry Miller may face more jail time.

B. Read the following article published in *USA Today*. Write **V** beside *five* inferences supported by the ideas in the article.

Audubon Comes to the Inner City

[1]The National Audubon Society wants to help people connect to nature. [2]The society plans to open 1,000 nature centers by 2020. [3]The nature centers will offer shows, events, and programs. [4]These centers will teach about local birds, other animals, and the natural world. [5]These centers will be opened in poorer neighborhoods across the country.

[6]The nature centers will take old **reservoirs** and turn them into places that are friendly to birds and small wildlife. [7]These birdwatching centers will be filled with sounds of many types of birds, bullfrogs, bats, or even coyotes.

[8]The first center will open in Brooklyn. [9]Audubon President John Flicker says, "It's important if people are going to care about the **environment** that they have some connection to it."

[10]The Audubon Society was named for wildlife painter John Audubon. [11]With 500,000 members, the Audubon Society has become one of the most powerful nature groups in the nation. [12]But most of its members are older and more white than the overall USA's population. [13]The society hopes to attract young people, immigrants, and people of color.

[14]"It's going to change us a lot, because we're going to have to reflect the communities we serve," Flicker says. [15]"That is probably the best thing that could happen to us."

— Charisse Jones, "Audubon Comes to the Inner City," *USA Today*, 10 Apr. 2002, p. A3. Copyright © 2002, *USA Today*. Reprinted with permission.

_____ The government is going to pay for nature centers.

_____ The word **reservoirs** in sentence 6 refers to basins, ponds, or pools.

_____ The word **environment** in sentence 9 refers to the world of nature.

_____ John Audubon was a scientist.

_____ John Audubon was an artist.

_____ John Audubon loved wildlife.

_____ One goal of the Audubon Society is education.

_____ Members of the Audubon Society are mostly young and of various races.

Read the following passage. Write V beside ten inferences that are based on the information in it.

¹The local cable television company ran a **promotion** to sign up more homes to high-tech television. ²The high-tech offer included the following: a smart box for digital TV access to hundreds of channels, a modem, and Road Runner high-speed cable connection to the Internet. ³The offer also promised free hookup and free service for one month. ⁴Shantel tried both the TV and Internet service for a few weeks. ⁵Before the end of the one-month trial period, she returned the smart box and canceled Road Runner. ⁶Her bill for that month showed that she was charged for a month. ⁷She called the cable company and had the following discussion:

⁸"Thank you for choosing Acme Cable. ⁹My name is Dorothy. ¹⁰How may I help you?" the customer service woman said in a cool, polite voice.

¹¹"My name is Shantel Adams, and I have a question about my bill," Shantel began in a cheerful voice.

¹²"Yes, ma'am," Dorothy cut her off. ¹³"Could you please give me your phone number and the last three numbers of your Social Security number."

¹⁴Shantel, surprised at being cut off, gave the information and listened to the clicking sounds of typing at the other end of the line.

¹⁵"Yes, Ms. Adams, how may I help you?" Dorothy asked with a stifled yawn.

¹⁶"Well," Shantel explained, "I heard your ad on the TV about a one-month free trial offer for smart box digital TV and Road Runner . . ."

¹⁷"Yes, that is our upgrade package," Dorothy interrupted.

¹⁸"Well," Shantel continued, "I tried both of them for a couple of weeks. ¹⁹But I don't want the services, so I took the **equipment** back to your office before the month was up."

²⁰"So you returned the digital smart box and the modem?" Dorothy interrupted again.

²¹"Yes, ma'am," Shantel said, frustrated. ²²Then she snapped, "But my bill shows I owe a month's fee for the smart box and Road Runner."

²³"We charge a month in advance," Dorothy explained.

²⁴"What does that mean?" Shantel asked, surprised.

²⁵"We charge a month in advance," Dorothy repeated, saying each word very slowly as if talking to a child.

457

²⁶"So I was billed for next month? ²⁷I didn't know you charge a month in advance. ²⁸How could you possibly know if I would keep the stuff after the free trial was up?" Shantel asked in a puzzled voice. ²⁹Then she added in a sharp tone, "When I returned it, you should have taken it off my bill."

³⁰"Ms. Adams, most people keep the service," Dorothy said.

³¹Shantel cut Dorothy off and said sharply, "It's not really a free month, is it, if you are billing a month in advance."

³²"Ms. Adams, we will correct your bill," Dorothy replied.

³³"Good thing I called," Shantel said tersely, "or I would be paying for something I don't owe!"

³⁴"Please accept our apologies . . . ," Dorothy began.

³⁵Shantel hung up abruptly.

_____ The word **promotion** in sentence 1 means "a raise in rank or status on a job."

_____ Shantel's attitude changed as she talked with Dorothy.

_____ Shantel was rude to Dorothy.

_____ Dorothy was rude to Shantel.

_____ Shantel doesn't like to be interrupted.

_____ Dorothy became angry during the conversation.

_____ The word **equipment** in sentence 19 refers to a smart box and a modem.

_____ Shantel placed an order to upgrade her service from the cable company.

_____ Shantel received a free month's trial of upgraded service.

_____ According to the cable company, few people cancel the upgrade when the free trial month is up.

_____ The cable company charges for services not yet used.

_____ The cable company acted illegally.

_____ The cable company charged Shantel without her approval.

A. Read the following paragraph from the textbook *Introduction to Mass Communications*. Write **V** beside *five* inferences that are supported by the details in the paragraph.

15 Minutes of Fame

Textbook
Skills

[1]Pop artist Andy Warhol's quip that every person will have 15 minutes of fame has a certain ring of reality. [2]At least some people do get their 15 minutes in the **limelight**, whether they earn it or not. [3]Persons unknown to the public sometimes become involved in a news situation, often by accident. [4]And they suddenly find themselves starring in the highly competitive media. [5]An example is Brian "Kato" Kaelin, a would-be actor who was living in O. J. Simpson's guesthouse the night Simpson's ex-wife and her friend were murdered. [6]Kaelin testified at the trial and suddenly was a national figure. [7]He tried later (with only modest success) to cash in on his short-lived fame. [8]During the trial, Judge Lance Ito noted caustically that some potential jurors he'd dismissed were riding around Los Angeles in stretch limousines, which were taking them from one interview to another.

—Adapted from Agee, Ault, & Emery, *Introduction to Mass Communications*, 12th ed., p. 28.

_V_ The word **limelight** in sentence 2 means "scandal."

_V_ The word **limelight** in sentence 2 means "spotlight."

_____ Kato Kaelin was famous for his acting abilities.

_V_ O. J. Simpson is innocent of the murder of his ex-wife.

_____ Fame can come by accident.

_____ The media were not interested in getting potential jurors from O. J. Simpson's trial on their television shows or in their magazines.

_V_ Everybody is famous or will be famous.

_V_ Some people who had been potential jurors in O. J. Simpson's trial gave interviews to the media.

_____ Kato Kaelin tried to profit from the attention he received during the O. J. Simpson trial.

_____ Anybody can become famous unexpectedly.

B. Read the following paragraph from the textbook *The Dynamics of Drug Abuse.* Write **V** beside *five* inferences that are supported by the details in the paragraph.

Treatment of Alcoholism

Textbook
Skills

[1]Many believe the alcoholic must hit bottom before he or she will look for or accept help. [2]"Hitting bottom" generally occurs when the alcoholic loses his or her job or family. [3]Some alcoholics are able to reach a "high bottom" and find help before their lives are totally destroyed. [4]This high bottom can be brought on through **intervention**. [5]Intervention occurs when loved ones confront the alcoholic. [6]People who care (such as family members, friends, or an employer) create a crisis for the alcoholic, forcing him or her to admit to the alcoholism. [7]This forced crisis is so alarming and painful that the person may be moved to seek help.

—Adapted from Fishbein & Pease, *The Dynamics of Drug Abuse,* p. 125.

_____ Alcoholics hit bottom when they lose a job or their family because of drinking problems.

_____ It is impossible for alcoholics to find ways to quit drinking and live sober.

_____ Alcoholics are bad people.

_____ Family members and friends can help an alcoholic.

_____ **Intervention** is a form of help.

_____ Fear often drives alcoholics to get help.

_____ Alcoholism is a treatable condition.

A. Read the following passage from a communications textbook. Write **V** beside *five* inferences that are supported by the details in the passage.

Democracy's Crucial Freedoms

Textbook
Skills

[1]Democratic society is built on four basic freedoms:

- Freedom of speech
- Freedom of the press
- Freedom of assembly
- Freedom of petition

[2]These four freedoms are the basis for other freedoms. [3]For example, religious and political choices are based on freedom of assembly (the ability to meet in public) and freedom of speech. [4]Religious and political choices also rely on the freedom of the press to spread ideas. [5]These four freedoms are basic to the freedom to share information and ideas. [6]The history of journalism and the mass media begins with the story of the long struggle of people for these freedoms. [7]In a society without these freedoms, the magic of print and electronic technology means little.

—Adapted from Agee, Ault, & Emery, *Introduction to Mass Communications,* 12th ed., p. 44.

 _____ Freedom is an important aspect of a democratic society.

 _____ A democratic society is one that is run by the people.

 _____ The ability to get and give information is based on the freedoms of speech, press, and assembly.

_____ Too much freedom is dangerous.

_____ Many people have struggled to gain these freedoms.

_____ The press misuses its freedoms.

 _____ Print and electronic technology are tools that should be used to share information; in other words, they can be tools of freedom.

B. Read the following passage from the textbook *Family Communication*. Write **V** beside *five* inferences that are supported by the details in the passage.

461

Textbook
Skills

Self-Disclosure

[1]**Self-disclosure,** the act of revealing oneself to another person, serves as a major way of gaining closeness within a relationship. [2]But it can also be used as a power strategy. [3]The **power play** occurs when one person tries to control the other with the "information power" gained from that person's previous self-disclosure. [4]For example, when a self-disclosure is thrown back at a spouse during a fight, that person loses power. [5]The statement, "Well, you had an affair, so how can you talk?" places the focus of the fight on a past event and reminds the spouse of his or her wrongdoing.

[6]Self-disclosure is often difficult for parents, but the mother in the following example gained greater closeness with her daughter:

[7]"One of the most meaningful times in my life occurred when my teenage daughter and I had an all-night session talking about love, sex, and growing-up problems. [8]It was the first time I honestly told her about what I went through growing up and how we faced some of the same things. [9]I had always kept those things to myself. [10]But I suddenly realized that she shouldn't feel like she was different or bad because of her feelings. [11]It's scary to tell your daughter your faults or fears, but it certainly resulted in a closer relationship between us."

—Galvin & Brommel, *Family Communication: Cohesion and Change,* 5th ed., pp. 199–200.

___✓___ Self-disclosure can be risky.

___✓___ People who self-disclose are selfish.

___✓___ Self-disclosure is telling someone else about your own fears or failures.

_____ Some people are afraid to self-disclose.

___✓___ Children feel guilty when they hear about their parents' struggles.

_____ Power plays may hinder intimacy.

___✓___ Self-disclosure can be misused.

Name *Phryl Lawrence* _____ Section _____

Date *1/10/09* Score (number correct) _____ × 10 = _____ %

A. Read the following paragraph from a college psychology textbook. Write **V** beside *five* inferences that are supported by the details in the paragraph.

Stress: A Response

Textbook
Skills

[1]Physical stressors, such as a piece of glass stuck in your bare foot, are generally easy to identify, but the definition of a psychological or social stressor is more subjective. [2]Maya is not bothered about the recent firings in her company because she wants to spend more time with her children. [3]Part of her wouldn't mind being out of work (and collecting unemployment) so that she could stay home for a while. [4]Between savings and her husband's paycheck, the family could get by for a few months. [5]So for Maya, the threat of being fired is not a psychological stressor. [6]It is the **perception** of whether or not a stimulus is a stressor that is crucial for determining whether the stress response will occur.

—Kosslyn & Rosenberg, *Psychology: The Brain,
The Person, The World*, p. 434.

_V_ An injury or wound is an example of a physical stressor.

_V_ A stressor can be physical or psychological.

_____ Maya is in no danger of being laid off from her job.

_V_ Maya is afraid of losing her job.

_____ Unemployment benefits will give Maya time to be with her children.

_V_ Maya is lazy.

_V_ The word **perception** in sentence 6 means "thought, idea, view."

_____ Thoughts, ideas, and views about a situation can cause stress.

B. Read the following passage from the college textbook *Listening*. Write **V** beside *five* inferences that are supported by the details in the passage.

Two Views

Textbook
Skills

[1]Linda Chou is a new receptionist at a busy downtown office. [2]She started work only two weeks ago after a week of orientation. [3]Lily Thomson is

463

the office manager, and she supervised Linda's orientation and training. [4]She was satisfied with Linda's performance during training, but she has kept an eye on Linda, particularly during peak hours. [5]For the past week, Lily has noticed that Linda sometimes hesitates to greet customers with a warm smile, as she was asked to do. [6]In fact, many times Linda doesn't even look at the male customers who come up to her desk. [7]In addition, she often speaks too softly and avoids dealing with the problems and questions that arise.

Manager's Viewpoint: [8]It has always been a policy for the receptionist to greet customers with a warm smile and friendly hello. [9]Linda acts almost uncaring when customers enter. [10]Therefore, Lily feels the need to coach Linda on this point. [11]She believes that Linda's behavior is likely the result of getting used to the workplace.

Employee Viewpoint: [12]Linda was brought up in a traditional Asian family. [13]She has always been taught that it is wrong for a woman to smile or look directly at a man. [14]Speaking too loudly is thought to be rude. [15]Therefore, Linda feels uneasy greeting customers the way Lily suggested, particularly since she did not have to do so when she worked in a similar position in Hong Kong.

—Adapted from Brownell, *Listening: Attitudes, Principles, and Skills*, 2nd ed., p. 349.

_____ Lily does not like Linda.

_____ Lily believes Linda is deliberately rude.

_____ A warm smile and a friendly hello are required behaviors for a receptionist in this office.

_____ Polite receptionist behavior is defined differently in Asia than it is in America.

_____ Linda was born and raised in America.

_____ Customers in Hong Kong do not expect a smile and a greeting.

_____ Linda has had experience working as a receptionist.

_____ It is helpful for managers to understand an employee's cultural background.

A. Read the following passage from the college textbook *Introduction to Mass Communications*. Answer the question in the photo caption, and then write **V** beside *four* inferences that are supported by the details in the passage.

Audiences Targeted on the Basis of Their Values and Lifestyles

[Textbook Skills]

¹A research firm based in California created a system to study audiences based on their needs and desires. ²This system is called the Values and Lifestyles Program (VALS 2). ³The system divides people into two large groups. ⁴The first large group is inner-directed; they take their cues from their own beliefs and values. ⁵The second large group is outer-directed; they look to society to guide their choices.

⁶In addition, VALS 2 divides people into subgroups. ⁷The research goal is to find out whether consumers in each of these subgroups can afford the things they need and want. ⁸Advertisers use these categories as they design their advertising and marketing programs. ⁹A few of the subgroups are described here:

¹⁰*Actualizers* are successful people with many resources; they are concerned with social issues and are open to change.

¹¹*Experiencers* are young, enthusiastic, and impulsive; they savor the new, the offbeat, and the risky. ¹²They are avid consumers.

¹³*Makers* are action-based and love to be self-supporting. ¹⁴They are often found building their own houses, canning vegetables, or working on the car.

¹⁵*Strugglers* are almost fully concerned with meeting urgent needs of the moment.

—Agee, Ault, & Emery, *Introduction to Mass Communications*, 12th ed., p. 73.

_____ ▲ Which audience group does the photo want to appeal to?
a. Actualizers
b. Experiencers
c. Makers

___✓___ Actualizers are better and stronger people than Strugglers.

___✓___ Actualizers probably earn high wages.

___✓___ Experiencers probably don't mind spending their money to have a good time.

___✓___ Makers are good with their hands.

___(✓)___ Makers do not like to work.

_____ Strugglers are driven by crisis.

B. Read the following passage from the college textbook *Listening*. Write **V** beside *five* inferences that are supported by the details in the passage.

Textbook
Skills

Listening to the Elderly

[1]Recognize that talking to an elderly person may take more time than talking to a young person. [2]If you need an answer in a hurry, try asking "closed" rather than "open" questions. [3]Or put your questions in an either-or format. [4]You cannot expect a quick answer to a question such as "What would you like to do tonight?" [5]Asking a more direct question such as "Would you like to take a ride after lunch?" or "Would you rather go look for that book you were talking about?" is less stressful and gives you more information.

[6]Let the older person know that she is important. [7]Rather than shouting a question from across the room, stand next to the person whenever you can. [8]People who have trouble hearing will appreciate the ability to see you as you speak with them.

[9]Ask questions. [10]Take the time to be interested in what an older person is doing and thinking. [11]Put yourself in the role of listener as much of the time as possible. [12]Share when it seems appropriate, but otherwise develop the attitude that you will gain more by listening than speaking.

—Adapted from Brownell, *Listening: Attitudes, Principles, and Skills,*
2nd ed., p. 319.

___✓___ When talking with the elderly, a "closed" question is better than an "open" question.

___✓___ An example of a closed question is "Would you like to take a ride after lunch?"

_____ An example of an open question is "What would you like to do tonight?"

___✓___ Most older people are able to keep up with the activities of their families.

_____ Most older people ask a lot of questions.

_____ Older people often need extra time and attention.

___✓___ You can benefit from listening to older people.

READING 1

Shoulders

Nels Gould

Each of us has a deep need to be loved and to belong; we need the cycle of connection that comes from both receiving and giving respect and acceptance. And we spend much time and energy seeking to fill these needs. The following essay taken from a psychology textbook explores the significance of the human need for connectedness. The author Nels Gould, Indiana University-Purdue University at Indianapolis, offers his insights about our compelling need for each other.

Vocabulary Preview

modified (paragraph 2): adapted, changed
ungratified (paragraph 4): unmet
perseverance (paragraph 4): resolve, determination
obligatory (paragraph 4): required, mandatory
omnipotence (paragraph 5): all powerful
pseudosolution (paragraph 5): fake, or false, solution
alienation (paragraph 5): isolation
contemplations (paragraph 6): thoughts

1   I was about six years old when my parents took me to a parade. Standing there in a crowd of giants all I could see were knees and belt buckles. The bands, floats, and zany clowns passed by unseen. "I can't see! I want to see!" I yelled. Within a couple of seconds two strong arms lifted me up high above the crowd. I had the best seat in the house up there on my father's shoulders. He didn't seem to mind at all that he was half strangled each time I got excited.

2   Two weeks ago I took some college students through a **modified** Outward Bound initiatives course. One task was to figure out how to get over a sheer 13-foot wall using only their minds and bodies. Gradually they decided to place a couple of people at the base of the wall. Sandy was elected to climb up on their shoulders. Sandy stretched and still was six inches from reaching the upper ledge. The two classmates she was standing on then pushed her up until she caught hold of the ledge and scrambled over. The rest of the class cheered Sandy. No one gave a hand to the two below with dirty shirts and sore shoulders.

3   It took actual shoulders to see the parade and climb the wall. Shoulders come in many other forms—teachings, models and

mentors, others' past efforts. Our most accomplished persons readily acknowledged shoulders. "Many times a day I realize how much my life is built upon the labors of my fellow men, both living and dead," said Einstein. Eddie Robinson, immediately before the game which made him college football's winningest coach, said to his players "It's a record made up of men like you for the last 40 years."

4   Why is it, then, that most of us, most of the time, forget that we stand on shoulders? It appears that once our foundations are established, they are dropped from waking consciousness. Our attention becomes fully focused on current struggles, unattained goals, and **ungratified** needs. Successes are seen as the result of personal resourcefulness, **perseverance,** and possibly a few breaks. Occasionally we might throw in a plaudit for those we stand on, but it generally rings of the **obligatory.** I was reminded of this when someone asked me how I achieved a certain style of trumpet playing. My response centered on individual effort and practice. Later reflection revealed gaping holes in this answer. I forgot my shoulders. Any current trumpeting skill would have to be traced to my mom's encouragement while hearing me butcher pieces like "The Carnival of Venice" in the back room; to Hendrik Buytendorp, the music teacher who made it clear that trumpet scales were just as important as little league practice; and to Ferguson, Severinsen, Hirt, Mangione.* An honest and true answer would have to acknowledge all these influences. Try it yourself—just attempt to fully explain how you are able to do something well. The answer will unveil a vast network of shoulders.

5   Forgetting shoulders may be linked to distorted notions of self-sufficiency. We value and reward self-direction, individual initiative, and taking responsibility. A healthy person possesses these qualities. It is when these traits are exaggerated out of proportion that problems begin. Healthy autonomy turns into neurotic self-reliance. A person gradually begins to believe he/she can master life's challenges by relying solely on personal resources, and that to even acknowledge the help of others is a "weakness." It may even work for awhile. Then prices must be paid. Some develop illusions of **omnipotence** or step into the trap Karen Horney called the **pseudosolution** of mastery. This "I don't need anybody, never had, never will" orientation propels one to the outpost of **alienation.**

6   One does not lose uniqueness by tracing an accomplishment or ability to the influence of others. The actual idea and action is an individual one; it has your stamp. That is what shoulders are for; they permit a stretching of the limits of what has gone on before. By remembering shoulders while perched up there, you get the bonus of profound sense of belonging. One may even realize Thoreau's advice: "If I devote myself to pursuits and **contemplations,** I must first see, at least, that I do not pursue them sitting upon another man's shoulders. I must get off him first, that he may pursue his contemplations, too."

7   Sometimes I realize my part in this shoulders network in simple ways. I am

---

*The last names of four accomplished trumpeters.

watching the Indianapolis 500 parade with 250,000 other giants. The bands, floats, and clowns pass by and I hear my four year old son hollering, "I can't see! I want to see!" I hoist him up on my shoulders and he half strangles me.

—Gould, Nels. "Shoulders." From Gould, Nelson and Abe Arkoff, *Psychology and Personal Growth*, 6th ed. Allyn & Bacon, 197–98

Fill in the blank in each sentence with a word from the "Vocabulary Preview."

Vocabulary Preview

1. Sticking to a physical fitness program requires *ungratified* based on resolve.

Vocabulary Preview

2. Lanedra enjoys keeping a journal of her *contemplations* or thoughts about current events and daily life.

Vocabulary Preview

3. Maria *modified* her work schedule by switching to the late night shift so that she could spend time with her children before and after school.

Vocabulary Preview

4. Roderick overcame social *alienation* by taking responsibility for and changing the angry and rude behavior that isolated him from others.

Vocabulary Preview

5. Heather gladly wrote the *obligatory* thank you notes to her family and friends who had showered her with wedding gifts.

Write the letter of the best meaning of each of the words in *italics*. Use context clues to make your choice.

Vocabulary in Context

c

6. "The bands, floats, and *zany* clowns passed by unseen." (paragraph 1)
   a. stupid   c. funny
   b. embarrassing   d. tall

Vocabulary in Context

7. "Our most *accomplished* persons readily acknowledged shoulders." (paragraph 3)
   a. fearful   c. hopeful
   b. successful   d. grateful

Vocabulary in Context

a

8. "Occasionally we might throw in a *plaudit* for those we stand on, but it generally rings of the obligatory." (paragraph 4)
   a. criticism   c. compliment
   b. gift   d. glance

Vocabulary in Context   _c_   **9.** "Healthy *autonomy* turns into neurotic self-reliance." (paragraph
   a. immune system
   b. dependence
   c. independence
   d. relationship

Vocabulary in Context   _a_   **10.** "One does not lose *uniqueness* by tracing an accomplishment (
   ability to the influence of others." (paragraph 6)
   a. individuality
   b. humility
   c. uniformity
   d. curiosity

Implied Central Idea   _d_   **11.** Which sentence is the best statement of the implied central idea (
   the passage?
   a. Successes are seen as the result of personal resourcefulness, per
      severance, and possibly a few breaks.
   b. Forgetting shoulders may lead to distorted notions of self
      sufficiency.
   c. Our successes come because we stand on the shoulders of others
   d. One must have strong "shoulders" to survive in this world.

Implied Main Idea   _b_   **12.** Which sentence is the best statement of the implied main idea of
   paragraph 2?
   a. It takes everyone working together to succeed.
   b. Those who give a helping hand are often overlooked when suc-
      cess occurs.
   c. Outward Bound is an excellent initative course.
   d. Sandy is a young lady of determination.

Supporting Details   _a_   **13.** Speaking of his winning record, football coach Eddie Robinson said,
   a. "Many times a day I realize how much my life is built upon the
      labors of my fellow men."
   b. "I can't see! I want to see."
   c. "We stand on the shoulders of giants."
   d. "It's a record made up of men like you for the last 40 years."

Supporting Details   _b_   **14.** The author knows how to play
   a. football.
   b. the corporate game to get ahead.
   c. on the guilt of other people.
   d. trumpet.

Thought Patterns ___*b*___ **15.** The main thought pattern for the overall passage is
   a. a list and explanation of examples of those who have made the author successful.
   b. an argument that gives supports for the point that each of us has relied on others to become the person we are today.
   c. a discussion of the causes of belonging.
   d. a comparison and contrast between self-reliance and dependence on others.

Thought Patterns ___*b*___ **16.** The thought pattern for paragraph 2 is
   a. cause and effect.
   b. generalization and example.
   c. time order.

Transitions ___*a*___ **17.** "Our most accomplished persons readily acknowledged shoulders. 'Many times a day I realize how much my life is built upon the labors of my fellow men, both living and dead,' said Einstein." The relationship of ideas between these two sentences is
   a. time order.
   b. contrast.
   c. example.

Transitions ___*a*___ **18.** "It appears that once our foundations are established, they are dropped from waking consciousness." (paragraph 4) The relationship of ideas within this sentence is
   a. time order.
   b. example.
   c. cause and effect.

Inferences ___*d*___ **19.** Which of the following statements is a valid conclusion based on the ideas in paragraph 7?
   a. The author is annoyed at his son.
   b. The author is an avid Indianapolis 500 fan.
   c. The author is happily married.
   d. The author understands that his son's success in life will be in part because of his own successes.

Inferences ___*c*___ **20.** From the passage, we can conclude that
   a. we need each other in order to succeed.
   b. the author is a successful businessman.
   c. even some level of self-reliance is an impossible goal.
   d. we have the potential to do each other great harm.

Mapping

Complete the following concept map. Fill in the blanks with the central id
and the missing major supporting details from "Shoulders."

Author sits on the shoulders of his father to see parade.

Shoulders have many different meanings.

Standing on shoulders help them become stronger.

Central idea: Shoulders

Shoulders come in many different forms.

One doesn't lose uniqueness by giving credit to those who helped along the way.

we stand on Shoulders

Once foundations are established, shoulders are forgotten.

Questions for Discussion and Writing

1. Write a paragraph that summarizes the author's central idea and major supporting details.
2. Discuss your reasons for agreeing or disagreeing with Gould's point about the origin of our successes. Discuss the origin of one of your accomplishments or skills.
3. Apply Gould's suggestion of tracing the origin of a skill or accomplishment of a public figure (current or historical).

4. Why do some people think it is a sign of weakness to give credit to those who have helped them? What are some other reasons people don't give credit to others?

5. Reread the quote from Thoreau in paragraph 6. What do you think he means? Is his view accurate? Why or why not?

VISUAL VOCABULARY

Nels Gould uses "shoulders" as

a _____ for giving

another

person a boost to success.

    a. method
    b. symbol

SKILLED READER **Scorecard**

"Shoulders"

Skill	Number Correct		Points		Total
Vocabulary Preview (5 items)	_____	×	10	=	_____
Vocabulary in Context (5 items)	_____	×	10	=	_____
			Vocabulary Score		_____
Implied Central Idea and Implied Main Idea (2 items)	_____	×	8	=	_____
Supporting Details (2 items)	_____	×	8	=	_____
Thought Patterns (2 items)	_____	×	8	=	_____
Transitions (2 items)	_____	×	8	=	_____
Inferences (2 items)	_____	×	8	=	_____
Mapping (4 items)	_____	×	5	=	_____
			Comprehension Score		_____

READING 2

Doryl Lawrence
12/03/09

Finding My Voice

Maria Housden

Have you ever witnessed an injustice and felt too afraid to speak up or take a public stand? Have you cared more about fitting in than about doing the right thing? In the following essay, published in *Self* magazine, Maria Housden chronicles her journey from silent bystander to involved activist. How does a woman accustomed to avoiding confrontation learn to stand up for what she believes in?

Vocabulary Preview

lacrosse (paragraph 1): a game in which players use a long stick with a pouch attached to catch and carry the ball to the goal.
oblivious (paragraph 1): completely unaware
disparaging (paragraph 7): critical, negative
integrity (paragraph 13): honesty
solidarity (paragraph 13): unity

---

1   My eyes were on my son, Will, and the other 14-year-old boys racing up and down the field, tossing and chasing the **lacrosse** ball, but I was listening to the women in front of me gossiping about their friends. Although I couldn't hear every word, their conversation was ripe with intrigue as they leaned into each other, sometimes covering their mouths with their hands. The two seemed **oblivious** to my presence, and I couldn't help feeling as if I had, briefly, become privy to the secrets of an inner circle, the kind to which I'd sometimes longed to belong.

2   Just then, a gaggle of teenaged girls, some of whom I knew from Will's class, made their way toward the bleachers. Most were giggling, unaware of anything but each other, though a few averted their eyes self-consciously as they crossed in front of the adults. Suddenly, one of the whispering women turned to the other and said, "Can you believe how fat some of those girls are getting?"

I felt my heart sink into my gut at her insensitivity. I knew I should say something, but in the tumble of my emotions, I couldn't decide what. So I sat there, the rough wood of the bleachers cutting into my thighs, choking back all the things I might have, *should* have, said.

I've always applauded the efforts of women willing to speak out against injustice. I've wished for the same courage but have often been ashamed of how I fall short. Hesitant to consider myself a feminist or an activist, I have mostly shied away from supporting too loudly any one thing.

5   It took a single moment at a lacrosse game for that habit to begin to change.

6   In the weeks that followed, as I washed dishes, pruned the jasmine and waited for red lights to turn green, I found myself returning again and again to the rage and shame I'd felt that afternoon. The intensity of my reaction puzzled me. Certainly I had witnessed women criticizing other women before, yet something about this felt different. Part of it was that I wished I'd called these women's attention to how their gossiping was a form of violence against those girls. But at the same time, I knew that my pointing an accusing, self-righteous finger wasn't the solution.

7   I had to admit I'd been all of those women at one time or another: the critical ones; the awkward teenagers; and the woman watching in silence, wanting to be included— me. It was conceivable, probable even, that my silence in the face of that woman's **disparaging** comment stemmed from the same feeling of insecurity that compelled her to utter it.

8   I have known the shame of not belonging. I was in the sixth grade the first time Cheryl Wainwright (I've changed her name) invited me to her house. Cheryl could effortlessly toss her long hair over her shoulder, and she'd been wearing a bra long before any of us needed one. I remember one afternoon at her house, nibbling on a freshly baked cookie, bouncing lightly on the edge of her canopied bed. I knew then that I wanted to *be* Cheryl Wainwright, and barring that, I wanted to be her best friend. For about six months I was. Then something happened: I've forgotten what. But I haven't forgotten how, for the next two years, Cheryl pointed at me whenever she saw me in the hall at school and whispered into the ear of whoever was standing beside her.

9   The pain of that rejection still stings, nearly 30 years later, and in the wake of the lacrosse game moment, I realized a part of me would do anything to avoid feeling it again. Each of us, no matter our intentions, is occasionally governed by a fear of not belonging, by a wish, above all, to be loved. When I'm honest with myself, I can admit that I, too, have said insulting things about someone behind her back, that sometimes, when I hear women gossiping, I feel relief that they're not talking about me.

10   Until now, I wanted to believe this reaction was a harmless symptom of being human. But while seeing one woman taking aim at another is as familiar to me as the pause of my heart between beats, it wasn't until the sights were trained on a 13-year-old girl that I saw it for what it had been all along.

11   Ultimately, when we undermine the strength and beauty of someone else, we undermine our own. All my life, I have yearned to be truly loved, to find clothes that fit, to have bigger breasts. By defending those young women, I could have honored all the ways that I, too, am vulnerable and imperfect, struggling to know who I am. What bothered me most about that moment on the bleachers, it turns out, wasn't that I hadn't known what to say, but that I *had* known yet was too afraid to speak the words aloud. My fear of making a fool of myself had kept me from being everything I am capable of being.

12   Every woman is another woman's daughter, and as a mother, I have instinctively tried to minimize the pain my children experience in their lives and not

revisit my sins on them. I've encouraged them to feel good about their bodies, to be proud of their abilities and to respect others. When my oldest daughter, Hannah, died of cancer at age 3, one of the lessons her death offered me was that everything we say and do matters. I was reminded of that truth at the lacrosse game. It wasn't enough for me to teach my children to love themselves and respect others; I had to do it, too.

13   Our history as women is filled with writers, dreamers, artists and activists whose fierce **integrity** shines through everything they do. I am ready to become a part of that history, to champion that **solidarity**. Increasingly, I have begun to make new choices, to base my self-worth more on my willingness to take a stand and less on whether others agree. Rather than simply stating my positions privately, I am speaking out in a way I wasn't able to at the lacrosse game. Since then, I have sign controversial petitions, participated in t launch of an international peace initiati and lectured publicly on how our cultu copes with and understands death. I do know if my efforts will ever make a me surable contribution to the world, b they've infused my life with a sense of po sibility that continues to inspire me. R cently, for instance, I was asked to lead workshop for bereaved parents. I agree though I felt little passion for the assign topic, long-term illness. In the end, I ove rode the voice within that wanted me to nice and took a leap. I told the board would be honored to participate, but wanted to talk about something else. To n surprise and delight, they agreed to n proposal—a workshop titled Don't F with Me, My Child Died: Making a Li That Matters on the Other Side of Grie I'm proud to finally be in the game.

VISUAL VOCABULARY

Gossip is a form of _____.

a. emotional abuse
b. harmless behavior

Fill in the blank in each sentence with a word from the "Vocabulary Preview."

Vocabulary Preview

1. The drug Oxycontin made Sonji _oblivious_ to the intense pain in her lower back.

Vocabulary Preview

2. With one _disparaging_ look, Scott's mother silenced his excited, childish chatter.

Vocabulary Preview

3. Unions are groups of workers who use _solidarity_ to bargain for pay and benefits.

Vocabulary Preview

4. According to historical records, _lacrosse_ was a sport that trained Native American men for war.

Vocabulary Preview

5. Employers list personal _integrity_ as a highly valued trait in prospective employees.

For items 6 and 7, choose the best meaning of each word in *italics*. Use context clues to make your choice.

Vocabulary in Context

_d_ **6.** "Although I couldn't hear every word, their conversation was ripe with *intrigue* as they leaned into each other, sometimes covering their mouths with their hands." (paragraph 1)
   a. conspiracy
   b. crime
   c. silliness
   d. meanness

Vocabulary in Context

_b_ **7.** "The two seemed oblivious to my presence, and I couldn't help feeling as if I had, briefly, become *privy to* the secrets of an inner circle, the kind to which I'd sometimes longed to belong." (paragraph 1)
   a. shut out of
   b. immune to
   c. let in on
   d. part of

Implied Central Idea

_a_ **8.** Which sentence is the best statement of the implied central idea of the passage?
   a. One woman grows from a person who shies away from taking a stand to a person who is willing to speak out.
   b. Women should be more supportive of one another.
   c. Speaking out takes courage and maturity.
   d. The need to belong often outweighs the desire to take a stand.

Main Idea   *d*   **9.** Which sentence best states the main idea of paragraph 6?

a. In the weeks that followed, as I washed dishes, pruned the j
    mine and waited for red lights to turn green, I found mys
    returning again and again to the rage and shame I'd felt th
    afternoon.

b. The intensity of my reaction puzzled me.

c. Part of it was that I wished I'd called these women's attention
    how their gossiping was a form of violence against those gir

d. But at the same time, I knew that my pointing an accusing, se
    righteous finger wasn't the solution.

Supporting Details   *c*   **10.** The incident that caused the author to find her voice was

a. the death of her daughter.

b. gossip overheard at a lacrosse game.

c. remembering the women of history who had fierce integrity.

d. launching an international peace initiative.

Supporting Details   *b*   **11.** What bothered the author most about the moment on th
bleachers was

a. her act of eavesdropping, that is, listening in on someone else
    conversation.

b. her own negative feelings toward the young girls.

c. that she knew what to say but was too afraid to say it.

d. young girls being gossiped about by older women.

Thought Patterns   *a*   **12.** The main thought pattern of the overall passage is

a. a list of important issues about which women should speak up
    and take strong stands.

b. an argument against gossiping.

c. a discussion of the causes of peer pressure.

d. a narration of the author's emotional journey of finding her voice.

Thought Patterns   *c*   **13.** The thought pattern of paragraph 1 is

a. cause and effect.

b. definition.

c. time order.

Transitions   *c*   **14.** "Part of it was that I wished I'd called these women's attention to
how their gossiping was a form of violence against those girls. But
at the same time, I knew that my pointing a self-righteous finger
wasn't the answer." (paragraph 6)

The relationship of ideas between these two sentences is
a. time order.
b. contrast.
c. example.

Transitions **15.** "I had to admit I'd been all of those women at one time or another: the critical ones; the awkward teenagers; and the woman watching in silence, wanting to be included—me." (paragraph 7)

The relationship of ideas within this sentence is
a. time order.
b. listing.
c. cause and effect.

Fact and Opinion **16.** "It was conceivable, probable even, that my silence in the face of that woman's disparaging comment stemmed from the same feeling of insecurity that compelled her to utter it."

This sentence from paragraph 7 is a statement of
a. fact.
b. opinion.
c. fact and opinion.

Fact and Opinion **17.** "I was in the sixth grade the first time Cheryl Wainwright (I've changed her name) invited me to her house."

This sentence from paragraph 8 is a statement of
a. fact.
b. opinion.
c. fact and opinion.

Inferences **18.** From the article, we can conclude that
a. the author is resentful toward other women.
b. the author has become a woman unafraid to speak her mind.
c. the rejection the author experienced from Cheryl Wainwright no longer bothers her today.
d. the author is self-righteous.

Inferences **19.** From the details in paragraph 1, we can conclude that
a. the author is willing to speak up against injustice.
b. even as an adult, the author still struggles with the need to belong.
c. the author is interested in the lacrosse game.
d. she knows the women who were gossiping.

Inferences   ___C___ **20.** The details in paragraph 13 imply that

        a. the author still fights the urge to stay quiet instead of speaki
           out against injustice.
        b. the author wants to make a measurable difference in the wor
        c. all women should become more actively involved in public
           sues of importance.
        d. the author has not changed much since the lacrosse game.

Mapping

Add the ideas needed to complete this concept map of the article "Finding I
Voice." Wording may vary.

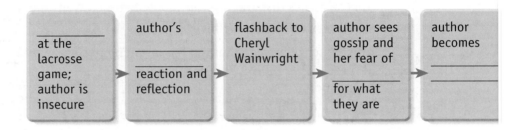

Questions for Discussion and Writing

1. Write a paragraph that summarizes the author's central idea and maj
   supporting details.
2. Have you ever been the object of gossip? What was its effect on you? Ha
   you ever been the one who gossips? How does gossiping about someo
   else make you feel?
3. Housden asserts that gossip is a form of violence. Do you agree? Why
   why not?
4. Have you ever been afraid to stand up for a principle or belief? How c
   the experience affect you?
5. Who are some well-known public figures who have not been afraid
   speak up? Discuss whether or not these well-known figures made a me
   surable contribution through their forthrightness.

SKILLED READER Scorecard

"Finding My Voice"

Skill	Number Correct		Points		Total
Vocabulary Preview (5 items)	_____	×	4	=	_____
Vocabulary in Context (2 items)	_____	×	4	=	_____
Implied Central Idea and Main Idea (2 items)	_____	×	4	=	_____
Supporting Details (2 items)	_____	×	4	=	_____
Thought Patterns (2 items)	_____	×	4	=	_____
Transitions (2 items)	_____	×	4	=	_____
Fact and Opinion (2 items)	_____	×	4	=	_____
Inferences (3 items)	_____	×	4	=	_____
Mapping (4 items)	_____	×	5	=	_____
			Comprehension Score		_____

READING **3**   *Daryl Lawrence*   12/08/09

A Dad at the Final Frontier

Marc Parent

Change has affected all aspects of our lives, from how we conduct our business to how we keep in touch with one another to how we cook our food. Families and the roles each member plays are also changing. The following essay appeared in the *New York Times*. In it, Marc Parent talks about society's reactions to his view of his role as a new kind of father.

Vocabulary Preview

accounting for (paragraph 1): explaining
nanny (paragraph 2): children's caregiver
provider (paragraph 2): supplier of income, goods, or services
putting in the hard time (paragraph 6): enduring a punishment
queasiness (paragraph 6): uneasiness
peppering (paragraph 10): showering, overwhelming

1   Things may be getting easier for me and my kind. In the last 10 years the number of fathers acting as primary custodians of children under 18 rose 62 percent—there are now 2.2 million of us, **accounting for** 2.1 percent of all American households. Of course, national statistics are one thing, and the midday grocery aisles are quite another.

2   If you want to assess America's adjustment to care-giving fathers, step into a city playground on a Wednesday afternoon and watch the reaction of the nearest **nanny**. As a stay-at-home father to sons 1 and 3 years old, I was often approached by well-meaning women who were certain I was between child-care **providers,** "Excuse me, do you need a nanny?"

3   "No thanks," I'd tell them. "I'm the father and the nanny."

4   And then I'd leave to go see the man at the deli, who asked every day, no matter what time, no matter how draped with children or how weighed down with stroller and diaper bag I was, "You on your lunch break?"

5   The curiosity is always the same: What business could a man in his mid-30's, midweek and midday, possibly have with his children?

6   Of course, some people see nothing at all remarkable about a man caring for his children, but most men **putting in the hard**

time will tell you there are many who seem to harbor an unspoken **queasiness** about it.

7   My wife is a teacher with a paycheck like a small, steady train. I'm a writer who brings feast or famine. There are no hidden agendas surrounding our decision about who stays home—you keep the job with the better health plan.

8   Still there's a feeling that if a man dons a baby carrier, he does so at the cost of some measure of manhood. It's perhaps no coincidence that I became obsessed with hand-splitting wood around the same time I got really good with a Diaper Genie.

9   The problem is that unless men find their own way to care for their children, they are left to imitate their wives or their own mothers. There are still very few well-worn paths to full-time fatherhood. In our household, we've found that the parent who spends the time does it better. I'm better with the demands of parenting in winter, and my wife is better on summer break. But though I've found a way to make fatherhood relevant before the first game of catch, the rest of the world may not buy it yet.

10   I recently joined a conversation with a group of mothers as we waited to pick up our children from preschool. One of them was pregnant, and the women were **peppering** her with advice. I stayed quiet through the part about breast pads and swollen ankles but spoke up when they reached the topic of diaper rash.

11   "I don't suggest using powder for a rash," I said, hoisting my youngest to my hip. They smiled and nodded politely with eyes wide, as if I'd just told them I liked to rob banks. "And the cream is much better than the ointment," I continued as they looked from my son to my two-day beard. "I use it with every diaper."

—Parent, "A Dad at the Final Frontier," *New York Times,* op-ed page. Originally published in the *New York Times,* June 16, 2001.

Fill in the blank in each sentence with a word from the "Vocabulary Preview."

Vocabulary Preview   **1.** Jerome always felt a *queasiness* in his stomach after he rode the roller coaster.

Vocabulary Preview   **2.** It is very important to check the references of a *nanny* before you hire one.

Vocabulary Preview   **3.** Dr. Nancy Bailey is an excellent *provider* for her family.

Vocabulary Preview   **4.** The boxer Muhammad Ali was known for *peppering* his opponents with quick, hard blows.

Vocabulary Preview   **5.** The police had all the family members *accounting* their actions over the past few days.

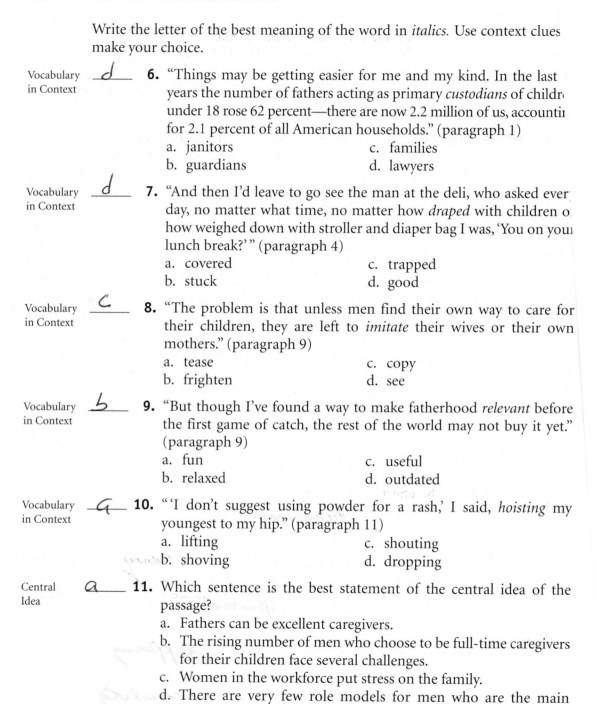

Write the letter of the best meaning of the word in *italics.* Use context clues
make your choice.

Vocabulary
in Context   *d*   **6.** "Things may be getting easier for me and my kind. In the last
years the number of fathers acting as primary *custodians* of childr(
under 18 rose 62 percent—there are now 2.2 million of us, accountii
for 2.1 percent of all American households." (paragraph 1)
a. janitors   c. families
b. guardians   d. lawyers

Vocabulary
in Context   *d*   **7.** "And then I'd leave to go see the man at the deli, who asked ever
day, no matter what time, no matter how *draped* with children o.
how weighed down with stroller and diaper bag I was, 'You on you:
lunch break?'" (paragraph 4)
a. covered   c. trapped
b. stuck   d. good

Vocabulary
in Context   *c*   **8.** "The problem is that unless men find their own way to care for
their children, they are left to *imitate* their wives or their own
mothers." (paragraph 9)
a. tease   c. copy
b. frighten   d. see

Vocabulary
in Context   *b*   **9.** "But though I've found a way to make fatherhood *relevant* before
the first game of catch, the rest of the world may not buy it yet."
(paragraph 9)
a. fun   c. useful
b. relaxed   d. outdated

Vocabulary
in Context   *a*   **10.** "'I don't suggest using powder for a rash,' I said, *hoisting* my
youngest to my hip." (paragraph 11)
a. lifting   c. shouting
b. shoving   d. dropping

Central
Idea   *a*   **11.** Which sentence is the best statement of the central idea of the
passage?
a. Fathers can be excellent caregivers.
b. The rising number of men who choose to be full-time caregivers
for their children face several challenges.
c. Women in the workforce put stress on the family.
d. There are very few role models for men who are the main
caregivers for their children.

Implied
Main Idea

_C_ **12.** What is the implied main idea of the final paragraph?
    a. The author gets along well with the other mothers.
    b. The author wants to go back to work outside the home.
    c. The author is an experienced caregiver for children.
    d. The author's children are often sick.

Supporting
Details

_d_ **13.** The author stays home to care for his children because
    a. as a writer, he doesn't bring in a regular paycheck or have benefits.
    b. his wife insists on working outside the home.
    c. he is unemployed.
    d. he and his wife cannot afford child care.

Supporting
Details

_C_ **14.** The author is a stay-at-home father to
    a. one son and one daughter.
    b. two daughters.
    c. two sons.
    d. two sons and one daughter.

Thought
Patterns

_c_ **15.** The main thought pattern for paragraphs 2 through 5 is
    a. comparison.
    b. time order.
    c. cause and effect.
    d. listing.

Thought
Patterns

_a_ **16.** The thought pattern for paragraphs 10 and 11 is
    a. comparison.
    b. effect.
    c. cause and effect.
    d. time order.

Transitions

_d_ **17.** "Of course, some people see nothing at all remarkable about a man caring for his children, but most men putting in the hard time will tell you there are many who seem to harbor an unspoken queasiness about it." (paragraph 6)

The relationship of ideas in this sentence is one of
    a. time.
    b. effect.
    c. contrast.
    d. comparison.

Transitions _____b_____ **18.** "I recently joined a conversation with a group of mothers as waited to pick up our children from preschool." (paragraph 10)

The relationship of ideas within this sentence is one of
a. time order.   c. addition.
b. effect.   d. comparison.

Inferences   Choose the two inferences that are most clearly based on information from th following passage.

"Still there's a feeling that if a man dons a baby carrier, he does so at th cost of some measure of manhood. It's perhaps no coincidence that I becam obsessed with hand-splitting wood around the same time I got really goo with a Diaper Genie." (paragraph 8)

19. _C_

20. _b_

a. The author felt that he had to prove he was manly.
b. Others may think of a man as less than manly if he is the main care-giver for his children.
c. The author is embarrassed to be the main caregiver for his children.
d. The author refused to change diapers.

Outlining

Complete the following outline with ideas from the passage.

Central Idea: **(1)** _the ratio and percentage of people that hire nannies._

I. More men than ever are the primary caregivers of their children.

   A. The number of fathers acting as primary caregivers rose

      (2) _18 to 62_ in the last 10 years.

   B. 2.2 million men are primary caregivers of their children.

   C. 2.1 percent of all American households have fathers as the primary care-givers of the children.

II. Society does not expect men to be the primary caregivers of their children.

   A. In the park, **(3)** _nanny_ often approach the author to offer their services.

B. The man at the deli assumes the author with his children is on a lunch break.

C. Some men harbor an unspoken queasiness about being a primary caregiver.

D. Even when men find a way to make (**4**) _easy_ relevant before the first game of catch, the rest of the world may not understand.

Questions for Discussion and Writing

1. Write a paragraph that summarizes the author's central idea and major supporting details.

2. What are the usual roles men and women have been expected to fulfill as parents? How do these roles differ from each other?

3. Why would people be surprised at a man's desire to be a caregiving father?

4. How might the children benefit from having their father as the main caregiver? How do men and women differ in their approach to parenting?

5. What are some of the unexpected roles women are beginning to take on? Why are women's roles changing?

6. Are there specific jobs or roles that are better suited to men or women? Why or why not?

SKILLED READER Scorecard

"A Dad at the Final Frontier"

Skill	Number Correct		Points		Total
Vocabulary Preview (5 items)	_____	×	10	=	_____
Vocabulary in Context (5 items)	_____	×	10	=	_____
			Vocabulary Score		_____
Central Idea and Implied Main Idea (2 items)	_____	×	8	=	_____
Supporting Details (2 items)	_____	×	8	=	_____
Thought Patterns (2 items)	_____	×	8	=	_____
Transitions (2 items)	_____	×	8	=	_____
Inferences (2 items)	_____	×	8	=	_____
Outlining (4 items)	_____	×	5	=	_____
			Comprehension Score		_____

READING **4**   *Daryl Lawrence* 12/09/09

Close Again

Marion Bond West

> After World War II, the return of America's victorious soldiers to wives and girlfriends resulted in a "boom" in births. Seventy-six million babies were born nationwide between 1946 and 1964. As the baby boom generation ages, so do their parents. As both generations grow older, they must find new ways to relate to each other. The author of this article tells about her mother's transition into an assisted-living home. The article appeared in the online version of *Guideposts*.

Vocabulary Preview

recurrence (paragraph 2): return
unbidden (paragraph 3): unasked, uninvited
interaction (paragraph 5): contact
brooding (paragraph 17): thinking in an anxious or gloomy way
tremendous (paragraph 18): great
pathetic (paragraph 31): sad, pitiful

---

1   I poured prune juice into a small glass, cranberry juice into another. From five different boxes of cereal lined up on my kitchen counter, I measured precise amounts into a bowl and added sliced bananas, sugar, and milk. Then I arranged everything on a tray along with a napkin, silverware, and a fresh cup of coffee.

2   For four years, ever since Mother had come to live with my husband, Gene, and me after a **recurrence** of cancer at age 85, I had prepared the same breakfast. I could put it together with my eyes closed.

3   Carrying the tray, I walked carefully down the hall to Mother's bedroom. I paused at her closed door and glanced at the meal I was about to bring in to her. **Unbidden** memories of other breakfasts—those Mother had prepared for me long ago—surfaced, rising like the steam off the oatmeal she used to set before me every morning. I never had much appetite early in the day, so she tried to make breakfast special, adding raisins and brown sugar to my oatmeal, serving it in a special bowl decorated with a cheerful red rooster.

4   The best part was that she sat at the breakfast table with me and told me a story while I ate. Even as a little girl, I understood those moments were daily blessings. Mother's job was our livelihood, and she put in long days at the office. She worked just as hard to make sure our relationship remained close— harder, truthfully—and she succeeded so well that to me, her only child, it seemed as if we'd been given all the time in the world together.

5   Now many years later, my mother and I were once again living under one roof. Things had gone well when she first moved in. I wasn't sure how or when it began, or even why, but gradually the distance—and the tension—between us grew. We drifted. We talked less and less, and Mother withdrew into her room more often. If it weren't for Veronica Hunter, the health care worker who came by every day to look in on her and help her bathe and dress, Mother would've had almost no **interaction** with other people. That worried me, especially since I felt I was doing a poor job as a companion—and as a daughter.

6   I held the tray and glared at her bedroom door. Lately, I'd been so frustrated I wanted to shout, "I can't stand this anymore, Mother! I want us to be close again." But I couldn't. We didn't have that kind of relationship. We'd hardly ever had a minor tiff, let alone a full-blown fight, and I wasn't about to start one now. Stifling a sigh, I knocked, then eased the door open. "Good morning, Mother."

7   "Good morning, dear!" she said. "Mannie," she murmured, using my childhood nickname, "you don't have to go to all this trouble."

8   It was obvious she had gotten up early to put on makeup and brush her hair so she would be presentable when I came in. That was Mother, always putting a good face on things.

9   "Do you need anything else?" I asked.

10   "No, thank you. This is marvelous," she replied, giving me her patented smile. She spread the napkin across her lap. That was my clue to leave, so I did, closing the door behind me.

11   Back in the kitchen, I sank down at the table. Gene saw my expression and shook his head. I knew what was on his mind. For a while he'd been telling me, "You can't go on like this, Marion. You're not happy, and even though she never complains, I don't think your mother is either."

12   But how could I tell Mother our living together wasn't working anymore? She'd been unfailingly loving and gracious to me. Didn't I owe it to her to treat her the same way? Mother was as strong-willed and independent-minded as ever, but she could no longer live on her own. Though recent tests showed no signs of cancer, she couldn't walk easily, and she'd fallen several times. She needed someone to look after her. And who better than family?

13   I was the only one Mother had. She lost my father to a swift and deadly infection when I was just 22 months old. Never one to depend on handouts, she got a job at Granite City Bank in Elberton, Ga., as a junior book-keeper. She worked there for 38 years, retiring as an assistant vice president.

14   On my way home from school, I always stopped at the bank and knocked on her office window. Mother knew I'd be by; still, her whole face lit up as if it were the most wonderful surprise in the world. I could hardly wait for the janitor to unlock the door so I could run in and hug her and have her say, "Mannie, I'm so glad to see you! Tell me about your day."

15   I loved Mother to the point of fierceness for all she'd done for me. She made sure I wanted for nothing growing up. She led a rich life, full of friends and interesting experiences, and she shared all of them with me. She devoted so much attention to me I never felt as if I were missing out because I didn't have both parents around. Why, then, couldn't I seem to give her what she needed now? I longed for her to have new stories, new

friends, new experiences. She deserved to be living a rich life still, not spending her days closeted in her room.

16 "Hi, hon!" a voice rang out. It was Veronica, making her usual house call. She gave me a smile and headed to Mother's room. From down the hall I heard the two of them talking and laughing, old friends after nearly four years together. Mother should be enjoying herself like this all the time, I thought guiltily.

17 On her way out Veronica caught me **brooding.** "Marion, you might not want to hear this," she began, "but I have to say, it just doesn't feel right in this house anymore. Your mother needs to be in her own place. I told her so today."

18 It hurt to hear that, but at the same time I felt a **tremendous** sense of relief. Maybe now Mother and I could get the whole thing out in the open.

19 The next day, when I brought her breakfast, I asked as nonchalantly as I could, "What do you think of Veronica's suggestion?"

20 "What suggestion?" Mother said, snapping her napkin open on her lap.

21 Taking a deep breath, I replied, "About your moving into your own place . . . a home where you can mix with other folks."

22 "Forget it!" she declared, in a voice the whole neighborhood could probably hear. "I'm not moving."

23 "But, Mother, you might like . . ."

24 "Leave me alone."

25 "That's the problem," I said. "You're a people person. You're not made to spend all day alone. And I worry about what this is doing to us."

26 "You don't seem worried to me."

27 "Well, I am. We hardly talk, and we're getting short with each other."

"Then I'll go back to my house in [ ]berton," Mother said.

"You can't live on your own anymore I reminded her. She glared at me. "Mothe please give this some thought," I said. "OK:

Although she didn't answer, when closed her door behind me, the tension be tween us didn't seem as impenetrable as be fore. We'd actually had our version of a fight and it wasn't as bad as I had dreaded.

I made inquiries about Magnolia Estates, a new assisted-living home right down the road. They were having an open-house picnic the following Sunday. I showed Mother the handsomely printed invitation. She glanced at it, then flung it into her wastebasket. "I'm not about to go to some picnic for **pathetic** old ladies nobody wants."

"Gene and I want you to come with us," I said. I walked over to her closet. "What would you like to wear?"

"Oh, just shut up," she snapped. 3

She'd never said anything like that to me 34 before, but this was the spunky mother I loved. "You know what?" I said, hiding a smile. "You're never going to turn into a pitiful old lady. That's just not you." I hung the outfit I'd given her the previous Mother's Day on the closet door, a silent ultimatum—we would attend that picnic.

Folding her arms, Mother regarded me 35 coolly. "If you and Gene are set on going to that picnic," she allowed, "I guess I might go along."

When I went to her room Saturday 36 morning, Mother was waiting, perfectly made-up, coiffed and dressed in the outfit I'd given her, looking like a *Modern Maturity* cover girl.

At the picnic we were greeted by the 37 tangy aroma of barbecue and the tune of

"Georgia on My Mind." I saw a smile cross Mother's lips. Then she started waving eagerly. Two ladies at a picnic table waved back. "Jewette Grogan," they called to her, "you'd better be coming to sit by us!" They were old friends of hers from Elberton. Gene and I went to get some food, and by the time we came back so many people were enjoying Mother's company I could hardly squeeze in at the table to hand her a plate.

38 Not long after that, Mother moved to Magnolia Estates, into a room that Gene and I decorated with some of her favorite things from her home in Elberton.

39 I visit her every day, and honestly, I think we spend more time together now than when she lived with me. I should have known our relationship was strong enough to survive even that test; after all, Mother had instilled in me the courage to do difficult things.

40 One afternoon recently, I was standing outside Mother's door, my hand lifted to knock, when an old, familiar feeling came over me. Looking at the "Bless This Home" lace banner she'd hung on the door, I realized what it was. That same delicious sense of love and anticipation I felt blessed by years ago, every time I'd stopped by the bank after school.

41 I knocked. "Come in," Mother called out.

42 When I walked into her room, her face lit up. "Mannie," she exclaimed, "I'm so glad to see you!"

43 I wasn't a bit surprised.

—"Close Again" by Marion Bond West, *Guideposts*, February 2000. Reprinted with permission from *Guideposts*. Copyright © 2000 by *Guideposts*, New York 10512. All rights reserved. www.guideposts.com

Fill in the blank in each sentence with a word from the "Vocabulary Preview."

Vocabulary Preview

1. The champion skater fell three times and stumbled twice; his performance was _____.

Vocabulary Preview

2. After years of taking medicine to prevent anxiety attacks, last week Jamie suffered a(n) _____.

Vocabulary Preview

3. _____ about a problem doesn't help find its solution.

Vocabulary Preview

4. Jerome enjoyed the _____ with other students he gained by working with the student government association.

Vocabulary Preview

5. Development of the vaccine against smallpox was a _____ scientific achievement.

Write the letter of the best meaning of the word in *italics*. Use context clues to make your choice.

Vocabulary in Context _____ **6.** "From five different boxes of cereal lined up on my kitch counter, I measured *precise* amounts into a bowl and added slic bananas, sugar, and milk." (paragraph 1)
    a. small   c. large
    b. exact   d. daily

Vocabulary in Context _____ **7.** "I held the tray and *glared* at her bedroom door." (paragraph 6)
    a. looked lovingly
    b. looked angrily
    c. looked as though disappointed
    d. looked patiently

Vocabulary in Context _____ **8.** "I hung the outfit I'd given her the previous Mother's Day on the closet door, a silent *ultimatum*—we would attend that picnic." (paragraph 34)
    a. plea   c. demand
    b. question   d. thought

Vocabulary in Context _____ **9.** "At the picnic we were greeted by the tangy *aroma* of barbecue and the tune of 'Georgia on My Mind.'" (paragraph 37)
    a. sight   c. taste
    b. sound   d. smell

Vocabulary in Context _____ **10.** "That same delicious sense of love and *anticipation* I felt blessed by years ago, every time I'd stopped by the bank after school." (paragraph 40)
    a. eagerness   c. peace
    b. regret   d. anger

Central Idea _____ **11.** Which sentence is the best statement of the central idea of the passage?
    a. Close relationships are the result of love, patience, and communication.
    b. Mothers and daughters often disagree.
    c. Growing older is difficult for most people.
    d. Caregivers are often under a great deal of stress.

Main Idea _____ **12.** Which sentence is the best statement of the main idea of paragraph 15?
    a. I loved Mother to the point of fierceness for all she'd done for me.
    b. She made sure I wanted for nothing growing up.
    c. She led a rich life, full of friends and interesting experiences, and she shared all of them with me.
    d. I longed for her to have new stories, new friends, new experiences.

Supporting Details _____ **13.** When the author was a young girl, her mother
   a. worked late and neglected her.
   b. punished her often.
   c. fixed her breakfast and sat and talked with her as she ate.
   d. stayed home to raise her.

Supporting Details _____ **14.** When the author took her mother to visit the assisted-living home for the first time, her mother
   a. sat by herself and brooded.
   b. ignored her daughter.
   c. met old friends and enjoyed meeting new people.
   d. moved in and stayed.

Thought Patterns _____ **15.** The main thought pattern for paragraph 1 is
   a. comparison.   c. cause and effect.
   b. classification.   d. time order.

Thought Patterns _____ **16.** The overall thought pattern for the entire passage is
   a. comparison.   c. cause and effect.
   b. listing.   d. time order.

Transitions _____ **17.** "When I went to her room Saturday morning, Mother was waiting, perfectly made-up, coiffed and dressed in the outfit I'd given her, looking like a *Modern Maturity* cover girl." (paragraph 36)

   The relationship of ideas in this sentence is one of
   a. time order.   c. contrast.
   b. effect.   d. classification.

Transitions _____ **18.** "Mother was as strong-willed and independent-minded as ever, but she could no longer live on her own." (paragraph 12)

   The relationship of ideas in this sentence is one of
   a. time order.   c. contrast.
   b. cause and effect.   d. comparison.

Inferences Choose the two inferences that are most clearly based on information from the passage.

19. _____

20. _____

   a. The author felt guilty that her mother was being cut off from other people.
   b. The author and her mother often fought.
   c. The author's mother was a successful career woman.
   d. The author disliked her mother.

Outlining

Complete the outline with details from the passage.

"Close Again"

    I. Fixing _____ for mother (paragraphs 1–2)

   II. Memories of closeness (paragraphs 3–4)

  III. Tension in the house (paragraphs 5–7)

   IV. Talking to _____ (paragraphs 8–10)

    V. Brooding in the kitchen (paragraphs 11–18)

   VI. Suggesting a visit to _____ (paragraphs 19–35)

 VII. Visiting Magnolia Estates (paragraphs 36–38)

VIII. Close _____ (paragraphs 39–43)

Questions for Discussion and Writing

1. Write a paragraph that summarizes the author's central idea and major supporting details.
2. The author describes a complex relationship with her mother. Discuss the different emotions she feels toward her mother. What was the source of the author's guilt?
3. What caused the author's mother to withdraw into her room? How did the author cope with her mother's withdrawal?
4. What are some of the concerns people face as they care for their elderly parents?
5. Have you witnessed or experienced the demands of caring for an elderly person? How was that experience different or similar to Bond West's expectations? What kind of advice would you give caregivers to deal with some of these issues?
6. What are some of the challenges the elderly face as they grow older? How can we prepare ourselves as we face the aging process?

SKILLED READER Scorecard

"Close Again"

Skill	Number Correct	Points		Total
Vocabulary Preview (5 items)	_____	$\times$ 10	=	_____
Vocabulary in Context (5 items)	_____	$\times$ 10	=	_____
		Vocabulary Score		_____
Central Idea and Main Idea (2 items)	_____	$\times$ 8	=	_____
Supporting Details (2 items)	_____	$\times$ 8	=	_____
Thought Patterns (2 items)	_____	$\times$ 8	=	_____
Transitions (2 items)	_____	$\times$ 8	=	_____
Inferences (2 items)	_____	$\times$ 8	=	_____
Outlining (4 items)	_____	$\times$ 5	=	_____
		Comprehension Score		_____

READING 5

I've Seen the Worst That War Can Do

Nikolay Palchikoff

The following essay appeared in *Newsweek* magazine toward the end of 2001. Each issue of *Newsweek* features an essay written by a reader of the magazine, in a regular column called "My Turn." In an introduction to this essay, the author summarizes his firsthand experience with the horrors of war by saying, "One month after the bomb dropped on Hiroshima, I stepped off the train and into a nuclear ground zero."

Vocabulary Preview

psychologically (paragraph 1): mentally
indescribable (paragraph 2): beyond words
begets (paragraph 3): causes, leads to
tsar (paragraph 4): emperor of Russia until 1917
imprisoned (paragraph 5): locked up, confined
preconditions (paragraph 7): requirements, terms to be met
negotiating (paragraph 9): bargaining, attempting to reach agreement

1   I remember getting off the train in Hiroshima in September 1945, one month after the city had been destroyed by the atom bomb. I was 21 years old. I stood there in my U.S. Army uniform, looking around at the world's first nuclear ground zero. The ground was covered with ashes that had once been my hometown. There were no search-and-rescue squads or policemen recovering bodies because there were none to recover. There were no memorial shrines, noisy tractors or visitors flocking to the site. Instead there were images of bodies burned like photographic negatives into the concrete and an utter silence so **psychologically** traumatic that it would be 40 years before I ever spoke about it.

2   When the train rolled away, I was overwhelmed by an **indescribable** emotion. Flashbacks of my childhood ran through my mind: drinking green tea and laughing with my mother; running through the local Sentai gardens; going to the annual cherry blossom festival each spring. As I looked at the wasteland where I once rode my bicycle, I wondered what had happened to the food vendors who brought tofu and fish to our house every week.

3   Watching the television coverage of the September 11 attacks brought back the agony of that day. The scenes of devastation made me remember what it was like to be able to see clear across Hiroshima to the bay on the

other side because there was nothing left standing in between. I can relate to the pain and confusion of the families who lost loved ones. My heart goes out to them. But 56 years after the tragedy of Hiroshima, I've come to the conclusion that violence only **begets** more violence, and war is not a solution to anything.

4 I didn't always think this way. For many years war was a part of my life. I was born in Hiroshima in 1924. My father was an officer in the **tsar's** White Army, a member of the Russian nobility who moved to Japan with my mother after the revolution in 1917. He would tell me bedtime stories about what it was like to fight in Siberia and encourage me to become an officer. My friends and I loved to imitate the Japanese soldiers marching off to the Manchurian War. We would run around the yard with sticks pretending to conquer our imaginary enemies.

5 When I was 16, a group of missionaries offered to take me to the United States so that I could continue my education. I arrived in San Francisco by ship. I wanted to become a doctor, so I went to high school during the day and worked as a janitor in a hospital each night. Within the year, two things happened that changed my plans: the Japanese bombed Pearl Harbor and **imprisoned** my father because I was living in America. My native country was now the enemy, and I was eager to join the war effort. Because of my ability to speak fluent Japanese, I became a member of U.S. Army intelligence.

6 I was translating Japanese radio in the Philippines on August 6, 1945, when they announced that the entire city of Hiroshima had been destroyed by a single bomb. I was shocked. I never thought that war might mean death for innocent civilians like my family, and for other living creatures whose only crime was to be in the wrong place at the wrong time.

7 The Army sent me to Japan to make sure its government was meeting the **preconditions** of the peace treaty. I took the opportunity to pay my last respects to my family. When I arrived in Hiroshima, I walked from the train station to the site where our home had stood. I recognized the fish-shaped pond that had been in the front yard and the twisted metal that was once my wrought-iron bed. Later that same day, I came across a family friend who had survived the attack by jumping into the river. He explained that my family had left the city just two days before the bomb was dropped. Miraculously, my parents and my brother and sister had survived and were living just a few miles away.

8 Despite the horror I had witnessed, I returned to America believing that a strong military was needed to maintain world peace. But by the mid-'80s, my perspective began to change. The arms race was out of control, and I felt something had to be done. In 1986 I returned to Hiroshima with my wife as part of an anti-nuclear peace mission and to put to rest my emotions about that tragic event, something that has proved impossible.

9 Now, at 77, I continue to work for peace. I believe that all countries, including the United States, must stop using the threat of war as a **negotiating** tool and find a way to solve global conflicts without killing more people. It is my hope that by speaking out about the horror of Hiroshima, I will help ensure that it is never repeated.

—"I've Seen the Worst That War Can Do," by Nikolay Palchikoff from *Newsweek*, December 3, 2001. All rights reserved. Reprinted by permission.

Fill in the blank in each sentence with a word from the "Vocabulary Preview"

Vocabulary
Preview
1. Stress affects us both physically and _____.

Vocabulary
Preview
2. _____ a deal with the car salesman saved Rob and Sue $2,00(

Vocabulary
Preview
3. French silk pie is so delicious, it's _____.

Vocabulary
Preview
4. Some very rich people set _____ before they marry to protec
their wealth in case of a divorce.

Vocabulary
Preview
5. Many convicted criminals are _____ for years while thei
cases are appealed.

Write the letter of the best meaning of the word in *italics*. Use context clues to
make your choice.

Vocabulary
in Context
_____ **6.** "There were no memorial *shrines*, noisy tractors or visitors flocking
to the site." (paragraph 1)
a. churches
b. speeches
c. sacred places
d. crowds of mourners

Vocabulary
in Context
_____ **7.** "Instead there were images of bodies burned like photographic
negatives into the concrete and an utter silence so psychologically
traumatic that it would be 40 years before I ever spoke about it."
(paragraph 1)
a. hurtful   c. important
b. fatal   d. helpful

Vocabulary
in Context
_____ **8.** "As I looked at the wasteland where I once rode my bicycle, I wondered what had happened to the food *vendors* who brought tofu
and fish to our house every week." (paragraph 2)
a. cooks   c. buyers
b. sellers   d. customers

Vocabulary
in Context
_____ **9.** "Because of my ability to speak *fluent* Japanese, I became a member
of U.S. Army intelligence." (paragraph 5)
a. a little   c. smooth and clear
b. no   d. broken

Vocabulary
in Context

10. "But by the mid-'80s, my *perspective* began to change." (paragraph 8)
a. viewpoint
b. love
c. career
d. fortune

Central Idea

11. Which sentence is the best statement of the central idea of the passage?
a. Hiroshima in 1946 and New York on September 11, 2001, had many similarities.
b. War is brutal.
c. Speaking about horrors such as the bombing of Hiroshima may help prevent war in the future.
d. War is not a solution to anything.

Implied
Main Idea

12. Which sentence is the best statement of the implied main idea of paragraph 8?
a. The author works for peace.
b. The author is still upset about Hiroshima.
c. The author is trying to deal with his pain by working for world peace.
d. The author is opposed to the military.

Supporting
Details

13. When the author saw the nuclear destruction at Hiroshima, his hometown, he was
a. 77 years old.
b. 16 years old.
c. 21 years old.
d. 56 years old.

Supporting
Details

14. The author's father was imprisoned in Japan because
a. his father was a war criminal.
b. his father tried to escape Japan.
c. the author was a war criminal.
d. the author lived in America.

Thought
Patterns

15. The main thought pattern of the passage is
a. comparison.
b. time order.
c. contrast.
d. listing.

Transitions _____ **16.** "There were no memorial shrines, noisy tractors or visitors floc[...]ing to the site. Instead there were images of bodies burned li[...] photographic negatives into the concrete and an utter silence [...] psychologically traumatic that it would be 40 years before I ev[...] spoke about it." (paragraph 1)

The relationship of ideas between these two sentences is one of
a. contrast.   c. time order.
b. cause and effect.   d. listing.

Transitions _____ **17.** "When I arrived in Hiroshima, I walked from the train station t[...] the site where our home had stood." (paragraph 7)

The relationship of ideas in this sentence is one of
a. time order.   c. addition.
b. cause and effect.   d. comparison.

Transitions _____ **18.** "Despite the horror I had witnessed, I returned to America believ-ing that a strong military was needed to maintain world peace." (paragraph 8)

The relationship of ideas in this sentence is one of
a. time order.   c. contrast.
b. cause and effect.   d. comparison.

Inferences   Choose the two inferences that are most clearly based on information from the following passage.

"Despite the horror I had witnessed, I returned to America believing that a strong military was needed to maintain world peace. But by the mid-'80s, my perspective began to change. The arms race was out of control, and I felt something had to be done. In 1986 I returned to Hiroshima with my wife as part of an anti-nuclear peace mission and to put to rest my emotions about that tragic event, something that has proved impossible." (paragraph 8)

19. _____

20. _____

a. The author no longer believes military force ensures peace.
b. The author believes that military force ensures peace.
c. The author still struggles with the trauma of Hiroshima.
d. The author refuses to return to his homeland.

Mapping

Complete the following timeline with details from the passage.

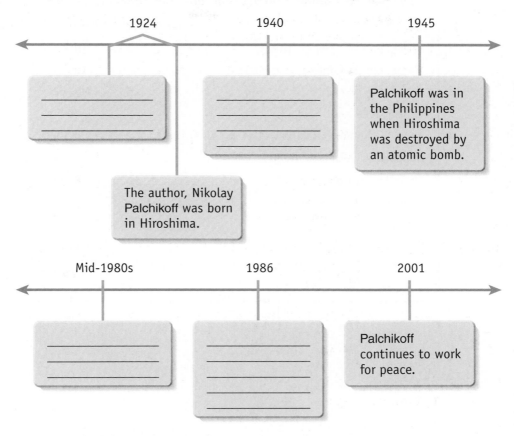

Questions for Discussion and Writing

1. Write a paragraph that summarizes the author's central idea and major supporting details.
2. In what ways were the atomic bombing of Hiroshima and the September 11 attacks on New York similar? How were they different?
3. What are some of the unexpected effects of war?
4. Why did the author change his mind about the use of military force to ensure peace? Do you agree with his current view about military force? Why or why not?
5. Have you ever had an experience in life that changed the way you thought about or believed in something? What was your first belief? What happened to change your view? What is your current view about that idea?

SKILLED READER Scorecard

"I've Seen the Worst That War Can Do"

Skill	Number Correct		Points		Total
Vocabulary Preview (5 items)	_____	×	10	=	_____
Vocabulary in Context (5 items)	_____	×	10	=	_____
			Vocabulary Score		_____
Central Idea and Implied Main Idea (2 items)	_____	×	8	=	_____
Supporting Details (2 items)	_____	×	8	=	_____
Thought Patterns (1 item)	_____	×	8	=	_____
Transitions (3 items)	_____	×	8	=	_____
Inferences (2 items)	_____	×	8	=	_____
Mapping (4 items)	_____	×	5	=	_____
			Comprehension Score		_____

READING 6

Growing Up With Two Moms

Megan McGuire

Fear of rejection, embarrassment, and confusion are common feelings shared by those who differ from the norm. Megan McGuire records her own childhood struggles with these feelings as the daughter of a gay mother. When she was eighteen years old, McGuire published this essay about her childhood experiences in *Newsweek* magazine.

Vocabulary Preview

tolerant (paragraph 1): open-minded, accepting
assumed (paragraph 2): understood, believed
straight (paragraph 2): slang for heterosexual
socially (paragraph 4): within society, publicly
literature (paragraph 4): written material
Ph.D. (paragraph 5): an abbreviation for the degree Doctorate of Philosophy

---

1   When I was growing up, the words "fag" and "queer" and "dyke" were everywhere, even though we lived in a relatively **tolerant** community, Cambridge, Mass. I even used them myself to put down someone I didn't like. If you were a fag or a dyke, you were an outcast. All that changed when I was 12. My mother had a friend, Barb, who started spending the night, though she lived minutes away. One night when Barb wasn't there, I asked my mother, "Are you gay?" I can only remember the "yes"—and the crying. All I could think was that she couldn't be gay. It wasn't fair. She was one of "those" people.

2   I always thought my family was normal. By the time I was 5, my mother and father no longer lived together. My brother and I split our time between our parents. My father remarried, and my mother dated men. We **assumed** our parents were **straight.** That's all you see on TV.

3   As it turned out, we didn't have a stereotypical family. The years after my mother came out to me were very difficult for me and my brother. We had just moved from Washington, D.C. We had to start over, and at the same time we had to lie about our mom. In school I wanted to be liked, so I laughed at the jokes about gays. I had yet to figure out how to make a friend I could trust with my secret. I wasn't ready to talk about my family because I wasn't ready to deal with it myself.

4   High school was the hardest. I was into all kinds of clubs, but I was afraid everything

I had gained **socially** would disappear if any-one ever found out that while they went home after volleyball practice to their Brady Bunch dinners with Mom and Dad, I went home to two *moms.* My brother and I would never allow Mom and Barb to walk together or sit next to each other in a restaurant. We wouldn't have people spend the night; if we did have friends over, we would hide the gay **literature** and family pictures. When a friend asked about the pink triangle on our car, my brother told him it was a used car and we hadn't had time to take the sticker off. We lived like this for three years, until we moved to a house with a basement apartment. We told our friends Barb lived there. It was really a guest room.

5   Ironically, our home life then was really the same as a straight family's. We had family meetings, fights, trips and dinners. My brother and I came to accept Barb as a par-ent. There were things she could never have with us the way our mother did. But she

helped support us while my mother got h **Ph.D.** in public health. And she pushed n brother and me to succeed in school, just li a mom.

With the help of a really great counsel and a friend who had a "it's not a big deal an I knew anyway" attitude, I started to becom more comfortable with my two-mom famil The spring of my junior year, a local newspa per interviewed me for an article on gay fami lies. I was relieved, but also afraid. The day th article appeared was incredibly tense. I fel like everyone was looking at me and talking about me. One kid said to my brother, "I saw the article, you fag." My brother told him to get lost. Some people avoided me, but most kids were curious about my family. People asked if I was gay. I chose not to answer; as teenagers, most of us can't explain the feelings in our minds and bodies.

Last year, in my final year of high school, I decided to speak at our school's National Coming Out Day. Sitting up front

VISUAL VOCABULARY

Some believe that the Brady Bunch represents a _____ family.

a. tolerant
b. stereotypical

were my best friend, my mother, my brother and my counselor, Al. That day was the best. I no longer had to laugh at the jokes or keep a secret. I hoped I was making a path for others like me: a kid with a gay parent, scared and feeling alone. After my speech, I lost some friends and people made remarks that hurt. But that only made me stronger. The hardest thing to deal with is other people's ignorance, not the family part. That's just like any other family.

—*Newsweek*, November 4, 1996.

Fill in the blank in each sentence with a word from the "Vocabulary Preview."

Vocabulary Preview

1. Jerome _____ that Angelina was shy because she was quiet.

Vocabulary Preview

2. Kate and Matt are _____ parents with few strict rules.

Vocabulary Preview

3. Miguel enjoys reading _____ about adventure in the outdoors.

Vocabulary Preview

4. Rhodella earned a _____ in mathematics.

Vocabulary Preview

5. Driving while under the influence of alcohol is not _____ or legally acceptable.

Write the letter of the best meaning of the word in *italics*. Use context clues to make your choice.

Vocabulary in Context

_____ **6.** "As it turned out, we didn't have a *stereotypical* family." (paragraph 3)
   a. traditional
   b. harmful
   c. happy
   d. unusual

Vocabulary in Context

_____ **7.** "*Ironically*, our home life then was really the same as a straight family's." (paragraph 5)
   a. sincerely
   b. easily
   c. unexpectedly
   d. lovingly

Vocabulary in Context _____ **8.** "With the help of a really great *counselor* and a friend who had 'it's not a big deal and I knew anyway' attitude, I started to becon more comfortable with my two-mom family." (paragraph 6)
a. person
b. family
c. attitude
d. therapist

Vocabulary in Context _____ **9.** "The day the article appeared was *incredibly* tense." (paragraph 6
a. somewhat
b. extremely
c. less
d. hardly

Vocabulary in Context _____ **10.** "After my speech, I lost some friends and people made *remarks* tha hurt." (paragraph 7)
a. comments
b. threats
c. gestures
d. noises

Central Idea _____ **11.** Which sentence is the best statement of the central idea of the passage?
a. As it turned out, we didn't have a stereotypical family.
b. I always thought my family was normal.
c. Ironically, our home life then was really the same as a straight family's.
d. The hardest thing to deal with is other people's ignorance, not the family part.

Main Idea _____ **12.** Which sentence is the best statement of the main idea of paragraph 4?
a. High school was the hardest.
b. My brother and I would never allow Mom and Barb to walk to- gether or to sit next to each other in a restaurant.
c. We wouldn't have people spend the night; if we did have friends over, we would hide the gay literature and family pictures.
d. We lived like this for three years, until we moved to a house with a basement apartment.

Supporting Details _____ **13.** According to paragraph 5, who earned a Ph.D.?
a. the author
b. Barb
c. the author's mother
d. the author's brother

Supporting
Details
_____ **14.** How old was the author when she learned that her mother was gay?
  a. 5
  b. 14
  c. 12
  d. a senior in high school

Supporting
Details
_____ **15.** The local newspaper interviewed the author for an article on gay families
  a. when the author was twelve years old.
  b. when the author moved to Washington, D.C.
  c. during the author's final year of high school.
  d. in the spring of the author's junior year.

Thought
Patterns
_____ **16.** The overall thought pattern for the passage is
  a. time order.
  b. contrast.
  c. cause and effect.
  d. definition.

Transitions
_____ **17.** "I was relieved, but also afraid." (paragraph 6)

The relationship of ideas within this sentence is one of
  a. addition.
  b. cause and effect.
  c. comparison and contrast.
  d. time order.

Transitions
_____ **18.** "The years after my mother came out to me were very difficult for me and my brother. We had just moved from Washington, D.C." (paragraph 3)

The relationship of ideas between these sentences is one of
  a. time order.
  b. cause and effect.
  c. addition.
  d. contrast.

Inferences   Choose the two inferences that are most clearly based on the information in the following passage.

"My brother and I would never allow Mom and Barb to walk together or sit next to each other in a restaurant. We wouldn't have people spend the night; if we did have friends over, we would hide the gay literature and family pictures. When a friend asked about the pink triangle on our car,

my brother told him it was a used car and we hadn't had time to take th
sticker off. We lived like this for three years, until we moved to a hou:
with a basement apartment. We told our friends Barb lived there. It was real
a guest room." (paragraph 4)

19. _____

20. _____

    a. The author and her brother didn't want others to know their mothe
       was gay.

    b. The author and her brother did not love their mother.

    c. The author resented her mother for being gay.

    d. A pink triangle is a symbol for the gay lifestyle.

Mapping

Complete the concept map using details from the narrative.

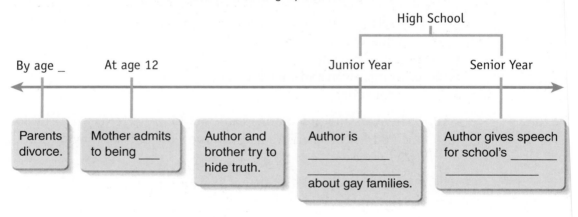

Timeline of Growing Up With Two Moms

Questions for Discussion and Writing

    1. Write a paragraph that summarizes the author's central idea and major
       supporting details.

    2. Why did the author try to hide the truth about her mother for so long?

    3. What caused the author to change her mind and speak publicly about her
       family?

    4. Has society become more accepting and tolerant of gay families since this
       article was published in 1996? Why or why not?

SKILLED READER Scorecard

"Growing Up With Two Moms"

Skill	Number Correct	Points			Total
Vocabulary Preview (5 items)	_____	×	10	=	_____
Vocabulary in Context (5 items)	_____	×	10	=	_____
			Vocabulary Score		_____
Central Idea and Main Idea (2 items)	_____	×	8	=	_____
Supporting Details (3 items)	_____	×	8	=	_____
Thought Patterns (1 item)	_____	×	8	=	_____
Transitions (2 items)	_____	×	8	=	_____
Inferences (2 items)	_____	×	8	=	_____
Mapping (4 items)	_____	×	5	=	_____
			Comprehension Score		_____

READING 7

Textbook
Skills

Want to Do Better on the Job? Listen Up!

Diane Cole

Have you ever found yourself wondering if the person you are talking to is really listening? Or have you found it difficult to concentrate when someone is talking to you? The following reading, reprinted in a college communication textbook, offers useful suggestions for listening more effectively in business situations. The suggestions, however, can easily be applied to the classroom or the home.

Vocabulary Preview

dividends (paragraph 6): benefits
perceptive (paragraph 7): aware
deliberate (paragraph 16): thoughtful
reluctant (paragraph 19): unwilling
studiously (paragraph 20): carefully

---

1   When Linda S., an Ohio banking executive, learned she would not be promoted, she asked her boss why. He had barely begun to speak when she blurted out, "I know whatever the reason, I can do better."

2   Exasperated, he replied, "You always interrupt before you even know what I'm going to say! How can you do better if you never listen?"

3   "Most people value speaking—which is seen as active—over listening, which is seen as passive," explains Nancy Wyatt, professor of speech communication at Penn State University and coauthor with Carol Ashburn of *Successful Listening.*

And there are other reasons we might fail to tune in.

We may become so fixed on what *we* think that we tune out important information. Or we may react emotionally to a phrase or style the speaker uses and miss the main point. Or we're just too busy to pay attention to what is being said.

6   Sound familiar? If so, listen up, for changing your ways will pay big **dividends.**

7   You'll stop wasting time on misunderstood assignments at work. People will start to see you as a **perceptive,** smart, and sensitive person who understands their needs. And that will open new opportunities on the job,

suggests Lyman K. Steil, Ph.D., president of Communication Development Inc., a consulting firm based in St. Paul, Minnesota.

8   You can also develop an ear for the crucial but unspoken words in conversation that signal problems in your business relationships. Here are some suggestions for learning to listen to what is said—and not said—more effectively.

9   • *Control distractions:* Give a speaker your full attention, or you're likely to miss the main point. Many interruptions can't be avoided, but you can limit their effect.

10   If you must take a call while a co-worker is explaining something important, make a choice and devote yourself to one conversation at a time.

11   • *Identify the speaker's purpose:* Tune in to the speaker's agenda. Is he or she there to let off steam, solve a problem, share information, or just schmooze?

12   Once you know, you can respond in the way he or she wants and expects. Learning to listen may also keep you from inadvertently getting caught in the crossfire of office politics.

13   • *Don't finish other people's sentences:* Many people have this bad habit. Just observe yourself: Do you cut people off before they finish a thought? Are you so busy thinking about what you want to say that you can't resist breaking in?

14   "That often happens because the interrupter is bright, thinks she has grasped the point, and wants to show off how much she knows," says Dee Soder, Ph.D., president of Endymion, a New York City–based executive consulting firm. "What happens instead is that interrupters are perceived as being arrogant and interested only in themselves."

15   To break the habit of interrupting, bite your tongue and follow up with your comments only after the other person has had his or her say. Soder suggests you might even have to literally sit on your hands to keep your gestures from speaking for you. Finally, if you're not certain that the speaker has finished, ask!

16   • *Don't let the speaker's style turn you off:* It's easy to tune out when less-than-favorite speakers clear their throats. One high school teacher confesses that for a long time she found a colleague's slow, **deliberate** drawl so grating that she simply could not listen to him.

17   "It was only when I was forced to work with him and had to concentrate on what he was saying rather than how that I realized how smart and helpful he was, and now we're best friends at work."

18   • *Don't be distracted by buzzwords:* What springs to mind when you hear the label "feminist" or "right-to-life"? If you're like most people, emotions take over, and you stop paying careful attention to the point the speaker is trying to make.

19   • *Listen to what is not being said:* Sometimes it's important to hear between the lines. "Many people like to avoid conflict, and so the person speaking is very **reluctant** to say anything negative," says Soder.

20   When you suspect that a delicate or negative subject is being **studiously** avoided, you have to be prepared to delve deeper and ask the speaker, "Tell me more about that. Could you please explain?"

21   • *Show you are listening:* Think about what your body language is revealing. Are you making good eye contact and

leaning slightly forward in a way that indicates "I'm open to what you're saying"? Or are you tapping your foot and looking out the window as if to say, "I have more important things to do than listen to you"?

22 • *Make a note of it*: Jotting down a word or two can remind you later of the main purpose behind the assignment your boss is giving you. A brief note

can also help you remember the poi you would like to raise after the speak finishes.

• *Make sure you heard it right*: Many mi understandings could be prevented we'd just make sure we heard what w thought we heard. So when in doub don't be afraid to ask, "Let me make sur I understand what you are saying." It's hearing test well worth taking.

—"Want to Do Better on the Job? Listen Up!" by Diane Cole as appeared
in *Working Mother*, Mar. 1991. © 1991 Diane Cole

Fill in the blank in each sentence with a word from the "Vocabulary Preview."

Vocabulary
Preview
1. Janine was _____ to drink the milk after it had been left on the counter all day.

Vocabulary
Preview
2. Many people invest in the stock market hoping for large _____.

Vocabulary
Preview
3. Maxine is _____ about her children's needs and strengths.

Vocabulary
Preview
4. Trey _____ recopies his class notes as a review of the day's lesson.

Vocabulary
Preview
5. Tiger Woods is _____ and accurate when he makes his putts.

Write the letter of the best meaning of the word in *italics*. Use context clues to make your choice.

Vocabulary
in Context
_____ **6.** "*Exasperated*, he replied, 'You always interrupt before you even know what I'm going to say! How can you do better if you never listen?'" (paragraph 2)
  a. annoyed   c. interested
  b. pleased   d. patiently

Vocabulary
in Context
_____ **7.** "Most people value speaking—which is seen as active—over listening, which is seen as *passive* . . ." (paragraph 3)
  a. bored   c. interested
  b. inactive   d. rude

Vocabulary in Context _____ **8.** "What happens instead is that interrupters are perceived as being *arrogant* and interested only in themselves." (paragraph 14)
- a. humble
- b. confident
- c. smart
- d. conceited

Vocabulary in Context _____ **9.** "Are you making good eye contact and leaning slightly forward in a way that *indicates* 'I'm open to what you're saying'?" (paragraph 21)
- a. denies
- b. shows
- c. hopes
- d. discourages

Vocabulary in Context _____ **10.** "Many misunderstandings could be *prevented* . . ." (paragraph 23)
- a. helped
- b. seen
- c. stopped
- d. twisted

Implied Main Idea _____ **11.** Which sentence is the best statement of the implied main idea of paragraphs 1 and 2?
- a. Linda S. wanted a promotion.
- b. Linda S.'s boss does not like her.
- c. Linda S. is a good example of someone who does not know how to listen.
- d. Linda S. interrupted her boss.

Central Idea _____ **12.** What is the central idea of the passage?
- a. Good listening skills are important, and you can take several steps to improve your ability to listen well.
- b. Always control distractions when you listen.
- c. Poor listening skills cause problems and waste time.
- d. Repeat what you have heard to make sure you have heard it correctly.

Supporting Details _____ **13.** Based on the information in paragraphs 3–5, how many reasons does the author list for poor listening?
- a. one
- b. two
- c. three
- d. four

Supporting Details _____ **14.** People who interrupt are seen as
- a. bright.
- b. petty.
- c. arrogant.
- d. informed.

Thought Patterns _____ **15.** The main pattern of organization for paragraphs 9–23 is
- a. comparison.
- b. time order.
- c. cause and effect.
- d. listing.

Thought   _____ **16.** The pattern of organization for paragraph 9 is
Patterns
            a. contrast.   c. cause and effect.
            b. listing.   d. time order.

Transitions   _____ **17.** "People will start to see you as a perceptive, smart, and sensitiv⟨e⟩ person who understands their needs. And that will open new opportunities on the job, suggests Lyman K. Steil, Ph.D., presiden⟨t⟩ of Communication Development Inc., a consulting firm based in St. Paul, Minnesota." (paragraph 7)

        The relationship of ideas in this sentence is one of
        a. time.   c. addition.
        b. effect.   d. comparison.

Transitions   _____ **18.** "When you suspect that a delicate or negative subject is being studiously avoided, you have to be prepared to delve deeper and ask the speaker, 'Tell me more about that. Could you please explain?'" (paragraph 20)

        The relationship of ideas in this sentence is one of
        a. time order.   c. comparison and contrast.
        b. cause and effect.   d. listing.

Inferences   Choose the two inferences that are most clearly based on information from the passage.

        "To break the habit of interrupting, bite your tongue and follow up with your comments only after the other person has had his or her say. Soder suggests you might even have to literally sit on your hands to keep your gestures from speaking for you. Finally, if you're not certain that the speaker has finished, ask!" (paragraph 15)

19. _____

20. _____

        a. To be a good listener, you must be polite.
        b. Hand gestures are a sign of interrupting.
        c. Interrupting is sometimes an important and necessary part of listening.
        d. It's always easy to know when a speaker is finished.

Mapping

Complete the idea map with details from the passage.

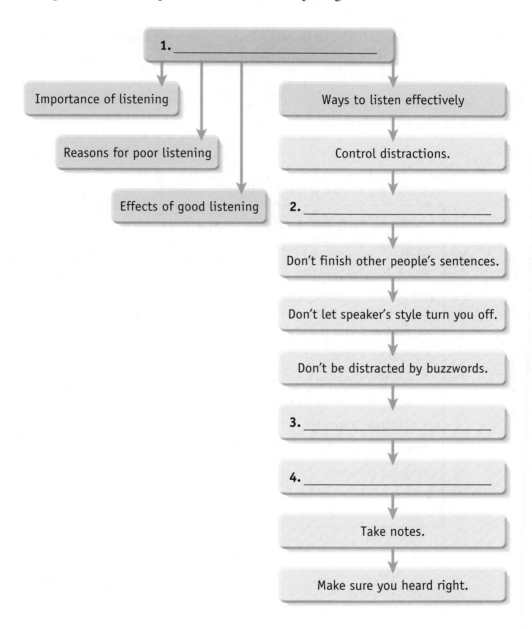

1. _____

Importance of listening

Reasons for poor listening

Effects of good listening

Ways to listen effectively

Control distractions.

2. _____

Don't finish other people's sentences.

Don't let speaker's style turn you off.

Don't be distracted by buzzwords.

3. _____

4. _____

Take notes.

Make sure you heard right.

Questions for Discussion and Writing

1. Write a summary that states the author's central idea and major suppor[t]ing details.

2. Why is listening important in personal relationships?

3. What topics of conversation other than "feminism" or "right to life" mig[ht] make it a challenge to listen closely?

4. What is the impact of body language on the listening process?

5. How can speakers help others listen to them?

SKILLED READER Scorecard

"Want to Do Better on the Job? Listen Up!"

Skill	Number Correct	Points	Total
Vocabulary Preview (5 items)	_____	× 10 =	_____
Vocabulary in Context (5 items)	_____	× 10 =	_____
		Vocabulary Score	_____
Implied Main Idea and Central Idea (2 items)	_____	× 8 =	_____
Supporting Details (2 items)	_____	× 8 =	_____
Thought Patterns (2 items)	_____	× 8 =	_____
Transitions (2 items)	_____	× 8 =	_____
Inferences (2 items)	_____	× 8 =	_____
Mapping (4 items)	_____	× 5 =	_____
		Comprehension Score	_____

READING 8

Sojourner Truth

John A. Garraty and Mark C. Carnes

The authors of the history textbook *The American Nation* think of the past as a collection of stories about specific people. "The personality, words, and actions of its people in large part made the American nation what it is." To understand the people is to understand the nation. The following essay from this textbook shares the actions and deeds of Sojourner Truth, a former slave who turned into a fiery advocate for human rights.

Vocabulary Preview

flax (paragraph 1): a plant grown for its fiber and seeds
siblings (paragraph 1): brothers and sisters
decrepit (paragraph 3): feeble, frail
diligence (paragraph 7): hard work
reneged (paragraph 7): broke a promise
ferment (paragraph 9): uproar, confusion
amalgam (paragraph 9): mixture
asceticism (paragraph 9): plainness, simplicity
patriarchs (paragraph 9): forefathers, founders
gravitated (paragraph 11): drifted
embarked (paragraph 12): started out

1   Isabella was the youngest of ten, or perhaps twelve, children; she was born in 1797, or perhaps 1799. Most details of her early life are unknown. No one bothered to record them because she was a slave. We do know that she was born in Ulster County, New York, and that her owner was Colonel Ardinburgh, a Dutch farmer. He grew tobacco, corn, and **flax.** Because the rocky hills west of the Hudson River could not sustain large farms, he could make use of only a handful of slaves. He therefore sold most of the slave children, including Isabella's **siblings,** when they were young.

2   Isabella's mother used to tell her of the time when Ardinburgh had gathered up her five-year-old brother and three-year-old sister to take them for a sleigh ride. They were initially delighted, but when he tried to lock them into a box, the boy broke free, ran into the house, and hid under a bed. He was found, and both children were dragged away,

▲ Sojourner Truth

never to be seen by their parents again. Isabella lived in terror of being similarly torn from her parents.

3   In 1807, Ardinburgh died. His heirs sold his "slaves, horses, and other cattle" at auction. A local farmer bought Isabella for $100. Her parents, too old and **decrepit** to be of value, were given their freedom. Destitute and virtually homeless, they died shortly afterward.

4   Isabella, who spoke only Dutch, found herself at odds with her new master and his family. Sometimes she did not understand what they wanted her to do. "If they sent me for a frying pan, not knowing what they meant, perhaps I carried them the pothooks," she recalled. "Then, oh! How angry mistress would be with me." Once for an order that she did not understand, the master whipped her with a bundle of rods. The lacerations permanently scarred her back.

5   In 1810, she was sold to John Dumont, a farmer. She remained with him for nearly

eighteen years. Though she came to regar him "as a God," she claimed that his wife sub jected her to cruel and "unnatural" treatmen What exactly transpired, she refused "fror motives of delicacy" to say. Historian Nell Painter contends that the mistress likel abused her sexually.

In 1815, Dumont arranged for Isabell to marry another of his slaves. (Slave mar riages were recognized by law in most north ern states but not in the South.) Isabella had no say in the choice of a husband, who had previously been mated to at least two othe slaves. She had five children by him.

Isabella labored in the fields, sowing and harvesting crops. She also cooked and cleaned the house. In recognition of her **diligence,** Dumont promised to set her free on July 4, 1826, exactly one year prior to the date set by the New York State legislature to end slavery. But during that final year, Isabella injured her hand and could not work as effectively as before. On the promised date of liberation, Dumont **reneged** on his promise to release her. Isabella chafed at his decision but said nothing. She dutifully spun 100 pounds of wool—the amount of labor she thought she owed him—and then, as winter was setting in, she heard the voice of God tell her to leave. She picked up her baby and walked to a neighbor's house. When Dumont came to collect her, the neighbor—Isaac Van Wagenen—paid him $25 for Isabella and the baby and set them free. In gratitude, Isabella took the surname Van Wagenen.

8   But Isabella learned that her five-year-old son, Peter, had been sold to a planter in Alabama, where no date had been set for the ending of slavery. She angrily confronted the Dumonts, who scoffed at her concern for "a paltry nigger." "I'll have my child again,"

Isabella retorted. She consulted with a Quaker lawyer, who assured her that New York law forbade such sales. He filed suit in her behalf, and in 1828, the boy was returned.

9   Now on her own, Isabella went to New York City. During these years, New York City, like much of the nation, was awash in religious **ferment.** Isabella, whose views on religion were a complex **amalgam** of African folkways, spiritualism, temperance, and dietary **asceticism,** was attracted to various unorthodox religious leaders. The most curious of these was Robert Matthews, a bearded, thundering tyrant who claimed to be the Old Testament Matthias. He proposed to restore the practices of the ancient **patriarchs,** especially an insistence that men dominate women. Matthews converted Elijah Pierson, a wealthy New York merchant, and persuaded him to finance a religious commune. Matthews acquired a house in the town of Sing Sing, named it Mount Zion, housed nearly a dozen converts, and ruled it with an iron hand. Isabella was among those who joined the commune.

10   In 1834, Pierson died. Local authorities, who had heard stories of sexual and other irregularities at Mount Zion, arrested Matthews on charges of poisoning Pierson. This sensational story boosted sales of the city's penny press, then in its infancy. When one published story accused Isabella of the murder, she sued the author for libel and collected a judgment of $125.

11   Isabella then **gravitated** to William Miller, a zealot who claimed that the world would end in 1843. When it did not, his movement did.

12   Although she had nearly always been subject to the authority of powerful men, Isabella had by this time become a preacher. Tall and severe in manner, she jabbed at the air with bony fingers and demanded the obedience she had formerly given to others. Now she changed her name to Sojourner Truth—a journeyer conveying God's true spirit—and **embarked** on a career of antislavery feminism.

—Garraty & Carnes, "American Lives: Sojourner Truth," in
The American Nation: A History of the United States,
10th ed., pp. 296–97.

Fill in the blank in each sentence with a word from the "Vocabulary Preview."

Vocabulary Preview   **1.** Rayanne worked with _____ to complete the project on time.

Vocabulary Preview   **2.** Louis _____ on his promise to take Michelle to the park.

Vocabulary Preview   **3.** Marci moves like a _____ old woman.

Vocabulary Preview   **4.** The newlyweds _____ on a three-week cruise to the Cayman Islands.

5. Sam's attraction to Marie was so strong that he _____ toward her whenever she entered the room.

Write the letter of the best meaning of the word in *italics.* Use context clues t make your choice.

_____ **6.** "*Destitute* and virtually homeless, they died shortly afterward. (paragraph 3)

    a. sad   c. poor

    b. angry   d. rejected

_____ **7.** ". . . she claimed that his wife subjected her to cruel and 'unnatural treatment. What exactly *transpired,* she refused 'from motives o delicacy' to say." (paragraph 5)

    a. happened   c. jumped

    b. recorded   d. hurt

_____ **8.** "Isabella *chafed* at his decision but said nothing." (paragraph 7)

    a. became rich   c. became free

    b. became annoyed   d. became smart

_____ **9.** "Matthews converted Elijah Pierson, a wealthy New York merchant, and persuaded him to finance a religious *commune.* Matthews acquired a house in the town of Sing Sing, named it Mount Zion, housed nearly a dozen converts, and ruled it with an iron hand. Isabella was among those who joined the commune." (paragraph 9)

    a. a place where things are sold

    b. a place where people learn

    c. a place where people go who are abused

    d. a place where people live and work together

_____ **10.** "Now she changed her name to *Sojourner* Truth—a journeyer conveying God's true spirit—and embarked on a career of antislavery feminism." (paragraph 12)

    a. troublemaker   c. traveler

    b. peacemaker   d. speaker

_____ **11.** Which sentence is the best statement of the implied main idea of paragraph 7?

    a. Isabella feared her master.   c. Isabella earned her freedom.

    b. Isabella bought her freedom.   d. Isabella was a hard worker.

Central Idea _____ **12.** What is the central idea of the passage?
  a. Sojourner Truth was a former slave who bravely survived and confronted the injustices of her time.
  b. Sojourner Truth faced great difficulties as a slave.
  c. Sojourner Truth became a well-known preacher.
  d. Sojourner Truth was one of the first people to fight for women's rights.

Supporting Details _____ **13.** Isabella took the last name of Isaac Van Wagenen because
  a. she was his slave.
  b. she was grateful to him for setting her free.
  c. she was the mother of his children.
  d. she became his wife.

Supporting Details _____ **14.** How many lawsuits did Isabella file and win?
  a. one   c. three
  b. two   d. four

Thought Patterns _____ **15.** The main thought pattern of the passage is
  a. comparison.   c. cause and effect.
  b. time order.   d. listing.

Transitions _____ **16.** "Because the rocky hills west of the Hudson River could not sustain large farms, he could make use of only a handful of slaves. He therefore sold most of the slave children, including Isabella's siblings, when they were young." (paragraph 1)

The relationship of ideas in these sentences is one of
  a. comparison and contrast.   c. listing.
  b. cause and effect.   d. time order.

Transitions _____ **17.** "Isabella labored in the fields, sowing and harvesting crops. She also cooked and cleaned the house." (paragraph 7)

The relationship of ideas in this sentence is one of
  a. time order.   c. addition.
  b. cause and effect.   d. comparison and contrast.

Transitions _____ **18.** "Tall and severe in manner, she jabbed at the air with bony fingers and demanded the obedience she had formerly given to others. Now she changed her name to Sojourner Truth—a journeyer conveying God's true spirit—and embarked on a career of antislavery feminism." (paragraph 12)

The relationship of ideas between these sentences is one of
a. time order.
c. comparison and contrast.
b. cause and effect.
d. listing.

Inferences Choose the two inferences that are most clearly based on information from the following passage.

"But Isabella learned that her five-year-old son, Peter, had been sold to a planter in Alabama, where no date had been set for the ending of slavery. She angrily confronted the Dumonts, who scoffed at her concern for 'a paltry nigger.' 'I'll have my child again,' Isabella retorted. She consulted with a Quaker lawyer, who assured her that New York law forbade such sales. He filed suit in her behalf, and in 1828, the boy was returned." (paragraph 8)

19. _____

20. _____

a. Slaves had certain rights protected by New York law.
b. Isabella hated the Dumonts.
c. Slaves were considered the property of their owners.
d. Quaker lawyers frequently helped freed slaves.

VISUAL VOCABULARY

Sojourner Truth was the name given to this woman when she was born in 1797 or 1799.

_____ True

_____ False

Outlining

Complete the outline with details from the passage.

"Sojourner Truth"

   I. 1797 or _____

     A. Isabella (later known as Sojourner Truth) is born.

     B. Isabella is owned by Colonel Ardinburgh.

  II. 1807

     A. Ardinburgh dies.

     B. Isabella is sold to a local family who beats her.

 III. 1810

     A. Isabella is sold to John Dumont.

     B. Mrs. Dumont abuses her.

  IV. _____

     A. Isabella is married.

     B. Isabella labors in the fields and cooks and cleans in the house.

   V. 1826

     A. Isabella gets her freedom.

     B. Her 5-year-old son is sold to a planter in Alabama.

     C. Isabella sues to get him back.

  VI. 1828

     A. Isabella's son is returned to her.

     B. Isabella goes to New York City.

     C. Isabella joins a commune with Robert Matthews and Elijah Pierson.

 VII. _____

     A. Pierson dies.

     B. Matthews is charged with Pierson's murder.

     C. A newspaper links Isabella to the scandal.

     D. Isabella sues the newspaper and wins $125.

VIII. _____

    A. Isabella meets William Miller.

    B. Isabella changes her name to Sojourner Truth.

    C. Sojourner Truth begins a career of antislavery feminism.

Questions for Discussion and Writing

   1. Write a paragraph that summarizes the author's central idea and major supporting details.

   2. In what ways did her hard life make Sojourner Truth strong?

   3. What facts about Sojourner Truth do you find surprising?

   4. Why did Isabella change her name to Sojourner Truth? What is the significance of her new name?

   5. What impact has slavery had on American society? Discuss several specific examples.

SKILLED READER Scorecard

"Sojourner Truth"

Skill	Number Correct	Points		Total
Vocabulary Preview (5 items)	_____	× 10	=	_____
Vocabulary in Context (5 items)	_____	× 10	=	_____
		Vocabulary Score		_____
Implied Main Idea and Central Idea (2 items)	_____	× 8	=	_____
Supporting Details (2 items)	_____	× 8	=	_____
Thought Patterns (1 item)	_____	× 8	=	_____
Transitions (3 items)	_____	× 8	=	_____
Inferences (2 items)	_____	× 8	=	_____
Outlining (4 items)	_____	× 5	=	_____
		Comprehension Score		_____

9

Confessions

Amy Tan

Daryl Lawrence   12-10-10

Born in the United States to immigrant parents from China, Amy Tan is a best-selling and award-winning author. Her novels are *The Joy Luck Club, The Kitchen God's Wife, The Hundred Secret Senses, The Bonesetter's Daughter,* and *Saving Fish from Drowning.* Her work has been translated into 35 languages, including Spanish, French, Finnish, Chinese, Arabic, and Hebrew. Her works often deal with the relationship between mother and daughter and the issues of being a first generation Asian American.

Vocabulary Preview

preposterously (paragraph 2): unbelievably
chalet (paragraph 2): cottage, cabin
tinderbox (paragraph 2): an explosive place
cleaver (paragraph 13): butcher's knife, chopper
gusting (paragraph 13): blowing

1   My mother's thoughts reach back like the winter tide, exposing the wreckage of a former shore. Often, she's mired in 1967, 1968, the years my older brother and my father died.

2   1968 was also the year she took me and my little brother—Didi—across the Atlantic to Switzerland, a place so **preposterously** different that she knew she had to give up grieving simply to survive. That year, she remembers, she was very, very sad. I too remember. I was sixteen then, and I recall a late-night hour when my mother and I were arguing in the **chalet,** that **tinderbox** of emotion where we lived.

3   She had pushed me into the small bedroom we shared, and as she slapped me about the head, I backed into a corner, by a window that looked out on the lake, the Alps, the beautiful outside world. My mother was furious because I had a boyfriend. She was shouting that he was a drug addict, a bad man who would use me for sex and throw me away like leftover garbage.

4   "Stop seeing him!" she ordered.

5   I shook my head. The more she beat me, the more implacable I became, and this in turn fueled her outrage.

VISUAL VOCABULARY

This _____ is a favorite resort for those who love to ski.

a. chalet
b. tinderbox

6   "You didn't *love* you daddy or Peter! When they die you not even sad."

7   I kept my face to the window, unmoved. What does she know about sad?

8   She sobbed and beat her chest. "I rather kill myself before see you destroy you life!"

9   Suicide. How many times had she threatened that before?

10   "I wish you the one die! Not Peter, not Daddy."

11   She had just confirmed what I had always suspected. Now she flew at me with her fists.

12   "I rather kill you! I rather see you die!"

13   And then, perhaps horrified by what she had just said, she fled the room. Thank God that was over. I wished I had a cigarette to smoke. Suddenly she was back. She slammed the door shut, latched it, then locked it with a key. I saw the flash of a meat **cleaver** just before she pushed me to the wall and brought the blade's edge to within an inch of my throat. Her eyes were like a wild animal's, shiny, fixated on the kill. In an excited voice she said, "First, I kill you. Then Didi and me, our whole family destroy!" She smiled, her chest heaving. "Why you don't cry?" She pressed the blade closer and I could feel her breath **gusting**.

14   Was she bluffing? If she did kill me, so what? Who would care? While she rambled, a voice within me was whimpering, "This is sad, this is so sad."

15   For ten minutes, fifteen, longer, I straddled these two thoughts—that it didn't matter if I died, that it would be eternally sad if I did—until all at once I felt a snap, then a rush of hope into a vacuum, and I was crying, I was babbling my confession: "I want to live. I want to live."

16   For twenty-five years I forgot that day, and when the memory of what happened surfaced unexpectedly at a writers' workshop in which we recalled our worst moments, I was shaking, wondering to myself, Did she really mean to kill me? If I had not pleaded with her, would she have pushed down on the cleaver and ended my life?

17   I wanted to go to my mother and ask. Yet I couldn't, not until much later, when she became forgetful and I learned she had Alzheimer's disease. I knew that if I didn't ask her certain questions now, I would never know the real answers.

18   So I asked.

19   "Angry? Slap you?" she said, and laughed. "No, no, *no*. You always good girl, never even need to spank, not even one time."

20   How wonderful to hear her say what was never true, yet now would be forever so.

—Amy Tan, "Confessions." Copyright © 2000 by Amy Tan. From *The Opposite of Fate* published by G.P. Putnam's Sons, 2003. First appeared in *Confession* (PEN/Faulkner Foundation). Reprinted by permission of the author and the Sandra Dijkstra Literary Agency.

Fill in the blank in each sentence with a word from the "Vocabulary Preview."

Vocabulary Preview   **1.** Our family rented a vacation _chalet_ on the lake.

Vocabulary Preview   **2.** A drought has made Florida a _tinderbox_ ready to be set off by lightning.

Vocabulary Preview   **3.** In one swift move, grandmother's _cleaver_ ended the rooster's life.

Vocabulary Preview   **4.** The _gusting_ wind toppled power lines and trees.

Vocabulary Preview   **5.** The lie was so _preposterous_/obvious that no one believed it.

Write the letter of the best meaning of the word in *italics*. Use context clues to make your choice.

Vocabulary in Context   _A_   **6.** "The more she beat me, the more *implacable* I became, and this in turn fueled her outrage." (paragraph 5)
   a. stubborn   c. sad
   b. depressed   d. happy

Vocabulary in Context   _C_   **7.** "'First, I kill you. Then Didi and me, our whole family destroy!' She smiled, her chest *heaving*." (paragraph 13)
   a. tightening   c. rising and falling
   b. stopping   d. coughing

Vocabulary in Context _____ **8.** "While she *rambled*, a voice within me was whimpering, 'This is sad, this is so sad.'" (paragraph 14)
   a. talked nonsense
   b. walked
   c. cried
   d. stumbled

Vocabulary in Context _____ **9.** "While she rambled, a voice within me was *whimpering*, 'This is sad, this is so sad.'" (paragraph 14)
   a. hoping
   b. shouting
   c. denying
   d. crying

Vocabulary in Context _____ **10.** "For ten minutes, fifteen, longer, I *straddled* these two thoughts—that it didn't matter if I died, that it would be eternally sad if I did—until all at once I felt a snap . . ." (paragraph 15)
   a. rejected
   b. balanced
   c. loved
   d. hated

Implied Main Idea _____ **11.** Which sentence is the best statement of the implied main idea of paragraph 3?
   a. Amy Tan and her mother hated each other.
   b. Amy Tan faced many difficulties as a first generation Asian-American.
   c. Amy Tan was a rebellious daughter.
   d. Amy Tan and her mother were engaged in a mother-daughter conflict.

Implied Main Idea _____ **12.** What is the best statement of the implied main idea of paragraph 16?
   a. Amy Tan did not know if her mother would have killed her.
   b. Amy Tan was afraid of her mother.
   c. Amy Tan chose not to remember this terrible incident.
   d. Amy Tan has bitter memories.

Supporting Details _____ **13.** Amy Tan's mother was angry because
   a. the family had to move to Switzerland.
   b. Amy had stayed out too late.
   c. Amy had a boyfriend.
   d. her mother had Alzheimer's disease.

C

Supporting Details _____ **14.** Peter was the name of Amy Tan's
  a. boyfriend.
  b. father.
  c. brother.
  d. uncle.

d

Thought Patterns _____ **15.** The main thought pattern for the passage is
  a. comparison and contrast.
  b. cause and effect.
  c. classification.
  d. time order.

Transitions _____ **16.** "I kept my face to the window, unmoved." (paragraph 7)

The relationship of ideas within this sentence is one of
  a. time order.
  b. contrast.
  c. cause and effect.
  d. spatial (space) order.

Transitions __b__ **17.** "My mother was furious because I had a boyfriend." (paragraph 3)

The relationship of ideas within this sentence is one of
  a. time order.
  b. cause and effect.
  c. comparison and contrast.
  d. listing.

Transitions __a__ **18.** "I wished I had a cigarette to smoke. Suddenly, she was back." (paragraph 13)

The relationship of ideas between these sentences is one of
  a. time order.
  b. contrast.
  c. cause and effect.
  d. definition.

Inferences Choose the two inferences that are most clearly based on the information in the following passage.

"I wanted to go to my mother and ask. Yet I couldn't, not until much later, when she became forgetful and I learned she had Alzheimer's disease. I knew that if I didn't ask her certain questions now, I would never know the real answers.

So I asked.

'Angry? Slap you?' she said, and laughed. 'No, no, *no*. You always good girl, never even need to spank, not even one time.'

How wonderful to hear her say what was never true, yet now would be forever so." (paragraphs 17–20)

19. ___b___

20. ___c___

a. Amy Tan remains bitter towards her mother.
b. Amy Tan has forgiven her mother.
c. Amy Tan's mother has forgotten about the incident.
d. Her mother never meant to hurt Amy Tan.

Summary

Complete the summary using details from the narrative.

"In 1967 and 1968, Amy Tan's ___brother___ and father died. In 1968, her mother took her and her little brother, Didi, to Switzerland. That year, a horrible fight occurred between Amy Tan and her mother who was angry because Amy had a boyfriend. Their disagreement grew violent, and Mrs. Tan attacked her daughter with a ___cleaver___. Amy pleaded for her life. Amy did not remember this painful incident for many years."

Questions for Discussion and Writing

1. What point is the author trying to communicate? Write the author's central idea in one sentence. Then provide key details to explain the central idea.
2. What was the main source of conflict between Amy Tan and her mother? What was the long-term effect of the conflict on their relationship?
3. Amy Tan recreates a vivid emotional experience. What was her mother's state of mind? What was Tan's state of mind? In what ways did Tan's emotional state of being change throughout the essay? What does the last sentence of the essay suggest about her relationship with her mother?
4. What is the significance of the title? What was Tan's confession?

SKILLED READER Scorecard

"Confessions"

Skill	Number Correct		Points		Total
Vocabulary Preview (5 items)	_____	×	10	=	_____
Vocabulary in Context (5 items)	_____	×	10	=	_____
		Vocabulary Score			_____
Implied Main Idea (2 items)	_____	×	8	=	_____
Supporting Details (2 items)	_____	×	8	=	_____
Thought Patterns (1 item)	_____	×	8	=	_____
Transitions (3 items)	_____	×	8	=	_____
Inferences (2 items)	_____	×	8	=	_____
Summary (2 items)	_____	×	10	=	_____
		Comprehension Score			_____

READING 10

To Walk in Beauty

Bear Heart

> According to his Web site, Marcellus Williams, 87, is a spiritual leader of the Muskogee Nation-Creek Tribe. One of the last traditionally trained medicine men, Bear Heart speaks thirteen native languages, is an American Baptist Minister, and holds an honorary Ph.D. in humanities. He served for seven years as a member of the advisory board for the Institute of Public Health-Native American and Alaskan Natives at Johns Hopkins School of Medicine. He is the author of *The Wind Is My Mother*, Random House, which is now published in fourteen languages. "To Walk in Beauty" is the opening passage of his inspirational book about his life and the wisdom of his people.

Vocabulary Preview

elements (paragraph 1): parts
environment (paragraph 8): climate, atmosphere, surroundings
ravines (paragraph 13): gullies, valleys
endurance (paragraph 13): staying power, stamina
dilapidated (paragraph 14): rundown, decaying
intentionally (paragraph 14): on purpose
gangrene (paragraph 16): death of soft tissue due to loss of blood supply

---

1   When I was three days old, my mother took me to a hilltop near our home and introduced me to the **elements**. First she introduced me to the Four Directions—East, South, West, and North. "I'm asking special blessings for this child. You surround our lives and keep us going. Please protect him and bring balance into his life."

2   Then, she touched my tiny feet to this Mother Earth. "Dear Mother and Grandmother Earth, one day this child will walk, play, and run on you. I will try to teach him to have respect for you as he grows up. Wherever he may go, please be there supporting and taking care of him."

3   I was introduced to the sun. "Grandfather Sun, shine upon this child as he grows. Let every portion of his body be normal and strong in every way, not only physically but mentally. Wherever he is, surround him with your warm, loving energy. We know that there will be cloudy days in his life, but you, are always constant and, shining—please shine through to this child and keep him safe at all times."

4   She lifted me up to be embraced by the breeze as she spoke to the wind: "Please

recognize this child. Sometimes you will blow strong. Sometimes you'll be very gentle, but let him grow up knowing the value of your presence at all times as he lives upon this planet."

5   Next I was introduced to the water. "Water, we do not live without you. Water is life. I ask that this child never know thirst."

6   She put some ashes on my forehead, saying, "Fire, burn away the obstacles of life for this child. Make the way clear so that he will not stumble in walking a path of learning to love and respect all of life."

7   And that night, I was introduced to the full moon and the stars. These elements were to watch over me as I grew up, running around on the carpet of grass that my Mother and Grandmother Earth provided, breathing in the air that sustains life and flows within my body, taking away all the toxins as I exhaled.

8   I had a sense of belonging as I grew up because of my people's relationship with these elements, and I imagine that's why most of our people related to the **environment** so easily. We recognized a long time ago that there was life all around us—in the water, in the ground, in the vegetation. Children were introduced to the elements so that as we grew up, we were not looking down upon nature or looking up to nature. We felt a part of nature, on the same level. We respected each blade of grass, one leaf on a tree among many other leaves, everything.

9   My name is *Nokus Feke Ematha Tustanaki*—in your language it means "Bear Heart." I'm also known as Marcellus Williams and I was born in the state of Oklahoma in 1918.

10   My tribe is Muskogee, and we originally lived along the waterways of what is now Georgia and Alabama. The Europeans who eventually settled in that area didn't know of us as Muskogeans; they simply referred to us by our habitat, "the Indians who live by the creeks." The name prevailed, so we are commonly known as Creek Indians, but in fact we are the Muskogee Nation.

11   In 1832, President Andrew Jackson signed an order to remove the native tribes from the southeastern United States, and it was then that the Muskogee were moved, along with the Chickasaws, Choctaws, and Cherokees. We walked all the way from our homes to "Indian Territory," which later became *Oklahoma*—that's a Choctaw word meaning "land of the red man." History has recorded that removal, but never once have the emotions been included in that record— what our people felt, what they had to leave behind, the hardships they had to endure.

12   The removal was forced; we were given no choice about it. When our people refused to leave their homes, soldiers would wrench a little child from the arms of his mother and bash his head against a tree, saying, "Go or we'll do likewise to all the children here." It's said that some of the soldiers took their sabers and slashed pregnant women down the front, cut them open. That's how our people were forced from their homeland.

13   Our people walked the entire distance, from sunup to sundown, herded along by soldiers on horseback. When our old people died along the way, there was no time allowed to give them a decent burial. Many of our loved ones were left in **ravines,** their bodies covered with leaves and brush because our people were forced to go on. It was a long walk, people got very tired, and the young children could not keep *up* with the adults, so

people would carry them, handing them back and forth. But they didn't have the **endurance** to carry them all the time, so some children and their mothers had to be left behind. Those are just some of the hardships our people endured on that walk, and out of those injustices came much lamenting and crying, so our people called it "The Trail of Tears."

14   I knew a man who went on that long walk as a child and he told me about it. At one point the people and the few horses they had were put on twelve **dilapidated** ferryboats to cross the Mississippi River. The ferry started sinking; so he grabbed his little sister, got on a horse, and headed for shore, all the while chased by soldiers who didn't want him riding. He was trying to hurry but the horse had to swim and was frightened from the commotion, so it was slow going. He had seen how brutal the soldiers could be and how the ferries were **intentionally** overloaded to make them sink, so he was making a break for his life. Someone came up behind him on another horse and grabbed his sister. "I was crying when I got to the shore," he said, "because I thought the soldiers took my sister, but I found out later one of my own people had helped me out."

15   Many of our people died crossing the Mississippi. When the survivors got across the river, many were soaked from swimming and it was freezing cold. One old woman, confused and exhausted from the ordeal, had no idea where she was—she thought she was back home and started giving instructions to the young ones. "Follow that trail and where it forks. There's some dry sticks on the ground. Gather them and build a fire to warm the people." She remembered where to find firewood at home and, in her own mind, she thought she was there. Surely she wished she was there.

16   My great-great-grandmother was on that forced march. No matter what kind of weather, they had to go on and, walking in the snow without any shoes, her feet froze. **Gangrene** set in and her feet literally dropped from her legs. She's buried at Fort Gibson, Oklahoma; but there's no name on those markers, just many, many crosses where our people died without recognition. I don't know where her grave is, but she's there among them.

17   Even after we were settled, that was not the end of our problems. Our children were taken from their parents and forced to go to boarding school, where they were not allowed to speak their native tongues—they had to speak English. The boarding school was a government school, so they had to march to and from class, make up their beds, do everything as if it were a military camp. This was forced upon our young children. Back then Native people took pride in their long hair, but the children had to have their hair cut short. Sometimes the administrators would just put a bowl over a child's head and cut around it. Then they would laugh at the child.

18   Those are just some of the things that we endured. And yet today in our ceremonies, many of our people still pray for all mankind, whether they be black, yellow, red, or white. How is it possible, with a background like that among our people, to put out such love?

—Heart, Bear. *The Wind Is My Mother*. Berkley Books: NY 1996. pp. 3–7.

VISUAL VOCABULARY

A real estate developer plans to turn this _____ neighborhood into a place to live.

   a. gangrene
   b. dilapidated

Fill in the blank in each sentence with a word from the "Vocabulary Preview."

Vocabulary
Preview
1. Ari Swari bought a _____ house, fixed it up, and sold it for a profit.

Vocabulary
Preview
2. Josiah trained to build his _____ in preparation to run a marathon.

Vocabulary
Preview
3. To graduate in the spring, Justine _____ registered for six classes.

Vocabulary
Preview
4. Many animals change colors to blend into their _____.

Vocabulary
Preview
5. The _____ of water are hydrogen and oxygen.

Write the letter of the best meaning of the word in *italics*. Use context clues to make your choice.

Vocabulary
in Context
_____ **6.** "History has recorded that removal, but never once have the emotions been included in that record—what our people felt, what they had to leave behind, the hardships they had to *endure*." (paragraph 11)
   a. suffer
   b. create
   c. see
   d. enjoy

Vocabulary
in Context   _____   **7.** "When our people refused to leave their homes, soldiers would *wrench* a little child from the arms of his mother and bash his head against a tree, saying, 'Go or we'll do likewise to all the children here.'" (paragraph 12)
a. turn
b. give
c. yank
d. hold

Vocabulary
in Context   _____   **8.** "Those are just some of the hardships our people endured on that walk, and out of those injustices came much *lamenting* and crying, so our people called it 'The Trail of Tears.'" (paragraph 13)
a. talking
b. singing
c. remembering
d. mourning

Vocabulary
in Context   _____   **9.** "The ferry started sinking; so he grabbed his little sister, got on a horse, and headed for shore, all the while chased by soldiers who didn't want him riding. He was trying to hurry but the horse had to swim and was frightened from the *commotion,* so it was slow going." (paragraph 14)
a. current
b. disturbance
c. quarrel
d. soldiers

Vocabulary
in Context   _____   **10.** "One old woman, confused and exhausted from the *ordeal,* had no idea where she was—she thought she was back home and started giving instructions to the young ones." (paragraph 15)
a. hardship
b. memory
c. walk
d. society

Implied
Main Idea   _____   **11.** Which sentence is the best statement of the implied main idea of paragraph 18?
a. Native people have many reasons to be bitter.
b. Native people are able to love and pray for those who mistreated them.
c. Native people still celebrate their traditional ceremonies.
d. Native people pray for all mankind.

Implied   _____ **12.** What is the best statement of the implied central idea of the passage?
Central Idea
 a. The Muskogee tribe are a spiritual people.
 b. Bear Heart is a wise medicine man.
 c. The Muskogee tribe are a spiritual people who have overcome brutal oppression and prejudice.
 d. The Muskogee tribe were forced to walk the "Trail of Tears."

Supporting   _____ **13.** The Muskogee tribe is also known as
Details
 a. Creek Indians.   c. Cherokee.
 b. Choctaws.   d. Chickasaws.

Supporting   _____ **14.** Who first called the Muskogee tribe "the Indians who live by the creeks"?
Details
 a. Andrew Jackson   c. the Europeans
 b. the Americans   d. Marcellus Williams

Thought   _____ **15.** The main thought pattern for paragraphs 1–8 is
Patterns
 a. comparison and contrast.   c. classification.
 b. cause and effect.   d. time order.

Transitions   _____ **16.** "But they didn't have the endurance to carry them all the time, so some children and their mothers had to be left behind." (paragraph 13)

 The relationship of ideas between these sentences is one of
 a. time order.   c. cause and effect.
 b. contrast.   d. definition.

Transitions   _____ **17.** "When I was three days old, my mother took me to a hilltop near our home and introduced me to the elements." (paragraph 1)

 The relationship of ideas within this sentence is one of
 a. time order.
 b. cause and effect.
 c. comparison and contrast.
 d. listing.

Transitions   _____ **18.** "Back then Native people took pride in their long hair, but the children had to have their hair cut short." (paragraph 17)

 The relationship of ideas within this sentence is one of
 a. time order.
 b. cause and effect.
 c. addition.
 d. contrast.

Inferences   Choose the two inferences that are most clearly based on the information in the following passage.

> "The ferry started sinking; so he grabbed his little sister, got on a horse, and headed for shore, all the while chased by soldiers who didn't want him riding. He was trying to hurry but the horse had to swim and was frightened from the commotion, so it was slow going. He had seen how brutal the soldiers could be and how the ferries were intentionally overloaded to make them sink, so he was making a break for his life. Someone came up behind him on another horse and grabbed his sister. 'I was crying when I got to the shore,' he said, 'because I thought the soldiers took my sister, but I found out later one of my own people had helped me out.'" (paragraph 14)

19. _____

20. _____

     a. The speaker had difficulty controlling the horse as they crossed the river.
     b. The speaker was a coward.
     c. The soldiers wanted the ferry to sink.
     d. The speaker owned the horse he was riding.

Mapping

Complete the concept map using details from the narrative.

Timeline of Events in "To Walk in Beauty"

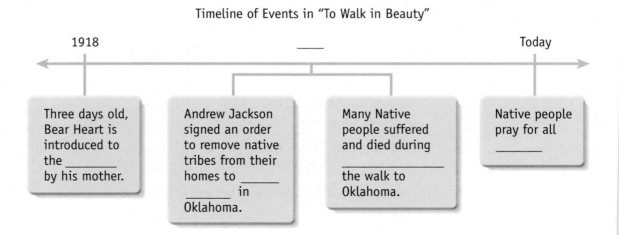

1918   _____   Today

Three days old, Bear Heart is introduced to the _____ by his mother.

Andrew Jackson signed an order to remove native tribes from their homes to _____ _____ in Oklahoma.

Many Native people suffered and died during _____ the walk to Oklahoma.

Native people pray for all _____

Questions for Discussion and Writing

1. What point is the author trying to communicate? Write the author's central idea in one sentence. Then provide key details to explain the central idea.
2. Why did Bear Heart's mother introduce him to the elements when he was only three days old?
3. In the conclusion, Bear Heart asks the question, "How is it possible, with a background like that among our people, to put out such love?" Write a paragraph in which you give an answer to his question.
4. What is the significance of the title of the narrative? What title would you give it? Why?

SKILLED READER Scorecard

"To Walk in Beauty"

Skill	Number Correct	Points		Total
Vocabulary Preview (5 items)	_____ ×	10	=	_____
Vocabulary in Context (5 items)	_____ ×	10	=	_____
		Vocabulary Score		_____
Implied Main Idea and Central Idea (2 items)	_____ ×	8	=	_____
Supporting Details (2 items)	_____ ×	8	=	_____
Thought Patterns (1 item)	_____ ×	8	=	_____
Transitions (3 items)	_____ ×	8	=	_____
Inferences (2 items)	_____ ×	8	=	_____
Mapping (5 items)	_____ ×	4	=	_____
		Comprehension Score		_____

PART THREE

Combined-Skills Tests

Part Three contains 15 tests. The purpose of these tests is twofold: to track your growth as a reader and to prepare you for the formal tests you will face as you take college courses. Each test presents a reading passage and questions that cover some or all of the following skills: vocabulary in context, main ideas, supporting details, thought patterns, and inferences.

Test 1

Read the paragraph, and answer the questions that follow it.

Textbook
Skills

Triple E Communicators

¹Dynamic professionals are usually smart readers. ²They seek out new ideas. ³No wonder others compete to include them on teams and join forces with them in business. ⁴These lifelong learners have the same amount of time as everyone else does. ⁵Their power lies in their ability to find excellent material. ⁶Good research skills support ethical, effective and expressive communication. ⁷These three traits help us to inform and persuade others. ⁸"Triple E communicators" have all three traits. ⁹First, ethical communicators care about the quality of information that they give to others. ¹⁰And they respect the length of time a listener has to give to them. ¹¹Next, effective communicators think about the amount of information that is needed to make a point. ¹²They know enough to back the claims they make. ¹³And they know how the information fits together reasonably. ¹⁴Finally, expressive communicators choose meaningful material for their listeners. ¹⁵They use interesting information. ¹⁶They also allow listeners to see the speaker's connection with the material.

—Adapted from Kelly, Marylin S. *Communication@work.*
Allyn & Bacon., 2006, p. 139.

Vocabulary _____ **1.** The best meaning of the word *dynamic* as used in sentence 1 is
  a. powerful.   c. explosive.
  b. controlling.   d. changing.

Vocabulary _____ **2.** The best meaning of the word *ethical* as used in sentence 9 is
  a. informed.   c. unfair.
  b. expert.   d. moral.

Main Idea _____ **3.** Choose the sentence that best states the main idea of the paragraph.
  a. Dynamic professionals are usually smart readers. (sentence 1)
  b. Good research skills support ethical, effective and expressive communication. (sentence 6)
  c. "Triple E communicators" have all three traits. (sentence 8)
  d. Finally, expressive communicators choose meaningful material for their listeners. (sentence 14)

Main Idea/ _____ **4.** Sentence 11, "Next, effective communicators think about the amount
Details   of information that is needed to make a point," is a
  a. main idea.   c. minor supporting detail.
  b. major supporting detail.

Thought
Patterns
_____
5. The thought pattern for this paragraph is
   a. cause and effect.   c. definition.
   b. classification.   d. comparison and contrast.

Inference
_____
6. Choose the inference that is most clearly based on sentence 4. "These lifelong learners have the same amount of time as everyone else does."
   a. Lifelong learners are busier than other people.
   b. Lifelong learners manage their time wisely.
   c. Lifelong learners make time for learning.
   d. Lifelong learners are smarter than other people.

Use ideas from the passage to complete the outline.

Triple E Communicators

7. I. _____

   A. care about quality of information.

   B. respect the length of time a listener has to give.

8. II. _____

   A. think about the quantity of information.

   B. know enough to back the claims they make.

9. III. _____

10.   A. _____

   B. use interesting information.

   C. allow listeners to see the speaker's connection with the material.

Test 2

Read the paragraph, and answer the questions that follow it.

How Learners Learn

[1]Too many people believe the ability to learn is a gift received at birth and measured by intelligence. [2]Actually, learning is a process. [3]This process consists of seven steps. [4]First, learners set goals based on the need to know. [5]The need to know goes beyond learning facts and looks at the

value of what is being learned. [6]Second, learners think about what they already know. [7]Third, learners identify what they don't know or don't understand. [8]Fourth, learners investigate. [9]If they don't know because of lack of information, they find the needed information. [10]Fifth, learners read and ask questions. [11]If they don't understand the information, they figure out exactly where their comprehension ends. [12]Sixth, learners listen. [13]Finally, learners think about what they have just learned. [14]Learners revisit their learning goal. [15]They compare what they think about the topic after learning to what they thought about the topic before studying. [16]Learners think about ways in which the information can be used. [17]Learners use the information.

Vocabulary _____ 1. The best meaning of the word *investigate* as used in sentence 8 is
    a. cope.   c. learn.
    b. search for information.   d. hope for.

Vocabulary _____ 2. The best meaning of the word *comprehension* as used in sentence 11 is
    a. understanding.   c. intelligence.
    b. confusion.   d. common sense.

Main Idea _____ 3. What is the best statement of the main idea of this paragraph?
    a. Learners don't work hard.
    b. Intelligent people are born with the gift to learn.
    c. Learning is a learned process.
    d. Learning is rewarding and fun.

Main Idea/ _____ 4. Sentence 4, "First, learners set goals based on the need to know," is a
Details
    a. main idea.   c. minor supporting detail.
    b. major supporting detail.

Thought _____ 5. The thought pattern for this paragraph is
Patterns
    a. comparison.   c. time order.
    b. contrast.   d. classification.

Inference _____ 6. Choose the inference that is most clearly based on the information in the paragraph.
    a. Learning cannot be learned.
    b. Learning is hard and difficult work.
    c. Learning is a gift.
    d. Most people can learn.

7. _____

8. I. _____

II. They think about what they already know.

III. They identify what they don't know.

9. IV. _____

V. They read and ask questions.

VI. They listen.

10. VII. _____

Test 3

Read the passage, and answer the questions that follow it.

Passive Resistance

[1]**Passive resistance** is the use of noncooperation to oppose a government authority. [2]Henry David Thoreau chose to go to prison in 1846 instead of paying a poll tax to fund the Mexican War. [3]In his famous essay "Civil Disobedience," Thoreau argued that passive resistance was an effective means of protest. [4]In the first half of the 20th century, Mahatma Gandhi used passive resistance to win India's freedom from Great Britain. [5]In the 1960s, civil rights leaders such as Dr. Martin Luther King Jr. used the power of passive resistance. [6]Marches, boycotts, and sit-ins were their weapons against hate and cruelty.

[7]Dr. King's students had been well trained in the methods of passive resistance. [8]They had attended workshops about how to protect themselves, stay calm, and not strike back. [9]They expected to be beaten and arrested. [10]In 1960, these determined young African Americans took their seats at white-only lunch counters across the South. [11]Immediately, they were shouted at, jerked from their chairs, and kicked to the floor. [12]Food was dumped on them, and cigarettes were ground out on their skin. [13]Not one of them struck back. [14]The students, well dressed and polite, submitted to violence and arrest without a fight. [15]Nor did they attempt to post their own bail. [16]As each group of African Americans who took their seats was beaten and arrested, a new group took their place.

opyright © 2008 Pearson Education, Inc.

Vocabulary _____ **1.** The best meaning of the word *passive* as used in the title and sentence 1 is
    a. weak.
    b. silent.
    c. nonviolent.
    d. hateful.

Vocabulary _____ **2.** The best meaning of the word *protest* as used in sentence 3 is
    a. strong disagreement.
    b. approval.
    c. embarrassment.
    d. victory.

Vocabulary _____ **3.** The best meaning of the expression *submitted to* as used in sentence 14 is
    a. created.
    b. avoided.
    c. reacted against.
    d. endured.

Central Idea _____ **4.** What is the best statement of the central idea of this passage?
    a. Thoreau, Gandhi, and King all used passive resistance.
    b. Passive resistance is a powerful way to confront an unfair society.
    c. African American students in the South used passive resistance.
    d. Passive resistance does not often bring about the needed change.

Thought Patterns _____ **5.** The thought pattern for this passage is
    a. time order.
    b. definition.
    c. comparison and contrast.
    d. cause and effect.

Inference _____ **6.** Choose the inference that is most clearly based on the information in the passage.
    a. Passive resistance is nonviolent.
    b. Passive resistance uses violence as its force.
    c. Passive resistance is not effective.
    d. Passive resistance was used by Thoreau, Gandhi, and King.

Complete the concept map, based on the information in the passage.

7. _____
_____

Three leaders:
8. _____
9. _____
10. _____

Example:
African American students in the South

Test 4

Read the paragraph, and answer the questions that follow it.

Good and Poor Listeners

[1]Good listeners and poor listeners can be recognized by their behavior. [2]Good listeners look at the speaker, for they know that eye contact is a way to stay focused on what the speaker is saying. [3]In contrast, poor listeners allow their eyes to wander all over the place. [4]As their eyes wander, so do their minds. [5]Once their mind wanders, they miss important information. [6]Good listeners wait to hear the speaker's point, and they don't interrupt. [7]In contrast, poor listeners constantly interrupt with their own ideas, requests for information to be repeated, or premature questions that would be answered by listening. [8]Good listeners do ask questions at the appropriate time. [9]However, unlike poor listeners, good listeners ask questions that bring out more details or clarify confusing ideas. [10]Good listeners stay on the same subject as the speaker. [11]In contrast, poor listeners use the speaker's words as an opportunity to jump off into a topic of their own choice. [12]Good listeners keep their emotions under control so that they can understand the speaker's point of view. [13]In contrast, poor listeners become agitated or upset at ideas that are different from their own. [14]Finally, good listeners make the speaker feel valued; poor listeners show little respect for others or their ideas.

Vocabulary _____ **1.** The best meaning of the word *wander* as used in sentence 3 is
- a. focus.
- b. blink.
- c. move around.
- d. stare.

Vocabulary _____ **2.** The best meaning of the word *clarify* as used in sentence 9 is
- a. stir up.
- b. clear up.
- c. question.
- d. study.

Vocabulary _____ **3.** The best meaning of the word *agitated* as used in sentence 13 is
- a. calm.
- b. sad.
- c. disturbed.
- d. hurtful.

Inference _____ **4.** Sentence 9, "However, unlike poor listeners, good listeners ask questions that bring out more details or clarify confusing ideas," implies that
- a. good listeners ask questions that clarify.
- b. poor listeners don't usually ask good questions.
- c. poor listeners can ask good questions.
- d. good listeners can ask poor questions.

Transitions _____   **5.** The relationship of sentence 11 to sentence 10 is one of
  a. time order.   c. example.
  b. effect.   d. contrast.

Main Idea _____   **6.** What is the best statement of the main idea of this paragraph?
  a. The world needs more good listeners.
  b. Poor listeners miss important information.
  c. Good listeners are more successful than poor listeners.
  d. There are several important differences between good and poor listeners.

Complete the chart, based on the information in the paragraph.

Contrast Between Good and Poor Listeners

Good Listeners	Poor Listeners
Look at the speaker	**8.** _____
Wait to hear the speaker	Interrupt with their own ideas
Ask questions at the right time	Ask premature questions
Stay on topic	Jump to their own ideas
7. _____	**9.** _____
Value the speaker	**10.** _____

Test 5

Read the passage, and answer the questions that follow it.

Textbook
Skills

Sibling Status Effects

[1]What is the optimal spacing between children's births? [2]Most children are born within two or three years of a sibling's birth. [3]Research suggests that this is the least optimal spacing pattern. [4]However, family planning should not be affected too much by this finding. [5]Working mothers, for example, might not want to draw out their child-rearing years by spacing children several years apart.

[6]There do seem to be benefits in spacing intervals of either less than two years or more than five years. [7]Short times between births lessens the effect of dethronement. [8](Dethronement is the loss of attention and status due to the arrival of another child.) [9]Infants cannot grasp the impact of a new sibling on

their special position. [10]Resentment and rivalry are more likely results after two years of age. [11]The child might miss the undivided attention from parents that she is used to receiving. [12]Five- and six-year-olds usually are self-reliant enough to cope with or avoid these feelings.

[13]There is another positive effect of longer spacing intervals (more than four years). [14]Parents will treat a newborn as specially as they treated the firstborn. [15]Middleborns, too, seem to feel more special when there are longer intervals between them and their siblings. [16]A time span of about five years seems optimal. [17]The parent is free from having to meet the demands of two children close together in age. [18]Thus, parents and children have more time for one-to-one contact. [19]As a result, the relationship is more supportive and relaxed. [20]Parents who pay for their children's college education will experience less crunch when there is only one child in college at a time.

[21]There is a trend toward greater spacing between siblings. [22]Part of this trend is due to the growing rate of remarriage following divorce. [23]Fertility problems also contribute to longer spacing intervals. [24]A negative effect of very long spacing is that the siblings may have few if any interests in common. [25]For parents, this is almost like having two only children. [26]It is not likely that spacing affects children's personalities. [27]It is a weak factor compared to other family variables. [28]Spacing seems to work together with other factors. [29]These factors include birth order, family size, and parental beliefs about sibling status. [30]The quality of the individual relationship between the parent and child is more powerful than these other factors, even in combination.

—Adapted from Jaffe, Michael L. *Understanding Parenting*,
2nd ed., Allyn & Bacon, 1997, pp. 223–224.

Vocabulary _____ **1.** The best meaning of the word *status* as used in the title is
    a. role.   c. value.
    b. rank.   d. acceptance.

Vocabulary _____ **2.** The best meaning of the word *siblings* in sentence 21 is
    a. parents.   c. brothers.
    b. brothers or sisters.   d. sisters.

Implied _____ **3.** What is the best statement of the implied central idea of this passage?
Central Idea
    a. Sibling status is the chief factor in a child's life.
    b. Older children are dethroned by a new sibling.
    c. The length of time between births affects the status of siblings.
    d. Parents care more about their firstborn child.

Main Idea/ _____ **4.** "Infants cannot grasp the impact of a new sibling on their special
Details   position" (sentence 9) is a
                  a. main idea.
                  b. minor supporting detail.
                  c. major supporting detail.

Thought _____ **5.** The overall thought pattern used in the passage is
Patterns   a. time order.   c. cause and effect.
                  b. comparison.   d. contrast.

Inference _____ **6.** The details in the second paragraph (sentences 6–12) imply that
                  a. it is better to have children less than two years or more than five
                     years apart.
                  b. infants require a great deal of time and attention.
                  c. five-year-olds are jealous of a new baby.
                  d. it is harder to have children that are spaced two years apart.

Complete the following list, based on the information in the passage.

Positive Effects of Longer Spacing Intervals between Births

7. Five- and six-year olds can better cope with _____

8. Parents will treat a newborn _____

9. Parents and children have more _____

10. Only one child at a time will be _____

Test 6

Read the passage, and answer the questions that follow it.

Types and Treatment of Migraine Headaches

[1]Migraine headaches plague nearly 10 percent of the population. [2]Experts classify migraine headaches as one of two types: classic or common. [3]A classic migraine is signaled 10 to 30 minutes before its onset with neurological symptoms known as an aura. [4]An aura may cause the person to experience flashing lights or zigzag lines, temporary loss of vision, difficulty speaking, weakness in an arm or leg, tingling in the face or hands, and confused thinking. [5]A classic migraine headache causes intense, throbbing or pounding pain in the forehead, temple, ear, eye, or jaw. [6]A classic migraine

starts on one side of the head but may spread to the other side. [7]An attack usually lasts one to two days.

[8]In contrast, a common migraine is not signaled by an aura. [9]Instead, sufferers complain of mental fuzziness, mood changes, fatigue, and water retention. [10]Once the headache develops, a person may experience diarrhea, increased urination, nausea, and vomiting. [11]Common migraines can last as long as three or four days.

[12]Several methods are commonly used to prevent and control both types of migraines. [13]First, to prevent migraines from occurring, those who are prone to these painful headaches use drug therapy, stress reduction, and diet restrictions. [14]Regular exercise, such as swimming or vigorous walking, may also reduce the frequency and severity of migraine headaches. [15]Next, once the migraine occurs, pain is controlled in the short term by applying cold packs to the head or a hot water bottle on the neck and resting quietly in a dark room.

Vocabulary _____ **1.** The best meaning of the word *aura* in sentence 3 is
    a. color.
    b. neurological symptoms.
    c. visual disturbances.
    d. moodiness.

Vocabulary _____ **2.** The best meaning of the phrase *prone to* in sentence 13 is
    a. lying flat.
    b. likely to experience.
    c. free from all.
    d. certain to avoid.

Main Idea _____ **3.** The best statement of the main idea of this passage is
    a. Many people suffer from migraine headaches.
    b. Migraines are classified into two groups: classic and common.
    c. Several methods are used to prevent and control migraine headaches.
    d. The pain and discomfort of the two types of migraine headaches leads to a variety of treatments in search of relief.

Transitions _____ **4.** The relationship between sentences 7 and 8 is one of
    a. time.
    b. effect.
    c. contrast.
    d. example.

Main Idea/ Details   _____ **5.** Sentence 12 is a
   a. main idea.
   b. major supporting detail.
   c. minor supporting detail.

Inference   _____ **6.** Choose the inference most soundly based on the information in the third paragraph (sentences 12–15).
   a. Food and drink always affect headaches.
   b. People who suffer with migraines risk drug addiction.
   c. Relaxation techniques help everyone who suffers with headaches.
   d. Some migraines can be avoided.

Complete the outline below based on the information in the passage.

Types and Treatment of Migraine Headaches

7.   I. _____

8.   A. _____

9.   B. _____

10. II. _____

       A. To prevent migraine headaches

       B. To control the pain of migraine headaches

Test 7

Read the passage, and answer the questions that follow it.

Manatees Face Rough Waters Around the Globe

[1]Manatees getting hit by boats in Florida may be grabbing most of the media attention, but the Sunshine State is not the only place in the world where sea cows face threats.

[2]In countries around the world, many dangers claim the lives of these gentle marine mammals. [3]They are hunted, snagged in fishing nets and faced with a loss of habitat. [4]And in some countries, such as Jamaica, scientists say manatees could soon become extinct.

[5]Experts believe that the basic problem is human overpopulation. [6]Daryl Domning, a professor who spent several years in Brazil studying manatees, says, "There are just too many people everywhere."

■ **West African Manatee**

Similar in size and appearance to the West Indian manatee, they range from 10 to 12 feet long. Little is known about this species.

■ **Dugong**

Related to manatees, but belongs to a different family of animals. They range in size from 8 to 10 feet, with smooth skin and notched tail fluke. Lives in the Indo-Pacific.

■ **West Indian Manatee**

There are two subspecies: the Florida manatee and the Antillean manatee. Both are found in salt, fresh or brackish water. They range in size from 10 to 13 feet long and feed on vegetation.

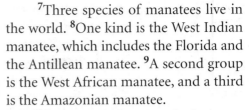

■ **Amazon Manatee**

Found in fresh waters of the Amazon River and its tributaries. Smallest of all manatees, with longest recorded at 9.2 feet. It has no nails on its flippers and feeds on freshwater vegetation.

[7]Three species of manatees live in the world. [8]One kind is the West Indian manatee, which includes the Florida and the Antillean manatee. [9]A second group is the West African manatee, and a third is the Amazonian manatee.

[10]Most countries in which manatees live have passed laws to protect the animals. [11]These laws make killing and hunting sea cows illegal. [12]But laws don't always help. [13]Even in Jamaica, where there may be fewer than 100 manatees left, sea cows are dying out even though they have been protected since 1971.

[14]In some countries, manatee meat is still sold for food. [15]Sometimes, even the local wildlife officials eat sea cow meat. [16]In parts of West Africa, for example, manatees are served as a main dish during special celebrations.

[17]Boating also poses a major danger for manatees. [18]As boat traffic increases all over the world, experts hope Florida will serve as an example. [19]Just like Florida, the country of Belize created refuges for the manatees and speed zones for boats. [20]Belize is one of the last harbors for the Antillean manatees that live in Central and South America.

—Lerman, "Manatees Face Rough Waters Around the Globe," *Daytona News-Journal*, 1 Oct. 2002, p. C1+.

Vocabulary _____ **1.** The synonym of the term *sea cows* in sentence 1 is
  a. animals.   c. manatees.
  b. mammals.   d. dolphins.

Vocabulary _____ **2.** The best meaning of the word *species* as used in sentence 7 is
  a. types.   c. parts.
  b. numbers.   d. dolphins.

Thought Patterns _____ **3.** What is the thought pattern used in the fourth paragraph (sentences 7–9)?
  a. cause and effect   c. time order
  b. comparison and contrast   d. classification

Main Idea/
Details

_____ **4.** "In parts of West Africa, for example, manatees are served as a main dish during special celebrations" (sentence 16) is a
a. main idea.
b. major supporting detail.
c. minor supporting detail.

Central
Idea

_____ **5.** What is the best statement of the central idea of this passage?
a. Manatees are getting hit by boats in Florida.
b. Manatees face dangers around the world.
c. There are three types of manatees.
d. Some countries hunt manatees for food.

Inferences   Based on the pictures of manatees and the captions below them, mark the following statements either **T** for true or **F** for false.

_____ **6.** The dugong is a kind of manatee.

_____ **7.** There is only one kind of West Indian manatee.

_____ **8.** Manatees live in salt, fresh, or brackish water.

_____ **9.** The largest manatees live in Florida.

_____ **10.** The smallest manatees live in the Amazon River region.

Test 8

Read the passage, and answer the questions that follow it.

Dia de las Hermanas Mirabal

[1]The novel _In the Time of the Butterflies_ by Julia Alvarez captures the heroic lives of four sisters from the Dominican Republic. [2]Three of these sisters became icons of courage who have inspired the world by giving their lives for the good of their country. [3]And every year on the 25th of November, the anniversary of their murder, Dominicans honor their sacrifice in tribute to their lives.

[4]The Mirabal sisters were Minerva, Patria, Maria Teresa, and Beligica, also known as Dedé. [5]Born into a rich family and raised in the Cibao region, they and their family lost most of their fortune and land under the dictatorship of Rafael Trujillo. [6]While in college, Minerva became friends with many people who had been devastated by Trujillo's cruelty. [7]During this time, she

fell in love with a man who shared her values. [8]He became her husband. [9]Together they became politically active. [10]In the late fifties, they joined a rebel group called The Movement of the Fourteenth of June. [11]Patria and Maria Teresa also joined the resistance movement. [12]They took the code name *las mariposas* (the butterflies) for their work with the movement. [13]Several times, the sisters were put in prison and tortured. [14]The husbands of Patria and Maria Teresa also aided in the rebellion. [15]At one point, Trujillo placed all three husbands in jail.

[16]Then, Trujillo ordered the murder of the sisters. [17]Minerva, Patria, and Maria Teresa met their deaths on the road to the Puerto Plata prison to see their husbands. [18]On November 25, 1960, Trujillo's soldiers ambushed the sisters' jeep. [19]Trujillo's soldiers strangled and beat them to death. [20]Trujillo's soldiers stuffed their bodies back into their jeep. [21]Finally, Trujillo's soldiers pushed the jeep off a cliff. [22]The public, however, did not believe in the *staged* accident. [23]And an outcry rose up against the dictator. [24]Within the year, an assassin killed Trujillo.

[25]The Dominicans still commemorate the sacrifice of *las mariposas*. [26]Every year on the 25th of November, the sisters' lives are honored throughout the Dominican Republic in civic, religious, and personal activities.

[27]The surviving sister, Dedé currently lives in Salcedo, Dominican Republic. [28]She has dedicated her life to preserving the memory of her slain sisters through the "Museo Hermanas Mirabal." [29]The museum, the Mirabal family home, has become a shrine to many.

[30]Reflection upon and reverence for the sisters inspired Alvarez to write her novel. [31]As a Dominican, her own father had worked for the resistance. [32]Eventually, his efforts against the dictator were discovered. [33]As a result, her family had been forced to flee the country a few months before the sisters were murdered. [34]"Needless to say, this book is one I felt compelled to write," Alvarez states on her website. [35]The Mirabal sisters have often been compared to Martin Luther King. [36]All of them were martyred for their devotion to civil rights. [37]*Las Mariposas* have come to be honored worldwide. [38]November 25th, has been declared by the United Nations, International Day Against Violence Against Women. [39]Alvarez encourages us to start "a tradition of wearing a butterfly on that day!"

—Adapted from Menard, Valerie. *The Latino Holiday Book.* Marlow & Co., 2004, pp. 210-211

Vocabulary _____ **1.** The best meaning of the phrase *resistance movement* as used in sentence 11 is
a. an exercise routine.   c. a work group.
b. a rebellion.   d. a gang.

Vocabulary _____ **2.** The best meaning of the word *shrine* as used in sentence 29 is
 a. church.   c. memorial.
 b. idol.   d. god.

Main Idea/ _____ **3.** "As a result, her family had been forced to flee the country a few
Details   months before the sisters were murdered" (sentence 33) is a
 a. main idea.   c. minor detail.
 b. major detail.

Transitions _____ **4.** The relationship between sentences 32 and 33 is one of
 a. contrast.   c. cause.
 b. addition.   d. time.

Central _____ **5.** What is the best statement of the central idea of this passage?
Idea   a. The novel *In the Time of the Butterflies* by Julia Alvarez captures
     the heroic lives of four sisters from the Dominican Republic.
     (sentence 1)
    b. These three icons of courage have inspired the world by giving
     their lives for the good of their country. (sentence 2)
    c. And every year on the 25th of November, the anniversary of their
     murder, Dominicans honor their sacrifice in tribute to their lives.
     (sentence 3)
    d. Alvarez encourages us to start "a tradition of wearing a but-
     terfly on that day!" (sentence 39)

Test 9

Read the passage, and answer the questions that follow it.

Ask Yourself: Would I Do This for Free?

[1]A story out of Berlin, N.H., caught my eye the other day. [2]It seems that the town librarian, Yvonne Thomas, decided to retire and volunteer rather than cut the public library's book budget by 8 percent.

[3]So Thomas, who has worked at the library for 28 years, retired one day and returned as a volunteer the next. [4]She was quoted in the *Manchester Union Leader* as saying, "If there's no money for books, this becomes a bad museum." [5]I don't know Yvonne Thomas, but I'd like to buy her a drink. [6]Or a book. [7]Both, if she wants.

[8]Would I volunteer to write this column for free if the publisher said he couldn't pay me any longer because of budget cuts? [9]Well, I do like to eat. [10]And I do have a weakness for nice hotels. [11]But, you know, I would.

^{12}Thomas and I are among the blessed who actually like what we do for a living. ^{13}Enough so that we'd do it for free.

^{14}Years ago, I'd go to the office Christmas party, and a colleague's husband would always corner me.

^{15} "You know, Craig, I only have 12 more years to go before I retire," he'd say. ^{16}And then it would be 11 years, and then 10. ^{17}He was counting down the months from a decade out. ^{18}The annual conversation was a bit of a downer for me, so I began avoiding him, something I feel a little bad about now because he finally retired and then promptly died.

^{19}Whenever I'm walking the dog in the morning, watching people head off to work, I wonder if where they're going is where they want to be. ^{20}Would they be on the way to the subway or the freeway if they weren't getting paid?

^{21}Would you work just for the love of what you do? ^{22}What would you be willing to do for free? ^{23}Open a bookshop in Boulder? ^{24}A coffeehouse in Santa Fe?

^{25}I was talking to a recent university graduate the other day. ^{26}He didn't know what he was going to do, although he thought he'd go to New York and work at a big investment house. ^{27}How long had he been interested in high finance? I asked.

^{28} "I'm not," he replied. ^{29} "I just want to make tons of money."

^{30}I think there's a librarian up in New Hampshire he needs to meet.

—Adapted from Craig Wilson, "Ask Yourself This Morning: Would I Do This for Free?"
USA Today. Wednesday May 15, 2002. p. D1.

Vocabulary _____   **1.** The best meaning of the word *colleague's* as used in sentence 14 is
        a. friend's.   c. employee's.
        b. boss's.   d. coworker's.

Vocabulary _____   **2.** The best meaning of the word *promptly* as used in sentence 18 is
        a. never.   c. slowly.
        b. quickly.   d. sadly.

Central Idea _____   **3.** What is the best statement of the central idea of this passage?
        a. Working at what you love brings rewards greater than money.
        b. Money is the root of all evil.
        c. Libraries are often underfunded.
        d. Most people die unfulfilled and unhappy.

Main Idea/ Details _____   **4.** Sentence 12 is a
        a. minor supporting detail.   c. main idea.
        b. major supporting detail.

Inference _____ **5.** "It seems that the town librarian, Yvonne Thomas, decided to retire and volunteer rather than cut the public library's book budget by 8 percent" (sentence 2) implies that

    a. the library is poorly run.

    b. the library is located in a low-income area.

    c. Thomas's salary will go toward purchasing new books.

    d. Thomas was ready to retire.

Test 10

Read the passage, and answer the questions that follow it.

Identity Theft: Deter, Detect, Defend

(NAPS)—[1]Identity theft is a serious crime. [2]It costs Americans billions of dollars and countless hours each year. [3]Identity theft is the use of your personal information without your permission to commit fraud or other crimes. [4]You can't fully control whether you will become a victim. [5]However, you can take several steps to lower your risk. [6]According to the Federal Trade Commission (FTC), you should Deter, Detect and Defend to fight against identity theft.

Deter

[7]Deter identity thieves by safeguarding your information:

- [8]Shred financial documents and paperwork with personal information before you discard them.
- [9]Protect your Social Security number. [10]Give it out only if absolutely necessary or ask to use another identifier.
- [11]Don't give out personal information via the phone, mail or the Internet unless you know who you are dealing with.

Detect

[12]Detect suspicious activity by routinely checking your financial accounts and billing statements. [13]Be alert to signs that require immediate attention, such as these: bills that do not arrive as expected; unexpected credit cards or account statements; denials of credit for no apparent reason; and calls or letters about purchases you did not make.

Defend

[14]If you think your identity has been stolen, here's what to do:

1.[15]Contact the fraud departments of any one of the three consumer reporting companies (Equifax, Experian, and TransUnion). [16]These companies will place a fraud alert on your credit report. [17]The fraud alert tells creditors to contact you before opening any new accounts or changing your current accounts. [18]You only need to contact one of the three companies to place an alert.

2.[19]Close the accounts that you know or believe have been tampered with or opened fraudulently.

3.[20]File a report with your local police or the police in the community where the identity theft took place. [21]Get a copy of the report, or the number of the report, to submit to those who may require proof of the crime.

4.[22]File your complaint with the FTC. [23]The FTC maintains a database of identity theft cases used by law enforcement agencies for investigations. [24]Filing a complaint also helps officials learn more about identity theft and the problems victims are having. [25]The more they know, the better they can better assist you.

[26]To learn more, visit ftc.gov/idtheft.

—Adapted from Federal Trade Commission. 15 May 2007.
"Fight Back Against Identity Theft."
<www.ftc.gov/bcp/edu/multimedia/press/naps03.pdf>.

Vocabulary _____ **1.** The best meaning of the word *permission* as used in sentence 3 is
    a. refusal.   c. agreement.
    b. denial.   d. receipt.

Vocabulary _____ **2.** The best meaning of the word *deter* as used in sentence 7 is
    a. frighten.   c. prevent.
    b. trick.   d. encourage.

Vocabulary _____ **3.** The best meaning of the word *tampered* as used in sentence 19 is
    a. kept.   c. altered.
    b. destroyed.   d. bribed.

Central Idea _____ **4.** The central idea of this passage is found in
    a. sentence 2.   c. sentence 5.
    b. sentence 4.   d. sentence 6.

Thought Patterns _____ **5.** The thought pattern used in this passage is
    a. classification.   c. definition.
    b. comparison and contrast.   d. time order.

Test 11

Read the passage, and answer the questions that follow it.

The A-B-C's of Airbag Safety

Air Bag Safety: Buckle Everyone! Children in Back!

[1]Air bags save lives. [2]They work best when everyone is buckled and children are properly restrained in the back seat. [3]Children riding in the front seat can be seriously injured or killed when an air bag comes out in a crash. [4]An air bag is not a soft, billowy pillow. [5]To do its important job, an air bag comes out of the dashboard at up to 200 miles per hour—faster than the blink of an eye. [6]The force of an air bag can hurt those who are too close to it. [7]Drivers can prevent air bag-related injuries to adults and children by following the critical safety points.

Child Safety Points

- [8]Children 12 and under should ride buckled up in a rear seat.
- [9]Infants in rear facing child safety seats should NEVER ride in the front seat of a vehicle with a passenger side air bag.
- [10]Small children should ride in a rear seat in child safety seats approved for their age and size.
- [11]If a child over one year old must ride in the front seat with a passenger side air bag, put the child in a front facing child safety seat, a booster seat, or a correct fitting lap/shoulder belt—AND move the seat as far back as possible.

Adult Safety Points

- [12]Everyone should buckle up with both lap and shoulder belts on every trip. [13]Air bags are supplemental protection devices.
- [14]The lap belt should be worn under the abdomen and low across the hips. [15]The shoulder portion should come over the collar bone away from the neck and cross over the breast bone. [16]The shoulder belt in most new cars can be adjusted on the side pillar to improve fit.
- [17]Driver and front passenger seats should be moved as far back as practical, particularly for shorter stature people.

—"A-B-C's of Airbag Safety." National Highway Traffic Administration.
United States Department of Transportation. Online. 15 May 2007.

Vocabulary _____ **1.** The word *supplemental* as used in sentence 13 means

a. necessary.   c. important.

b. additional.   d. expensive.

Vocabulary _____ **2.** The word *stature* as used in sentence 17 means
         a. build.   c. looking.
         b. temper.   d. sighted.

Central
Idea _____ **3.** The central idea of the passage is
         a. Knowing how airbags work will ensure safety.
         b. Airbags should be used in addition to seat belts.
         c. Airbags can cause harm when they are deployed.
         d. Drivers can take precautions to minimize the risks of airbags.

Details _____ **4.** Sentence 4 is a
         a. major supporting detail.
         b. minor supporting detail.

Thought
Patterns _____ **5.** The thought pattern used in sentences 8–17 is
         a. time order.   c. listing.
         b. comparison and contrast.   d. cause and effect.

Test 12

Textbook Skills

Read the following passage, adapted from the college textbook *Access to Health,* and answer the questions that follow it.

Communicating as a Couple

[1]Lack of communication in intimate relationships is often a source of trouble. [2]When two people cannot communicate, the couple's ability to solve problems is harmed. [3]Two skills—leveling and editing—can help couples talk and listen to each other.

[4]*Leveling* refers to sending your partner a clear, simple, and honest message. [5]Leveling serves several purposes. [6]The overall purpose is to make communications clear. [7]The next purpose is to make clear the expectations partners have of each other. [8]Another purpose is to clear up unpleasant feelings and thoughts from past incidents. [9]A similar purpose is to make clear what is relevant and what is irrelevant. [10]And the final purpose is to become aware of the things that draw you together or push you apart. [11]Telling your partner that you expect a phone call if he or she is going to be late is an example of leveling.

[12]*Editing* or censoring remarks is another useful skill. [13]Couples should hold back comments that are hurtful or irrelevant. [14]Often when people are upset, they let everything fly. [15]Bringing up old issues and incidents causes pain and puts the partner on the defensive. [16]Editing means taking the time and

making the effort not to say inflammatory things. [17]Leveling and editing are ways for couples to be caring and sensitive as they communicate with each other.

—Adapted from Donatelle, *Access to Health,* 7th ed., pp. 136–37.

Vocabulary _____ **1.** The best meaning of the word *leveling* as used in sentence 4 is
   a. sending clear, simple, honest messages.
   b. demanding attention.
   c. facing disappointments.
   d. clearing up problems.

Vocabulary _____ **2.** The best meaning of the word *censoring* as used in sentence 12 is
   a. oppressing.   c. whispering.
   b. leaving parts out.   d. sharing.

Central _____ **3.** The central idea of the passage is found in
Idea
   a. sentence 1.   c. sentence 3.
   b. sentence 2.   d. sentence 4.

Thought _____ **4.** The relationship between sentences 7 and 8 is
Patterns
   a. cause.   c. addition.
   b. effect.   d. time order.

5. Complete the concept map with a detail from the passage.

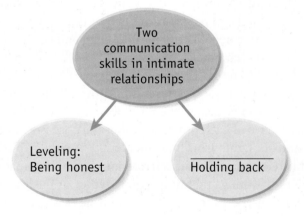

Test 13

Read the following passage, adapted from a college psychology textbook, and answer the questions that follow it.

Effects of Stress on the Immune System

[1]Stress can affect the immune system, which functions to defend the body against infection. [2]Two types of white blood cells are critical to the immune system. [3]The B cells mature in the bone marrow. [4]And the T cells mature in the thymus, an organ located in the chest. [5]Some of the T cells detect and destroy damaged or altered cells, such as precancerous cells, before they become tumors. [6]Glucocorticoids, which are released when the stress response is triggered, can kill or stop the growth of new white blood cells.

[7]Even day-to-day events and stresses, such as taking exams, can affect the functioning of the immune system. [8]A study looked at the relationship between stress and catching a cold. [9]The study found that the more stress a participant reported before exposure to a cold virus, the more likely he or she was to catch a cold. [10]The aspects of stress that best predicted whether participants would get a cold were how likely they were to experience negative feelings like guilt, anger, and being upset. [11]Another factor was how out of control and unpredictable they rated their lives.

[12]Stress can play a role in the length of time it takes a wound to heal. [13]The wounds of women who experienced high levels of stress by caring for a relative with Alzheimer's disease took nine days longer to heal than those of women of similar age and economic status who were not engaged in such caretaking.

—Adapted from Kosslyn & Rosenberg, *Psychology: The Brain, the Person, the World*, p. 443.

Vocabulary _____ **1.** The best meaning of the expression *exposure to* as used in sentence 9 is
      a. uncovering of.   c. holding of.
      b. contact with.   d. removal of.

Vocabulary _____ **2.** The best meaning of the word *status* as used in sentence 13 is
      a. style.   c. level.
      b. need.   d. goal.

Thought _____ **3.** The thought pattern for this passage is
Patterns
      a. time order.   c. cause and effect.
      b. classification.   d. comparison and contrast.

Main Idea/
Details
_____ **4.** Sentence 4 is a
   a. main idea.   c. minor supporting detail.
   b. major supporting detail.

Central
Idea
_____ **5.** What is the best statement of the central idea of this passage?
   a. White blood cells are crucial to the immune system.
   b. Stress affects the immune system.
   c. Stress lengthens the time it takes a wound to heal.
   d. Catching a cold is often stress-related.

Test 14

Textbook
Skills

Read the following passage, adapted from a college history textbook, and answer the questions that follow it.

Indian-Settler Relations in Colonial North America

[1]The colonists of early America learned a great deal about how to live in the American forest from the Native American Indians. [2]The Indians taught the colonists the names of plants and animals (hickory, pecan, raccoon, skunk, moose). [3]The Indians taught the colonists what to wear (leather leggings and moccasins). [4]The Indians taught them what to eat in their new home and how to catch or grow it. [5]The Indians taught the settlers how best to get from one place to another, how to fight, and in some respects how to think.

[6]One of the most important gifts given by the Indians to the colonists was corn. [7]Corn, which the Indians had developed, was the staple of the diet of agricultural tribes. [8]Corn played a vital role in the success of the colonies. [9]The colonists also took advantage of that marvel of Indian technology, the birchbark canoe.

[10]For their part, the Indians eagerly used the tools and products that the colonists brought over from Europe. [11]Indians took on many of the whites' attitudes along with their tools, clothing, weapons, alcohol, and knickknacks. [12]Some tribes used these items to oppress other tribes in more remote areas. [13]During wars, Indians often fought beside whites against other Indians.

[14]The fur trade shows the level of the Indian-white contact. [15]It was in some ways a perfect business arrangement. [16]Both groups profited greatly. [17]The colonists got "valuable" furs for "cheap" European products. [18]The Indians got "priceless" tools, knives, and other trade goods in exchange for "cheap" beaver pelts and deerskins.

[19]The demand for furs caused the Indians to become better hunters and trappers. [20]Hunting parties became larger. [21]Farming tribes shifted the location of their villages in order to be near trade routes and waterways. [22]Early in the 17th century, Huron Indians in the Great Lakes region, who

had likely never seen a Frenchman, owned French products obtained from eastern tribes in exchange for Huron corn.

—Adapted from Garraty & Carnes, *The American Nation: A History of the United States,* 10th ed., p. 30.

Vocabulary _____ **1.** The best meaning of the word *agricultural* as used in sentence 7 is
a. rural.
b. country.
c. farming.
d. larger.

Vocabulary _____ **2.** The best meaning of the word *marvel* as used in sentence 9 is
a. comic.
b. strength.
c. failure.
d. wonder.

Transitions _____ **3.** The relationship between the second and third paragraphs (sentences 6–9 and sentences 10–13) is one of
a. time order.
b. comparison and contrast.
c. classification.
d. effect.

Main Idea _____ **4.** What is the best statement of the main idea of the third paragraph (sentences 10–13)?
a. The colonists ruined the Indian culture.
b. Indians were seldom enemies of other Indians.
c. The Indians both accepted and were influenced by the colonists.
d. Indians and whites did not like or trust each other.

Main Idea/ _____ **5.** Sentence 11 is a
Details
a. main idea.
b. major supporting detail.
c. minor supporting detail.

Test 15

Textbook
Skills

Read the following passage, adapted from the college textbook *Introduction to Mass Communications,* and answer the questions that follow it.

Printing the News

[1]This is how a news story is born, edited, and put into print at a large newspaper:

[2]*Covering the story.* [3]A reporter covers a "beat" such as police or the environment and is responsible for all the news that happens in that area. [4]Or the reporter is sent out by the city desk on a specific assignment. [5]He or she uses the telephone extensively to gather and cross-check information.

[6]*Writing the story.* [7]The reporter writes the story at a computer in the office or perhaps on a personal computer in the field. [8]On an urgent story, the reporter may telephone the facts to a writer in the office.

[9]*Editing the story.* [10]The story is transferred to a computer terminal at the city desk, where the city editor or an assistant reads it on the screen. [11]The editor corrects errors, smooths out the writing, and looks for story "angles" that should be included. [12]When approved, the story is moved by computer to the news desk.

[13]*Writing the headline.* [14]The news editor assigns the story a headline size and style and marks it into position on a designated page. [15]The editor then turns over the story by computer to one of the editors at the copy desk. [16]The copy editor gives it a final polish, writes the headline, and returns the story to the news editor.

[17]*Putting the story into type.* [18]After getting final approval, the story is moved through the system to the production department. [19]There it flashes through electronic typesetting machinery and comes out as printed words on strips of paper. [20]A printer pastes the story into the chosen place on a cardboard page form. [21]This form is sent to the platemaking department. [22]There it is moved onto a thin metal sheet that is locked into the press for printing.

—Adapted from Agee, Ault, & Emery, *Introduction to Mass Communications*, 12th ed., p. 131.

Vocabulary _____ **1.** The best meaning of the word *terminal* as used in sentence 10 is
a. dying.   c. place.
b. workstation.   d. desk.

Vocabulary _____ **2.** The best meaning of the word *designated* as used in sentence 14 is
a. chosen.   c. back.
b. hit.   d. small.

Thought Patterns _____ **3.** The thought pattern for the passage is
a. the effects of the news.
b. the process or steps in publishing a news story.
c. the differences between writing and editing a news story.
d. the traits of a good news reporter.

Details _____ **4.** Sentence 11 is a supporting detail that gives information about
a. a reason for publishing a news story.
b. an example of a news story.
c. a person who helps in the process of publishing a news story.
d. the traits of a good reporter.

Central Idea _____ **5.** The central idea of this passage is found in
a. sentence 1.   c. sentence 7.
b. sentence 3.   d. sentence 18.

PART FOUR
Reading Enrichment

ESL Reading Tips

Knowing more than one language is a tremendous advantage. A language is closely tied to the culture of its people. Thus, when you learn an additional language, you learn about the values and customs of a way of life different from your own. The differences among cultures can be seen in the differences among their languages. For example, three of the most frequently used words in the English language are the articles *the, an,* and *a.* Yet many other languages do not use articles at all. Some say that learning English as an additional language offers some specific challenges.

English as a Second Language (ESL) refers to teaching English to a person whose native or main language is not English. The following ESL reading tips are designed to aid you in your admirable quest to acquire English.

General Hints

Every chapter of *The Skilled Reader,* Second Edition, teaches specific skills and strategies that are helpful to students learning to read English. The following chart lists a few of the specific lessons that directly support ESL instruction. Use this chart to survey or review information that will help you learn to read English. Complete the chart by writing in the page numbers you will study.

> **Skills and Strategies in *The Skilled Reader* that support ESL**
>
> Use a reading plan like SQ3R. [Chapter 1] Pages 8–22
> Skim or read rapidly for main ideas. [Chapter 4] Pages 141–144
> Scan or read rapidly for specific details. [Chapter 6]
>   Pages 212–220
> Use the general sense of the passage to figure out the meaning
>   of unfamiliar words and phrases. [Chapter 2] Pages 48–57
> Annotate the passage. [Part II] Pages 470–472
> Create graphic organizers based on thought patterns from
>   information in the text. [Chapters 7-9] Pages 249–376

In addition, form a study group that includes native speakers of English. The more you hear and speak the language, the more quickly you will learn it.

Figurative Language: Idioms, Similes and Metaphors

Consider the following well-known phrases:

catch some Zs	sharp as a tack	eats like a bird
burn the midnight oil	an icy stare	raining cats and dogs

Each one of these sayings creates a vivid word picture that deepens the reader's understanding of the author's meaning. To understand how an author creates and uses vivid word pictures, you need to know about literal and figurative language.

> **Literal language** uses the exact meaning of a word or phrase.
> **Figurative language** uses a word or phrase to imply or mean something different from its literal definition; also known as "figures of speech."

Literal language expresses the exact meaning of a word or phrase. For example, if you were out hiking with a friend and told him to "go jump in a lake," he could take your words *literally* and immerse himself in a nearby body of water. However, if you were having an argument and said, "Go jump in a lake," your friend would understand that you were using **figurative language** and were saying something like "go away." Hundreds of figures of speech exist, but understanding three commonly used types will make you a more skilled reader. The three types are *idioms, similes* and *metaphors*.

> **Idiom**—a phrase (a group of words) that cannot be understood based on the individual words in the phrase
> **Simile**—an indirect comparison between two ideas that uses *like, as, as if,* or *as though*
> **Metaphor**—a direct comparison between two ideas that does not use *like, as, as if,* or *as though*

Idiom

An **idiom** is a phrase (a group of words) that cannot be understood based on the individual words in the phrase.

EXAMPLE   Read the following two sentences. Underline the idioms in each sentence. Use your own words to write the meaning of the idioms.

1. Last night, Enrico and Carlos burn the midnight oil studying for final exams.

_____

2. Enrico was exhausted after the exam, so he went home to catch some Zs.

_____

EXPLANATION The phrases *burn the midnight oil* and *to catch some Zs* are idioms. In sentence 1, the phrase *burn the midnight oil* implies that Enrico and Carlos stayed up late into the night studying. The expression refers to the time before electricity when oil lamps were used for light. In sentence 2, the phrase *to catch some Zs* implies sleep. This meaning is implied with the context clue "exhausted." The expression most likely came from the way cartoons depict the sound of someone snoring with a string of Zs coming from a character's mouth: Zzzzzzzzz indicates snoring.

PRACTICE **1** Idioms

Use your own words to write the meaning of each idiom in bold print. Compare and discuss your answers with those of your classmates.

1. After working 10 hours organizing the office, Jamal decided **to call it a day**.

Jamal decided _____

2. Margaret thought the final exam would be hard, but it was **a piece of cake**.

Margaret thought the test was _____

3. As a hardworking employee, Robert is **worth his salt**.

Robert is _____

4. Kathleen, who gossips instead of doing her work, is **a bad egg**.

Kathleen _____

5. Don't listen to Lynn's complaints. She is full of **sour grapes** because she didn't get the promotion.

Lynn is _____

Simile

A **simile** is an indirect comparison between two ideas that uses *like, as, as if,* or *as though*.

EXAMPLE   Read the following two sentences. Underline the similes in each sentence. Use your own words to write the meaning of the similes.

1. Jamie is sharp as a tack; she always knows the right thing to say.

_____

2. Elaine, who is always worried about her weight, eats like a bird.

_____

EXPLANATION   The phrases *sharp as a tack* and *eats like a bird* are similes. They use the words *like* and *as,* which are words of indirect comparison. In sentence 1, the phrase *sharp as a tack* means that Jamie is smart or quick-minded. Jamie is not a tack. Perhaps Jamie is compared to a sharp tack because her ideas pierce through to the main point. In sentence 2, the phrase *eats like a bird* implies that Elaine eats small portions. Elaine is not a bird. Perhaps Elaine's eating style is compared to a bird's because she picks at her food and takes tiny bites of it. In both examples, Jamie and Elaine are described in *similes* as *similar* to these things.

Because a simile is a figure of speech that cannot be taken literally, the skilled reader must interpret the author's implied meaning.

PRACTICE 2 Similes

Write the meaning of each simile in bold print. Compare and discuss your answers with those of your classmates.

1. A gallbladder attack feels **like labor contractions during the last phase of childbirth.**

A gallbladder attack is _____

2. Justine accepts new ideas **as well as a cat accepts a bath.**

Justine accepts a new idea with _____

3. New love breaks into one's life **like a brilliant sunrise.**

New love is _____

4. The tornado sounded **as though a freight train were coming straight at me**.

The tornado had a _____ sound.

5. One stage of grief is **like the eye of a hurricane**.

One stage of grief is _____

Metaphor

A **metaphor** is a direct comparison between two ideas that does *not* use *like, as, as if*, or *as though*. Often a metaphor is created by using the verb *is* to set up a direct comparison between ideas.

EXAMPLE   Read the following three sentences. Underline the metaphors in each sentence. Use your own words to write the meaning of the metaphors.

1. Alita gave the naughty child an icy stare.

_____

2. It is raining cats and dogs.

_____

3. Faith is my anchor in life.

_____

EXPLANATION   The three metaphors are an *icy stare, raining cats and dogs,* and *Faith is my anchor.* Note that none of these examples uses the word *like* or *as*. Instead, the first idea in each metaphor is directly compared to the second idea. In sentence 1, the word *icy* is used to directly describe Alita's stare, to paint a picture of a "cold look." In sentence 2, the phrase *raining cats and dogs* makes a comparison between cats and dogs and rain and wind. In some ancient myths, cats represented rain and dogs represented wind (for example, in Nordic mythology, both animals were associated with the storm god, Odin). The author's purpose is to suggest a storm.

Often a metaphor uses words such as *is, are,* or *were* to make the direct comparison between the two ideas. In sentence 3, *Faith is my anchor* sets up a direct link between faith and the traits of an anchor. Thus the metaphor paints a picture of faith as an ideal that lies beneath a person's everyday life, out of sight, yet holds that person's life steady so that it cannot drift.

Because a metaphor is a figure of speech that cannot be taken literally, the skilled reader must figure out the author's implied meaning.

PRACTICE 3 Metaphors

Write the meaning of each metaphor in bold print. Compare and discuss your answers with your classmates.

1. Parenting **is a roller-coaster ride**.

Parenting _____

2. His looks were **daggers he threw around the room** to silence others.

His looks were _____

3. Grandmother Lewis is **a walking encyclopedia**.

Grandmother Lewis is _____

_____

4. Jonathan is **a lion** on the football field.

Jonathan is _____

5. My mentor Rhodella is **my Rock of Gibraltar**.

_____

VISUAL VOCABULARY

The Rock of Gibraltar has become a well-known _____ for dependability and strength.

a. figure of speech
b. simile
c. metaphor

Distinguishing Between Similes and Metaphors

Both similes and metaphors use comparisons between ideas to deepen meaning. Almost any expression that can be worded as a simile could also be worded as a metaphor. Remember the main difference between a simile and a metaphor is the use of the words *like, as, as if,* and *as though*. Similes use these words; metaphors do not. Authors must carefully choose whether the indirect comparison of a simile or the direct comparison of a metaphor is better suited for their purposes. Thus skilled readers pay close attention to the author's careful application of these two figures of speech.

EXAMPLE   Read the following two sentences. Underline the figures of speech. Identify each one as a metaphor or a simile. Write **M** for metaphor and **S** for simile.

_____   **1.** The stock market sank like a rock.

_____   **2.** His mop of hair hung limp and stringy.

EXPLANATION   In sentence 1, the phrase *sank like a rock* is a simile (**S**). The word *like* sets up an indirect comparison between the behavior of the stock market and a rock. In this case, both fall rapidly from high places. In sentence 2, the phrase *mop of hair* is a metaphor (**M**) that directly compares his hair to a *limp and stringy mop*.

PRACTICE 4

Each of the following sentences contains a figure of speech. Identify each figure of speech as a metaphor or a simile. Write **M** for metaphor and **S** for simile.

_____   **1.** Marie was as frightened as a deer caught in a car's headlights on a dark country road.

_____   **2.** Some military leaders are hawks; others are doves.

_____   **3.** Karl Marx said, "Religion is the opiate of the masses."

_____   **4.** Your words skim across my heart like small stones skipping across the smooth surface of water.

_____   **5.** I am as hungry as a horse.

REVIEW Test 1 UNDERSTANDING FIGURES OF SPEECH

A. Idioms   Use your own words to write the meaning of each idiom in bold print.

1. Samantha is **fed up with** Anita because Anita is always late.

Samantha is _____

2. Ricky almost missed the deadline to file his taxes, but he made it **by the skin of his teeth**.

Ricky _____

B. Similes   For each simile choose a meaning from the box. Use each meaning once.

boastful	discipline	grow	valuable

3. Wisdom is as good as gold.

Wisdom is _____

4. Talent is like a plant that needs to be fed, watered, and pruned.

Talent can _____

5. William struts like a rooster.

William is _____

6. Achieving success is like training for a marathon.

Success requires _____

C. Metaphors   For each metaphor, choose a meaning from the box. Use each meaning once.

confusing	guardian	painful	short time

7. In George Orwell's novel *1984*, government becomes everybody's feared "Big Brother."

Government becomes everyone's _____

8. The thorn of failure pricks self-confidence.

Failure is _____

9. Grief is but a passing season.

   Grief lasts a _____

10. Surely life is a jewelry box; yet guilt, fear, love, and hope are tangled neck-laces, hopelessly knotted together.

    Life is _____

REVIEW Test 2 UNDERSTANDING FIGURES OF SPEECH

A. Idioms   Use your own words to write the meaning of each idiom in bold print.

1. I can't **make up my mind** about what to cook for dinner.

   I can't _____

2. Miguel didn't study for the exam. He **paid the piper** with a low grade.

   Miguel _____

3. Joanne called in to say she wouldn't be able to work today. She is **feeling under the weather**.

   Joanne feels _____

4. Jim gets **hot under the collar** when he sees a careless driver talking on a cell phone.

   Jim gets _____

B. Similes and Metaphors   Each of the following quotations contains a figure of speech. Identify each one as either a simile or a metaphor. Write **S** for simile and **M** for metaphor.

_____ 5. "How dreary—to be—somebody! How public—like a frog—to tell your name—the livelong June—to an admiring bog!"—Emily Dickinson.

_____ 6. "Character is destiny."—Heraclitus

_____ 7. "A dream that is not interpreted is like a letter that is not read."—Talmud

_____ **8.** "Fame is like a river, that beareth up things light and swollen, and drowns things weighty and solid."—Francis Bacon

_____ **9.** "Everyone is a moon, and has a dark side which he never shows to anybody."—Mark Twain

_____ **10.** "Paying alimony is like feeding hay to a dead horse."—Groucho Marx

Devyn Lawrence

12/08/09

Reading Graphics

Reading comprehension involves reading more than just words. Authors also use visual images such as photographs, cartoons, and graphics to relay ideas. Graphics are helpful for several reasons. First, graphics can simplify difficult ideas and make relationships easier to see. Second, graphics can sum up ideas so that they can be more quickly digested. Third, graphics can sway a reader by pointing out trends or gaps in information. A skilled reader should know how to read different types of graphics. This appendix will discuss three basic types: tables, graphs, and diagrams. Although a variety of graphics exist, a few basic guidelines can be applied as a reading process for any graphic.

Basic Guidelines for Reading Graphics

Graphics give a great deal of information in a smaller space than it would take to write the ideas in the form of words. The following suggestions will help you understand the general format of a graphic. Apply the SQ3R strategies discussed in Chapter 1. Remember to skim, question, read, recite, and review the information.

Read the Words Printed with the Graphic

Just as in a paragraph or passage, a graphic has a main idea and supporting details.

Read the title or caption. The title or caption is usually at the top of the graphic. The title or caption states the main idea of the graphic.

Ask: What is this graphic about? What is being described?

Note the source. The source is usually at the bottom of the graphic. The source is the author or publisher of the ideas in the graphic.

Ask: Who collected the information? Is the source a trusted authority? If the graphic reports the results of a survey, how many people took part? Who were they?

Read any footnotes. Footnotes are also found at the bottom of a graphic. Footnotes can include important supporting details.

Ask: Do the footnotes explain what any numbers or headings mean? How was the data collected?

Read the labels. Many graphics use columns and rows. Other graphics use horizontal or vertical axes. Columns, rows, and axes are labeled. These labels give important supporting details for the graphic's main idea. Look up any words you do not know in a dictionary.

Ask: Do the labels tell what the columns and rows represent? Are any symbols or abbreviations used? If so, what do they mean?

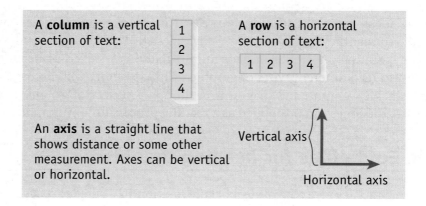

A **column** is a vertical section of text:

A **row** is a horizontal section of text:

An **axis** is a straight line that shows distance or some other measurement. Axes can be vertical or horizontal.

Vertical axis

Horizontal axis

Analyze the Graphic

Analyze the format. Each type of chart has its own organization. For example, a table uses columns and rows. A pie chart is a circle divided into parts.

Ask: How is the graphic organized? Why did the author use this type of graphic?

Analyze the unit of measurement. Study the legend. A legend will list and explain symbols used as labels. Study the labels of rows, columns, and axes.

Ask: Do the numbers represent hundreds? Thousands? Millions? Inches? Feet? Miles? Pounds? Ounces? Are metric units used?

Analyze trends and patterns. Trends and patterns suggest or imply important ideas that support the graphic's main idea.

Ask: What are the extremes? How do the extremes compare to the total? What are the averages? What and how much are the increases? What and how much are the decreases?

EXAMPLE   Study the graphic. Complete the statements that follow it with information from the graph.

Percentage of U.S. Households with a Computer, by Annual Income and by Race

	Under $15,000	$15,000–$34,999	$35,000–$74,999	$75,000+
White, Not Hispanic	15.4	28.0	55.1	76.3
Black, Not Hispanic	6.3	18.2	40.2	64.1
Other, Not Hispanic	19.1	38.5	62.6	81.0
Hispanic	7.8	16.6	36.8	72.8

Source: National Telecommunications and Information Administration, U.S. Department of Commerce, "Falling through the Net II: New Data on the Digital Divide" (1997).

"Other, Not Hispanic" includes Asians and Pacific Islanders, American Indians, Eskimos, and Aleuts.

1. The title of the table is _____ _____.

2. The source of the table is _____ _____.

3. Income is measured in _____.

4. "Hispanic" means _____ _____.

5. The highest percentage of households with a computer have an annual income of _____.

6. The lowest percentage of households with a computer have an annual income of _____.

7. The percentage of "White, Not Hispanic" households with annual incomes of $15,000 to $34,999 who own a computer is _____.

8. The percentage of "Other, Not Hispanic" households with annual incomes of $35,000 to $74,999 who own a computer is _____.

9. "Other, Not Hispanic" includes _____

_____ .

10. Based on the information in the table, what is the impact of income on

owning a computer? _____ .

EXPLANATION

1. The title of the table is "Percentage of U.S. Households with a Computer, by Annual Income and by Race." The title is located above the table.

2. The source of the table is the National Telecommunications and Information Administration, U.S. Department of Commerce. This information is located at the bottom of the table. This is a reliable government source.

3. Income is measured in dollars. The income ranges from under $15,000 to $75,000 and above. We know the range goes above $75,000 because of the plus sign after that number.

4. "Hispanic" means a person of Latin American origin who lives in the United States. If you did not know the meaning of this term, you should have looked it up in a dictionary. Always look up terms that you do not know.

5. The highest percentage of households with a computer has an annual income of $75,000 or more. To find this answer, a skilled reader would skim for the highest number in all the rows and columns. That number is 81.0, which is found in the "$75,000+" column.

6. The lowest percentage of households with a computer has an annual income of under $15,000. To find this answer, a skilled reader would skim for the lowest number in all the rows and columns. The lowest number in the entire table is 6.3, which is found in the "Under $15,000" column.

7. The percentage of "White, Not Hispanic" households with annual incomes of $15,000 to $34,999 who own a computer is 28.0.

8. The percentage of "Other, Not Hispanic" households with annual incomes of $35,000 to $74,999 who own a computer is 62.6.

9. "Other, Not Hispanic" includes Asians and Pacific Islanders, American Indians, Eskimos, and Aleuts. You had to read the footnote to understand the meaning of this label.

10. The report that was published with the graphic answered this question. Compare your answer to the following summary of the answer based on the report: "Income has a great effect on owning a computer. Members of all income groups may own a computer, but those with higher incomes

Daryl Lawience 12/08/09

are more likely to own one. As a result, the gap between owning a computer and not owning a computer is quite large between high-income households and low-income households."

Three Basic Types of Graphics

Many magazines, newspapers, and textbooks use tables, graphs, and diagrams. These graphics call attention to key concepts. Thus a skilled reader takes time to study the ideas within them.

Tables

The graphic on U.S. households that have computers is a table. Social science, health, and business textbooks often use tables. A **table** is a systematic ordering of facts in rows and columns for easy reference. The purpose of a table is to allow the reader to compare the given facts. Often the facts are given as numbers or statistics. The basic guidelines to reading graphics apply to reading a table. In addition, some tables require that you study the places where columns and rows intersect.

EXAMPLE Study the following table. Based on the data in the table, mark each numbered statement **T** if it is true, **F** if it is false, or **DK** if you don't know, based on the given data.

Calculated Body Mass Index for Selected Heights and Weights for Individuals Aged 2 to 20 Years: 48"–57" and 114 lbs.–124 lbs.

Height Cm	In	Weight Kg	51.7	52.6	53.5	54.4	55.3	56.2
		Lb	114	116	118	120	122	124
121.9	48		34.8					
124.5	49		33.4	34.0	34.6			
127.0	50		32.1	32.6	33.2	33.7	34.3	34.9
129.5	51		30.8	31.4	31.9	32.4	33.0	33.5
132.1	52		29.6	30.2	30.7	31.2	31.7	32.2
134.6	53		28.5	29.0	29.5	30.0	30.5	31.0
137.2	54		27.5	28.0	28.5	28.9	29.4	29.9
139.7	55		26.5	27.0	27.4	27.9	28.4	28.8
142.2	56		25.6	26.0	26.5	26.9	27.4	27.8
144.8	57		24.7	25.1	25.5	26.0	26.4	26.8

Source: U.S. Department of Health and Human Services, Centers for Disease Control and Prevention, June 2000.

The body mass index (BMI) is used to decide if a person is within a normal growth range, overweight, at risk of becoming overweight, or underweight. BMI is determined as follows: English formula: Weight in pounds divided by height in inches divided by height in inches times 703 = BMI. Metric formula: Weight in kilograms divided by height in meters divided by height in meters = BMI.

_____ **1.** The source of this table is a reliable source.

_____ **2.** This table charts the BMI of elderly adults.

_____ **3.** 48 inches equals 121.9 centimeters.

_____ **4.** The BMI of a person who is 57 inches tall and weighs 120 pounds is 26.0.

_____ **5.** A child who is 48 inches tall and weighs 114 pounds is overweight.

EXPLANATION

1. T: This table was published by a government agency, the Centers for Disease Control and Prevention. This information is found in the source note at the bottom of the table.

2. F: The title of this chart clearly states that it gives data for people 2 to 20 years old.

3. T: The chart gives both metric and English measurements. 121.9 centimeters is listed in the same row as 48 inches; they are therefore equal.

4. T: You can check this answer in several ways. First, begin in the row that lists 57 inches; follow that row over to the number 26.0; then travel up that column to its heading, where you will find 120 pounds listed. You could have begun with the 120 pounds column and traveled down to the BMI of 26.0 and then over to the matching row of 57 inches. If you had only the weight and height of the child, you would have to find where the row that shows the child's height and the column that lists the child's weight meet to find the child's BMI.

5. DK: This chart does not give us the guidelines to determine if a child is overweight. The footnote tells the reader that the body mass index is used to determine healthy growth, but it does not tell the reader how to do so.

PRACTICE 1

Study the following table. Then mark each numbered statement **T** if it is true, **F** if it is false, or **DK** if you don't know, based on the given data.

Dietary Guidelines for Americans, 2000

Recommended Number of Servings

	1,600 Calories	2,200 Calories	2,800 Calories
Grains group	6	9	11
Vegetables group	3	4	5
Fruit group	2	3	4
Milk group	2 or 3	2 or 3	2 or 3
Meat and beans group	2 (5 oz. total)	2 (6 oz. total)	3 (7oz. total)

Source: USDA Center for Nutrition Policy and Promotion.

_____ **1.** Eleven servings of grains is recommended for a diet of 1,600 calories.

_____ **2.** Four servings of fruit is recommended for a diet of 2,800 calories.

_____ **3.** Six ounces is recommended for one serving of meat for a diet of 2,200 calories.

_____ **4.** A healthy diet should include two or three servings from the milk group.

_____ **5.** Individuals who need to lose weight should follow the recommendations for a 1,600-calorie diet.

Graphs

Graphs show the relationship between two or more sets of ideas. The most common types of graphs you will come across in your reading are line graphs, bar graphs, and pie charts.

Line Graphs A **line graph** plots two or more sets of facts on vertical and horizontal axes. The vertical axis sets out a scale to measure one set of data, and the horizontal axis offers another scale to measure the other set of data. These features make a line graph ideal to show the curve, shifts, or trends in data. As the information varies, the line changes to show dips and surges. If the information does not change, the line remains steady. Remember to use the guidelines for reading graphics from pages 585–586, and pay special attention to the labels on the vertical and horizontal axes.

EXAMPLE Study the following line graph. Based on the data in the graph, mark each numbered statement **T** if it is true, **F** if it is false, or **DK** if you don't know, based on the given data.

Prisoners on Death Row, by Race, 1968–2001

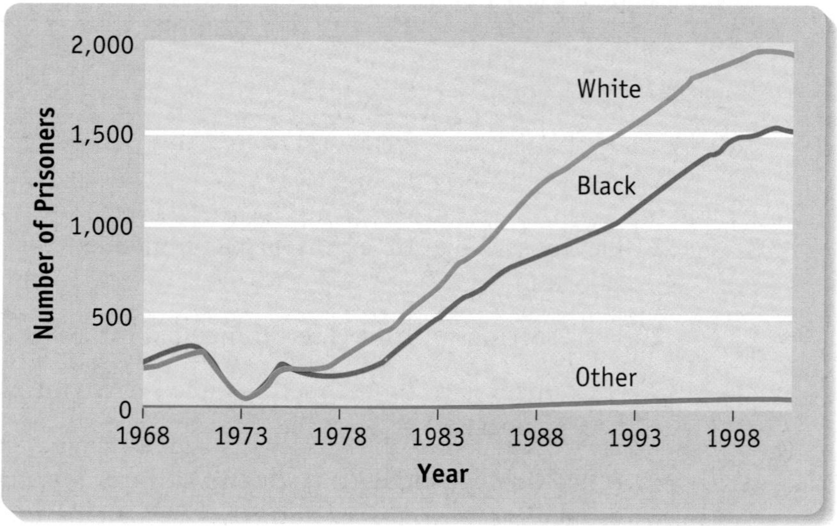

Source: *Capital Punishment, 2001.* U.S. Department of Justice, Bureau of Justice Statistics.
The death penalty was reinstated by the U.S. Supreme Court in 1976.

_____ **1.** Only two groups of people on death row are tracked on this line graph.

_____ **2.** The horizontal axis plots the timeline of death row in ten-year periods.

_____ **3.** The vertical axis plots the numbers of people on death row.

_____ **4.** The number of people on death row began to rise around 1976 when the U.S. Supreme Court reinstated the death penalty.

_____ **5.** Whites are more violent than blacks.

EXPLANATION   Compare your answers to the ones that follow.

1. F: Three groups of people by race are tracked on this graph. The third group is labeled "other."

2. F: The horizontal axis does plot the timeline of the death penalty, but it is plotted by five-year, not ten-year, periods. The time span is important because it gives the reader a sense of how many people face the death penalty during a given time.

3. T: The vertical axis does plot the number of people on death row. The numbers are marked off in groups of 500.

4. T: The line indicating the number of inmates on death row begins to take a sharp and steady curve upward around this time. The footnote tells the reader that the Supreme Court reinstated the death penalty in 1976. Notice that the line dips sharply down in the early 1970s. During this time, there was great pressure to end the death penalty. A Supreme Court decision in 1972 brought executions to a halt nationwide. The graph does not explain these shifts in the lines. The footnote does, however, suggest that executions had been halted previously, because the word *reinstated* means "put back in place."

5. DK: It may be tempting to jump to this conclusion. Yet based on the data given, we cannot possibly know whether whites are more violent than blacks. All the graph tells us is that more whites than blacks are on death row. The information in this graph does not mention why they are on death row.

Bar Graphs A **bar graph** presents a set of bars. Each bar stands for a specific quantity, amount, or measurement of information. The bars allow you to compare the quantity of each item represented on the graph. The bars on bar graphs can be arranged horizontally or vertically. Remember to use the guidelines for reading graphics (pages 585–586) when you read bar graphs.

EXAMPLE Study the following bar graph. Based on the data in the graph, mark each numbered statement **T** if it is true, **F** if it is false, or **DK** if you don't know, based on the given data.

Percentage of People Under 65 Years of Age Without Health Insurance Coverage: United States, 1998.

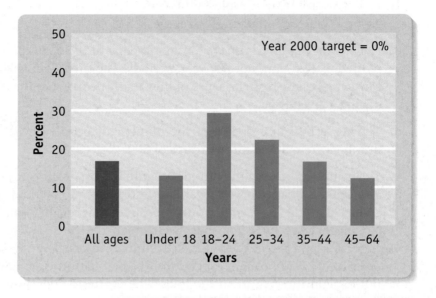

	All ages	Under 18 years	18–24 years	25–34 years	35–44 years	45–64 years
People without health insurance	16.6%	12.7%	29.0%	22.2%	16.4%	12.2%

Source: *Healthy People 2000*. Centers for Disease Control and Prevention, National Health Interview Survey.

_____ **1.** The idea stated as "Year 2000 target = 0%" means that the government wanted all people to have insurance by the year 2000.

_____ **2.** The horizontal axis shows the number of people without insurance as percentages.

_____ **3.** The horizontal axis shows people grouped by race.

_____ **4.** The highest percentage of people without health insurance in 1998 were under the age of 18.

_____ **5.** About 12 percent of the people aged 45 to 64 years were without health insurance in 1998.

EXPLANATION

1. T: The idea stated as "Year 2000 target = 0%" means that the government wanted no one to be without insurance coverage, which would mean that everyone would have had insurance by the year 2000.

2. F: The *vertical* axis shows the number of people as percentages.

3. F: The horizontal axis groups people by age, not race.

4. F: The group with the highest bar shows the largest group without health insurance, which is the 18- to 24-year-old group.

5. T: The table under the graph clearly states the actual percentage. The 45- to 64-year-old group is the group that has the smallest percentage of people without insurance. In other words, this group has the largest number of people covered by health insurance.

Pie Charts   A **pie chart**, also known as a *circle graph,* shows a whole group as a circle and divides the circle into smaller units that look like slices of the pie. Each smaller slice is a part, percentage, or fraction of the whole. Pie graphs are used to show proportions and the importance of each smaller unit to the whole.

EXAMPLE   Study the following pie charts. Based on the data shown, mark each numbered statement **T** if it is true, **F** if it is false, or **DK** if you don't know, based on the given data.

Extent of Internet Use by Fourth and Eighth Graders, 2001

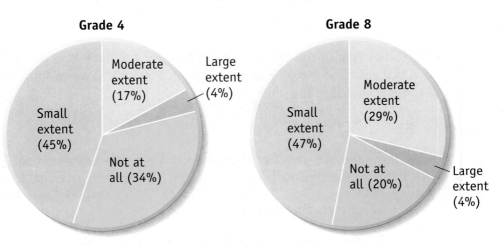

Source: Data from National Center for Education Statistics, *The Nation's Report Card* (2001).

_____ **1.** Both circle graphs are divided into five parts.

_____ **2.** More eighth graders than fourth graders used the Internet "not at all" in 2001.

_____ **3.** The same percentage of fourth graders and eighth graders used the Internet to a "large extent."

_____ **4.** The majority of fourth graders used the Internet to a "small extent."

_____ **5.** The fourth graders who didn't use the Internet at all began using the Internet to a small extent by the time they were eighth graders.

EXPLANATION

1. F: Each pie chart is divided into four groups based on what percentage of children in each group uses the Internet. The four groups are labeled "small extent," "moderate extent," "large extent," and "not at all."

2. F: The fourth graders had the higher percentage of children who use the Internet "not at all." The percentage of fourth graders represented by the "not at all" slice of the pie is 34 percent. The percentage of eighth graders represented by the "not at all" slice of the pie is 20 percent.

3. T: Four percent of each group used the Internet to a "large extent."

4. F: The word *majority* means a number more than half of the total, or greater than 50 percent. But only 45 percent of fourth graders used the Internet to a "small extent."

5. F: The title of the graph includes the year the data were gathered: 2001. Students who were in fourth grade in 2001 could not also have been in eighth grade in the same year.

PRACTICE 2

Study the following graphic. Then mark each numbered statement **T** if it is true, **F** if it is false, or **DK** if you don't know, based on the given data.

_____ **1.** This graphic is a line graph.

_____ **2.** The vertical axis shows that most of the new jobs are in seven main areas.

Where the New Jobs Will Be, 1994–2010

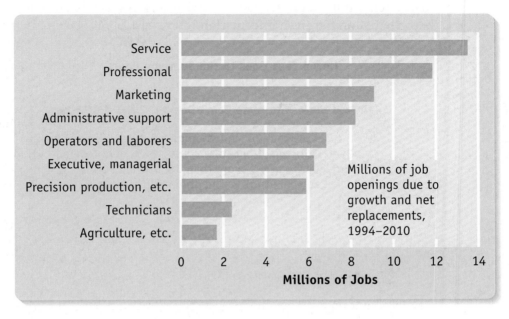

Source: Carol D'Amico. "Understanding the Digital Economy." U.S. Department of Commerce, April 12, 2003.
[http://www.ta.doc.gov/digeconomy/powerpoint/carol/sld005.htm].

_____ **3.** Most of the new jobs will be in the service field.

_____ **4.** Farm-related jobs will make up less than 2 million of the new jobs.

_____ **5.** Service jobs will offer the best salaries.

Diagrams

A **diagram** is a graphic that explains in detail the relationships of the parts of an idea to the whole idea. Diagrams include flowcharts, pictograms, and drawings.

Flowcharts A **flowchart** is a diagram that shows a step-by-step process. Each step or phase of the process is typically shown in a box or circle, and the shapes are connected with lines and arrows to show the proper order or flow of the steps. Flowcharts are used in a number of subject areas, including social sciences, science, history, and English.

EXAMPLE Study the following flowchart. Based on the data in the diagram, mark each numbered statement **T** if it is true, **F** if it is false, or **DK** if you don't know, based on the given information.

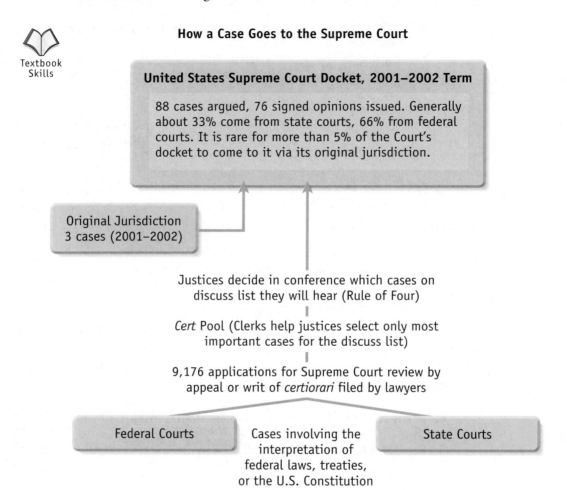

How a Case Goes to the Supreme Court

Textbook Skills

> **United States Supreme Court Docket, 2001–2002 Term**
>
> 88 cases argued, 76 signed opinions issued. Generally about 33% come from state courts, 66% from federal courts. It is rare for more than 5% of the Court's docket to come to it via its original jurisdiction.

Original Jurisdiction 3 cases (2001–2002)

Justices decide in conference which cases on discuss list they will hear (Rule of Four)

Cert Pool (Clerks help justices select only most important cases for the discuss list)

9,176 applications for Supreme Court review by appeal or writ of *certiorari* filed by lawyers

Federal Courts   Cases involving the interpretation of federal laws, treaties, or the U.S. Constitution   **State Courts**

Over 92 million cases initially filed in U.S. state and federal trial courts

Source: Karen O'Connor and Larry J. Sabato, *American Government: Continuity and Change* (New York: Longman, 2004), Fig. 10.6.

_____ **1.** Either a federal or state court can apply for a case to be heard by the Supreme Court.

_____ **2.** Most of the cases the Supreme Court argues come from state courts.

       3. Clerks of the Supreme Court have an important role in deciding which cases are heard by the Supreme Court.

       4. Most of the Supreme Court cases deal with the Bill of Rights.

       5. A single Supreme Court justice can insist that the Supreme Court hear a case.

EXPLANATION

1. T: The lines that are drawn from the boxes that are labeled "Federal Courts" and "State Courts" show that both courts can send cases to be considered by the Supreme Court.

2. F: The information in the box at the top of the flowchart states that most of the cases (66 percent) argued come from federal courts. Only 33 percent come from state courts.

3. T: The flowchart states that when cases reach the "*cert* pool," clerks help justices select "only the most important cases" for the justices to discuss as a group.

4. DK: The flowchart does not reveal the types of cases the Supreme Court considers. Most likely that idea is addressed in the textbook in the same section in which this flowchart appears. When a skilled reader studies a graphic, unanswered questions often arise that the text can most likely answer.

5. F: The justices decide in conference on which cases to hear. The "rule of four" is also noted in the flowchart at this stage. The rule of four means that at least four of the justices must agree to hear the case, or the case will not be heard. (The text tells the reader that the Supreme Court is made up of nine justices.)

Pictograms A **pictogram** is a diagram that uses pictorial forms to represent data. Usually statistics are used in pictograms.

EXAMPLE Study the following pictogram. Based on the ideas in the diagram, mark each numbered statement **T** if it is true, **F** if it is false, or **DK** if you don't know, based on the given information.

Cascades Eruptions During the Past 4,000 Years

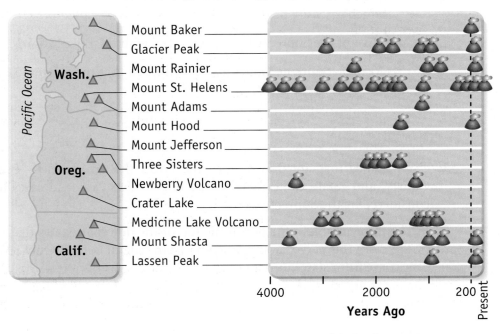

Source: Cascades Volcano Observatory, U.S. Geological Survey, Department of the Interior, 2000.

The Cascade Range includes numerous volcanoes and covers about 1,000 miles from Mount Garibaldi in British Columbia, Canada, to Lassen Peak in northern California.

_____ **1.** The Cascade Range is a mountain range that stretches 1,000 miles across three states and part of Canada.

_____ **2.** Mount St. Helens has had more eruptions over the past 4,000 years than the other volcanoes of the Cascades.

_____ **3.** Newberry Volcano has had the fewest eruptions over the past 4,000 years.

_____ **4.** The volcano Three Sisters is located in the state of Washington.

_____ **5.** In the last 200 years, Mount St. Helens has had the most violent and destructive eruptions of any of the volcanoes in the Cascade Range.

EXPLANATION

1. T: This information is found in two places on the pictogram. The map shows that the range covers three states. The footnote tells you that the range is also in Canada and covers a distance of about 1,000 miles.

2. T: The pictogram shows a total of 15 eruptions for Mount St. Helens, more than any of the other volcanoes. Each volcano picture represents one eruption.

3. F: Newberry Volcano has two volcano icons. However, both Mount Baker and Mount Adams have only one each. So Mount Baker and Mount Adams have had the fewest number of eruptions.

4. F: The line from Three Sisters to the map points to a volcano in the middle of the state of Oregon.

5. DK: The pictogram depicts only the number of eruptions over the past 4,000 years, not their force or their effects. Mount St. Helens has had more eruptions than the other volcanoes during the past 200 years, but the pictogram doesn't tell us how destructive those eruptions were.

Drawings A **drawing** is an artist's illustration of a complicated process or idea. The drawing shows the relationships among all the details in the picture. Often these drawings are dependent on the matching text, and a skilled reader must move back and forth between the drawing and the text for full understanding.

EXAMPLE Study the following drawing, and read its matching text. Based on the ideas in the diagram, mark each numbered statement **T** if it is true, **F** if it is false, or **DK** if you don't know, based on the given information.

Coral Reef Structure

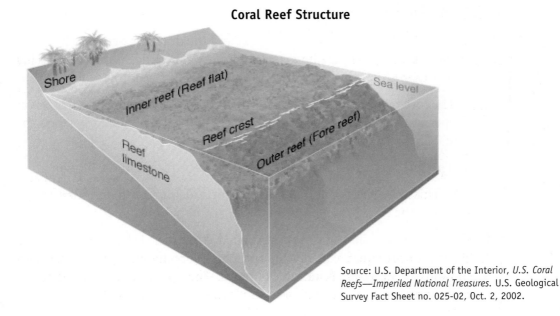

Source: U.S. Department of the Interior, *U.S. Coral Reefs—Imperiled National Treasures*. U.S. Geological Survey Fact Sheet no. 025-02, Oct. 2, 2002.

Coral Reefs Develop in Clear, Warm Seas

[1]Colonial "hard corals" can take on several different forms. [2]Hard corals become elaborate finger-shaped, branching, or mound-shaped structures. [3]These structures can create masses of limestone that stretch for tens or even hundreds of miles. [4]Many coral reefs fringing coasts consist of near-shore inner reef flats. [5]These inner reefs slope to deeper water fore reefs farther offshore. [6]The reef crest lies in very shallow water between the inner reef flat and outer fore reef. [7]The reef crest may be exposed during the lowest tides. [8]Waves commonly crash against or break on the reef crest.

—Adapted from U.S. Department of the Interior, *U.S. Coral Reefs— Imperiled National Treasures*. U.S. Geological Survey Fact Sheet no. 025-02, Oct. 2, 2002.

_____ **1.** Coral reefs have a limestone base.

_____ **2.** The fore reef lies close to shore.

_____ **3.** The reef crest lies between the inner reef and the fore reef.

_____ **4.** Coral reefs are home to 25 percent of all marine species.

_____ **5.** All coral reefs develop into a mound shape.

EXPLANATION

1. T: This idea is verified in both the text and the drawing. Sentence 3 tells us that coral structures "create masses of limestone." In addition, the drawing clearly shows that the living coral is supported by "reef limestone."

2. F: The fore reef is another name for the "outer reef," which is farther out in deeper water. Sentence 5 states this idea, and the drawing clearly labels the fore reef as the outer reef in deeper water.

3. T: This fact is clearly stated in sentence 6 and depicted in the drawing.

4. DK: This may well be a fact; however, this idea is not mentioned in the text, and the drawing gives us no details for its support.

5. F: The drawing shows a mound-shaped coral reef. However, sentence 2 states that coral reefs can develop into three shapes: finger, branching, and mound. The drawing is just an example of one type.

PRACTICE **3**

Study the following graphic. Then mark each numbered statement **T** if it is true, **F** if it is false, or **DK** if you don't know, based on the given information.

**2005 Total Waste Generation
245 Million Tons
(before recycling)**

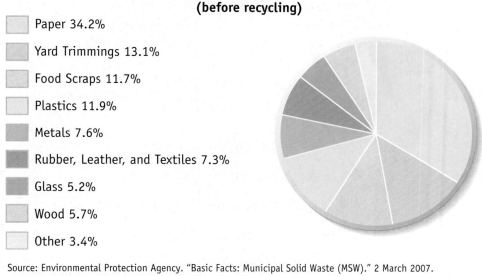

Paper 34.2%

Yard Trimmings 13.1%

Food Scraps 11.7%

Plastics 11.9%

Metals 7.6%

Rubber, Leather, and Textiles 7.3%

Glass 5.2%

Wood 5.7%

Other 3.4%

Source: Environmental Protection Agency. "Basic Facts: Municipal Solid Waste (MSW)." 2 March 2007.
<http://www.epa.gov/epaoswer/non-hw/muncpl/facts.htm>.

_____ **1.** This graphic is a pie chart, also known as a circle graph.

_____ **2.** Food waste makes up the majority of our trash.

_____ **3.** Paper makes up the highest percentage of daily trash.

_____ **4.** Plastic items make up the smallest percentage of daily trash.

_____ **5.** The United States is running out of landfills in which to dump trash.

REVIEW **Test 1**

A. Based on the ideas in the following graphic, mark each numbered statement **T** if it is true, **F** if it is false, or **DK** if you don't know, based on the given information.

Source: U.S. Department of Agriculture, Center for Policy and Promotion. Home and Garden Bulletin no. 267-1.

_____ **1.** This graphic is a pictogram.

_____ **2.** A healthy diet is mostly made up of meats and beans.

_____ **3.** A healthy diet contains a number of servings from each food group.

_____ **4.** Exercise is an important part of a healthy diet.

_____ **5.** A healthy diet avoids all fat.

B. Based on the ideas in the graphic, mark each numbered statement **T** if it is true, **F** if it is false, or **DK** if you don't know, based on the given information.

Sample Food Portions Larger Than One Pyramid Serving

Food Grains Group	Sample Portion You Receive	Compare to Pyramid Serving Size	Approximate Pyramid Servings in This Portion
Bagel	1 bagel 4$\frac{1}{2}$" in diameter (4 ounces)	$\frac{1}{2}$ bagel 3" in diameter (1 ounce)	4
Muffin	1 muffin 3$\frac{1}{2}$" in diameter (4 ounces)	1 muffin 2$\frac{1}{2}$" in diameter (1$\frac{1}{2}$ ounces)	3
English muffin	1 whole muffin	$\frac{1}{2}$ muffin	2
Sweet roll or cinnamon bun	1 large from bakery (6 ounces)	1 small (1$\frac{1}{2}$ ounces)	4
Pancakes	4 pancakes 5" in diameter (10 ounces)	1 pancake 4" in diameter (1$\frac{1}{2}$ ounces)	6
Burrito-sized flour tortilla	1 tortilla 9" in diameter (2 ounces)	1 tortilla 7" in diameter (1 ounce)	2
Individual bag of tortilla chips	1$\frac{3}{4}$ ounces	12 tortilla chips ($\frac{3}{4}$ ounce)	2
Popcorn	16 cups (movie theater, medium)	2 cups	8
Hamburger bun	1 bun	$\frac{1}{2}$ bun	2
Spaghetti	2 cups (cooked)	$\frac{1}{2}$ cup (cooked)	4
Rice	1 cup (cooked)	$\frac{1}{2}$ cup (cooked)	2

Source: U.S. Department of Agriculture, Center for Policy and Promotion. Home and Garden Bulletin no. 267-1.

_____ **6.** This graphic is a flowchart.

_____ **7.** The purpose of this graphic is to show how easy it is to eat more than the food pyramid recommends for a healthy diet.

_____ **8.** One 4$\frac{1}{2}$-inch-sized bagel is equivalent to four servings as defined by the food pyramid.

_____ **9.** The column labeled "Approximate Pyramid Servings in This Portion" refers to the column labeled "Sample Portion You Receive."

_____ **10.** People who eat the portions of food listed in the column "Sample Portion You Receive" are overweight.

REVIEW Test 2

A. Study the following graphic. Then mark each numbered statement **T** if it is true, **F** if it is false, or **DK** if you don't know, based on the given information.

Textbook
Skills

Stages of Conflict Resolution

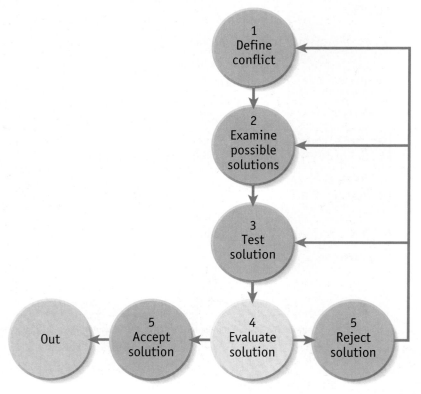

Source: De Vito, *Messages: Building Interpersonal Communication Skills,* 4th ed., p. 300. Published by Allyn and Bacon, Boston, MA. Copyright © 1999 by Pearson Education, Inc. Adapted by permission of the publisher.

_____ **1.** This graphic is a flowchart.

_____ **2.** Step 5 shows that a solution can be either accepted or rejected.

_____ **3.** If a solution is rejected, the process ends.

_____ **4.** If a solution is rejected, a person can repeat any one or all of the first three steps.

_____ **5.** Most tested solutions are accepted.

B. Study the following graphic. Then mark each numbered statement **T** if it is true, **F** if it is false, or **DK** if you don't know, based on the given information.

Textbook
Skills

Women and Minorities in Congress

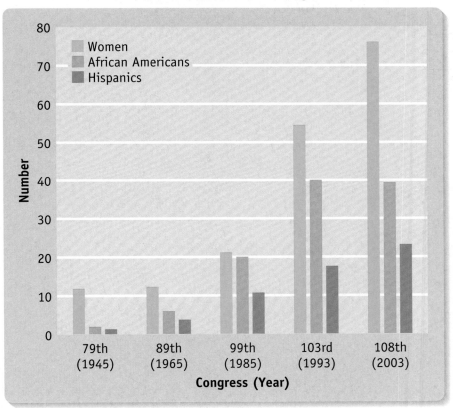

Source: Karen O'Connor and Larry J. Sabato, *American Government: Continuity and Change* (New York: Longman, 2004), p. 231.

_____ **6.** This graphic is a line graph.

_____ **7.** The 79th Congress had the fewest numbers of women and minorities of the Congresses shown.

_____ **8.** Between 1985 and 1993, the number of African Americans in Congress nearly doubled.

_____ **9.** The number of Hispanics in Congress has remained the same over the years.

_____ **10.** The 108th Congress had nearly 40 women.

Word Parts

Roots

Root	Meaning	Example
alter	change	altercation
ama	love	amorous
anima	breath, spirit	animated
anno	year	annual
aqua	water	aquifer
aster, astro	star	asteroid
aud	hear	auditory
bene	good	beneficial
bio	life	biology
cap	head	decapitate
cap, capt	take	captivate
card, cor, cord	heart	cardiologist, core
ced, ceed, cess	go	proceed
cosmo	order, universe	cosmos
cresc	grow, increase	crescendo
cryp	secret, hidden	crypt
dent	tooth	dentist
derm	skin	epidermis
dict	say	predict
duc, duct	lead, guide	conductor
dynam	power	dynamic
ego	self	egotistical
equ, equal	equal	equilibrium
err, errat	wander	erratic
ethno	race, tribe	ethnic
fac, fact	do, make	factory
fer	carry	transfer

Root	Meaning	Example
flu, fluct, flux	flow	influx
fract	break	fracture
frater	brother	fraternal
gene	race, kind, sex	genetics
grad, gres	go, take steps	graduate
graph	write, draw	autograph
gyn	woman	gynecologist
hab, habi	have, hold	habitat
hap	change	happenstance
helio	sun, light	heliograph
ject	throw	eject
lat	carry	translate
lic, liqu, list	leave behind	liquidate
lith	stone	monolith
loc	place	relocate
log	speech, science, reason	logic
loquor	speak	colloquial
lumen, lumin	light	luminary
macro	large	macroeconomics
manu	hand	manual
mater	mother	maternal
med	middle	mediator
meter	measure	thermometer
micro	small	microorganism
miss, mit	send, let go	transmit
morph	form	morpheme
mort	die	mortal
mot, mov	movement	demote
mut, muta	change	mutation
nat	be born	natural, native
neg, negat	say no, deny	negate, negative
nomen, nym	name	antonym, synonym
pel, puls	push, drive	propel
philo	love	philanthropy
ocul	eye	monocle
ortho	right, straight	orthodontist
osteo	bone	osteoporosis
pater	father	paternal

Root	Meaning	Example
path	suffering, feeling	pathology
ped	child	pediatrician
ped, pod	foot	podiatrist
phobia	fear	claustrophobia
phon	sound	telephone
photo	light	photograph
plic	fold	implicate
pneuma	wind, air	pneumonia
pon, pos, posit	put, place	dispose
port	carry	import
pseudo	false	pseudonym
psych	mind	psychology
press	press	compress
pyr	fire	pyromaniac
quir, quis	ask	inquire
rog	question	interrogate
scope	see	microscope
scrib, script	write	inscription
sect	cut	dissect
sequi	follow	sequence
sol	alone	solitude
soma	body	somatotype
somnia	sleep	insomnia
soph	wise	sophisticated
soror	sister	sorority
spect	look	inspect
spers	scatter	disperse
spir	breathe	inspire
struct	build	construction
tact	touch	tactile
tain, tent	hold	contain
tempo	time	temporary
the, theo	God	theology
therm	heat	thermometer
tort	twist	contort
tract	drag, pull	extract
verbum	word	verbatim
vis	see	revise

Prefixes

Prefix	Meaning	Example
a-, ab-	away, from	abduct
a-, an-	not, without	asexual
ac-, ad-	to, toward	accept, admit
ambi-, amphi-	both, around	ambivalent, amphitheater
ante-	in front of, before	antecedent
anti-	against, oppose	antisocial
auto-	self	automatic
bi-	two, twice	bifocal
cata-, cath-	down, downward	catacombs
cent-	hundred	centennial
chrono-	time	chronological
circum-	around	circumspect
col-, com-, con-	with, together	collate, combine, connection
contra-	against	contradict
de-	down away, reversal	destruction
deca-	ten	decade
demi-	half	demigod
di-, duo-	two	dioxide
dia-	between, through	diagonal, dialogue
dis-	apart, away, in different directions	dismiss
dys-	ill, hard	dysfunctional
e-, ex-	out, from	emerge, expel
epi-	on, near, among	epidemic
eu-	good	euphoric
extra-	beyond, outside	extramarital
hecto-	hundred	hectogram
hemi-	half	hemisphere
hetero-	other, different	heterosexual
homo-	same	homonym
hyper-	above, excessive	hyperactive
hypo-	under	hypodermic
il-, im-, in-	not	illogical, impossible
im-, in-	in, into, on	implant, inject
infra-	lower	infrastructure
inter-	between, among	intercede
intra-	within	intranet
iso-	equal	isometric

Prefix	Meaning	Example
juxta-	next to	juxtapose
mal-	wrong, ill	malpractice
meta-	about	metaphysical
micro-	small	microscope
mil-	thousand	millennium
mis-	wrong	mistake
mono-	one	monotone
multi-	many	multimedia
non-	not	nonactive
nona-	nine	nonagon
octo-	eight	octopus
omni-	all	omniscient
pan-	all	panorama
penta-	five	pentagram
per-	through	pervade
peri-	around	periscope
poly-	many	polygon
post-	after, behind	postscript
pre-	before	precede
pro-	forward, on behalf of	promote
proto-	first	prototype
quadri-	four	quadrant
quint-	five	quintuplets
re-	back, again	retract
retro-	backward	retrospect
semi-	half	semicircle
sesqui-	one and a half	sesquicentennial
sex-	six	sextet
sub-, sup-	under, from below	subgroup, support
super-	above, over, beyond	supervise
sym-, syn-	together, with	symmetry, synonym
tele-	far, from a distance	telegraph
tetra-	four	tetrahedron
trans-	across	transport
tri-	three	triangle, triplet
ultra-	excessive, beyond	ultrasonic
un-	not	unnecessary
uni-	one	uniform
vice-	in place of	viceroy

Suffixes

Suffix	Meaning	Example
Noun suffixes	*People, places, things*	
-acle, -acy, -ance	quality, state	privacy
-an	of, related to	American
-ant, -ary	one who, one that	servant
-arium, -ary	place or container	auditorium
-ation	action, process	education
-ator	one who	spectator
-cide	kill	homicide
-eer, -er, -ess	person, doer	collector
-ence, -ency	quality, state	residence, residency
-ent	one who, one that	president
-hood	quality, condition, state	brotherhood
-ician	specialist	statistician
-ism	belief	modernism
-ist	person	extremist
-ity	quality, trait	sincerity
-logy	study of	biology
-ment	act, state	statement
-ness	quality, condition, state	illness
-or	person, doer	juror
-path	practitioner; sufferer of a disorder	osteopath; psychopath
-ship	quality, condition, state	relationship
-tion	action, state	fraction
-tude	quality, degree	multitude
-y	quality, trait	apathy
Adjective suffixes	*Descriptions of nouns*	
-able	capable of	reusable
-ac, -al, -an, -ar, -ative	of, like, related to, being	logical
-ent	of, like, related to, being	persistent
-ful	full of	fearful
-ible	capable of	defensible
-ic, -ical, -ile, -ious, -ish, -ive	of, like, related to, being	feverish
-less	without	luckless

Suffix	Meaning	Example
Adjective suffixes	*Descriptions of nouns*	
-ly	having the quality of	manly
-oid	resembling	tabloid
-ose, -ous	of, like, related to, being	hideous
Verb suffixes	*Action or states of being*	
-en	cause to have or increase the stated quality	blacken
-ify	create, increase the stated quality, become	simplify
-ize	cause to become	modernize
Adverb suffixes	*Descriptions of verbs and adjectives*	
-ally, -ly	in that manner	basically, quickly
-ward	direction	toward, backward
-wise	direction	clockwise
-wise	with respect to	pricewise

Text Credits

Agee, Warren, Phillip H. Ault, and Edwin Emery. *Introduction To Mass Communication,* 12th ed. Published by Allyn and Bacon, Boston, MA. Copyright © 1997 by Pearson Education. Adapted by permission of the publisher.

Alpert, Lukas I. Adapted from "Panhandling Moves into the Internet Age," *Daytona Beach News-Journal,* November 11, 2002, p. 2A. Reprinted with permission of the Associated Press.

Ambert, Anne-Marie. *Families in the New Millennium.* Boston, MA: Allyn and Bacon, 2001.

Anson, Chris M., and Robert A. Schwegler. *The Longman Handbook for Writers and Readers.* New York: Longman, 1997.

Aronson, Elliot, Timothy D. Wilson, and Robin M. Akert. *Social Psychology,* 4th ed. Upper Saddle River, NJ: Prentice Hall, 2002.

Associated Press. "Oviedo Boy Dies of Amoeba Infection." *The Ledger,* July 27, 2002. Reprinted with permission of the Associated Press.

Aulette, Judy Root. *Changing American Families.* Boston, MA: Allyn and Bacon, 2001.

Barker, Larry L., and Deborah Roach Gault. *Communication,* 8th ed. Boston, MA: Allyn and Bacon, 2002.

Blasengame, Bart. "Justin Timberlake: The new King of Pop wants to give his title back," *MEN.STYLE.COM/The Online Home of Details and GQ,* April 2007. http://men.style.com/details.

Brownell, Judi. *Listening: Attitudes, Principles, And Skills,* 2nd ed. Published by Allyn and Bacon, Boston, MA. Copyright © 2002 by Pearson Education. Adapted by permission of the publisher.

Campbell, Neil A., and Jane B. Reece. *Essential Biology.* Copyright © 2001 by Benjamin Cummings. Reprinted by permission of Pearson Education, Inc., Glenview, IL.

Campbell, Neil A., Jane B. Reece, Martha R. Taylor, and Eric J. Simon. *Biology: Concepts & Connections,* 5th ed. Published by Pearson Benjamin Cummings. Copyright © 2006 by Pearson Education, Inc. Reprinted by permission of Pearson Education, Inc., Glenview, IL.

Cole, Diane. "Want to Do Better On the Job? Listen Up!" *Working Mother Magazine,* March 1991. Reprinted by permission of Reprint Management Services.

Condon, John C. *With Respect to the Japanese: A Guide for Americans.* Yarmouth, ME: Intercultural Press, a Nicholas Brealey Publishing Company, 1984

DeVito, Joseph A. *Essentials of Human Communication,* 5th ed. Boston, MA: Pearson Allyn and Bacon, 2005.

DeVito, Joseph A. *Interpersonal Communication: Relating to Others,* 11th ed. Published by Allyn and Bacon, Boston, MA. Copyright © 2005 by Pearson Education. Adapted by permission of the publisher.

De Vito, Joseph. *Messages: Building Interpersonal Communication Skills,* 4th ed. Published by Allyn & Bacon, Boston, MA. Copyright © 1999 by Pearson Education. Adapted by permission of the publisher.

Dickinson, Emily. "I'm Nobody! Who are You?" Reprinted by permission of the publishers and the Trustees of Amherst College from *The Poems of Emily Dickinson,* Thomas H. Johnson, ed., Cambridge, Mass.: The Belknap Press of Harvard University Press, Copyright © 1951, 1955, 1983 by the President and Fellows of Harvard College.

Donatelle, Rebecca J. *Access to Health,* 7th ed. San Francisco, CA: Benjamin Cummings, 2002. Reprinted by permission of Pearson Education, Inc., Glenview, IL.

Dove/Unilever. "Only Two Percent of Women Describe Themselves as Beautiful." Press Release published by Dove/Unilever on September 29, 2004.

Edwards, George C., III, Martin P. Wattenberg, and Robert L. Lineberry. *Government in America: People, Politics and Policy,* 5th ed., Brief Version. Addison Wesley Educational Publishers, 2000.

Eshleman, J. Ross. *The Family,* 9th ed. Boston, MA: Allyn and Bacon, 2000.

Fishbein, Diana H., and Susan E. Pease. *The Dynamics Of Drug Abuse.* Published by Allyn and Bacon, Boston, MA. Copyright © 1996 by Pearson Education. Adapted by permission of the publisher.

Folkerts, Jean, and Stephen Lacy. *The Media In Your Life: An Introduction To Mass Communication,* 2nd ed. Published by Allyn and Bacon, Boston, MA. Copyright © 2002 by Pearson Education. Adapted by permission of the publisher.

Galvin, Kathleen M., and Bernard J. Brommel. *Family Communication: Cohesion and Change,* 5th ed. New York: Longman, 2000.

Gamble, Teri Kwal, and Michael W. Gamble. *The Gender Communication Connection.* Boston, MA: Houghton Mifflin, 2003.

Garraty, John A., and Mark C. Carnes. *The American Nation: A History of the United States,* 10th ed. New York: Longman, 2000. Reprinted by permission of Pearson Education, Inc., Glenview, IL.

Gould, Nels. "Shoulders" from Nelson Gould and Abe Arkoff. *Psychology and Personal Growth,* 6th ed. Published by Allyn and Bacon, Boston, MA. Copyright © 2003 by Pearson Education. Reprinted by permission of the publisher.

Heart, Bear and Molly Larkin. From *The Wind Is My Mother* by Bear Heart and Molly Larkin, copyright © 1996 by Bear Heart and Molly Larkin. Used by permission of Clarkson Potter/Publishers, a division of Random House, Inc.

Housden, Maria. "Finding My Voice. " Reprinted by permission of the author.

Jaffe, Michael L. *Understanding Parenting,* 2nd ed. Published by Allyn and Bacon, Boston, MA. Copyright © 1997 by Pearson Education. Adapted by permission of the publisher.

Janero, Richard Paul, and Thelma Altschuler. *The Art of Being Human,* 7th ed. New York: Longman, 2003.

Jones, Charisse. "Audubon Comes to the Inner City: Group Plans to Open 1000 Centers in Low-Income Areas." *USA Today,* April 10, 2002. Copyright © 2002, USA TODAY. Reprinted with permission.

Kelly, Marilyn S. *Communication @ Work.* Published by Allyn and Bacon, Boston, MA. Copyright © 2006 by Pearson Education.

Kemper, Steve. From "Clippety-Clopping Along," *Smithsonian,* March 2001, pp. 38–40. Reprinted by permission of the author.

Klein, Allen. *The Healing Power of Humor.* Copyright © 1989 by J. P. Tarcher. The Putnam Publishing Group.

Kossyln, Stephen M., and Robin S. Rosenberg. *Psychology: The Brain, The Person, The World.* Published by Allyn and Bacon, Boston, MA. Copyright © 1999 by Pearson Education. Adapted by permission of the publisher.

Leathers, Dale G. *Successful Nonverbal Communication: Principles and Applications,* 3rd ed. Boston, MA: Allyn and Bacon, 1997.

L'Engle, Madeleine. "Act III, scene ii" (poem). From *The Weather of the Heart.* Published by Harold Shaw Publishers. Copyright © 1969, 1978 by Crosswicks, Ltd. Reprinted by permission of Lescher & Lescher, Ltd. All rights reserved.

Lerman, Ivona. "Manatees Face Rough Waters Around Globe," *Daytona Beach News-Journal,* October 10, 2002, p. C1. Reprinted by permission of the *Daytona Beach News-Journal.* Illustrations used with the permission of Save the Manatee Club, Maitland, FL 32751.

Lieberman, Senator Joseph (CT). "The Social Impact of Music Violence." Nov. 6, 1997. Governmental Affairs Committee On Oversight. http://www.senate.gov/member/ct/lieberman/releases/r110697c.htm1 (9-30-2002).

Map of Tornado Alley reprinted from www.tornadochaser.net. Reprinted by permission of Tim Baker.

Martin, James Kirby, Randy Roberts, Steven Mintz, Linda O. McMurry, and James H. Jones. *America and Its Peoples: A Mosaic in the Making,* 3rd ed. Published by Longman. Copyright © 1997 by James Kirby Martin, Randy Roberts, Steven Mintz, Linda O. McMurry, and James H. Jones. Reprinted by permission of Pearson Education, Inc., Glenview, IL.

McKissack, Patricia and Fredrick. "Sojourner Truth: Ain't I a Woman?" Copyright © 1992 by Scholastic, Inc.

Merriam-Webster's Collegiate® Dictionary, Eleventh Edition. Copyright © 2005 by Merriam-Webster, Incorporated (www.Merriam-Webster.com). Material used with permission.

Migon, Sylvia I., Calvin J. Larson, and William M. Holmes. *Family Abuse: Consequences, Theories, and Responses.* Boston, MA: Allyn and Bacon, 2002.

Nakamura, Raymond M. *Health in America: A Multicultural Perspective.* Boston, MA: Allyn and Bacon, 1999.

NASA. "Car Development." Adapted from NASA Systems Development at NASA Ames Research Center Sept. 9, 2001.

NASA. "Waste Collection System." NASA webpage 6-16-01. http://science.ksc.nasa.gov/shuttle/technology/sts-newsref/sts-eclss-wcl.html#sts-eclss-wcs

National Center for Health Statistics. *Healthy People 2000 Final Review.* Hyattsville, Maryland: Public Health Service, 2001.

Newman, Joseph W. *America's Teachers: An Introduction to Education,* 3rd ed. New York: Longman, 1998.

Novak, Mark. *Issues in Aging: An Introduction to Gerontology.* Boston, MA: Allyn and Bacon, 1998.

O'Connor, Karen, and Larry J. Sabato. *American Government: Continuity and Change,* 2000 Edition. New York: Longman, 2000. Reprinted by permission of Pearson Education, Inc., Glenview, IL.

O'Connor, Karen, and Larry J. Sabato. *American Government: Continuity and Change,* Texas Edition. New York: Longman, 2004. Reprinted by permission of Pearson Education, Inc., Glenview, IL.

"Oprah Winfrey" from AMERICAN DECADES CD-ROM/BIOGRAPHY RESOURCE CENTER by Gale Group, © 1998 Gale Group. Reprinted with permission of the Gale Group.

Palchikoff, Nikolay. "I've Seen the Worst That War Can Do." Reprinted with permission from the December 3, 2001 issue of *Newsweek.* © 2001 Newsweek, Inc. All rights reserved. For more information about reprints from *Newsweek,* contact PARS International Corp. at 212-221-9595.

Parent, Mark. "A Dad at the Final Frontier," *New York Times,* June 16, 2001. © 2001, The New York Times. Reprinted by permission.

Powers, Scott K., and Stephen L. Dodd. *Total Fitness: Exercise, Nutrition, and Wellness,* 2nd ed. Boston, MA: Allyn and Bacon, 1990.

Pruitt, B. E., and Jane J. Stein. *HealthStyles: Decisions for Living Well,* 2nd ed. Copyright © 1999 by Allyn and Bacon. Reprinted by permission of Pearson Education, Inc.

Renzetti, Claire M., and Daniel J. Curran. *Women, Men, And Society,* 4th ed. Published by Allyn and Bacon, Boston, MA. Copyright © 1999 by Pearson Education. Adapted by permission of the publisher.

Ruggiero, Vincent Ryan. *The Art of Thinking: A Guide to Critical and Creative Thought,* 7th ed. New York: Pearson Longman, 2004.

Smith, Thomas M., and Robert Leo Smith. *Elements of Ecology,* 4th ed. Update. San Francisco, CA: Benjamin Cummings,